Perspectives on contemporary printmaking

MANCHESTER
1824

Manchester University Press

Perspectives on contemporary printmaking

Critical writing since 1986

Edited by
Ruth Pelzer-Montada

Manchester University Press

Published by Manchester University Press
Altrincham Street, Manchester M1 7JA

www.manchesteruniversitypress.co.uk

British Library Cataloguing-in-Publication Data
A catalogue record for this book is available from the British Library

ISBN 978 1 5261 2575 0 paperback

First published 2018

Typeset
by Toppan Best-set Premedia Limited
Printed in Great Britain
by TJ International Ltd, Padstow, Cornwall

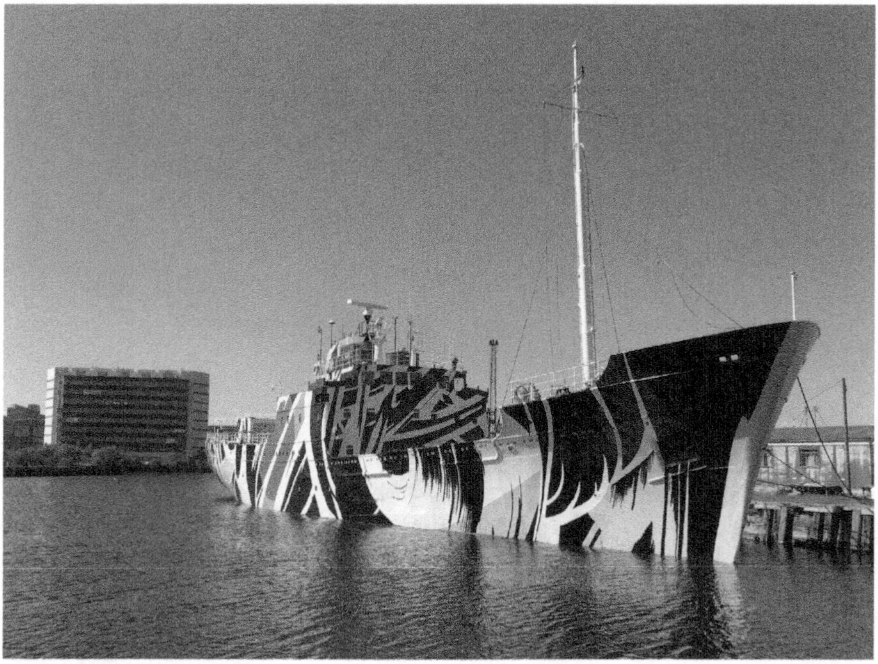

Ciara Phillips, *Every Woman*, 2016. Prince of Wales Dock, Harbour of Leith, Edinburgh, Scotland.

Contents

List of figures

Notes on contributors

Allora and Calzadilla (Jennifer Allora and Guillermo Calzadilla) are a collaborative team of visual artists who live and work in San Juan, Puerto Rico. Their work encompasses a variety of media including sculpture, photography, performance art, sound and video to reflect on contemporary and historical socio-political conditions. They have exhibited widely and in 2011 represented the United States at the Venice Biennale.

Barbara Balfour is an interdisciplinary and print media artist and curator who has exhibited her work and lectured across Canada and in the UK, China and Japan. In addition to print installations, artist's books and multiples, Balfour has incorporated writing, video and digital imaging into her art. She teaches in the School of the Arts, Media, Performance & Design at York University, Toronto, Canada.

Andrzej Bednarczyk is an artist and educator. He leads the Department of Painting at the Krakow Academy of Fine Art in Poland. His work encompasses painting, graphic arts, photography and drawing and he also creates objects, installations and book art. He has exhibited widely, both in Poland and abroad and his work is represented in public and private collections.

Deidre Brollo, PhD, is Lecturer in Printmedia at University of Newcastle, Australia. As an artist she works primarily with artist's books, print media and installation. Her work has been exhibited in Australia and internationally, and is represented in numerous collections including the National Library of Australia, the State Library of New South Wales, and the State Library of Queensland.

Catherine Brooks is an artist and master printmaker. She is the author of *Magical Secrets about Line Etching and Engraving, the Step-by-Step Art of Incised Lines*, 2007, published by Crown Point Press in San Francisco where she was a master printer. Previously, she was an apprentice in Paris with Maître d'Art René Tazé.

Sheryl Conkelton, PhD, is an art historian and curator. She has organised numerous exhibitions and is the author of many publications, among them a monograph on *Lewis Baltz* (RAM/Steidl/Whitney Museum of American Art, 2005). She has held senior curatorial positions, including at the Museum of Modern Art, New York and the Los Angeles County Museum of Art, and has lectured extensively in North America, Europe and Japan.

Nicky Coutts, PhD, is an artist and Reader in Fine Art at the Royal College of Art, London. Her work in photography, film and video has been exhibited widely in the UK, Europe and beyond. Writing, publishing and artist's books also form an important part of her practice. She was formerly Commissioning Editor of *Make, Magazine of Women's Art*.

Georges Didi-Huberman is a philosopher and art historian. As well as being a visiting professor at art institutions worldwide, he has been Professor at the Centre d'Histoire et de Théorie des Arts, École des Hautes Études en Sciences Sociales (EHESS) in Paris since 1990. He has published over thirty books on the history and theory of images in a wide field of study ranging from the Renaissance to contemporary art, has curated numerous exhibitions, and is the recipient of prestigious international awards, including the Adorno Prize (2015).

Johanna Drucker is an internationally renowned book artist, author, visual theorist and cultural critic. Her scholarly writing documents and critiques visual language: letterforms, typography, visual poetry, art and, lately, digital aesthetics. She is currently the Martin and Bernard Breslauer Professor in the Department of Information Studies at the Graduate School of Education and Information Studies at University of California, Los Angeles (UCLA).

Cai Feng, PhD, is Professor at the China Academy of Art in Hangzhou, Dean of the Printmaking Department, and a doctorate candidate instructor. Being an expert in print and oil painting, he has participated in many art exhibitions in and out of the country. Many of his art pieces are collected by art galleries in China, the US, Australia, the UK and Japan.

Richard S. Field is Curator Emeritus of Prints and Drawings at the Yale University Art Gallery, New Haven, Connecticut. He has written widely on fifteenth-century woodcuts as well as the prints of the late nineteenth (Gauguin, etc.) and late twentieth centuries (Jasper Johns, etc.).

Yara Flores is a New York-based artist. Recent projects include the solo show *Greebles* at Raygun (Toowoomba, Australia, 2016), as well as participation in *Fifteen People Present Their Favorite Book (after Kosuth)*, at Škuc (Ljubljana, Slovenia, 2016), and Asad Raza's *Home Show* (New York, 2015). She collaborated with D. Graham Burnett on *Pound vs. Stevens: The*

Rematch (an installation in the *Aesthetics of Information* exhibition at Princeton University, Princeton, USA, 2014).

K. E. Gover is Professor of Philosophy at Bennington College, Vermont. She has published scholarly articles in international journals of philosophy and aesthetics, as well as art criticism. Gover is the 2011 recipient of the John Fisher Memorial Prize in Aesthetics. Her book, *Art and Authority: Moral Rights and Meaning in Contemporary Visual Art*, was published in 2018.

Ana María Guerra is an Ecuadorian artist and researcher based in Barcelona. She is currently undertaking a PhD at the University of Girona, where she lectures in visual culture studies. Her practice analyses the evolution of photography from the materiality of silver gelatin to the virtuality of 3D technologies, while examining how technological progress has modified the appearance of nature and the devastating impact it has had on the environment.

Richard Hamilton (1922–2011) was a renowned British painter and printmaker and one of the pioneers of Pop art. An influential teacher, exhibition organiser and writer, he is best known for his montages featuring scenes of advertising and contemporary life, notably *Just what is it that makes today's homes so different, so appealing?* (1956, Kunsthalle, Tübingen).

Richard Harding, PhD, is an artist and educator who teaches at RMIT University in Melbourne. His focus is the practice and theories of reproducible technologies through the mediums of photography and printmaking to explore the homosexual closet. Harding's research examines sexual orientation, masculinity and codes of representation. His work has been exhibited in Australia and internationally.

Daniel F. Herrmann, PhD, is an art historian and Curator of Special Projects at the National Gallery, London. Formerly Curator at the Whitechapel Gallery, London, his exhibitions include: Eduardo Paolozzi (2017); Hannah Höch (2014); Laure Prouvost (2013); Gillian Wearing (2012) and John Stezaker (2011). He is currently preparing the catalogue raisonné of the prints of Eduardo Paolozzi.

Shang Hui, PhD, has worked as Assistant Director of Research at the Jiangsu Art Museum and Director of Collections at the Shanghai Art Museum. His present positions include Commissioner of the *China Artists Association*, Senior Editor and Chief Editor of *ART* magazine, Guest Professor of the College of Fine Arts of Shanghai University. He has won numerous prizes for his publications on twentieth-century and contemporary Chinese art.

Clare Humphries, PhD, is an artist based in Melbourne, Australia. She is Lecturer in Drawing and Print Media at the Victorian College of the Arts and her work is held in major public collections, including the National Gallery of Australia.

Susan Lambert was formerly Keeper of Word & Image comprising prints, drawings, paintings, photographs and the National Art Library, at the Victoria & Albert Museum, London. Her publications include *Drawing: Technique and Purpose* (1984); *The Image Multiplied: Five Centuries of Printed Reproductions* (1987); and *Prints: Art and Techniques* (2001). Professor Lambert is currently Head of the Museum of Design in Plastics, Arts University of Bournemouth, UK.

Jeremy Lewison is an independent curator and was previously Director of Collections at Tate, London, where he was also responsible for the print collection. He has organised many international exhibitions and written numerous texts on modern and contemporary art, among them Jackson Pollock, Barnett Newman, Alice Neel, Ben Nicholson, Wols, Sol LeWitt, Brice Marden and Anish Kapoor. He is a regular contributor to the *Burlington Magazine*.

Shen Ligong is an artist and educator who teaches in the Open Media Lab (OML) at the China Academy of Art in Hangzhou.

Cecilia Mandrile, PhD, is an artist, researcher and educator. She has exhibited in prestigious international venues such as El Museo del Barrio, NYC; the Victoria & Albert Museum, London; WPA Corcoran, Washington, DC; and the National Museum of Fine Arts, Buenos Aires, Argentina. She is the recipient of numerous fellowships, grants and awards. Her work is included in private and public collections around the world.

Chad McCail is a British artist. His interest in literature and communication frequently feature in his work and recall the sort of visual information that we come upon daily. Rather than using these modes as a figure of authority, McCail uses them to imagine and describe utopias. His recent work includes public commissions that provide perspectives on the intersections between art, activism and the built environment.

Frieder Nake's thinking is rooted in fine art and algorithms. He is a mathematician, computer scientist, semiotician and artist. Alongside G. Nees and A. M. Noll he belongs to the three earliest pioneers of generative art. An author in many fields of computing and aesthetics, his works are represented in major public and private collections. Having spent time in Germany and abroad he now lives and works in Bremen.

Paul Ogier is an artist and photographer. Born in South Auckland, New Zealand, he holds an MVA from the University of Sydney and recently completed a PhD at the University of New South Wales. His work was included in the touring exhibition *Black Mist, Burnt Country*, and his most recent solo exhibition was *The Prohibited Zone: Australian Atomic Landscapes*. His studio is in Brooklyn, New York.

Matthew Perkins is an Australian curator, writer and artist specialising in electronic media projects. He recently curated *Red Green Blue: A History of Australian Video art* (2017) and *Resistance: Peter Kennedy* (2016), both exhibitions highlighting the rich histories in Australian moving image practice. Perkins has also contributed to a number of recent publications including *Kiffy Rubbo and the George Paton Gallery: Curating the 1970s* (2016) and *Video Void: Australian Video Art* (2014), as writer and editor.

Ciara Phillips is a Canadian/Irish artist, based primarily in Glasgow, UK. Utilising traditional printmaking practices, she often works collaboratively, involving local artists and designers, as well as community groups. She draws much inspiration from the ideas of Corita Kent (1918–86). Phillips is the founder of the artist collective Poster Club and her ongoing project titled Workshop 2010– won her a nomination for the Turner Prize in 2014.

Carl Robert Pope is an African-American artist working in the mediums of photography and video. His work tackles the issues of race in America and other social concerns. He often develops his projects in relationship to specific locations. Utilising existing forms such as the billboard, the broadside and the letterpress poster, Pope animates them with a cacophony of individual and often opposing voices, transcribing local utterances as complicated poetics that define the public sphere.

Printeresting is an award-winning art blog collectively founded and edited by Amze Emmons (Philadelphia, PA), R. L. Tillman (Baltimore, MD), and Jason Urban (Austin, TX). The site published semi-daily insights about contemporary print practice from 2008 to 2015. Since then, Emmons, Tillman, and Urban have focused on their individual practices and continue to occasionally produce Printeresting projects.

Mari Carmen Ramírez, PhD, is Wortham Curator of Latin American Art at the Museum of Fine Arts in Houston (MFAH), Texas, and Director of the International Center for the Arts of the Americas (ICAA) at the Museum. She has curated numerous exhibitions and is the author of several books on Latin American art and artists.

Ernst Rebel is Professor Emeritus of Art History and its Didactics at the University of Munich, Germany. His main research and publications are: *The History and Technologies of Printmaking* (1981, 2003); *The Art of Albrecht Dürer* (1990, 1996) and *The Interrelationship between Art and the Philology of Art* (1996, 1998).

Kathryn Reeves is Professor Emerita of Art at Purdue University, USA. She also worked at Drake University and Harvard University's Fogg Museum.

Reeves works in print media, virtual assemblage and installation. She has exhibited worldwide and received numerous awards for her work. Reeves's essays on print theory have been published, for example, in *Contemporary Impressions: Journal of the American Print Alliance.*

Frances Robertson, PhD, has been Lecturer in Design History & Theory at Glasgow School of Art since 2002, with previous experience in art practice and theatre design. Her research and writing is cross-disciplinary, working between art and design theory and history and histories of science and technology, with a focus on the material cultures of drawing, mark making and visual culture.

Blair Robins is an artist based in Toronto and has exhibited in Canada and internationally. The work reproduced here is from a project called *The Money Supply*, a series of copper engravings and works on paper created with the assistance of computer software used for banknote production. Blair is currently exploring non-dual states of consciousness, and will return shortly to present his findings.

José Roca is a Colombian curator based in Bogotá. He is currently the Artistic Director of FLORA ars+natura, an independent space for contemporary art in Bogotá, and Curator of the LARA (Latin American Roaming Art) Collection. Roca was a Co-curator of the first *Poly/graphic* Triennial in San Juan, Puerto Rico (2004), the *27th Bienal de São Paulo*, Brazil (2006). In 2010 he was the Artistic Director of *Philagrafika* in Philadelphia, USA.

Gill Saunders, PhD, is Senior Curator of Prints at the Victoria & Albert Museum, London, specialising in twentieth-century and contemporary prints. Her publications include *Prints Now* (2006); *Walls are Talking* (2010); *Recording Britain* (2011); *In Black and White: prints from Africa and the Diaspora* (2013). She recently curated *Pop Art in Print*, a V&A exhibition which is touring UK venues until 2019. She teaches, lectures and broadcasts regularly.

Amanda Thomson, PhD, has an MFA from the School of the Art Institute of Chicago. She also has degrees in the social sciences. Her creative practice is ideas- and research-led and fuses traditional and digital printmaking techniques with photography, bookmaking, video, 3D and writing. She completed her practice-based PhD in Interdisciplinary Fine Art Practice in 2013. She is a lecturer at the Glasgow School of Art.

R. L. Tillman is an artist, teacher, writer and curator. Working in unusual venues, he uses graphic media, installation, performance, publication, writing and more and has exhibited his art throughout the US and abroad. Tillman is Professor at the Maryland Institute College of Art (MICA) in Baltimore, teaching in the printmaking department. He is also a co-founder of the popular web resource *Printeresting.org* (2008–15).

Eric Triantafillou is a sociocultural anthropologist who lives in Chicago. His research investigates the aesthetics and politics of social movement visual culture and the political economy of activist labour. He co-founded the *San Francisco Print Collective*, a group of graphic arts interventionists who work in solidarity with Bay Area social justice movements and *Mindbomb*, the first public sphere art activist collective in post-socialist Romania.

Ruth Weisberg is an artist, Professor of Fine Arts and former Dean at the USC (University of Southern California) Roski School in Los Angeles. She is currently the Director of the *USC Initiative for Israeli Arts and Humanities* and the founder and President of the *Jewish Artists Initiative of Southern California*. She has been the recipient of numerous awards and has exhibited widely.

Bill Woodrow is one of the British sculptors who emerged in the late 1970s on to the international art scene, together with fellow artists such as Richard Deacon and Tony Cragg. Woodrow's work has been exhibited nationally and internationally at major venues. In 2002 he was appointed a Royal Academician and in 2013–14 the Royal Academy, London, mounted a major retrospective of his work.

Beat Wyss is a Swiss art historian, living in Berlin and Venice. He is Professor Emeritus for Art History and Media Theory and a member of the Heidelberg Academy of Sciences and Humanities. His research interests include the history of ideas and mentalities, the orbit of poststructuralism, the historical expansion of the art system, colonialism and globalisation.

Acknowledgements

In addition to the artists and authors represented in this book, some of whom have spent considerable time revising or editing their texts, I would also like to thank everyone who shared their insight and knowledge so generously: Deidre Brollo, Marian Crawford, Claire Cuccio, Catherine de Breukelare, Amze Emmons, Annis Fitzhugh, Sue Forster, Helen Frederick, Bess Frimodig, Maria Fusco, Jo Ganter, Paul Harrison, Jessica Hemmings, Mary Hood, Eve Kask, Jenn Law, Enrique Leal, Steve Lovett, Philipp Maurer, Hugh Merrill, Carinna Parraman, Jon Pengelly, Jan Pettersson, Lisa Pon, Carol Pulin, Jennie Renton, Michael Schneider, Breda Škrjanec, Joanne Soroka, Lucy Soutter, Jo Stockham, Xiaobing Tang, Paul Thirkell, Paul Thompson, Dominic Thorburn, R. L. Tillman, Jenny Tobias, Jason Urban.

I would like to thank the various publishers, museums and galleries and their staff without whose support this project would have been impossible.

Special thanks are due to translators Hugh Keith and Dr Miranda Stewart and to Isla Robertson and Jude Browning for administrative support, as well as friends and family, above all Simon Coke.

Thanks to Edinburgh College of Art (ECA), The University of Edinburgh, and The Royal Society of Edinburgh for their financial support towards this project, as well as the ECA School of Art and my colleagues for making a sabbatical possible.

Last but not least, a big thank you to staff at MUP, especially my editor who kept her calm throughout.

A note on sources and copyright materials

As a general rule, spelling and referencing conventions in the original sources have been maintained.

Introduction

What purpose is there, one might ask, in a collection of texts on the meaning and status of print – in printed form – when we supposedly live in a 'post-print' culture, in which an immense number of sources are available at the click of a mouse? Moreover, what reason is there in dedicating a whole book to one – albeit greatly varied – discipline when art today is largely 'post-disciplinary'; when the majority of artists adopt a variety of media and processes rather than following the modernist ethos of disciplinary purity?

An early impetus for this anthology lay in the difficulty I encountered in finding Ruth Weisberg's frequently referenced essay of 1986.[1] The availability of rapid, digitally delivered interlibrary loans may have changed this situation; however, not everybody has access to an academic library. Also, not *all* texts are available at the click of a mouse. Writing on prints and printmaking has been, and often still is, published in geographically dispersed and not widely disseminated conference proceedings, biennale or exhibition catalogues, journals or specialist publications.

My intention with this project, therefore, is to provide a critical 'topography', a map of some of the debates on contemporary prints and printmaking since the 1980s – albeit a necessarily partial map.

Perspectives on contemporary printmaking is the first anthology of its kind. It therefore presents a unique resource. Although it is inevitably shaped by the editor's familiarity with the Anglo-Saxon context, it is not – unlike biennale and conference publications – bound by specific institutional or national agendas. Its framing of issues is based on a rigorous examination of the field.

It is important to stress that the anthology does not deliver a general survey for the simple reason that several such publications already exist.[2] Additionally, countless publications are available in the form of catalogues of international print biennales and major exhibitions – for example, the landmark shows by the Museum of Modern Art (MOMA) in New York – and increasingly conference proceedings, such as *IMPACT*.[3] These tend to be focused on a single and often topical, premise or theme. This anthology, by contrast, uses a four-part thematic structure – with further keywords in Parts III and IV – to highlight issues and questions as to the history, ontology, discourse and institutional–material 'fields' of printmaking practice as they have existed or have emerged over the course of the last thirty years.

Why this special publication when the subject has been and continues to be a solid, even if somewhat marginal, branch of art history?[4] Debates on contemporary prints are not new either. Just consider the large body of writing by art historians and art critics on – typically well-established – contemporary artists who make prints.[5] Artists themselves have spoken or written about their engagement with print for centuries. However, Weisberg's essay of 1986 can be taken to mark an increasing self-consciousness and broadening of the discourse among artist-printmakers themselves.[6] In particular, hers is a prominent example of an extended critical engagement by a print artist with the broader, philosophical and cultural framework of their own practice rather than mere attention to matters of style, motif or technique. The roots for this heightened critical engagement lie in the burgeoning and often heated cultural debates from the 1960s onwards. Echoes of this theoretical impact, for example of semiotics, can be found in the writings of authors such as Weisberg and others in this anthology. The chosen texts are informed by the critical debates of the last decades – on class, race, gender, aesthetics and ethics, the social mandate of art, new technologies, globalisation, etc. – even if not explicitly addressed in each contribution. In recent years, the increasing emphasis on research in art, not just in the academic context, and the changing self-definition of artists – who are as much writers, speakers, curators as well as the makers of their work – have furthered critical engagement with print from within the field itself.[7] There are a number of examples of this development represented in the book.

Also, during the period covered in this book, the number of print-specialist, research-focused symposia and conferences at art institutions but also at print workshops worldwide, has multiplied.[8]

By contrast, within the larger art context, recognition and critical appreciation of prints or printmaking still occur only marginally, if at all. As Canadian artist and printmaker Barbara Balfour (2016) has noted:

> When objects as diverse as the Shroud of Turin or Andy Warhol's 'paintings' are not discussed, expressly, in terms of their printed qualities, I long for clarification to be made – not to claim their inclusion in some definitive list of printed works or for the sake of bringing them into the print fold, but to acknowledge that part of what makes certain work interesting is connected to its printed nature. ... these situations make me want to call out, 'but it's a print!' (146–7)[9]

The marginal status of prints and printmaking is a phenomenon to which a number of texts in the anthology refer.[10] It continues to exist despite the fact that prints have been and are a crucial feature of many contemporary artists' multi-media practice. Increasingly, however, printmaking's 'ex-centricity' and its outsider status are regarded as a vantage point rather than a disadvantage.[11]

The new hegemony of the digital in culture at large has simultaneously fuelled interest in 'slow' media and processes, of which the older techniques of printmaking are considered to be one prominent example. The association of older processes with slowness is somewhat ironic, given that digital processes can be extremely protracted and time-consuming. Anyone who has undertaken digital image editing or 3D printing knows how painstakingly drawn-out they can be. Nevertheless, the identification of older processes as being 'slow' sticks. In Part I the re-emergence of the woodcut is cited as one such example. The crisis that was felt within the field of printmaking due to the appearance, during the 1990s, of digital technologies, especially imaging software and home printers, led often to either absurdly enthusiastic or despairing reactions in equal measure. These have now been superseded by a cautiously optimistic mood as to the future of printmaking, partly for the reasons mentioned, and also because digital technologies have been incorporated into or are complemented by – rather than having simply replaced – older technologies.[12]

Interestingly, if not surprisingly, print and its history is gaining critical and theoretical attention in the context of the study of new media and new media art. The brief historical overviews at the beginning of the collection by Ernst Rebel and Beat Wyss are both written from the perspective of a history of new media.[13] As the text by French art historian Georges Didi-Huberman (1997) on the notion of the imprint in Part III argues, a more complex understanding of history and temporality permits us to look into the past to discover the present and future alike and vice versa.

Several factors give prints and printmaking prominence today – over and above its specific manifestations – despite frequent proclamations of print's demise in culture at large:

- Self-publishing is gaining in importance and is widely practised in contemporary art;[14]
- contemporary art's emphasis on sociality, collaboration, ethics and political action can be argued to have been vital features of print practice for centuries;[15]
- the recognition of the importance of materiality, craft and manual touch, as currently theorised, for example, in craft and art theory, has given new credence to a physically demanding and – in some respects – technically 'outdated' discipline such as printmaking;[16]
- the inherently mechanical nature of print makes its practitioners exceptionally well-prepared to engage with and incorporate, as well as contest, new technologies;

- the recognition that no medium is stable or 'fixed' and should instead be regarded as 'multiple' and heterogeneous has gained currency;[17]
- the notion of an 'expanded print practice' or 'print media' as a collective term are indicators of this widening of the concept and practices of print that align it with contemporary multi-media art.

These factors, even if not explicitly addressed in the individual texts within the book, are referenced in the extensive further reading lists at the end of each of the four parts.

It is important to say what you will not find in this book: there are no technical discussions as such or texts dedicated to single print techniques. The reason for the omission is two-fold. There are countless publications, websites, blogs etc. dedicated to specific print techniques. Moreover, as several authors in this volume argue, printmaking is often primarily framed – by writers and makers alike – in terms of technology and techniques. I wanted to avoid the same overemphasis – a collusion with the 'techno-fetish' of printmakers, as it has been memorably called by Graeme Cornwell in 1992 and critiqued, more recently, by Luis Camnitzer (2011).[18] I do believe that the material aspects of a medium or media are vitally important. Indeed, as Ewa Lajer-Burchardt and Isabelle Graw (2016) have argued, 'the material and technical register of the work of art' must be regarded as 'the very site rather than the mere support of meaning' (8). Hence a number of texts pay close attention to the making and/or physical and technical make-up of prints. However, I hope that the various contributions in the anthology show that technology and technique are never purely 'technical', or mere 'tools', and that they are always mediated by multiple factors – economic, social, scientific, philosophical, cultural, aesthetic, personal – no matter how 'immediate' or pragmatically motivated they appear to an individual practitioner or indeed, an institution.

Also not included are critical texts on individual artists by art historians or critics, although such work is often of a high quality and proposes broader insights into the field. Instead, I have aimed to include a variety of voices and authors with different professional identities and affiliations. There are contributions by art historians, curators, critics, but equally by artists themselves. In addition to this authorial diversity I have also opted for different textual formats or modes of writing, from longer, in-depth academic discussions (by, for example, art historian Didi-Huberman, philosopher K. E. Gover, curator Susan Lambert) to writing that combines theory and practice (Barbara Balfour, Richard Harding, Clare Humphries, the former *Printeresting* team Amze Emmons, R. L. Tillman, Jason Urban). New modes of 'art writing' that elide the theoretical and the poetic are also included (Nicky Coutts, Yara Flores). This is to account for the fact that the conventional hierarchies between Theory with a capital T and theory with a small t, between academic and creative, specialist and amateur knowledge, are being re-drawn. Moreover, alternative modes of writing pay attention to their own texture and sensuous materiality and hence correspond more closely to the art itself than conventional models of writing.

The structure of the book

The texts are grouped into four themed sections or parts, each preceded by an introduction which gives a brief outline of the texts and their relevance. 'Part I: Genealogy' provides a brief contextualisation of print's broader history. It also includes an examination of its current functions in society at large. 'Part II: Debates' is chronologically organised. This is to give an indication of the different emphases of the debate about printmaking over the period of time covered in the anthology. The texts collected here – mostly written by artists – show both continuities and differences in the conception, positioning, concerns and practices of printmaking. 'Part III: Keywords' pinpoints some of the key concepts associated with prints and printmaking. 'Part IV: The field' identifies a range of printmaking's institutional and geographical locations, modes of production and examples of dissemination.

Inevitably, the topography that the anthology provides is far from comprehensive and not intended as a definitive recent history. Printmaking is now a truly global field with innumerable strands or force-fields. Many of these are well connected; however, it is important to bear in mind others that remain off the map. South African Dominic Thorburn's (unpublished) presentation at *IMPACT* 2011, titled 'Navigating the North–South Axis – Divide and Rule?' examined some of the geo-political imbalances that prevail in global print practices and exchanges.

The anthology should therefore be approached in a spirit of orienteering, prompting additional investigation and study, both practical and theoretical. Readers are encouraged to create their own map, or temporal and thematic trajectory through the material presented in this volume, and find the connections between different texts that are pertinent to them. By referring to the further reading lists at the end of each section, readers are then able to create a diverse, yet interconnected web of multiple intersecting lines that lead beyond the book itself.

Note: Some desirable texts were not available due to copyright restrictions or astronomical fees. These have, however, been included in the further reading lists. Overall, preference has been given to texts that may not be easily available but, as explained above, in some cases accessible texts have been included because they contribute to the discursive field that the anthology aims to create.

Notes

1 Weisberg's 'The Syntax of the Print: In Search of an Aesthetic Context' was published in 1986 in the legendary journal of the Tamarind Institute, *The Tamarind Papers*. Its influence prompted the conveners of the 2005 *IMPACT* Conference in Berlin-Posznan to invite Weisberg as a keynote speaker to revisit her earlier paper after almost twenty years.

2 The best-known in English are Tallman (1996), Miles and Saunders (2006) and Coldwell (2008).

3 *IMPACT* stands for 'International Multi-disciplinary Printmaking, Artists, Concepts and Techniques'. See the information on the website of the Centre for Fine Print Research (CFPR) at the University of the West of England, Bristol: www.uwe.ac.uk/sca/research/cfpr/dissemination/conferences/impact.html [Accesssed15 February 2017].

4 In addition to general art historical journals, specialist journals such as *Print Quarterly* or *Nouvelles de l'Estampe* approach prints and printmaking from a largely art historical perspective. As of 2015, a welcome forum for print specialists has emerged in the form of the Association of Print Scholars (APS). APS is focused on 'innovative and interdisciplinary methodological approaches to the history of printmaking' and aims to 'facilitate dialogue and community among its members and promotes the dissemination of their ideas and scholarship'. This is a fantastic initiative that welcomes both art historians and practitioners alike and is international in its remit. For an insightful assessment of the historiography of the study of prints, see APS's inaugural lecture by Peter Parshall, 'Why Study Prints Now?', 25 September 2015. A revised version of the lecture can be found in the September/October issue 2016 of *Art in Print*.

5 Susan Tallman's (2012) review of four landmark shows at MOMA, New York, gives an indication of the expanding discourse since the 1960s, through the lens of this important institution.

6 This is not to deny the important role of earlier figures, such as James McNeill Whistler (1834–1903) or Stanley W. Hayter (1901–88), and many others for a self-understanding of modern printmaking in the West.

7 For one example of such research within the academic context, see Amanda Thomson in this anthology, as well as references in the further reading list of Part IV.

8 The following few, largely European, examples give a small indication. They have occurred in addition to larger events associated with biennales and conferences such as the bi-annual *IMPACT* with changing locations world-wide or the annual *SGC International* in the US: The *FIRST EDITION* Print Symposium was hosted by Cork Printmakers print studio in Cork, Ireland, in June 2017; *RE:Print/RE:Present* was a one-day symposium and exhibition at Anglia Ruskin University Gallery, Cambridge, curated by Veronique Chance and Mark Graver in 2015; *Printmaking in the Expanded Field*, a three-day symposium organised by Jan Stefan Pettersson at the Oslo Academy of Art and Design, also occurred in 2015. The 2010 *Printopolis* symposium by Toronto's Open Print Studio yielded the eponymously titled publication, edited by Jenn Law and Tara Cooper (2016). The *SNAP* International Print Symposium at Kloster

Bentlage in Northern Germany is the only such event in Germany (2009, 2012, 2015).

On the changing identity of artists, see Singerman (1999).

Paul van der Lem (1999) considered the difference between artistic research (or 'search') and academic arts-based research in his presentation for the first *IMPACT* Conference, in Bristol in 1999.

9 See also Jenn Law's essay 'Notes from the margins of the empire' in the same publication, and Pelzer-Montada (2008).

10 See Weisberg, Roca, Reeves, Harding in this anthology. See also Parshall (2016) for an art-historical perspective.

11 Tallman (2013). Sarah Suzuki considered different print constituencies in her 2011 essay 'Print people'.

12 Printmaking even appears to have obtained the much-sought-after label of being 'cool' – at least in some quarters. See R. L. Tillman's (2010) wry blog 'On the faddishness of printmaking'.

13 See also Cubitt (2014). Precursors to a consideration of print in the context of media are, of course, William Ivins and Marshall McLuhan. A fascinating project is the digitisation and online publication of the Graphical Collection of the Göttweig Abbey, Austria. It is realised by the Department of Image Science of the Danube University Krems and aims to further research into the monastery's vast and significant historical print collection in the context of image science and new media art. www.gssg.at/gssg/displayProject.do [Accessed 16 January 2017]. See the essay by media theorist Oliver Grau (2014).

14 See Johanna Drucker's essay in Part IV.

15 See, for example, Marion Crawford (2016). See also the keyword 'Collaboration' in the further reading list in Part IV.

16 On the former, see Adamson (2013); on the latter, Buszek (2011). Further impulses for challenging and stimulating reconsiderations of materiality can be found in the field of material studies and the emerging field of 'new materialism'. In the art context, see Bolt and Barrett (2013).

17 See Susan Lambert's contribution in Part III of this book; for an example from another historic discipline, see photography historian Geoffrey Batchen's speech 'Double displacement: photography and its ghosts' at the NSW Art Gallery *Photography* symposium 2015.

18 See José Roca's essay in Part II of this volume.

References

Adamson, Glenn. 2013. *The Invention of Craft*. London: A & C Black Publishers.

Balfour, Barbara. 2016. 'The What and the Why of Print'. In: Law, Jenn and Cooper, Tara (eds), *Printopolis*. Toronto, Ontario: Open Studio, 142–57.

Batchen, Geoffrey. 2015. 'Double Displacement: Photography and its Ghosts'. Keynote speech at Photography symposium *Trafficking Images: Histories and Theories of Photographic Transmission*. The Power Institute for Art and Visual Culture and New South Wales Art Gallery, Sydney, Australia. https://soundcloud.com/artgalleryofnsw/double-displacement-photography-and-its-ghosts/ [Accessed 19 January 2017].

Bolt, Barbara and Barrett, Elizabeth. 2013. *Carnal Knowledge: Towards a New Materialism Through the Arts*. London: I. B. Tauris.

Buszek, M. E. (ed.). 2011. *Extra/ordinary: Craft and Contemporary Art*. Durham, NC: Duke University Press.

Camnitzer, Luis. 2006. 'Printmaking: A Colony of the Arts'. Re-printed in: Philagrafika et al. 2011. *The Graphic Unconscious*. Philadelphia, PA: Philagrafika, 1–4. www.philagrafika.org/pdf/WS/Printmakingacolony.pdf [Accessed 25 January 2018].

Chance, Veronique and Mark, Ganley (eds), 2018. *Re:print*. London: Marmalade Publishers of Visual Theory.

Coldwell, Paul. 2008. *Printmaking: A Contemporary Perspective*. London: Black Dog Publishing.

Cornwell, G. 1992. 'The Techno-Fetish in Printmaking'. Australian Print Symposium 1992. www.printsandprintmaking.gov.au/references/4852/ [Accessed 19 January 2017].

Crawford, Marion. 2016. 'The News and the Book'. In: *JAB:39*. Chicago: Columbia College, Center for Book and Paper Arts, 18–20.

Cubitt, Sean. 2014. *The Practice of Light: A Genealogy of Visual Technologies from Prints to Pixels*. Cambridge, MA: MIT Press.

Grau, Oliver. 2014. 'Druckgrafik bis Medienkunst. Neue Analyseinstrumente für die historisch vergleichende Bildforschung', *Rundbrief Fotografie*, 21 (1/2), S. 108–16. [From Graphic to Media Art. New Instruments of Analysis for Historical Comparative Image Science] www.digitalartarchive.at/database/literaturedetail.html?tx_vafe_pi1[lit]=3254&cHash=4583eaaed4cea73771e108f8f6fd4456 [Accessed 15 February 2017].

Lajer-Burcharth, Ewa and Graw, Isabelle (eds), 2016. *Painting Beyond Itself: The Medium in the Post-Medium Condition*. Berlin: Sternberg Press.

Law, Jenn. 2016. 'Notes From the Margins of the Empire'. In: Law, Jenn and Cooper, Tara (eds), *Printopolis*. Toronto, Ontario: Open Studio, 158–73.

Law, Jenn and Cooper, Tara (eds), 2016. *Printopolis*. Toronto, Ontario: Open Studio.

van der Lem, Paul. 1999. 'Search and Research in Fine Print: Creating Practice-Based and Theoretical Research for the Discipline of Fine Print'. In: Parraman, Carinna and Brewer, Emmeline (eds), *IMPACT International Multi-disciplinary Printmaking Conference Proceedings*. Bristol: Impact Press, 115–24. www.uwe.ac.uk/sca/research/cfpr/dissemination/conferences/IMPACT%20PROCEEDINGS%20copy.pdf [Accessed 15 January 2017].

Miles, Rosie and Saunders, Gill. 2006. *Prints Now: Directions and Definitions*. New York: V&A Publications.

Parshall, Peter. 2016. 'Why Study Prints Now? Or, the World according to Bartsch'. *Art in Print*, 6 (3): 5–12.

Pelzer-Montada, Ruth. 2008. 'The Discursivity of Print: Damien Hirst's Series *The Last Supper* (1999)'. *Visual Culture in Britain* 9 (1): 81–100.

Petterson, Jan (ed.). 2017. *Printmaking in the Expanded Field – A Pocketbook for the Future*. Oslo: Oslo Academy of the Arts.

Roca, José. 2011. 'The Graphic Unconscious or the How and Why of a Print Triennial'. In: Moor, et al. (eds), *The Graphic Unconscious*. Philadelphia, PA: Philagrafika, 21–9.

Singerman, Howard. 1999. *Art Subjects: Making Artists in The American University*. Berkeley, CA: University of California Press.
Suzuki, Sarah. 2011. 'Print people: A Brief Taxonomy of Contemporary Printmaking'. *Art Journal*, 70 (4): 6–25.
Tallman, Susan. 2013. 'Wallflower at the Artworld Ball'. In: Rehkopp, M. and Willich, K. (eds), *SNAP 3: 3rd International Printmaking Symposium*. Rheine: Kloster Bentlage, 14–17.
Tallman, Susan. 2012. 'The Elephant in the Room: MoMA's Print Surveys: 1966, 1980, 1996, 2012'. *Art in Print*, 2 (1): 31–9.
Tallman, Susan. 1996. *The Contemporary Print: Pre-Pop to Postmodernism*. London: Thames and Hudson.
Thorburn, Dominic. 2011. 'Navigating the North–South Axis – Divide and Rule?' Presentation at *Intersections and Counterpoints: IMPACT 7 International Multidisciplinary Printmaking Conference*. Melbourne: Monash University, 27–31 September 2011 (unpublished).
Tillman, R. L. 2010. 'On the Faddishness of Printmaking'. *Printeresting*. Blog 22 August 2010: http://archive.printeresting.org/2010/08/22/thoughts-on-the-faddishness-of-printmaking-gq/ [Accessed 19 January 2017].
Weisberg, Ruth. 1986. 'The Syntax of the Print: In Search of an Aesthetic Context'. *The Tamarind Papers: A Journal of the Fine Print* 9 (2): 52–60.

PART I

Genealogy

Introduction to Part I

Part I is titled 'Genealogy' instead of the more conventional 'history'. It signals the insight, following Michel Foucault, that historical accounts, far from being 'objective', exist as the result of discourses and are hence subject to change. In a recent essay, the eminent American Renaissance print scholar and curator Peter Parshall (2016) examined – across the course of several centuries – the changing focus of the discourses on prints and printmaking. His condensed overview of the historiography of print illuminated focal points, as well as exclusions, and demonstrated how discourses constitute, rather than simply describe their subject. Parshall noted the dominance – in art historical writing on print since the eighteenth century – of a connoisseurial approach, which focused on masterpieces, individual print techniques and individual artist monographs, accompanied by the quest for rare pieces or particular 'states' of certain prints. While this largely market-driven methodology still persists, it has also undergone changes. Yet Parshall emphasised that there is a continued necessity for a broader approach to prints that considers their historical significance 'as embedded in society and politics' as well as their cross-medial properties.[1] The texts in Part I allow the reader to gain an overview of such broader historical changes as played out in the wider field of prints and printmaking. All three texts approach their subject from the perspective of media history and 'print culture', rather than of connoisseurial art history. This is not to deny the relevance of aesthetics. The term 'print culture' here serves to highlight print's function as a mode of communication rather than aesthetics alone.

As the title of his chapter indicates, Swiss art historian and media theorist Beat Wyss suggests that specific technologies correspond to certain modes of cultural thought. According to media theorist Vilém Flusser, the invention of writing in the middle of the second millennium BCE and the invention of the technical image, i.e. photography, in the middle of the nineteenth century are to be considered the major cultural factors in media history. Wyss uses the analogy of a finer, 'halftone mesh' to bring into focus the economic, social, religious, political and artistic changes that occurred through the advent of the printing press, especially engraving, the medium of the book and reproducible images. He vividly outlines print's impact on religion, art and society – above all on the power structures associated with them.

The text by German art historian Ernst Rebel links the seemingly self-generative propensity of the new visual technology of photography in the early nineteenth century to earlier graphic processes. These exhibited a similar, if less comprehensive 'automatism' as photography did later. Rebel then traces the development of photography during the nineteenth century which he identifies as 'the second transmedialisation'. If the first transmedialisation is associated with an equality between painting and printmaking around 1500, the second transmedialisation is linked to industrial image production and reproduction at the turn of the twentieth century. Aesthetic forms and media that had previously been separate are made commensurate with each other through the technology of halftone printing. Computer technology is responsible for the third, current transmedialisation. It is characterised by the transmutation of multiple forms, phenomena and signs into binary code. Contemporary printmaking as an art form incorporates elements of this transmedialisation through its adoption of digital technologies. Hence, it can be argued to be supremely 'up-to-date', but there is a simultaneous focus by some artists on printmaking as an 'outdated' mode of technology. As Rebel argues, it can in this respect – as do other art forms – offer some resistance to the competitive drive of mere image innovation through ever newer technologies.

In the last chapter of her book *Print Culture*, Frances Robertson asks whether the widespread assertion of the 'death of print', that is, its displacement by digital technologies and media forms, is accurate. Indeed have the texts and images that we encounter daily become as dematerialised as is constantly argued? The chapter is included here to widen the scope of the notion of print beyond fine art and to explore some of the different material, social, economic and creative practices that have encompassed print in the last two hundred years. Robertson focuses especially on changes to everyday print practices in domestic, commercial and administrative contexts. Amongst other print forms she considers the role and format of the book and the use of paper in the office. She also touches on changes in graphic design, the issue of copyright and the creative commons. Robertson ends with the persuasive conclusion that it is premature to diagnose the 'death' of print culture.

Notes

1 Of course, William Ivins (1953) had famously regarded prints in terms of their communicative rather than merely aesthetic properties. See also Weisberg (1990).

References

Ivins, William M. Jr. 1953. *Prints and Visual Communication*. Cambridge, MA: Harvard University Press.

Parshall, Peter. 2016. 'Why Study Prints Now? Or, the World according to Bartsch'. *Art in Print*, 6 (3): 5–12.

Weisberg, Ruth. 1990. 'The Absent Discourse: Critical Theories and Printmaking'. *The Tamarind Papers*, 13: 8–10.

Beat Wyss

Fragments for an art history of media: electr(on)ic thinking*

The task is to think up a technological history of thought. It would match appropriate technologies with corresponding intellectual developments: imagine a kind of technical 'index fossil' in which contemporary modes of thinking are prefigured. During much of the modern age, clockwork was the dominant technology; its intellectual equivalent is thinking in terms of cause and effect, type and picture – the philosophy of Wilhelm Leibniz. Then the steam engine ploughed through the nineteenth century; its matching philosophy being that of Karl Marx who explains changes in society in terms of the dialectics of compression and rotation. At the end of the same century, electricity's invisible lightning replaced the heavy clouds of steam power. This unfathomable evanescence which is, simultaneously, energy could be linked to Nietzsche's ideas. His 'Gay Science' (German: *Die fröhliche Wissenschaft*) was published in 1882 when the first transformer station was built in New York. Without it no computer can function; electricity is the precondition for the digital image.

The mechanical power in clockwork is visible from the springs, cog wheels and axles that keep it running and transfer energy. The workings of electric power, by contrast, are not represented within the means by which it is produced and distributed. The invisible flow of energy, captured in a system of copper wires and silicon chips, expresses itself only as a *fait accompli* – destructively, if I bring my finger into contact with the electric current; productively, if I connect a hairdryer or a blender. As with the

* Wyss, Beat. 1997. *Die Welt als T-Shirt. Zur Ästhetik und Geschichte der Medien* [*The World as a T-Shirt. On Aesthetics and the History of Media*]. Köln: DuMont Buchverlag. Reproduced in: Wyss, Beat. 1997. 'Fragmente einer Kunstgeschichte der Medien'. In: Hirner, René (ed.), *Vom Holzschnitt zum Internet. Die Kunst und die Geschichte der Bildmedien von 1450 bis Heute* [*From Woodcut to Internet: The Art and History of Image Media from 1450 to Today*]. Ostfildern-Ruit: Cantz Editions, pp. 10–18. Reproduced by kind permission of the author and Hatje-Cantz. Translated by Hugh Keith and Ruth Pelzer-Montada.

hairdryer and blender, the computer, dependent on the electric current, redirects a highly energised nothing into a useful expression of power. On a computer screen, apparently aimless energy is channelled into a meaningful task.

The past as seen through the halftone image

In his *Philosophy of Photography* Vilém Flusser identifies two revolutions that have shaped our cultural behaviour: the invention of writing in the middle of the second millennium before Christ, and the invention of the technical image in the mid-nineteenth century. Different modes of thinking correspond to these two profoundly important time thresholds. This is because, according to Flusser, thought follows formally the conditions of its technical possibilities of expression. Despite the fact that it invents its own symbolic and technical media, thought adapts itself ever more perfectly to them in a virtual process of self-reproduction. While writing expresses the world through signs in a linear fashion, the technical image generates the world in a zigzag between black and white. A staccato of binary information of 'yes' and 'no', '0' and '1', the basis of all digital technologies, creates the image.

Since the invention of photography, according to Flusser, we have thought in binary terms; hence our notion of history is binary too: leaping from 'writing' to 'image'. Without wishing to change this grid pattern, let us – metaphorically speaking – intensify the image resolution, by increasing the enormous shadow dropped between the invention of writing and photography. Let us zoom in on the developments of the last six hundred years. If we view the grid under the magnifying glass, we recognise that although image and writing are two different sign systems for encoding the world, they do not simply follow one another historically, but rather occupy a parallel history, at least for the time period under consideration. Since my own mode of thinking can also only be represented in grids, it is to be marked by three tones of grey, as it were.

At the first level there is handwriting and the '*imago*': emanations of a god or law giver that represents the divine. '*Imago*' designates the concept of the image derived from the image traditions of antiquity and the Middle Ages that Hans Belting has developed in his book *Image and Art*. 'Imagines' – statues of gods and emperors, icons and portraits of the ancestors – are images before the advent of art. Writing and *imago* are produced by the hand of humans, but can also have materialised as a miracle of divine revelation. Writing and *imago* are manually reproduced and, wherever they are placed, represent the will of the gods and the lawmakers. Writing and *imago* were invented as an act of enlightenment against magic animism, which detected the divine and the law in the numinous itself. The cultural achievement of writing and *imago* lies in the separation of signifier and signified. However, populist fervour and awe thwart this imposed enlightenment by venerating established symbols as fetishes. From a theological point of view, the Black Madonna of a pilgrim church is merely the pictorial symbol of the 'mother of God', but the popular inclination towards animism recognises in this piece of dark wood a divine force that brings luck and healing. The animist reinterpretation of the symbol from below clashes with rational domination from above, vacillating between repression and tolerance.

Just as the first step was a reaction against primary animism, so the second step is an act of instruction against that secondary animism which misuses the symbol as a fetish. From the fourteenth century onwards the Renaissance starts to distance itself from the confusion between sign and signified by affirming the visual message unmistakably as an illusionistic representation. A pinnacle is reached in the generation of artists, such as Masaccio, Masolino und Mantegna, who turn space into a language according to mathematical rules, namely the system of central perspective by linear projection. At the same time, between 1434 and 1455, Johannes Gutenberg experiments with letterpress printing as a means to reproduce writing by setting movable type into lines. Writing, manually set in this way, becomes the technically reproducible text. At this point a possible objection can be easily defused, namely that writings other than holy scriptures on divine revelation or the law did exist in antiquity. Of course, there were wordly poets and thinkers such as Vergil, Horace and Cicero. But their work in text form only existed for such a miniscule audience that they are invisible under the broad lens that I am employing here. Vergil, Horace and Cicero only 'become visible' when texts begin to spread and determine the humanistic climate of the modern age. This makes it possible to disseminate an author's written ideas. If writing and *imago* appeared as emanations of the divine and its representatives, text and the reproduced image are created by authors.

One might think that this is still the case today. But here the finer grid coincides with the bigger epochal frame defined by Flusser. Text and the reproduced image change in the age of photography. Created by authors they become procedures and images, generated by machines. The lines you are reading, although produced on a laptop, sound a little 'woodcut-like'; for this reason I will now, in between the second and third steps, use the soft-focus lens of the art historian to ask what it is that connects the symbolic systems of text and process on the one hand and picture and image on the other. Contrary to Flusser's view, it is argued that linguistic and pictorial sign systems – at least during the six hundred years under consideration on our canvas, as it were – possess a parallel history. The end of the culture of writing, that is so frequently bemoaned, and the prognosis of future illiteracy in the digital age remain, figuratively speaking, on the surface of the screen. The user-friendly operating instructions of an interactive porn game rely on computing code: however optically convincing the playmate's movements are, he or she has been as thoroughly constructed as the perspectival space of the seemingly puzzling *Tribute Money* scene by Masaccio. The transitions from *imago* to picture and image run parallel to the transitions from writing, text and machine processes.

At the end of the fourteenth century, 'art', as we understand it when we regard an artificially created object, emerges. The *imago* is not art but an image that stands in for the divine and demands an appropriately devotional attitude from the viewer. Writing and *imago* are media of the divine and its law-making representatives. Texts and pictures are the media of authors. Processes and images are the media of machines. It seems opportune, at this point, to clarify the word 'medium' in pragmatic terms. 'Medium' means 'middle', 'means', 'mediation'. Every sign system has the mediatory task of spreading ideas within a society. Today's conventional use of the word 'medium' only refers to sign systems that have been mediated by technical means. This is a narrowing of the term that is typical for our time. It has even become customary to see a difference between art and media. Art educators and sociologists reflect on the problem of 'art education in the media'; art historians and philosophers are invited to speak about the problems of 'art in the context of the media'. But where is the problem? It lies in the linguistic conventions of those who ask the questions. Art has been a medium since its beginnings. The polarisation of 'art and media' wormed its way into thought when the mechanical apparatus began its cultural dominance. Since then, the representatives of 'art' see themselves as adversaries of the 'media'. Art means high cultural standards while the media in their technical, hence essentially superficial, mode of communication threaten culture and heritage. I will shortly sketch out how this anxiety occurred, but first of all let us return to a time period when art readily understood itself as a medium.

Mysticism and the printing press

Towards the end of the fourteenth century, signs of a media revolution appear whose artistic and societal consequences in no way lag behind those of the invention of the daguerreotype. *Imago* and writing as medial sign systems of divine revelation start to weaken. During major upheavals, cultural and technical developments enter into a productive force-field. It is pointless to ask whether cultural and social needs influence technology or, conversely, technical possibilities determine the cultural life of a society. Socio-cultural attitudes and technologies can co-exist side by side for centuries without cross-fertilisation. This was the case with the ingredients that led to the media revolution of 1500. Textile printing by means of wood blocks was already known in late antiquity. This technical process of reproduction was used for transferring ornaments onto wallpaper and fabric. At the same time, since early Christianity, there has been the mystical tradition of Gnosticism. What, you might ask, links a wooden printing block and mysticism?

The answer is: a lot, if the stars of history form a specific conjunction. When, in the fourteenth century, the Italians imported papermaking from Arabia, they were primarily interested in writing material that was more convenient than parchment. But which Tuscan ragman and paper maker would have thought then that his product would become the fuse that ignited the edifice of the Church? When the first German paper mill of Ulmann Stromer near Nuremberg went into production in around 1390, the time was ripe for the first fermentation between technology and thought. The first single leaf woodcut prints whose colour adhered well to paper were circulated. Small devotional images were printed. Cheap and increasingly in demand, they were bought by people as an aid to prayer within their own home. These reproduced, bought and sold devotional objects facilitated the renunciation of the *imago*, the icon in a holy place guarded by the clergy. The result was a kind of folk piety that freed itself from the Church's liturgical calendar. An example had been set by individual mystics, such as Heinrich Seuse, who had had pious miniatures painted by artists, in front of which he performed his prayers. The fact that Seuse, a pupil of Meister Eckhart, wrote the first autobiography in German is testimony of a new spirituality that is about to discover itself. Miniaturised devotional pictures endowed piety with mobility and accompanied the spirit on its journeys. Heinrich von Nördlingen and his spiritual friend, the Dominican nun Margaretha Ebner, sent each other small, edifying parchment pictures via courier. Such mystical long-distance traffic was a forerunner of the videophone.

Mystical contemplation corresponded to an emancipation of faith from the control of the clergy whose influence the common people now also began to escape. The privatisation of religious media triggered a deregulation of spirituality. The devotional picture as the reproduced image of signs from the world of the icon made itself available to a private desire for faith. These small pictures were initially distributed without accompanying text; carrying no commentary, their interpretation was therefore left to whichever practices their users chose. In the eyes of the Church, these cheap woodcuts, often carelessly slapped onto the paper, opened the floodgates to heresy. As this connection between technology and thought developed, there was an initial reverse impact on the medium. The printing process became rationalised in order to supply a market with a commodity that did not yet exist. As already mentioned, Johannes Gutenberg had been conducting experiments with a printing press since 1434. The first 42-line bible left the print shop in Mainz in 1455. Blockbook and movable type brought text and image into a flexible relationship that furthermore could be reproduced almost at will. From the perspective of writing and the *imago*, both these achievements were highly alarming: The possibility of a flexible association between text and imprint loosened the binding character of bible interpretation; private acquisition by the masses removed the encounter with the contents of belief from the control of the Church. Attending holy mass compared to devotional practice at home is like the relationship between going to the cinema and watching TV. The edifyingly illustrated prayer book for domestic use is a forerunner of the video.

These developments established the feedback loop between the new technical processes and the socio-cultural mindset. The Reformation utilised printed books and illustrated flyers as media in its struggle against the papacy. A popular format of the pamphlet was the dialogue: an early form of snapshot 'citizen journalism'. People love news reports that appear to come straight from 'real life'. Luther's Wittenberg became the media centre of the Reformation. By 1550, a hundred thousand copies of his bible had been sold. Illustrated with images from the Cranach workshop, the Luther bible represented a highpoint of medial progress. The example of the Luther bible demonstrates the parallel history of text and reproduced image. The printing matrix brings together Cranach's woodcut with lines of letter type. The word 'type' derives from the Greek 'typos' with its multi-faceted meanings of 'imprint', 'pattern', 'picture', 'model'. Text and pictures are reproductions drawn from typoi.

The *imago* is a manually created image object that we – although not in the sense of the monk for whom the icon was a representation of the divine – call an 'original'. In reproducing the *imago* it was necessary to observe as precise as possible a correspondence with the initial image that was, at best, regarded as having been directly handed down: an exact imprint of the immortalised, like Christ's Holy Shroud; an icon directly descended from heaven or painted under the guidance of an angel's hand; a contemporaneous picture painted by a key witness, like the apostle Lucas, for example, the patron saint of painters. An icon therefore is not an actual reproduction but a picture that stands in for the original image that is representative of God and His Saints.

Print significantly changes the religious idea of what an 'image' is. It becomes 'information': the imprinting of a conceptual idea onto matter. Already Aristotle had conceptualised the world as composed of 'hylae' and 'morphae', form and matter. His theory of hylomorphism, until then only comparable with the impression of seals and stamping of coins, encountered in book printing a new, manifest realisation. Within the printed 'information', form as 'patrix' lowers itself onto the 'matrix' of the material support. Information was represented as an act of procreation from the perspective of the men working in the print workshop. The male stamp, the type, presses the imprint of a new idea onto the female paper, the soul of which can be heard murmuring in the letter fonts. In the epoch of text and reproduced image that begins with modernity, the world appears as the reproduction of an idea. Everything that is visible and legible is the imprint of potently fertile models.

The media revolution around 1500

In the third decade of the fifteenth century, concurrently with the development of book printing, image processing was improved by the invention of copper engraving. One of the first artists who did not use the new technique for reproductive purposes only but also as an art form in its own right was Martin Schongauer (ca. 1450–91). He marked the printing plate with his monogram. Artistic ideas circulated throughout workshops in Europe in the form of engraved sample sheets, and thus changed artistic training. The apprentice was no longer obliged to journey in order to gain knowledge. In the sphere of artistic production, a reversal occurred: once images start to wander, the artist becomes more sedentary and may, in the best case scenario, remain at home. Even there he is able to acquire information faster and more comprehensively than a medieval stone mason, who had to earn his apprenticeship by journeying from building site to building site between Reims and Pisa. Sitting at home, the artist could now learn about the latest formal inventions from the artistic centres in Venice or Antwerp via pattern books and sample sheets. This network for the transmission of ideas resulted in a homogenisation of styles. Artists of the sixteenth century in the Netherlands, Germany and Italy were interconnected by graphic prints. As already mentioned, information was distributed faster and more widely but was also more superficial than before. One can trace this media-derived stylistic flattening due to greater sedentariness for example in German Renaissance architecture: it seems to be cut straight out of Italian pattern books.

A multitude of inventions crowded the media market around 1500: short-lived ones like the woodcut tone-block by Lucas Cranach the Elder and Hans Burgkmair; long-lasting ones like intaglio printing, which first of all became popular as drypoint and then through etching. As with many technical advances, engraving most likely derives from arms manufacture. The invention may have been an accidental result of the application of decorative engravings on armour by craftsmen. The earliest known engraving, dated 1513, was by Urs Graf who himself happened to be a mercenary.

At the beginning of the sixteenth century not just the sphere of production was extended, but also the sphere of distribution. Professional engravers emerged like Marcantonio Raimondi, who worked on the basis of originals by Dürer, Titian, Michelangelo and Raphael and also published reproductions of antiquities in Rome. Raimondi influenced the school of engravers of Raphael's pupil Giulio Romano, a branch of which opened in Antwerp with the workshop of Hieronymus Cock. As well as professional engravers, publishers became the new producers of the medium. Cock distributed print editions of up to 1,000; his publishing house was called – not without reason – 'To the Four Winds'.

One of the designers of Cock's originals for reproduction was Pieter Bruegel, a brilliant draftsman. In art as a system of representation, drawing now attained a new value as the prototype of the artistic idea. The distinctive, virtuoso drawing style of an artist achieved market value due to its recognisable particularity; and thanks to engraving it could be reproduced. The artist himself operated as the engraver of his work. By means of the 'original print' the first simulacrum of individuality was created: a serially produced expression of uniqueness.

As in the sphere of production, a countervailing trend appeared in the sphere of distribution: The larger the degree of dissemination of systems of reproduction, the smaller the circle of significant producers of ideas. The commercial distribution system of prints favoured the stars among the artists. Their ideas functioned as taste-makers and influenced the mid-field of production in the business of art through print media. The overwhelming influence of Dürer, Titian, Michelangelo and Raphael is due to print. They were quick to recognise the possibilities of the new medium in creating fame and attracting lucrative commissions. Titian was one of the first celebrity artists to employ an engraver in his workshop specifically to reproduce and publish his work. At the same time, leading artists had to make sure that their engravers did not exploit or usurp their ideas. Dürer deliberately travelled to Venice in order to safeguard his copyright from Raimondi's expansionist business acumen.

By means of the media and favouring celebrity artists, the system of image reproduction asserts a canon of normative values. This homogenisation of taste led, in the course of the modern age, to a dominance of Academicism that was only broken by the artistic rebels of the nineteenth century.

The media revolution around 1500 occurred through a chain of historical accidents, religious movements and inventions in the field of the reproduction of text and image. Its technical outcomes were the book and intaglio printing; its cultural consequences were the Reformation and Counter-Reformation. The medial system of text and reproduced image made it possible, through information, to standardise a society's mind-set and to influence and monitor it effectively.

Nevertheless, progress in media technologies generates uncontrollable side-effects which, from the view point of high culture, are either arrogantly ignored or actively fought against. The official perspective of elite culture regards them as entropic waste products of progress. Despite being a result of progress, they disrupt it. Officially they can never be declared socially acceptable, for in their amorality they are subversive; at the same time they are so persistently popular that only draconian laws could prohibit them. This, however, conflicts with the interests of media operators who make good money from popular, latently seditious products. The 'gameboy' of printmaking was the card game, whose negative influence, together with unbridled drinking deprived many a family of their possessions and landed them in the poorhouse. Somewhat more harmless was the sensationalist press, which brought reports of comets, bizarre birth defects and cannibals. The danger was that such extraordinary news might import heretic viruses into the mental programme of society. However, such amoral cravings for outlandish, cruel stories could be presented within an orthodox context – for example by a report of a massacre of fellow Christians by Turkish pirates. Delight in the gory was thus – to the benefit of state and Church – directed into hatred of the Other.

In 1524 the first printed porn was issued by Raimondi's workshop. He had an eye for a business opportunity beyond the confines of High Art. Based on originals by Giulio Romano he published nude couples cavorting in advanced erotic positions; none other than [the poet] Pietro Aretino delivered the soundtrack in form of adroitly wrought verses. Raimondi found himself in prison but was promptly released after a few days – thanks to protection from on high by those among whom his booklet circulated and had secretly found favour.

The [radical theologian and preacher] Thomas Müntzer could not count on such favours. His 'Sermon to the Princes' – also of 1524 – triggered the Peasants' War. The latters' defeat proved the historical law by which no media revolution starts from below. Luther's media machine was oiled from above – and not just from heaven.

Technical progress in the media generates contradictory processes, two of which we already know: In the sphere of production, where the images migrate and the artists become sedentary; in the sphere of distribution where dissemination increases and the circle of major suppliers of ideas diminishes. The third contradictory process is to be found in reception: mass publication promotes private encounters with information. Media do not, as commonly asserted, create a public sphere but are rather a means of addressing private individuals by circumventing it.

Ernst Rebel

The technical gaze: the parallel world of photography*

Photography is not a graphic technique. Strictly speaking it therefore does not belong to the purview of our topic. Nevertheless it needs to be mentioned here. Nowadays, the photographic image functions either as the initial medium or as an element of one. It is an essential constituent of our world of signs and images. 99 out of 100 images we encounter are mediated by photo-technical means. This also applies to the large number of woodcuts, engravings and etchings that have accumulated over the centuries. The historical prints that we see today exist for the most part in books, catalogues, journals, on postcards or posters. We encounter them as photographs, reproduced by industrial halftone printing, often in facsimile quality that comes close to the original. In other words, they are represented in a way that lets us forget about the difference between original and reproduction.

Today, this development towards apparent identity and authenticity is far from over – in the context of digital production it has only just begun. But there is another reason why photography must not be disregarded in the context of printed images. From an art historical perspective, photography can be regarded as the most instructive model of technical synthesis. It draws together several features which – partially stretching back into the mythic beginnings of our cultural memory – point towards the realisation of the dream of the self-replicating image. It is here that the connections with our actual topic lie. This is because the history of printmaking is filled with attempts at technical automation, efforts to transfer and replace at least some of its processes or parts thereof. As a brief reminder: Gutenberg's movable type had provided a variable and reproducible set of letters: a

* Ernst Rebel. 2003. *Druckgrafik. Geschichte, Fachbegriffe* [*Printmaking. History, Terminology*]. Ditzingen: Reclam, pp. 116–48. Shortened excerpt. Reproduced by kind permission of the author and Reclam Verlag. Translated by Hugh Keith and Ruth Pelzer-Montada.

compendium of the printable word. Etchers had replaced the work of deep manual incision of the plate by the chemical etching process. In this way they took partial control of inevitably occurring natural processes. Further, printmakers who used aquatint had obtained the etching of tonal values by means of the mechanical dusting of the plate with powdered rosin. By their use of multiple plates mezzotint artists anticipated the quasi-automatic synthesis of all colours achieved later through superimposition of tone and light components. Stereo- and galvanotypes made the automatic reproduction of the plate possible. However, none of these substitution or auto-technical components replaced the manual craft principle completely or led to the ultimate control of chance. Nevertheless, technical predictability increased gradually. Finally, in the nineteenth century, photography appears. In its basic premise it is nothing more than the technical control of the automatic action of those magical processes that had been observed for centuries in the *camera obscura*. [...] The world begins to divide into a twin chamber system of visible things: 'Outside' there is the real world of buildings, trees, humans: the world as an infinitely contingent space, and, separated from it is the 'interior' of the dark chamber. Into it tumbles – as if through an eye that is composed of aperture, mirror and lens – everything that the aperture can optically collect. This light materialises in the darkroom as an imprint of the outer world. [...] This is the point at which, between 1829 and 1839, the invention of photography begins. Its pioneers Nicéphore Niépce (1765–1833), Louis-Jacques Daguerre (1787–1851) and William Henry Fox Talbot (1800–87) brought the pictorial elements of the camera obscura under their productive control. They fixed the fleeting image by means of light-sensitive coatings – substances that hardened under the effect of light. In this way they transformed physical-optical processes into chemical ones, translating reflection and time into tangible permanence. The other aspects of the chamber were also gradually rationalised in terms of their image-generating and image-storing functions. The optical complex achieved synchronisation with the chemical transformation process. This occurred through extra light-sensitive mobile lenses and light-filtering aperture mechanisms. The chamber itself, originally a physical place, became a mobile device. (Only in the word 'dark room', the place for the completion of the analogue photographic process by means of developer and fixing baths, does a remnant of the original meaning of the word persist.) If the 'light-image' was at first fixed to glass or metal, pictures soon developed that were conveyed by gelatin-coated papers and foils und whose division into a positive and negative allowed them to be reproduced. Several 'positives' could be 'copied' from the 'negative' of a 'shot'. Photography thus approached, albeit distantly, graphic multiplication.

Up to the end of the century, all these constituents and factors underwent numerous and continuous improvements. Ultimately, they mirror the technical and commercial process of modernity as a dynamic of progress characterised by competition. Between the daguerreotype (1839) and the industrially produced Eastman-Kodak roll film (1894), photographic image production underwent a process of continuous improvement and functional expansion. The technical gaze was able to conquer the world with ever greater speed, accuracy and versatility, partly in competition with the art of the painter, partly in cooperation with it. The first big phase of the history of photography was completed around 1900. Alongside the existence of artistic images there were now uniquely technical images and, with the concurrent rise of amateur photography, the accessibility of all aspects of the visible, even to the lay person, became historical fact. Thanks to photography the spectrum of the *technical image* expanded significantly. Functions of the image that had grown across epochs, such as documentation, fiction, decoration, propaganda, entertainment, now, at the turn of the twentieth century, became amplified. Added to this were the reporting capabilities of photo journalism. At the same time, new modes of aesthetic experimentation developed that were only possible on the basis of photography, such as the snapshot and amateur 'snapping'. In particular, early snapshots show that novel pictorial participation in reality does not merely provide evidence of subjective freedom. The photographic DIY gaze onto a rainy scene in the centre of Vienna in approximately 1895* demonstrates exactly the opposite. The photo-eye 'sees' more and, above all, it sees differently from the human eye. Humans think, feel and remember while and because they are seeing. The more aimlessly, unintentionally and faster the photo-eye captures the world and its events, the more authentic and – literally – more objective the frozen arrested features turn out to be: a pavement mirrors wetness in more extensive and consistent detail than the natural eye would ever be able to perceive in such a short moment; humans [...] approach the camera – actors without composition or direction; an object in the foreground accidentally gains more weight than any human figure; cut-off features, arrested movements and gestures of the figures, light patterns, peripheral information [...] – there is only a rapid here and now, precise, yet permanently subject to chance: a picture-world that only attains independent existence in and for the photographic moment. The moment and its footprint coincide in the outcome. A unity of opposites briefly accumulates: subject – object, temporality – duration, intention – chance, contingence – necessity, everything becomes subject to the same technicised moment.

However, all this does not fully describe the technical gaze. Even the earlier developments of the graphic arts taught us that the principle of reproduction does not only represent quantitative but ultimately also qualitative changes in perception. Neither should one disregard this aspect in

* Editor's note: Rebel is referring to a typical snapshot of an urban scene.

relation to the history of photography. Only the *printed, mass-reproduced* photo contributes to a change in public consciousness and can become a 'public image' (Diers, 1997: 42). The paramount medium for this is the autotype, developed in 1881 by Georg Meisenbach (1841–1922). The operative core of this [halftone] process is a specially devised 'cross-line grid', which revolutionised commercial illustration worldwide around 1890 and is the final link with the sizeable, technological tool-kit of the nineteenth century. It is at this point that we return to the graphic core of our topic.

The second transmedialisation

Industrial halftone screens

In order to accurately combine typesetting and the authentic light-image, its rich halftones have to be broken down into printable elements that should be indiscernible to the human eye from the outset. This is to satisfy the large print runs of the book and newspaper publishing industry. In contrast to the pre-industrial rasters of mezzo- and aquatints, the photomechanical 'cross-line grid' introduces the precision and complexity of control that are indispensable for industrial demands. What is its main principle? A glass plate bearing a cross-hair grid is mounted in front of the photograph that is to be reproduced. During exposure, the lighter areas of the halftone sample reflect light more intensely than the darker ones. This leads to a greater overlay of the light cones within the micro-windows of the cross-line grid and effectively to smaller grid dots. Conversely it results in larger dots for the darker reflection areas. Following the usual developing and fixing processes, the continuum of these window contents (dots), which also essentially change between circular and square shapes, can be copied onto a zinc plate, etched in relief and then printed. Depending on the size of the grid the dots – that is the print particles – are invisible to the eye. Larger editions require – at least during the pioneer days of the process – coarser, more wear-and-tear resistant grids.

[...]

We can say that the authentic light and dark of photography is translated into a secondary – inauthentic – light and dark of the grid-exposure, in both cases according to the laws of mechanics, optics and photochemistry. Under a magnifying glass one can see how, for example, buildings, shadows and human figures in a photo become transformed into a seamlessly structured universe of continuously quantified graphic particles for the purposes of reproducibility. While the autotype reproduces the authenticity of representation in a controlled fashion, it does so fully and automatically as a function of objective facts and technically regulated mechanisms. Every optical phenomenon, regardless of the type and reality of the image, becomes the uniform material of raster quanta verging towards disappearance. At this level of possibilities the old utopian dreams of the four-colour print can suddenly be resolved. After 1900 even the colourful phenomenal continuum of reality can – on the basis of optically and photochemically precisely controlled colour filters – be defined in analogue terms, converted into a raster grid and graphically reproduced. Of course relief print, given all these rationalisations of the process, is not the only conveyor of progress. Intaglio (copper intaglio printing) and planographic processes (offset) contribute their own subtle variations and participate in the production of the industrial flood of images which now covers the entire globe. If, from today's perspective, one attempts to invest past developments with a historical 'logic' – in other words to recognise, within the growing complexity, a trend towards continuously improved performance – one arrives at surprising insights: A certain similarity of innovative processes at the turn of two different epochs and centuries becomes apparent. While around 1500 a first transmedialisation occurred on account of the equivalence between painting and printmaking, around 1900 a second transmedialisation materialises due to the equality that has been reached between the artistic and the industrial–public image of commercial graphics. To put it differently: just as around 1500 the 'original' arts became translated by means of reproductive printmaking into a multiplicatory form and were thus made available to a broader public, in around 1900 the full range of aesthetic manifestations, including its various mediatised forms, becomes multiplied and made public by means of a single technology that integrates all media and effects – industrial halftone printing. A multiplication of multiplication occurs, a *potentiation* of the image. The industrial halftone process around 1900 devours all previous media and forms, a quasi-authentic leveller of all differences in appearance. An art journal presents next to each other photos from art and life, architectural views, sculptures of stone and bronze, tapestries and frescoes, charcoal drawings, water-colours and oil paintings, their differences technically registered by autotype. Whether as a postcard or poster, as book or magazine illustrations: all images of art history, photos of contemporary events, inventions and codes of advertising – anything that can be documented somehow, all signs of the visible world now enter the media store of industrial halftone printing. This is what the term *transmedialisation* entails: individual media divest some of their properties to another, technically superior medium or are completely replaced by it.

Yet one must not merely list the negative aspects. The industrial halftone process not only generates a gigantic flood of images, but also acts as a means of regulation. Even the archives of our cultural image memory require reproducible evidence for the purpose of collection and organisation.

Without the flood of images today there would be no supply of images either! And since talk of a glut of images has taken on inflationary dimensions, one should add: it is not the glut as such that is the problem, but rather our way of dealing with it.
[…]

Transmedialisation once again

From the nineteenth century onwards, the history of the technical image cannot be solely tied to the experimental ventures of printmaking and photography. As we have already seen, in the particle universe of industrial halftone the graphic principle meets its secret apotheosis, albeit with the result of its becoming merely one element within a technology that spans different media. At the end of the twentieth century, two things of relevance emerge for our topic. Firstly, today, all previous pioneering functions of the technical image have been taken over by computer technology. Secondly, print continues to exist as part of a consolidated media system, and even operates at a high artistic level, though ultimately it is being historically superseded, and reduced to a subsidiary existence. Just as industrial halftone around 1900 reduced all manner of images to the most common, publicly efficient denominator of reproduction, after 1980, a third transformation (transmedialisation) occurred. In the electronic environment, the old polarities between 'public' and 'private', 'productive' and 'receptive', 'professional' and 'amateur' are increasingly disappearing, as they all become lumped together by the same algorithm-based system. Within the gigantic, globe-spanning binary code of digital virtuality, all signs become networked within a traceless data archive; one generates, saves, downloads, converts. Binary code resembles the grid above all grids. Only within the pixel field of the monitor or as a printout can it be sensed in its material form. There is no extra-digital 'art' which does not refer to the prevailing omnipotence of signs. This is the case even when it demonstratively rejects the latter's hegemony. There is no 'art history' that has not, in the meantime, expanded to become a 'history of the image'; no history of print that could still describe its own developments without referring to the horizon of the pixel universe.

Nevertheless it is also legitimate to pursue the impulses of transmedialisation within the heart of today's sidelined field of artistic printmaking. It is legitimate because it is not obligatory to discuss art and image only at the level of the technological vanguard, and because one may wish to discover, within the harsh competition for innovation, the gentle spirit of free exchange. Printmaking, like any art, can contribute powers of resistance to this goal.
[…]

Back to the future

From the 1980s onwards certain developments that concern many general areas of image cultures, right down to 'subculture' scenes such as techno-aesthetics, nevertheless have to be regarded as typical for the graphic field of printmaking. This is a trend with multiple strands, which resists the dominant slogans of progress. One could term it voluntary restraint, a conscious return to the manageable order of crafts, rules and respect for materials. If, for example, photographers today demonstratively cling to the production principles of black-and-white analogue photography, then they do so partly in order to cultivate an individual, manual intensity of picture-making in contrast to the new digital automatism. Or take young people in the computer-scene competing in sports-like fashion for the simplest and most efficient version of a piece of software-hacking (Botz, 2008: 207). Here, the crucial principle is that of voluntary self-regulation. It is not rule-breaking that is rewarded but rather creativity that aims to establish and maintain boundaries, because this is the only way to safeguard the comprehensibility of one's own procedures. The technical core of such competitions is not the latest piece of hardware on the market, but rather the 'old' cult hardware of the Commodore 64, built in 1983. In other words, complexity is renounced, 'craft' is prioritised over mere technical bravura. Printmaking now, however much it may have become a marginal form in a digitally dominated world of image reproduction, also appears to have become the refuge for such technical self-restriction. Take screen-printing: its experiments by now consist of applying the same photomechanical principles to infinitely varied support materials, more often than not for purely artistic reasons. In such cases the underlying rationale is, above all, pleasure in extending the controlled range of possibilities (Sienel, 2008: 164).

[...]*

It is within the space of graphically translated images that the contrasts between old and new media are temporarily resolved. As to its future value, making through craft is not so much a limitation as a condition of print's continued creative existence – an existence that does not wish to turn its back on the physical aspects of the craft.

* Editor's note: Rebel goes on to discuss the woodcuts of contemporary artists Gert and Uwe Tobias as an example of the creative potential that can be derived from the resistance of materials and the application of the rules of craftsmanship. He then concludes with the final paragraph reproduced here.

References

Botz, Daniel. 2008. *Hacker-Ästhetik. Die geschichtlichen, technischen und gestalterischen Voraussetzungen zum Verständnis des Mediums Computerdemo*. Dissertation, München.

Diers, Michael. 1997. *Zur politischen Ikonographie der Gegenwart*. Frankfurt a M.: Fischer Verlag.

Sienel, Uta Catharina. 2008. *Der Siebdruck und Seine Druckträger. Zur Materialität eines Jungen Druckverfahrens*. München: Utz.

Frances Robertson

Post-print culture?*

Print culture cannot be reduced to one narrative; for example the introduction of print culture in the Middle East or in India did not necessarily lead to the development of a Western humanist mindset, but was instead often adopted in order to attack colonial rule or secular values. 'Print culture' (as a kind of slogan) has also often been espoused by particular groups within the business of print, whether by printing house workers, publishers or academics, leading to very different characterisations of what print culture might be; and in the process, these views have often been attached to different mediums and visual languages. But below these assured professional voices, many printed objects have been produced in more informal circumstances or in different working spheres. Against the more powerful expression of designers and associated discourses of exhibitions, academic monographs and critical commentaries, discredited, outdated and 'merely decorative' items also have weight. The example of chromolithographs, whether in women's social exchanges in domestic spaces or in the development of 'photos of the gods' in India in the late nineteenth century (Pinney 2004), show that the worthy ideals of a single, progressive 'print culture' are simply the good taste of the ruling caste.

Breaking up print culture from any abstract overall meaning it may have, and looking at the particularities of printing techniques and mediums, also shows the social, political and economic costs and difficulties of change and innovation, combating more deterministic views of the march of print culture and indeed of visual culture in general. Looking at the materiality of specific mediums and examples shows those social negotiations in contact with the worlds of production, and the meanings of making objects in multiples. Printing techniques have always been derived from other

* Frances Robertson. 2013. 'Conclusion: Post-Print Culture?' In: Frances Robertson (ed.), *Print Culture*. New York: Routledge, pp. 118–32. Reproduced by kind permission of the author and Taylor & Francis.

procedures for making objects in multiples, some very ancient, such as stamping, branding and stencilling, and the development of printing reflects the state of surrounding technologies, whether these are expressed in steam and steel, chemistry, photographic imaging, or computing. Techniques for surface marking in print are at the very boundary of two- and three-dimensional making, and today some important applications of printing are sinking back into procedures for object crafting, and away from the production of textual content. For example, a Google search using the keyword 'photolithography' is now much more likely to throw up references to nanotechnology. Optical lithography is used for microfabrication of objects such as circuits (Sotomayor Torres 2003) in a continuation of the ways in which silk screen-printing was also harnessed for fuse and circuit production earlier in the twentieth century (Kosloff 1958), while digital three-dimensional printing is now used increasingly for design prototyping or individual bespoke fabrication of material objects (Gerschenfeld 2007).

But against these new applications of print procedures, the advent of digital communication technology, whether as cyberspace (Benedikt 1992) or hypertext (Landow 2006) has been seen, often gleefully, as the end of print culture (Joyce 2001). Many rapid response books on the death of print appeared around the turn of the millennium with titles such as *The Gutenberg Elegies: The Fate of Reading in an Electronic Age* (Birkerts 1994) or more bluntly (from the latecomer Jeff Gomez) *Print is Dead: Books in our Digital Age* (2008). Reviewers responded to this genre with their own crop of hackneyed jokes about the irony of this procedure, or the tonnage of dead trees. Sven Birkerts, for example, feared that the loss of printing would unweave the social fabric, erode language and destroy our sense of history (Birkerts 1994: 125–9), while more recent books such as *The Shallows: How the Internet is Changing the Way we Think, Read and Remember* (Carr 2010) seemed to invite mockery by setting out to prove that we now lack the concentration to follow a sustained argument. These books do nevertheless all reflect serious anxieties: that digital communications appear to threaten those core values of print culture of clear authorship, of the perceived stability and fixity of texts, or that hyperlinks will encourage jumping and browsing so that we will lose interest in following the thread of sustained linear arguments or narratives that are carried in books. The short life of most websites, and the open-access policies of most web servers, make digital content suspect to most academics. In short, digital communications threaten our social and consensual models of how information is to be made and agreed, and how knowledge is ordered. Other common fears about the death of print culture are more personal and subjective, usually focused directly on bookish pleasures that might be lost, such as the nostalgic atmosphere of old libraries, or the private pleasures of quiet reading in bed or the bath. Even before the development of commercially successful digital book readers, such as Sony's digital e-book reader (2006) or Amazon's Kindle (2007), many commentators feared that young people, 'digital natives', were no longer accustomed to reading or handling information in books (Thompson 2010: 312–68). Why would a student bother to walk to the library or consult an index with Google or Wikipedia at hand? While book historians Finkelstein and McCleery note a 'natural closure' of the 'old print revolution' in the electronic era (Finkelstein and McCleery 2005: 26), Elizabeth Eisenstein has claimed more boldly that print's 'sense of an ending' began right from the start of the twentieth century due to incursions of previous new media, so that digital books are only a final confirmation of the end of print's domination (Eisenstein 2011: 215).

Nevertheless, we can see that many of these fears are exaggerated and misdirected, and some of the cult of the 'physical book' is misleadingly rose-tinted. Not all books are fun to handle. William Morris's complaint about unwieldy books in 1894 is still only too recognisable today: 'you want a book to turn over easily, and to lie quiet while you are reading it ... the fact is, a small book seldom does lie quiet, and you either have to cramp your hand by holding it, or else put it on the table with a paraphernalia of matters to keep it down, a tablespoon on one side, a knife on the other, and so on, which things always tumble off at a critical moment' (Morris 1999 [1893]; Peterson 1991). With e-readers, why go through this performance? Geoffrey Nunberg suggests a massive but selective cull of printed material would not be a bad thing: 'books as such – that is, bound and printed documents – are not an interesting category. In modern industrial societies, the vast majority of books bear no cultural burden at all: they are parts catalogs, census reports ... repair manuals, telephone directories, airline schedules' (Nunberg 1993). But whatever one's stance, blanket statements such as 'print is dead' are still largely rhetorical and speculative. In relation to book use and production, print is still dominant. The volume of printed book sales has actually increased in the digital era, as communications and searching technologies support much more widespread browsing and buying, with online discussion groups and internet book sites such as Amazon. Used and out-of-print books are now much more easily available either through second-hand book sites such as Abebooks, or as facsimile copies through print-on-demand services. Even though e-book sales have increased significantly in the few years they have been available (for example, moving from around 3 per cent of total book sales in 2009 to around 8 per cent in 2010), those sales are only a small percentage of the total. Printed books and print culture are still central elements of cultural life, although patterns of use, marketing and consumption are changing (Nunberg 1996; Thompson 2010; Striphas 2011). In these circumstances, John B. Thompson has argued that concentrating on the fate of the 'physical book' does not in fact offer the most important analysis of the effects of digital communications on print culture. Instead, the real impact of digital technology is on the workflow and operating systems of print production (Thompson 2010: 321). Until the late 1990s, most publishers used offset lithographic printing that was expensive in terms of initial set-up costs to print large runs of books. Digital technologies such as Xerox DocuTech systems or scanned PDF facsimiles allow short-run print-on-demand strategies. Instead of selling large numbers of (it is hoped) startlingly new best-sellers, publishers can in theory maintain a large digital back catalogue of titles that would only be printed when desired (Thompson 2010: 324–7).

Nor is print culture just about book production. Ephemeral and everyday uses of print have increased in many domains in the digital era: in advertising, in commerce and packaging, and in the office. The printing industry is dominated by massive business corporations whose activities are rarely talked about outside the trade and financial press, but whose output spans a whole range of products such as security and banknote printing, mail order catalogues and packaging (Marshall 1983: 7, 54). If printers in craft unions have declined there is a still a vast workforce serving new species of printers (that is, machines), whether in large automated offset litho printing plants for newspapers and packaging, local copy shop equipment running both digital and offset operations or desktop printers. Workers in print culture include lower-skilled print workers, engineers, designers, marketing teams, and the buyers and users of printed products. The number of professional designers has increased enormously; creating a much more crowded labour market.

[...]

The field of design and typography practices [also] expanded and changed from the 1980s with increasing marketing of personal computers to ordinary buyers without technical expertise. Word processing and design software developed for these products, suitable for all computer users, meant that many non-specialists began to create graphic designs, or at the very least began to take an interest in typography and design to an unprecedented degree. Apple Macintosh computers, introduced in 1984, were equipped for the first time with word processing choices about fonts (such as Chicago and Geneva) and layout, prompting users to take account of their text's appearance. Such concentration on the visual, on appearance as a central factor in the writing process, marked a real change in way that readers evaluated their texts (Staples 2000: 20). All home software providers developed word processing packages and the number of font choices and layout options continued to increase. Default settings and 'style themes' impose structure and a somewhat bland uniformity. However, digital graphics and new methods of designing type also created unexpected appearances and layouts that formed a jarring contrast to established ideas of print layout and design.

[...]

Digital equipment allowed designers and writers to craft a postmodern form of expression that deliberately stressed the ambivalent quality of destabilised digital typography, demonstrating an indeterminacy of meaning to set against the fixity and trustworthiness of graphic design derived from traditional typesetting (Brannon 2007: 353–64), or to break with established good practice in other ways. Well-known examples include April Greiman's contribution 'Does It Make Sense?' to the magazine *Design Quarterly* (No 133: 1986). Here, an apparently normal issue of the magazine actually opened out to one single large poster, folded to the normal format size. When open, the poster presented unconventional graphic language laid out in unfamiliar style, designed and pasted-up entirely on computer. According to Heller and Pomeroy, this was completely new and astonishing. In 1986, most designers were accustomed to paste-up methods established in the era of photomechanical reproduction and felt that computers were 'arcane, expensive and unfriendly', producing uncongenial 'bit-mapped type and imagery'. Greiman's work asserted a 'new level of authorship for designers' using personal computers (Heller and Pomeroy 1997: 213–14). Such new graphic languages have quickly been assimilated into practice and into teaching, for example in the experimental and theoretical work of the graduate school of graphic design at Cranbrook Academy of Art under Katherine McCoy. Through the 1980s and 1990s, the school developed graphic languages in print that reflected digital methods of working (and thinking), with layers of embedded information, non-linear progression of ideas, and an exploration of the decorative and expressive qualities of type (Heller and Pomeroy 1997: 147–50; Lupton and Miller 2010 [1994]: 192–9).

[…]

The conceptual artist and graphic designer Blair Robins reflects on the multiple registers of print communication in his practice, with reference to contemporary digital graphic styles of assembly. For example in the project *The Money Supply* Robins presented a critical analysis on the ways in which both art and money are accorded value through agreed systems for creating surface markings, while also thinking about the instant visual recognition aimed for in brand identity.

[…]

In contrast to high-resolution prints in advertising and other commercial communications, digital design is also used to generate everyday and frequently low-resolution print outputs in domestic and office environments. In *The Myth of the Paperless Office* Sellen and Harper (2002) describe the changing uses of paper and print in digital office environments. The idea of the paperless office was, as they show, a journalistic future-gazing invention; nevertheless it caught hold with many business thinkers because paper was a 'symbol of old-fashioned practices and old-fashioned technologies' placed in unflattering contrast to new digital regimes of office computing

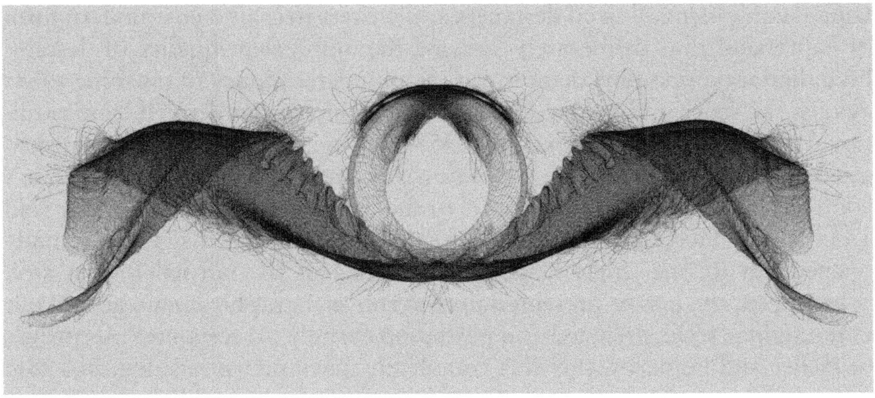

Blair Robins, *Gorgon*, 2007. Digital inkjet print. 17″ × 32″.

(Sellen and Harper 2002: 5). Office managers became sensitive to the sight of piles of paper that they associated with incompetence. Clear desks, to some bosses, signified their employees were clear thinkers and efficient workers. In reality, Sellen and Harper found that just as the volume of books on paper has increased in conjunction with digital technologies, so office paper use has also increased substantially in conjunction with digital office technologies.

[…]

The interaction between paper and digital ways of working has created new uses for an increased paper flow. According to Sellen and Harper, paper has certain 'affordances' (that is, possibilities for action) that are different from digital layouts of information. They found that paper is most useful for annotating, for shuffling around in a meeting, and for sharing and disseminating texts while working through a live project carried on by teams of people. In short, they asserted that printing on paper remains vital to 'knowledge work' but only for a very short period. It is a 'temporary medium' of creative development, whereas finished work tends to be stored digitally. Sellen and Harper predicted, correctly, that printers would increase in number, with smaller separate machines on individual desks in frequent use rather than there being one large communal printer. Equally they asserted, more playfully, the well-stuffed wastepaper basket ought to be recognised as the symbol of an effective and creative worker (Sellen and Harper 2002: 211–12). Their account of the print culture of the office challenges the idea that print leads to stability and fixity of texts; instead, in this usage, print becomes the forum for alteration, and digital storage is the medium of fixity. This description of paper use in Sellen and Harper was, however, focused on fairly private and hidden printing practices. Even though their findings may have been challenging to established managerial certainties, they were still interested in the same goal of efficient organisational function, and their account does not therefore address all the other more public and perhaps more frivolous uses of office printing technology that fill everyday environments. Ordinary home and office printers now churn out all kinds of posters and publicity materials. The same kinds of machines that are used to make Powerpoint presentations, memos and emails are also used to craft unofficial flypostings, lost pet signs, or the daily menus of bars or restaurants. Most productions like this are printed out on the cheapest setting possible, for printer ink is expensive, deliberately so, as the companies who make cheap individual printers are in business to sell disposable ink cartridges designed to fit only into their machines. As a result, much of the ephemeral printed material we encounter today has a mushy, greyed-out quality, quite different from the sharp glossy blacks of cheap low-grade photocopies or offset lithography of previous eras.

Such examples of everyday printing, from print-on-demand book production, to commercial packaging or corporate communications, to office or home printing, show that digital graphic media are linked in various specific and localised ways to the material expressions of print, and contradict a common assertion that we are now bombarded by texts and images that have somehow become dematerialised by new media developments.

Recently several digital media researchers such as Katherine Hayles (2002) and Matthew Kirschenbaum (2008) have begun to move away from 'virtuality', to the materiality of digital communications, looking at the 'actual "stuff" of media – the nuts, bolts, and silicon' (Kitzmann 2005: 681). Kirschenbaum, for example, has engaged with 'counterintuitive' evidence of textual stability and data recovery after traumatic damage, in order to challenge current assumptions of the ephemeral mutable nature of electronic textuality. He combats most writing on new media that remains focused on conceptual, textual layers of meaning imbued with a kind of 'screen essentialism', accepting current display technologies as an invisible window into virtuality. Instead Kirschenbaum investigates the material matrix governing electronic writing and inscription, examining physical processes of storage, inscription and processing (Kirschenbaum 2008: 1–35).

[...]

To environmentalists and human rights activists, 'cyberspace' is a deceptive lie that obscures both 'ecology and labor' in the production and life cycle of digital equipment (Markley 1996: 77, cited in Kirschenbaum 2008: 35). Equally the 'myth of the paperless office' or the 'death of books' also obscure the environmental and human labour questions that are connected with the materiality of digital-print interactions in all their forms. Many different kinds of hybrid print/digital cultures coexist, and not always easily, from the corporate to the home-made. Currently, optimists and book-lovers look to the notion of an easy-going 'post-digital' print culture that will encourage a 'return to civility' (Jenkins 2011) and would exploit digital technology for its convivial sociable qualities. The term first appeared around 2000 in works such as *The Postdigital Membrane: Imagination, Technology and Desire* (Pepperell and Punt 2000), which emphasised the values of live experience, asserting after the previous decade of techno-euphoria the virtues of being human rather than the dream of becoming a digital entity. In relation to books, 'post-digital' print culture attempts to be pragmatic, open and socially responsible, valuing some books, but trying to balance scarce resources. Publishers like OpenBook, for example, publish in a range of formats, as paper or e-books, and as downloadable PDFs. In addition, all their books are available free to read online through Creative Commons licence arrangements. Adherents of 'creative commons', like this publisher, believe that open access is not just socially useful but also is good business, increasing sales.

Printing enthusiasts also sustain a similar ethos of creative commons, maintaining presses and techniques in part-time printing practices. In art schools, many graphic design students still study letterpress, composing text by hand setting, and printing on hand presses as a part of their training, building on the letterpress revival of the 1980s (Lupton 1996: 33; Jury 2006; Rivers 2010). The creative ferment of this part of their lives remains, and many graduates maintain a fluid identity, working as designers, teachers and printers in turn, even though some parts of their work may not make much money.

[...]

Nevertheless, many current exhibitions and publications now take place with established artistic and academic sponsors somewhere in the background. For example, a recent publication *Splitting the Atom on Dalston Lane: The Birth of the Do-It-Yourself Punk Movement* in March 1977 (Williamson, 2009) presented an assembly of contributors that included printers, poets and artist collectives, and a text that gave testimony to the many stages on the way to publication. As a result, this very slim volume conjured two very distinct environments, both a psycho-geographical excursion around the shabby former stomping grounds of the band Desperate Bicycles, and a recent cultural event at the British Museum [in London], celebrating these past exploits. In Glasgow [Scotland] we can see a similar diversity of working environments in the practice of one typographic artist, Edwin Pickstone, who is a letterpress specialist. Like [Johanna] Drucker, Pickstone reflects on the long history of his medium, on its many revivals, and on previous avant-garde critiques of the role of printing and typography in society in his work. To do this, he maintains multiple roles as a typographic craftsman, conceptual artist, academic tutor, graphic designer and jobbing printer.

[...]

Copyright laws and agreements began with printing. Copyright issues, and battles for control of intellectual property continue but are changing in the digital era. To the opponents of tighter copyright legislation, the battle is still framed in the terms described by William St Clair, that is as a price-fixing and monopoly agreement in the merchant's favour (St Clair 2004: 43–5). The author and publisher copyright system established in the nineteenth century has now grown and ramified with new forms of mechanical reproduction such as photography, music, film and digital communications. Different national legal systems, and the values they uphold do not mesh together. New technologies do not fit easily into existing legal frameworks, giving enterprising poachers and pirates the chance to grab or share other people's work. In the digital era many artists and publishing corporations feel particularly endangered by the spectre of free copying and sharing on the internet because it allows instant worldwide communications and datacopying (Goldstein 2003; Lessig 2008; Johns 2009). Against these anxieties, general internet users value that 'free' content. In addition, many people value the empowerment of rapid and free exchange of information and debate. Currently, in the first decades of the twenty-first century, arguments about control versus freedom in the digital realm are complex and increasingly embittered. Potentially corporations and internet providers are in a position to exert much more copyright control over consumers than in recent print periods. For example, with the 'celestial jukebox' system, providers are in a position to limit the number of times that even a legitimate subscriber can access their downloaded content, in contrast to the amount of use that can be wrung from a book, LP record or videotape (Goldstein 2003: 25; Lessig 2004; 2008). In early 2012, while the United States legislature was considering two controversial bills, SOPA (Stop Online Piracy Act) and PIPA (Protect IP Act), the online encyclopaedia Wikipedia imposed a 24-hour protest blackout of service in opposition ('English Wikipedia anti-SOPA blackout' 2012), prompting vociferous counter-accusations from powerful corporation bosses against the 'political' involvement of this content provider.

More insidiously, the new litigious atmosphere of digital 'zero-tolerance' against piracy by large media corporations, defending their publishing and archive holdings, threatens 'fair use' conventions. 'Fair use' is the established legal convention that copying or quoting parts of works without copyright charges or penalties is legitimate for academic purposes. Without this neutral territory for operation, say defenders of fair use, no one could possibly operate in the vaunted knowledge economy that is supposed to replace manufacturing in the West. Increasingly, if there is any doubt about whether an image or quotation might annoy a copyright holder, it is now much more likely for publishers to self-police and censor themselves and their authors rather than risk a legal battle. Ted Striphas and Kembrew McLeod have argued that in current circumstances 'fair use' is a right that must be defended, not simply because of its importance in the academic sphere, but as a civic duty. Aggressive control of intellectual property by corporate interests now extends deeply into many aspects of everyday life. For example, battles about GM crops that are deemed to be eligible for copyright protection are important because at base this is a battle for control of food production and access to daily nourishment. The science of copyright protection now gives much more power to copyright holders, from 'terminator crops' to the coded working of digital information that limits the amount of access to material. With this in mind, say Striphas and McLeod, everyone should be alert to defend the principle of 'fair-use' in their own patch wherever possible (Striphas and McLeod 2006).

As well as the idea of copyright and the development of social systems for the defence of intellectual property, other concepts from print culture have been transported into the digital realm, notably the kind of technological determinism that claimed the development of printing formed a new kind of consciousness for humans. Adherents of 'visual culture' for example often dismiss the importance of print communications in our lives today because at some level they believe that non-linear digital thinking is now dominant (Mirzoeff 1999; Coupland 2010). This way of thinking rejects the idea of print culture not because it is technologically determined, but because it is an outmoded deterministic regime. Instead of fearing the death of print, many ecstatic visions of digital culture welcomed it, for example when *The Alphabet Versus the Goddess* (Shlain 1998) conjured the destruction of the patriarchy that would surely follow from new visual and non-linear communication on the web (Crow 2006).

With the numbers of practitioners, students, interested spectators, academic historians, and other contributors noted in this chapter, print culture as both practice, production and discourse about print is evidently not at all dead. Ordinary people now take an interest in design and the previously arcane topic of typography through exhibitions, books (Loxley 2004; Garfield 2010), television programmes and films, for example Gary Hustvit's *Helvetica* (2007). The approach of popularising texts often emphasises personal stories and anecdotes, as for example in Simon Loxley's narrative of 'Frederic Goudy, type star' (Loxley 2004: 93), in contrast to new approaches to print culture by scholars and academics who investigate wider systems and networks of practice in social and economic contexts. Johanna Drucker has argued that the expansion of resources for study is encouraging this change in method: 'as networked (and print) resources grow, the artefacts available for study expand ... as the available inventory of materials expands, this history will not be limited to an inventory of artefacts to be thought about, but will include a lively critical discourse about ways of thinking' (Drucker 2009: 72). Indeed, in relation to 'ways of thinking' it is important to assert cultures of print as a contemporary, and not simply a historical phenomenon. In contrast to the triumphalist celebration of print in the nineteenth century, the vast range of contemporary print activity is hidden by the deliberate anonymity of large corporations, and eclipsed by the excitement of digital culture to the extent that the older words for the workings of the mind, such as 'impress' and 'imprint' have been displaced by newer metaphors as we talk about 'hard-wiring' or 'programming' the brain. Currently digital and print mediums are mixed up in many ways, are expressed in many kinds of action, and invoke many different struggles for cultural and economic power, so that future print cultures remain to be made, and remade, neither 'impressed' nor 'hard-wired' into our brains.

This is an abridged version of the original chapter approved by the author.

Select bibliography

Benedikt, Michael, ed. (1992) *Cyberspace: First Steps*. Cambridge, Mass.: MIT Press.

Birkerts, Sven (1994) *The Gutenberg Elegies: The Fate of Reading in an Electronic Age*. London: Faber and Faber.

Brannon, Barbara A. (2007) 'The Laser Printer as an Agent of Change: Fixity and Fluxion in the Digital Age' in Baron, Sabrina Alcorn, Eric N. Lindqvist and Eleanor F. Shevlin, eds *Agent of Change: Print Culture Studies after Elizabeth L. Eisenstein*. Amherst, Boston and Washington, DC: University of Massachusetts Press and the Centre for the Book: 353–64.

Carr, Nicholas (2010) *The Shallows: How the Internet is Changing the Way we Read, Think and Remember*. London: Atlantic.

Cleveland, Paul (2004) 'Bound to Technology: The Telltale Signs in Print', *Design Studies* 25: 113–53.

Coupland, Douglas (2010) *Marshall McLuhan: You Know Nothing of My Work!* New York: Atlas & Co.

Crow, David (2006) *Left to Right: The Cultural Shift from Words to Pictures*. Lausanne: AVA Publishing.

Drucker, Johanna (2009) 'Reconsidering: Philip Meggs and Richard Hollis: Models of Graphic Design History', *Design and Culture*, 1 (1): 51–78.

Eisenstein, Elizabeth L. (2011) *Divine Art, Infernal Machine: The Reception of Printing in the West from First Impressions to the Sense of an Ending*. Philadelphia: University of Pennsylvania Press.

Finkelstein, David and Alistair McCleery, eds (2005) *An Introduction to Book History*. London: Routledge.

Garfield, Simon (2010) *Just My Type: A Book About Fonts*. London: Profile Books.

Gerschenfeld, Neil (2007) *FAB: The Coming Revolution on Your Desktop: From Personal Computers to Personal Fabrication*. New York: Basic Books.

Goldstein, Paul (2003) *Copyright's Highway: From Gutenberg to the Celestial Jukebox*. Stanford Calif.: Stanford University Press.

Gomez, Jeff (2008) *Print is Dead: Books in Our Digital Age*. London: Palgrave Macmillan.

Greiman, April (1986) 'Does It Make Sense?', *Design Quarterly* 133.

Hayles, N. Katherine (2002) *Writing Machines*. Cambridge, Mass.: MIT Press.

Heller, Steven and Karen Pomeroy (1997) *Design Literacy: Understanding Graphic Design*. New York: Allworth Press.

Jenkins, Simon (2011) 'Welcome to the Post-Digital World, an Exhilarating Return To Civility via Facebook and Lady Gaga' *The Guardian online*, 1 December 2011 [www.guardian.co.uk/commentisfree/2011/dec/01/post-digital-world-web accessed 17 January 2012].

Johns, Adrien (2009) *Piracy: The Intellectual Property Wars from Gutenberg to Gates*. Chicago: University of Chicago Press.

Joyce, Michael (2001) 'Notes Toward an Unwritten Non-Linear Electronic Text, "The Ends of Print Culture" (A Work In Progress)', *Postmodern Culture*, 2 (1) September.

Jury, David (2006) *Letterpress: New Applications for Traditional Skills*. Hove: RotoVision.

Kirschenbaum, Matthew G. (2008) *Mechanisms: New Media and the Forensic Imagination*. Cambridge, Mass.: MIT Press.

Kitzmann, Andreas (2005) 'Review Essay, the Material Turn: Making Digital Media Real (Again)', *Canadian Journal of Communication*, 30: 681–86.

Kosloff, Albert (1958) *Screen Process Printing*. Cincinnati, Ohio: The Signs of the Times Publishing Company.

Landow, George P. (2006) *Hypertext 3.0: Critical Theory and New Media in an Era of Globalization*. Baltimore: Johns Hopkins University Press.

Lessig, Lawrence (2004) *Free Culture: How Big Media Uses Technology and the Law to Lock Down Culture and Control Creativity*. London and New York: Penguin.

Lessig, Lawrence (2008) *Remix: Making Art and Commerce Thrive in the Hybrid Economy*. London: Bloomsbury Academic (also available to read online under the Creative Commons licence).

Loxley, Simon (2004) *Type: The Secret History of Letters*. London: I. B. Tauris.

Lupton, Ellen (1996) *Mixing Messages: Contemporary Graphic Design in America*. London: Thames and Hudson.

Lupton, Ellen and J. Abbott Miller (2010 [1994]). 'Deconstruction and Graphic Design: History Meets Theory' in Grace Lees-Maffei and Rebecca Houze, eds *The design history reader*. Oxford: Berg: 192–9.

Markley, Robert, ed. (1996) *Virtual Realities and Their Discontents*. Baltimore: Johns Hopkins University Press.

Marshall, Alan (1983) *Changing the Word: The Printing Industry in Transition*. London: Comedia.

Mirzoeff, Nicholas (1999) *An Introduction to Visual Culture*. London: Routledge.

Morris, William (1999 [1893]) 'The Ideal Book' in: Bierut, Michael, Jessica Helfand, Steven Heller and Rick Poynor, eds *Looking Closer 3: Classic Writings of Graphic Design*. New York: Allworth Press: 1–5.

Nunberg, Geoffrey (1993) 'The Place of Books in the Age of Electronic Reproduction' *Representations* 42 Special issue: Future libraries: 13–37.

Nunberg, Geoffrey, ed. (1996) *The Future of the Book*. BREPOLS Papers from Conference at Centre for Semiotic and Cognitive Studies at University of San Marino 1994.

Pepperell, R. and M. Punt (2000) *The Postdigital Membrane: Imagination, Technology and Desire*. Bristol: Intellect Books.

Peterson, William (1991) *The Kelmscott Press: A History of William Morris's Typo-Graphical Adventure*. Oxford: Clarendon Press.

Pinney, Christopher (2004) *'Photos of the Gods': The Printed Image and Political Struggle in India*. London: Reaktion.

Rivers, Charlotte (2010) *Reinventing Letterpress: Inspirational Pieces by Contemporary Practitioners*. Hove: RotoVision.

St Clair, William (2004) *The Reading Nation in the Romantic Period*. Cambridge: Cambridge University Press.

Shlain, L. (1998) *The Alphabet Versus the Goddess: The Conflict Between Word and Image*. New York: Penguin and Arkana.

Sellen, Abigail J. and Richard H. R. Harper (2002) *The Myth of the Paperless Office*. Cambridge, Mass.: MIT Press.

Sotomayor Torres, Clivia M. (2003) *Alternative Lithography: Unleashing the Potentials of Nanotechnology*. London: Kluwer Academic/Plenum.

Staples, Loretta (2000) 'Typography and the Screen: a Technical Chronology of Digital Typology', *Design Issues* 16 (3): 19–34.

Striphas, Ted (2011) *The Late Age of Print: Everyday Book Culture from Consumerism to Control*. New York: Columbia University Press.

Striphas, Ted and Kembrew McLeod (2006) 'Strategic Improperties: Cultural Studies, the Everyday, and the Politics of Intellectual Properties'. *Cultural Studies* Special issue: The Politics of Intellectual Properties 20 (2/3). [www.indiana.edu/bookworm/ip-toc.html accessed 17 January 2012].

Thompson, John B. (2010) *Merchants of Culture: The Publishing Business in the Twenty-First Century*. Cambridge: Polity Press.

Williamson, Aaron (2009) *Splitting the Atom on Dalston Lane: The Birth of the Do-It-Yourself Punk Movement in March 1977*. London: The Eel.

Part I Further reading

Beegan, Gary. 1995. 'The Mechanization of the Image: Facsimile, Photography, and Fragmentation in Nineteenth-Century Wood Engraving'. *Journal of Design History*, 8 (4): 257–74.

Briggs, Asa and Burke, Peter. 2010. *A Social History of the Media: From Gutenberg to the Internet.* 3rd ed. Malden, MA: Polity Press.

Dackerman, Susan. 2011. *Prints and the Pursuit of Knowledge in Early Modern Europe*. Cambridge, MA: Yale University Press.

Eichhorn, Kate. 2013. 'Late Print Culture's Social Media Revolution: Authorship, Collaboration and Copy Machines'. *Authorship 1.4.* www.authorship.ugent.be/article/view/792/806 [Accessed 3 March 2017].

Eisenstein, Elizabeth L. 2010. *Divine Art, Infernal Machine: The Reception of Printing in the West from First Impressions to the Sense of an Ending*. Philadelphia: University of Pennsylvania Press.

Eisenstein, Elizabeth L. 1984. *The Printing Revolution in Early Modern Europe.* New York: Cambridge University Press.

Eisenstein, Elizabeth L. 1979a. *The Printing Press as an Agent of Change: Communications and Cultural Transformations in Early-Modern Europe.* Cambridge: Cambridge University Press.

Eisenstein, Elizabeth L. 1979b. *The Printing Press as an Agent of Change: Volume 2: Communications and Cultural Transformations in Early-Modern Europe: V. 2*. Cambridge: Cambridge University Press.

Enszer, Julie R. 2013. 'The Whole Naked Truth of Our Lives: Lesbian-Feminist Print Culture from 1969 Through 1989'. Dissertation, University of Maryland.

Goldstein, Carl. 2008. 'Printmaking and Theory'. *Zeitschrift Für Kunstgeschichte* 71 (3). Deutscher Kunstverlag München Berlin: 373–88.

Griffiths, Antony. 1996. *Prints and Printmaking: An Introduction to the History and Techniques*. 2nd ed. Berkeley, CA: University of California Press.

Hirner, René, Heinlein, Stefan (eds) and Kunstmuseum Heidenheim. 1997. *Vom Holzschnitt Zum Internet: Die Kunst Und Die Geschichte der Bildmedien von 1450 Bis Heute*. Ostfildern-Ruit: Cantz Editions.

Hults, Linda. 1997. *The Print in the Western World*. Madison: University of Wisconsin Press.

Humphries, Tristan (ed.), 1996. *Transformations: The Fine Art Print and the Computer: The Integration of Computers Print Technology and Printmaking.* London: Chelsea College of Art and Design.

Johns, Adrian. 2014. *The Nature of the Book: Print and Knowledge in the Making.* Chicago, IL: University of Chicago Press.

Jule, Walter (ed.). 1997. *Sightlines: Printmaking and Image Culture.* Edmonton, Alberta: University of Alberta Press.

Kittler, Friedrich A., trans. Geoffrey Winthrop-Young and Michael Wutz. 2002. 'The Perspective of Print'. *Configurations*, 10 (1), Winter: 37–50.

Koschatzky, Walter. 1972. *Die Kunst der Graphik Technik, Geschichte, Meisterwerke.* Salzburg: Residenz Verlag.

MacGregor, William B. 1999. 'The Authority of Prints: An Early Modern Perspective'. *Art History* 22 (3): 389–420.

Mayor, Hyatt A. 1980. *Prints and People: A Social History of Printed Pictures.* New York: The Metropolitan Museum of Art.

Melot, Michel et al. 1981. *Prints, History of an Art.* Geneva: Skira; New York: Rizzoli.

Moro, Juan Martínez. 1998. *Un Ensayo Sobre Grabado [A Finales Del Siglo 20].* Santander: Creática, Ediciones.

Mukerji, Chandra. 1983. *From Graven Images: Patterns of Modern Materialism.* New York: Columbia University Press.

Parshall, Peter. 2016. 'Why Study Prints Now? Or, the World According to Bartsch'. *Art in Print* 6 (3): 5–12.

Prince, Patric D. 2009. 'Imaging by Numbers: A Historical View of Digital Printmaking in America'. *Art Journal* 68 (1): 91–103.

Platzker, David and Wyckoff, Elizabeth. 2000. *Hard Pressed: 600 Years of Prints and Process*, Manchester, US: Hudson Hills Press.

Poirée, Marie-Christine. 1997. *L'Empreinte Au XXe Siècle: de la Véronique Au Verre Ironique.* Paris: L'Harmattan.

Sandback, Amy. 2006. *Imagined Worlds: Willful Invention and the Printed Image 1470–2005.* New York: Axa Gallery and International Print Center.

Tallman, Susan. 2012. 'The Elephant in the Room: MoMA's Print Surveys: 1966, 1980, 1996, 2012'. *Art in Print* 2 (1): 31–9.

Wood, Frances and Barnard, Mark. 2010. *The Diamond Sutra: The Story of the World's Earliest Dated Printed Book.* London: The British Library.

Wye, Deborah. 1996. *Thinking Print: Books to Billboards, 1980–1995.* New York: The Museum of Modern Art, Abrams.

PART II

Debates

Introduction to Part II

If the anthology as a whole represents vital aspects of the general discourse on print, Part II offers texts that act as markers for some of the specific debates in the field of artistic printmaking over the last thirty years. They are written by artists who are also educators (Weisberg, Reeves, Bednarczyk, Harding, Balfour), as well as by a curator of contemporary art (Roca) and by an art historian/curator (Field).

The texts aim to define an ontology of print as image and of printmaking as an artistic mode of production and expression. They highlight questions around the role and function of print within art and the broader artistic and cultural context, and probe its relationship to other art forms as well as its intersection with digital technologies in recent years. They also touch on its 'expansion' as an art form and posit its – frequently ignored – relevance to contemporary art as a whole. Furthermore, they explicitly, as well as implicitly, aim to raise the level of the discourse on print.

Unlike the texts in the other parts of this volume, the pieces in this section appear in chronological order. This will permit the reader to follow the emergence of particular insights and concerns at certain points since the mid-1980s and to identify new as well as recurring themes during this period.

Ruth Weisberg's text from 1986, the earliest in this volume, has an almost legendary status among an older generation of printmakers. It was clearly written with the intention of 'upping the ante' of print discourse as it existed in the mid-1980s and of posing a challenge to curators and critics as well as printmakers themselves. It is informed by and touches on critical and philosophical debates at the time, such as semiotics and postmodern theory, but it also draws on earlier modernist and structuralist ideas, such as the search for a 'discipline-based aesthetic' and 'inherent categories'. Weisberg's focal categories are 'function, process and material'. These terms may have their roots in the methods of art history, but Weisberg writes from the perspective of what is now termed 'arts-based research', that is from the viewpoint of the practising artist. Many of the features of the 'process' highlighted by Weisberg still preoccupy printmakers today. As other contributions to the volume testify, they may even have come into closer focus since the essay was written: the role of the matrix and the displacement that it entails; its potential for multiplicity; the serial nature of printed images; the necessity or opportunity for collaboration. Weisberg identifies a conceptual aspect in the very process of printmaking which has surfaced again and again in the debate.[1] Her theme of the material qualities of 'making' has grown in recent years and benefited from insights in the area of material studies.[2]

Written from a US perspective, Weisberg's observations on the 'location' of prints within the artworld system – or rather their absence – find an echo in more recent publications, as in the contribution by José Roca. Weisberg already notes a point later developed by Roca, namely the prevalence of the 'syntax of the print' in contemporary artistic strategies in general.[3]

In 1994 art historian and curator Richard Field published his thirty 'sentences on printed art', inspired by Sol LeWitt's 'Sentences on Conceptual Art' of 1969. Ideally suited as a series of theses for further discussion, the sentences highlight, in a nutshell, many of the concrete features of the production of prints and their qualities as objects. They also signal the conceptual frameworks that have been constructed around prints as social and artistic products. Field's own historiographic position as a scholar writing at a particular time also becomes apparent: for example, he is indebted to media theorists such as Barthes and Baudrillard. This is evident in his emphasis on the concept of the simulacrum as well as the incipient focus on the binary base of the digital.

Kathryn Reeves presented her paper 'The re-vision of printmaking' at the first *IMPACT International Printmaking Conference* in Bristol in 1999. It was clearly intended, as the title suggests, as a challenge to the field. In many respects, her text took up the mantle from Weisberg's 1986 essay to which Reeves refers and whose critical-theoretical scope she expands. Employing the insights of critical theory, especially semiotics, psychoanalysis and feminism, Reeves demonstrates how these can be fruitfully employed to interrogate issues crucial to print, such as authorship, reproduction and originality. Viewing print through the lens of critical theories brings into focus hitherto neglected facets of print, such as the body and touch and especially the matrix. They also yield a convincing explanation of print's marginal status as a feminine-coded practice in a patriarchal or masculine-coded, hierarchical art world. Reeves expressly does not demand a 're-vision' of print with the aim of attaining a higher status for it in the arts, as this would entail an implicit acceptance of art's existing hierarchical structures. Instead, she calls for an acceptance of the heterogeneity and mutability of print and its position as a relational site or space. The text can be fruitfully read in conjunction with other texts in this volume, such as Harding and Balfour in Part II, and Didi-Huberman in Part III.

Polish artist Andrzej Bednarczyk's text serves to highlight an approach to print from a non-Anglo-Saxon country with its different philosophical and cultural traditions. The English translation of the text maintains the term 'graphic art', which is rather more prevalent in European languages than 'printmaking'.[4] The term itself indicates a breadth not as easily connoted by the word 'printmaking'. Furthermore, the author also highlights the importance of differentiating between 'graphic technique' and 'graphic art'. It is worth stressing this difference, since – as has often been argued – printmaking (as a graphic art form) is frequently not only defined by, but reduced to its techniques.

The value of Bednarczyk's analysis lies in the fact that he takes the situation of print in the twenty-first century as a starting point where existing models of analysis and definition are insufficient in talking about graphic art. Like other authors in this volume, Bednarczyk maintains the value of considering specific art forms even in today's post-medium situation. By paying close attention to the various parameters and processes of the graphic technique – such as matrix, receiving matter/substrate, flatness and two-dimensionality, the series and the edition – the author does justice to the changing aspects of what might – and might not – justifiably figure as graphic art. This applies to graphic art as an overall category or as an individual work. At the same time, he acknowledges the shading of graphic aspects into interdisciplinary work. In this respect, Bednarczyk's text corresponds to the next entry – despite the two authors' different approaches.

In his essay for *Philagrafika*, the inspirational print exhibition in Philadelphia, USA, in 2009/10, chief curator José Roca recounts the curatorial team's reflections on the purpose and format of biennales in general and of the print biennale in particular. The latter's medium-specific focus requires detailed attention in an art context that has challenged and to some extent eliminated single-medium forms.

Philagrafika set out to 'problematise print as a category' (Roca, 96). Therefore, Roca's text can be seen to function as a barometer of issues regarding print practices and their discourses in the early twenty-first century. Despite the display of 'traditionally defined' prints (96), the various exhibitions that comprised *Philagrafika* presented works in a variety of media; hence the curation adopted an 'expanded print' ethos. It also endeavoured to trace print qualities, such as multiplicity, dissemination and seriality within the broader field of contemporary art. The thesis was proposed that the characteristics of print form an important, if unacknowledged, part of contemporary art, albeit an 'unconscious' one. This concept was reflected in the title of the exhibition and catalogue. In other words, *Philagrafika* set itself the ambitiously conceived aim of 're-reading' contemporary art itself through printmaking. Roca – agreeing with the critique of conceptual artist Luis Camnitzer – lays at least some of the blame for the omission of print from the wider art discourse on printmaking or printmakers themselves.

Ultimately, by adopting a broad definition of print within contemporary art, Roca hoped to enliven print media and print discourse. Reviews, such as that in *Art in Print*, by associate publisher Julie Bernatz, who called the catalogue 'an essential building block in a new understanding of print', attest to the success of *Philagrafika's* goals.

Australian artist and educator Richard Harding explores print's position within contemporary art through the socio-political notion, developed in the context of postcolonial and queer theory, of 'otherness'. Viewed through the lens of identity and gender politics, print's matrixial and reproductive nature and its lack of 'originality' result in its 'queer' position within art's medium hierarchy. Harding is well aware that one could argue that the hierarchical normativity of painting and its affiliation with originality as the gold standard of art has all but disappeared in a post-medium art world. Nevertheless, the essay provides a conceptual 'handle' on theorising print's (still) marginal position. At the same time, 'queerness' is proposed as a compelling metaphor for the mutability of the future of print.

The final text in Part II is Canadian artist and educator Barbara Balfour's contribution to Toronto's Open Studio's 2010 symposium *Printopolis*. As with other authors in this book, in thinking about the ontology (the 'what' of the title) and the decision for the making of prints (the 'why') in a post-disciplinary art context, Balfour rejects the dominant focus on technical matters. Instead, she presents theoretically astute reflections on her chosen topics that are grounded in and informed by practice. While she demonstrates some of the key elements of the medium-specificity of print, and argues that it is possible to retain its 'printness' (120), this is not to be understood in a narrow way 'in terms of a set of defining forms and attributes' (121). Emphasising print as 'a particularly porous range of media' and its ability to incorporate others, she suggests instead the notion of a medium as an 'enabling agency' and stresses its 'capacity and mobility', rather than any fixed attributes and processes. As in Reeves's essay in this section, Balfour furthermore highlights the prospect of expanding print's relational potential *vis-à-vis* other media while embracing its specificities.

Notes

1 See, for example, Barfield, Barfield and Whale, 2001; Ganter, 2005 and Pelzer-Montada, 2004.

2 See Humphries 2013; see also Pelzer-Montada 2011. These two essays are written from the perspective of contemporary artist-practitioners. The Dutch artist and scholar of historical intaglio processes Ad Stijnman (2016) has critiqued art-historical methodologies for their lack of attention to the depths of making, and calls for a thorough training of art historians in historical print techniques in order to improve art historical scholarship from a material point of view.

3 See also Walker 2000.
4 The short text by Ernst Rebel in Part III provides a further explanation of the differences in terminology. On the use of the term 'graphics' in English, see *Art in Print*, 5 (2), July/August 2015, especially the introduction by Susan Tallman, 2.

References

Barfield, N., Barfield, R. and Whale, G. 2001. 'Defying Convention: Emergent Print Practices in Digital Printmaking'. *Point, Art and Design Research Journal* 1 (12): 4–14.
Bernatz, Julie. 2011. 'The State of the State'. *Art In Print* 1 (1), May/June: 35–6.
Ganter, Jo. 2005. 'Craft Versus Concept'. *Grapheion* 18 (1): 4–5.
Humphries, Clare. 2013. 'Relational Surfaces: The Tissue of Materiality'. In: Morgan, Luke (ed.), *Intersections and Counterpoints: IMPACT 7 International Multi-disciplinary Printmaking Conference Proceedings*. Clayton, Victoria: Monash University Publishing, 243–9.
Pelzer-Montada, Ruth. 2011. 'Sensing Print: Reflections on the Materiality of the Contemporary Art Print'. In: Hoskins, Stephen et al. (eds), *IMPACT 6 Multi-disciplinary Printmaking Conference Proceedings*. Bristol: Impact Press, 53–9.
Pelzer-Montada, Ruth. 2004. 'Technology Versus Concept, or the Site of Practice Versus the Bite of Theory',. *Contemporary Impressions* 12: 21–5.
Stijnman, Ad. 2016. 'It's All About Matter: Thoughts on Art History from the Perspective of the Maker'. *Art in Print* 6 (3), Sept./Oct.: 16–17.
Tallman, Susan. 2015. 'Introduction'. *Art in Print* 5 (2): 2.
Walker, Sam. 2000. 'Printmaking as Syntax of Contemporary Art'. *Contemporary Impressions* 8 (1): 2–5.

Ruth Weisberg

The syntax of the print: in search of an aesthetic context*

With a few but notable exceptions, critics and curators with powerful venues and easy access to publication have failed to provide printmaking with a theoretical framework. Recent books and exhibitions often disclaim responsibility for a comprehensive overview. An example is provided by Judith Goldman's *American Prints: Process & Proofs*, which 'looks at graphics by painters; it excludes printmakers, not because they have not made important graphic statements, but because historically painters have brought the major innovations to the graphic arts.'[1] While there is in her statement a suggestion of an underlying aesthetic theory, it is never elucidated, and it is never amplified or substantiated in her text. One is thus led to suspect that taste and selection are powerfully shaped by considerations of the marketplace, a suspicion further supported by Riva Castleman's recent book *American Impressions: Prints Since Pollock*. In her review of this book, Pat Gilmour notes that, 'Although a few of the better-known "printmakers" are mentioned, as one might expect from the print curator of a blue-chip museum, the emphasis in *American Impressions* is on the "star" system and particularly those who have "made it" in New York.'[2]

It is characteristic of most writing on contemporary printmaking that certain aesthetic theories and value systems are assumed and that these assumptions remain unsubstantiated. Although at symposiums and conference panels, statements are frequently made about concepts and sensibilities, contemporary printmaking seems to lack a broad philosophical context for aesthetic analysis. Examination of the literature of an analogous field such as ceramics reveals what printmaking lacks. In the 1940s Bernard Leach created a separate aesthetic category for ceramics based

* Ruth Weisberg. 1986. 'The Syntax of the Print: In Search of an Aesthetic Context'. *The Tamarind Papers: A Journal of the Fine Print* 9 (2): 52–60. Reproduced by permission of the author.

on its inherent values and intrinsic qualities. Since the mid-1950s several authors have attempted serious syntheses of ceramic tradition and contemporary art expression. One must ask whether it would be possible in the field of printmaking to compile a collection of critical essays such as those found in *Ceramic Art: Comment and Review 1882–1977*, edited by Garth Clark.[3]

Instead, the recent literature of printmaking leans toward the technical, the historical, and, especially, the socio-economic. This is understandable, given the print's function as consumer goods and as a mass medium which serves as transmitter of motifs, images, and ideas. The history of printmaking encompasses great contradictions; prints are at once intimate and political, private and public. While in the past thirty years printmaking reflected every style and trend, it was often a refuge for the artist whose work was figurative, narrative, socially conscious, or literary. It was a less rigid corner of the art world – one in which the formalist aspects of modernism could be circumvented. While the general tendency was toward more color and larger scale, this trend was resisted by printmakers who were nourished by the historical roots of their craft. It is interesting to note that in 1975 Richard Field could write in disparaging terms of etching as 'a medium that had more and more become fixated on its own capacities for representational and literary complexity.'

In the 1980s this anti-representational, anti-allegorical bias disappeared, but modernism continued to exert an enduring influence through its insistence upon the integrity of materials. Printmakers continued to highlight aspects of process, to reveal their struggle with the graphic material. Other artists reintroduced illusionary and narrative subject matter into their work. Bruce Richards, who was a minimalist painter, worked for a number of years on a trompe l'oeil series of enigmatic objects; Pamela Zwehl-Burke replicated a sketchbook page, creating art about the literal object as well as about the process of seeing; Warrington Colescott told the story of the history of printmaking in a manner both irreverent and engaging.

Since Plato, the ideal of aesthetic philosophy has been the all inclusive and the universal: ideas and theories that will endure through the ages, that will be applicable in all periods, and that will apply to all media. Even so, when one reviews the history of aesthetic theory and art criticism, one quickly realizes that the most influential ideas of an era are often doomed by their timeliness. There is a compelling historicity to aesthetic theory. Critics write insightfully only about the art of their own time, or about another time with which they have a clear affinity. The radii of their empathy and antipathy define their reach.

In the recent past, aesthetic analysis has been structured in innumerable ways, from media-based to iconographic, from stylistic to deconstructive. These discussions, however, often presume an accepted paradigm: a body of assumed ideas, an overview which provides a framework for speculative thought. I should like to locate my ideas in terms of a general paradigmatic structure, then move on to thoughts about a more specific, aesthetic understanding of historical and contemporary printmaking.

Since Heinrich Wölfflin's formulation of aesthetic theory in the early twentieth century, we have become wed to a pluralistic conception of style: to notions of periodicity, national character, media, and process. It is difficult to return to a pre-enlightenment mode of thinking, in which Beauty was thought to be the object or aim of art. The criteria for an objective conception of Beauty were to be found in such attributes as proportion, harmony, perfection, form, truth, and virtue. The major shift from this rule-based model occurred in the eighteenth century. Objective criteria were supplanted by a subjective analysis of aesthetic judgment, which was understood to reside in the realm of perception and in the workings of the mind. By the late nineteenth century, George Santayana could suggest that 'Beauty is pleasure regarded [that is, experienced] as the quality of a thing' or 'pleasure objectified.'[5]

Late in the twentieth century, we are still engaged in this method of disassociating ideas and analyzing their origins. The reflexive aspects of modernism are consistent with this subjective method. The apparent exhaustion of modernism has been followed by a liberating and feverish pluralism. Whether postmodernism represents a real shift in viewpoint is a matter of controversy. In trying to come to terms with the difference between the deconstructive impulse and the self-critical tendencies of recent modernism, Hal Foster writes that this distinction 'is crucial to the post-modernist break, and no doubt the two operations are different: self-criticism, centered on a medium, does tend (at least under the aegis of formalism) to the essential or "pure", whereas deconstruction, on the contrary, decenters, and exposes the "impurity" of meaning.'[6] In the end, he characterizes postmodernism as a rupture rather than a complete break.

Modernism, as defined by Clement Greenberg and Michael Fried, necessitates a very particular attitude toward the *media* of art. In their view, the medium gives the work its identity; therefore, a self-critical stance in dealing with the medium is a crucial factor in definition of one's aesthetic. Each medium thus has a code or nature to which one must be true. Postmodernism, according to some, stands in opposition to this purity of medium, existing 'between, across, or outside them, or in new or neglected mediums (like video or photography).'[7]

In practice, however, artists' attitudes toward media are still largely moulded by modernist ideas about intrinsic qualities, and even those who decode or deconstruct are reacting to the immediately preceding code or structure. The breadth and variety of actual artistic practice is an important touchstone, for theoretical constructs – and even historical analyses – are fictions, more coherent and unified than is the practice of art in any era. The structuralist search for inherent categories seems most useful here, given my approach, which is to explore a discipline-based aesthetic. I will use the categories of *function*, *process*, and *materials* which subsume among them all factors relevant to printmaking.

Function

Among these categories, function is best defined in relation to the history of the print. The multiplicity of prints gives them a role as communicators and disseminators of motifs and information. There is an impressive body of literature on the impact of the print as repeatable image and consumer product. When writers choose to emphasize these functions, the aesthetic aspects of the print usually become either incidental or extraneous. Walter Benjamin, William M. Ivins, Jr., David Kunzle, and, most recently, Chandra Mukerji have all written insightfully on the print as an artifact of material culture. When one examines the print from the viewpoint of modes of production and distribution, the rise of reproductive printmaking becomes predictable.

Reproductive work tended to degenerate or devolve aesthetically because of pressures to increase production and to standardize practices. Systems of crosshatching were evolved which allowed artisans to translate the subtleties of chiaroscuro into simplified and readable volumes, but such attendant losses were accepted to permit gains in market distribution. As Ivins observes of such a reproductive printmaker, 'he had learned to see in a particular way and to lay his lines in accordance with the requirements of some particular convention or system of linear structure, and anything that that way of seeing and that convention of drawing were not calculated to catch and bring out failed to be brought out in his statement.'[8]

Ivins inventories the profound effect the repeatable pictorial image had on the growth of technical and scientific knowledge.

> [By] the nineteenth century informative books usefully illustrated with accurately repeatable pictorial statements became available to the mass of mankind in western Europe and in America. The result was the greatest revolution in practical thought and accomplishment that had ever been known. This revolution was a matter as momentous from the ethical and political points of view as from the mechanical and economic ones.[9]

To our eyes, the illustrations in an early printed book, such as Robertus Valturius's *De re militari* (Art of War), published in Verona in 1472, have aesthetic merit. Its large schematic illustrations of catapults and moveable towers have a satisfying clarity on the pages; this appeal, however, was not intentional and was probably not evident to the author's fifteenth-century contemporaries.

Chandra Mukerji has expanded the implications of Ivins's thesis. For Mukerji, the special status of printmaking is due not just to its role as disseminator of information but primarily to its role as creator of culture and consumable goods:

> The artists and printmakers who established shops outside guild control in early modern Europe were taking advantage of the emerging systems of manufacture and international trade to create new kinds of pictures in Europe. With more efficient means of production, they helped to create a proliferation of material culture; by producing new types of goods (art and mass culture) for new types of consumers (the collector and the nonaffluent) they helped to spread the range of people recruited into the new consumerist culture.[10]

A vast category of prints somewhat neglected by art historians is the topical broadside, where a preponderance of image over text combined with cheap distribution to create a powerful vehicle of popular communication. Most of the prints that serve this function are without great pretensions. Although Callot's *Misères de la guerre*, Hogarth's *The Harlot's Progress*, and Goya's *Desastres de la Guerra* are among the inspired exceptions, their subject matter is not as uncommon as it once seemed. David Kunzle has gathered together a fascinating compendium of such narratives with an illuminating text in *The Early Comic Strip*.[11] His collection includes vivid depictions of Huguenot dissent, Jesuit intrigue, and Elizabethan plots. A section on personal morality contains diatribes against disobedient wives, some violent and some humorous, as well as images of what were perceived as the vices and follies of their age. One gets a lively impression of printmaking's relevance, its interaction with everyday life, its persuasive powers as propaganda, and its force in the externalization of beliefs. Some of the prints also have an unintentional appeal to the twentieth-century viewer, for example, the English engraving *The Escape of Jack Sheppard*, gridded with an inventory of locks, bolts, and doors broken or eluded by Sheppard in his escape from Newgate Prison.

In general, topical broadsides are a somewhat degraded reflection either of contemporary taste or of that of a preceding era. They are typically conservative or regressive in style, crude in execution, and provincial – as might be expected in printed matter which was intended to be hawked on the street for a few farthings. The print, whether by Dürer or by an anonymous *formschneider*, remained part of the accessible popular culture until the nineteenth century. As Peter Burke observed:

> [By 1500] popular culture was everyone's culture; a second culture for the educated, and the only culture for everyone else. By 1800, however, in most parts of Europe, the clergy, the nobility, the [wealthy] merchants, the professional men – and their wives – had abandoned popular culture to the lower classes, from whom they were now separated, as never before, by profound differences in world view.[12]

During the several centuries in which printmaking coincided with popular culture, it was also the most technically advanced means of reproduction.

When Alois Senefelder invented lithography, it was more efficient and economic than the media that preceded it. In the nineteenth century the connection begins to break down. Walter Benjamin pinpoints the change:

> But only a few decades after its invention, lithography was surpassed by photography. For the first time in the process of pictorial reproduction, photography freed the hand of the most important artistic functions which henceforth devolved only upon the eye looking into a lens. Since the eye perceives more swiftly than the hand can draw, the process of pictorial reproduction was accelerated so enormously that it could keep pace with speech. A film operator shooting a scene in the studio captures the images at the speed of an actor's speech. Just as lithography virtually implied the illustrated newspaper, so did photography foreshadow the sound film.[13]

So the print loses its identity as a state-of-the-art mass medium and gains the freedom to pursue more aesthetic ideals. Depending upon one's value system, these changes can be viewed either positively or negatively. For someone who values reproducibility and political purpose above all else (as does Benjamin), the new aestheticism is defined as a parasitical dependence on ritual. About art for art's sake, he writes:

> With the advent of the first truly revolutionary means of reproduction, photography, simultaneously with the rise of socialism, art sensed the approaching crisis which has become evident a century later. At the time, art reacted with the doctrine of *l'art pour l'art* [*sic*], that is, with a theology of art. This gave rise to what might be called a negative theology in the form of the idea of 'pure' art, which not only denied any social function of art but also any categorizing by subject matter.[14]

During the next hundred years, prints evolved into precious works of art, their rarity assured by the new convention of the signed and numbered, limited edition. Newspapers, television, reproductive photography, and film took over the functions that at one time were served principally by the print and town crier. A new class of patron developed for the limited edition print. The new printmaking demanded connoisseurs with erudition and disposable income.

More must be said at this point about the way in which patronage influences the status of a medium. Before the nineteenth century, a limited number of illustrated books, portraits, and print series (the *Sieges* of Jacques Callot, for example) were commissioned by princes, popes, and wealthy burghers. Most printed material, as has already been seen, went directly into a market economy or was distributed as political opinion. In retrospect, we can also appreciate how printmaking may have aided an artist's development of images, as well as compositional and visual syntax (I will discuss the reasons for this affinity under the rubric of process). Suffice it to say here that examples of such conceptual thematic and formal struggle are among the most prized prints in the history of the medium. The progressive states of Rembrandt's etchings and drypoints and the variants of Degas's compositions have gained their present prestige retroactively, however. Generally, it was the patronage of the rich and the powerful that enhanced the renown of an art object in its own day. In turn, factors such as place of a genre within the hierarchy, the fame of an artist, or the status and monetary value of the material influenced the projects chosen by patrons. A pecking order of media was institutionalized in the seventeenth century, the era of the academies. While we are amused today by that rigid hierarchy of preferred subjects, we are still affected by the beaux-arts traditions of the major and minor arts, of the fine arts and the crafts. Until very recently, I returned my printmaking slides at the University of Southern California to a tray marked 'Minor Arts.'

We are plagued by these hidden ideologies in the study of art history. Examples in printmaking abound. To this day, a certain nobility of the etching media overshadows the humble woodcut. These are adjectives we have inherited from the fifteenth century, when workers in precious metals had greater status than did those who worked with wood. A new patronage for the print has emerged in the mid-twentieth century; the locus of print collecting which earlier shifted from the person on the street to the connoisseur in the drawing room has shifted once again, this time to a new middle-class audience. As Barry Walker noted in his catalogue essay for the Brooklyn Museum's 24th National Print Exhibition, *Public and Private: American Prints Today:* 'In the 1950s, a small revolution in the way prints were produced, together with a broadened educational basis and a wider public awareness of art in general, led to a different type of print and a new kind of collector. … The crucial difference between the new and the old generations of print collectors was that the new generation of collectors bought contemporary prints to display them on the wall.'[15]

Prints destined to be framed had to compete with paintings and posters for impact and pride of place. This has led to large colorful images that are 'easy to read' at a distance. The latter characteristic has been reinforced by adoption of procedures in which much artwork is judged, selected, or purchased upon the basis of slides, transparencies, or photographs. Subtle nuances of surface and scale recede in importance. What Walker calls a 'public' print is not measured in terms of the social conscience of a Goya or Daumier; public here refers to the public nature of the viewing experience, in contrast with the privacy of contemplation of the hand-held sheet. While individual artists have contributed to this trend, print workshops and publishers have been particularly responsible for merchandising prints of this character. In terms of marketing practices, one might call these 'public' prints the reproductive prints of today, inasmuch as they serve as substitutes for paintings. Riva Castleman admits that 'the development of the workshop-publisher complex in America in the 1960s cannot be disassociated from the quality of the art produced within it. … Nevertheless, the preferences of publishers and workshop directors, like those of art dealers, have limited the number of artists and the sort of artistic styles or expressions that have been represented.'[16] This is an interesting statement, for Castleman, Judith Goldman, Richard Field, and others among the New York establishment have long been identified with the validation of the products of these workshops.

Process

Michael Rothenstein once remarked during a lecture that the irreducible essence of printmaking is an embrace, one body pressed against the other. He certainly got our attention, while at the same time he isolated the intrinsic feature common to all printmaking processes: the pressing of a matrix against a receptive surface. Whether the image is mechanically or chemically produced on the matrix, it is always once removed from the final work of art. It is this indirection, this displacement, which is the hallmark of the printmaker's art, whether one is thinking of a fifteenth-century engraving by Pollaiuolo or a photoscreen-print by Paolozzi. This reliance upon a matrix allows for many identical images, with resultant flexibility in their distribution and use.

The serial nature of the process through which a print is made has been much commented upon. The printmaking process allows the artist to record the discrete changes and developments in the image. The transcription of these revisions has been formalized over the centuries into a system of proofs and states. Most importantly, the artist's mode of concept is shaped by the possibility of successive proofs. The artist thinks differently when working on a print. There are often dramatic transformations of tone and color in the transfer from matrix to paper, as well as in the reversal of the image's direction. In intaglio, the bright metallic line revealed by a scratch in the grounded plate may become a black line on white paper. In lithography, one learns to calculate the value range of each color. When printed in yellow, pale washes of black tusche may disappear altogether. So while the engagement with the materials of printmaking may be immediate and visceral, much of the process is temporal and cerebral. The process unfolds through a series of controlled accidents. This is our delight and our challenge. The final image is the visible consequence of all one's decisions. As June Wayne recently remarked, 'I consider printmaking to be to other media what chamber music is to the symphony. It is very disciplined – there is no place to hide and no one covers your errors. Like chamber music, it can provide a subtlety of *extase* that makes other media feel gross by comparison.'[17] This self-conscious emphasis on conceptualization in printmaking opens the facture to analysis for both the artist and posterity. For the reviewer, the evidence of decisions, additions, alterations, and deletions can reveal directly the artist's intentions and mental process. The eight states of Rembrandt's *Ecce Homo* gives us access to Rembrandt's internal considerations. The decisive sixth state, in which a crowd of onlookers is replaced by a cavernous abyss, has a stunning effect on anyone who has really studied these prints. Imagine, by comparison, what it would be like if we were to have all the stages of underpainting, or all the alternative modes of resolution, for a painting such as Velasquez's *Las Meninas*.

Collaboration has almost always been a key aspect of the graphic arts. In the Orient and to a great degree in the West, printmaking has been a group effort, with tasks divided among artisans and artists. One need only think of Japanese Ukiyo-e to realize that collaboration need not compromise aesthetic accomplishment. Such artists as Rembrandt and Whistler, working alone, are really anomalies. While it is true that Whistler's *Nocturne: Palaces* from the Second Venice Set would be nothing but vague wisps without the artist's masterful wiping of the plate, even Whistler relied on others when making lithographs.

The consequences of collaboration seem to be twofold. It leaves the process vulnerable to the lowest common denominator. The artist's efforts can be compromised because he or she does not have total control. Because control or mastery by the individual is the preferred model of modern Western culture, contemporary collaboration demands special social skills and sensitivity on the part of team members. Leonard Lehrer provides a most insightful examination of this aspect of printmaking, while defining some of the crucial desiderata for the non-artist members of the team: 'Printers are a special breed, a breed which combines immense skill with diplomacy and endurance, patience with knowledge; they set the tone of the project, maintain its rhythm, and are expected to have answers for everything. ... It is a unique relationship and a unique component of the art world.'[18] How much visible effect collaboration should have on the finished print is a controversial matter. Tamarind Lithography Workshop espoused a non-interventionist position. The printer should 'detect the true spirit of the work and give it life, while at the same time avoiding any act which might tend to impose his own aesthetic upon that of the artist.'[19] In contrast, Ken Tyler believes the relationship between the artist and printer to be symbiotic: 'You can't separate it after a while and you don't know whether the suggestion came from the printer on the press or that it was the artist's idea. But you know that something's going on there and if it works, it's magic.'[20] The question that should be asked is what the effect of interventionist and non-interventionist modes of collaboration may be upon the quality of the work and the aesthetic choices of the artist. Another way to put this question is to ask whether the art is more important than the artist, or whether the artist's development is more significant than the success of a particular print.

My education and formation as an artist tend to put me in the non-interventionist camp. When I studied printmaking with Frank Cassara and Emil Weddige at the University of Michigan and at S. W. Hayter's Atelier 17 in Paris, I was taught to believe in printmaking as a process which allowed one to wrestle from incalcitrant if seductive materials one's personal vision. Authenticity, originality, and the artistic growth of the artist are important values for me, so while individual prints may benefit from the intercession of a printer or publisher, I feel the artist is impoverished in the long run. The workshop can become not just a technical resource but an aesthetic crutch.

Material

While it is difficult to divide completely material from process, it is valuable to consider each medium's intrinsic properties and visceral appeal. One's interaction with a process is strongly colored by its physical properties and their technical possibilities. In lithography one begins with the cool, sensuous surface of grained Bavarian limestone; the autographic qualities of crayon drawing and the myriad reticulations of tusche washes make lithography a rich and flexible medium for the artist. I have always felt that the sedimentation of lithographic washes was a reflection of the great macro-events of the earth: the eroding of mountains, the drying of lakes, and the silting up of the great river deltas. They also mirror the microcosms of life, as if viewed through a microscope.

Intaglio offers the swelling and tapering precision of the engraved line (too rarely mastered today), the eroded and insistent bitten line of etching, the grainy shadows of aquatint, and the velvet furrows of drypoint. For some, the making of an intaglio is just an excuse to work on the seductive metal plate. Zinc and (especially) copper present hard metallic surfaces that are still malleable enough to permit scraping, polishing, and all manner of surface manipulation. One develops the ability to 'read' the plate uninked, even before proofing it, intuitively measuring the degrees of darkness and the crispness of whites.

The directness of woodcut also has its partisans. One enjoys the pressure of the hand as it cuts into and overcomes the resistance of a woodblock. Human beings seem to have an inborn attraction for wood. Gauguin and Munch added the rich veining of wood grain to our repertoire of gouge, knife, and chisel.

As I have not made screenprints, it is hard for me to imagine the pleasures of that medium, but others speak of its speed and flexibility.

While each of the printmaking media has its own distinctive ink layer, varying from the raised lines of intaglio to the silky veils of lithography, they are more subtle and nuanced than is the surface of most paintings.

When connoisseurs viewed prints in albums or boxes, the hand-held sheet allowed an intimate scrutiny not possible through a protective sheet of glass. The downplaying of tactile qualities in contemporary prints is partly the result of a shift in viewing procedures. Scale, too, has contributed to change: when prints were small, they tended to be concise in their making. Artists drew more from the wrist than the elbow. As scale increases, so does the size of the gesture.

Just as we take for granted the convention of black-and-white representation of a multi-chromatic world, printmaking's scale infers a variable conceptual size. The grandeur of Piranesi's *Prisons* is not compromised by their actual dimensions. We more readily adopt the artist's imaginative projection of scale in a print than we do in a painting, where we often experience images that are larger than life.

Conclusion

How do the factors I have described under the rubrics of function, process, and materials manifest themselves in the present? In the 1980s, under pressure from printmaking workshops and the prestigious galleries that publish prints, artists have tended to produce large colorful prints. It was thus a stunning turnabout when, in a recent symposium at the Los Angeles County Museum of Art, Richard Solomon of Pace Editions, New York, called for prints to return to the values of intimacy and pure printmaking.[21] When other publishers at the symposium agreed as to the desirability of Solomon's suggestions, titters and guffaws broke out in the audience. Many artists in attendance found it somewhat hilarious and a little maddening that these men should endorse values they had previously undercut, with the consequence that what once had been a flourishing ecology of print galleries, national print exhibitions, and publications has been significantly diminished, so that prints are now either integrated into the general marketplace of the art world or all but totally marginalized. It follows that while a greater number of artists are making prints, there are fewer printmakers. Intrinsically, this change is neither good nor bad. The aesthetic consequence of the loss of a separate printmaking sphere seems to be a mixed bag: commercialism on the one hand, sophistication on the other.

We have yet to see a true reckoning of quality in relation to all layers of print production in the United States. I would contend that excellence is more widely dispersed than is currently acknowledged by the powers that be. When a curator can state: 'I don't see printmaking – and never have – as a way of working out the basic problems of art,' or: 'There's such a difference between New York and anywhere else. I always do try to be fair and get to other places and see all I can but I only prove to myself that the best gets to New York somehow,'[22] you know that any attempt at independent judgment is compromised.

For the artist, the relationship between printmaking and other media is far more complex and interactive. Pop Art borrowed mightily from print syntax. Printmaking has competed very directly with painting during the past twenty-five years. Current deconstructive strategies also place great emphasis upon the repeatability and diffusion of images.

Thoughtful artists who make prints are still caught in the dynamic tension between printmaking's socio-political function and its purely aesthetic possibilities. In each age, artists reanimate printmaking for their own purposes – mostly in hope of investing their images with the resonance which only the panoply of printmaking materials, techniques, and processes can provide.

Notes

1 Goldman, Judith. *American Prints: Process & Proofs* (New York: Harper and Row, 1981): 6.
2 Gilmour, Pat. Review of *American Impressions: Prints Since Pollock* by Riva Castleman. *TTP 8* (1986): 31.
3 Clark, Garth (ed.). *Ceramic Art: Comment and Review 1882–1977* (New York: E. P Dutton, 1978).
4 Field, Richard. *Recent American Etching* (Middletown, Conn.: Wesleyan University, 1975): 1.
5 Santayana, Georges. *The Sense of Beauty* (New York: Scribner's, 1896).
6 Foster, Hal. 'Re: Post,' in Brian Wallis (ed.), *Art After Modernism: Rethinking Representation* (New York: New Museum of Contemporary Art, 1984): 199–200.
7 Ibid.: 191.
8 Ivins Jr., William M. *Prints and Visual Communication* (Cambridge, MA: Harvard University, 1953): 60–1.
9 Ibid.: 20.
10 Mukerji, Chandra. *From Graven Images: Patterns of Modern Materialism* (New York: Columbia University, 1983): 46–7.
11 Kunzle, David. *The Early Comic Strip* (Berkeley: University of California, 1973).
12 Burke, Peter. *Popular Culture in Early Modern Europe* (London: Temple Smith, 1978): 270.
13 Benjamin, Walter. *Illuminations: The Work of Art in the Age of Mechanical Reproduction* (New York: Schocken Books, 1969): 219.
14 Ibid.: 224.
15 Walker, Barry. *Public and Private: American Prints Today* (Brooklyn Museum, 1986): 10.
16 Castleman, Riva. *American Impressions: Prints Since Pollock* (New York: Alfred Knopf, 1985): 51.

17 In conversation, 11 September 1986, Los Angeles. Through her use of the French *extase* (ecstacy), Wayne gives greater emphasis to a contemplative trance-like state.

18 Lehrer, Leonard. 'Artist and Printers: Some Matches Are Made in Heaven and Others...' *TTP 8* (1985): 49.

19 Gedeon, Lucinda. *Tamarind: From Los Angeles to Albuquerque* (Los Angeles: Grunwald Centre for the Graphic Arts, UCLA, 1985): 13.

20 Gilmour, Pat. *Ken Tyler – Master Printer, and the American Print Renaissance* (New York: Hudson Hills Press in association with the Australian National Gallery, 1986): 32.

21 Panel discussion, 'Contemporary Print Publishing,' Graphics Arts Council, Los Angeles County Museum of Art, 17 May 1986.

22 The quotations are from statements made by Riva Castleman on 10 May 1979 during a panel discussion, 'New Prints of Worth: A Question of Taste,' organized by *Print Collector's Newsletter* in relationship to the *21st National Print Exhibition* at the Brooklyn Museum. In a preface to the panel discussion, PCN's editor Jacquelyn Brody characterized the panel as 'the Open Establishment. ... Theirs are the criteria – like it or not – that artists must meet.' PCN10 (Sept.–Oct. 1979): 109–19.

Richard S. Field

Sentences on printed art*

Despite the obvious allusion to Sol LeWitt's 1969 'Sentences on Conceptual Art,' the following does not privilege idea over execution. Quite the contrary, it is an attempt to equate the contradictory attitudes we hold toward prints and to explore the opposites I believe are encoded in printmaking. What I owe to LeWitt's art and prose, most assuredly, is his wonderfully ironic pairing of the logical and the irrational.

1 Prints are metonymous statements about the pervasiveness of binary thought, opposites, reversals, and mirrors.
2 Prints represent a deeply transgressive mechanization of culture, i.e., the principles biological reproduction transferred to that of cultural reproduction.
3 The physical act of transferring information from one surface to another is analogous to the transfer of information from one linguistic field to another.
4 Prints arose in the context of the general pursuit of methods of 'mass production' during the 15th century.
5 Prints are multiples, the products of collaboration.
6 Prints are the natural expression of the masses because they are expressions of the means of production.
7 Prints are highly individualized statements within the confines of rigidly defined technical means; they embody a condition of modernism – the conflict between man and machine, the handmade and the replicated, the original and the copy.
8 Fine prints privilege the modernist notion of originality and authorship, of which the concept of the signed, limited edition is their sign, but popular prints privilege reproduction and communication, of which the very quantity of anonymous prints is their sign.

* Richard S. Field. 1994. 'Sentences on Printed Art'. *Print Collector's Newsletter* 25 (5): 171. Reproduced by kind permission of the author.

9 The print implies a chain of prototypes, something that always precedes; the print is an 'always already.'
10 Prints layer information embodying traces of past thought and acts: they are metaphors for the way in which memory traces impose themselves on all perceptions and thought.
11 Prints are demonstrations of the process of representation, that all pictures of the world are codified and conventionalized, never indexical reflections.
12 Prints are metalanguages – languages about language – whose codes are total abstractions. The more descriptive, the more abstract.
13 Prints embody exactly repeatable visual information, but the implication that they themselves are precise replications must be reexamined.
14 The codes (or 'syntax') of prints can modify or over-modulate the message so that the codes become the message.
15 Codeless prints do not exist. The codes may be invisible, but the properties of techniques always impact content.
16 The information in many prints is encoded in binary systems of 'on' and 'off,' of black and white. Grey does not exist.
17 Prints draw upon the nature and resistance of materials, signifying the opaqueness of languages.
18 The necessary delays between thought and image in printmaking are analogous to present-day information processing (CPU time) and serve as reminders that images are only relatively instantaneous just as they are only relatively codeless.
19 In printmaking, contour, light, and shadow are both particulate and linear.
20 The imperceptible space of the prints – evoked by the deformation of the paper by plates, blocks, and stones – is an important part of their content and operates as an analogue for mental space.
21 Prints made possible the propagation of the history of art as a history of style; for two centuries, prints privileged sculptural interpretation.
22 The print is an index of technological intention – prints represent the technology that made technology possible.
23 Prints have always implied a text and have traditionally conjoined that which originated from very similar impulses (printed imagery preceded and inspired printed text).
24 The historical burden of prints is communication, just as their subject has always been reproduction.
25 Prints are unique works of art, expressing the intentions of the artist.
26 Prints mediate art and craft, often locating meaning in process.
27 Prints are not site specific but the ultimate in transportable art.
28 Prints are multiples, implying reception by multiple viewers and public experience.

29 Prints are mechanical tools that mediate private thought and public experience; as such they comprise media, the means of cultural transmission.

30 Prints (and photography) prepared the ground for mass media and the overwhelming presence of surrogate experience in contemporary culture.

Kathryn Reeves

The re-vision of printmaking*

The re-vision of printmaking[1] is long overdue, especially at a time when theorists, historians, and practitioners in so many fields are intensely interested in rethinking the foundations of their disciplines. Psychoanalysts Margaret Black and Stephen Mitchell wrote, 'History is now understood by many as not a simple uncovering and assembling of facts, but as an active process between past and present, involving a selection and arrangement of some facts, from an infinite set of possibilities, to produce one among many possible understandings.'[2] The re-vision of printmaking, then, is not a simple revisionist exercise, but a process of re-looking, re-seeing, re-arranging, and redefining of both the historical and contemporary construction of the field. Little work has been done in printmaking related to semiotics, feminism, or psychoanalysis. This paper is a call for a new history and historiography of printmaking and, more than anything, is a call for dialogue that would examine the ways in which printmaking relates to the important theoretical issues of our time.

Re-visioning a printmaking historiography is an oxymoron of sorts: a history exists but the critical examination of its sources is missing. It doesn't take long to identify some big gaps in the body of information that constitutes the history of printmaking; nothing has been looked over and almost everything has been overlooked. Art historian Kathryn Kramer noted the lack of a historiography of printmaking (other than chronicles of technical practice) and a neglect of the medium in art theory and criticism. It is, as she put it, 'an especially puzzling slight when the medium seems so accessible

* Kathryn J. Reeves. 1999. 'The Re-Vision of Printmaking'. In: Parraman, Carinna and Brewer, Emmeline (eds), *IMPACT International Multi-disciplinary Printmaking Conference Proceedings*. Bristol: Impact Press, pp. 69–75. www.uwe.ac.uk/sca/research/cfpr/dissemination/conferences/IMPACT%20PROCEEDINGS%20copy.pdf [Accessed 25 January 2018]. Reproduced by kind permission of the author and Impact Press.

to debates surrounding notions of authorship, originality, social formation, [and] agency...that have dominated the critical discourse of western art since antiquity.'[3] Where is our discourse? Where are the questions concerning this medium, so accessible yet unexplored, to be located in theory and history? And where is theory to be located in our practice? These questions must not be asked by theorists alone and experience tells us that few questions specifically concerning printmaking have been located in the literature of theory. Walter Benjamin's germinal essay 'The Work of Art in the Age of Mechanical Reproduction', often cited, often misunderstood, must not be the sole theoretical basis of our historiography. And if it seems printmakers get mired in discussions of the same territory, perhaps it is because we are not looking in the right places or spaces for critical examination. James Clifford wrote, 'To theorise, one leaves home.'[4] So for a while let's leave the familiar territory, a place with boundaries but without a concrete, fixed location. Spaces have been left unexplored and open, and print artists must enter if we are to understand where our identities and our linguistic and cultural practices are located and how those have been constructed.

Homi K. Bhabha said, 'What theory does first of all is respond to a problem.'[5] Our problem, a misleading and inadequate history and a missing historiography, requires that we try to discover what is present or absent, what requires identification, what must be decoded. The body, the matrix, theory, location, and past and present coding, are the missing who, what, why, where, and when of our historical narratives. Woven throughout the narratives are questions of encryption, marginality, originality, and binary opposition. I say narratives (plural) because I feel we must strongly resist the production of a grand narrative with its homogenising effect and its implicit singular voice. As we approach the 21st century, the modernist project of constructing or discovering a totalizing structure surely ought to be abandoned once and for all.

Histories often begin with mapping and locating activities. In *Notes Towards a Politics of Location*, Adrienne Rich suggested beginning with the closest geography available – the body. She considered the body a locus, but not the centre of discourse. It is the 'site of more than one identity,' and at the same time, is 'a place in history.'[6] Many of us began our own experience and history with printmaking when as newborn infants a portion of our body was inked and a footprint taken. Touch always results in a print. It is safe to say that body prints, from fingers, lips, hands, feet, and skin exist in the billions. It is equally safe to say that the term 'print' means many things to many people, and that no other term substitutes for these multiple identities. 'Print' exists as trace, identity, evidence, and reproduction simultaneously.

That printmakers equate the print with the body is not in doubt. We 'bleed' when the margin of the print is excised. The margin, and the identification with the marginal, is deeply imbedded within the printmaking psyche. Excision of the pristine, virginal space surrounding a print image may function as an attempt to make a print more like a painting – but the language, the naming of the bleed print, acknowledges the depth of the loss. The printmaking corpus suffers the loss, but the loss is also one of the known identity. The margin is a discursive space, but, for the print artist, it exists largely as a tabula rasa and that must change if printmaking is to engage with the decentred perspective of contemporary thought.

Historians, curators, and we ourselves are active and vigilant in the maintenance of our identity. When paint is used in the production of our prints, we are all careful to call it hand-colouring. New Zealand artist Carole Shepheard wrote that 'print challenges the notion of authorship and originality by the very nature of its methods....But printmaking has a legacy of marginalisation and this needs to be recognised and addressed for any changes to occur.'[7] It must be said that printmakers support those same notions by avoiding infringement into the territory of painting. But this interpretation of the term 'hand-colouring,' while accurate in its own way, is limited and does not take into account the desire to invoke the body via the hand in the print. It acknowledges the absence of a colour printing element or matrix and, at the same time, constructs the printmaker's hand as another matrix.

Does the location of our artistic identity and practice also involve the print matrix – an inky middle ground between paper and pressure? Is this plane of activity a centre or a non-centre? And if the matrix is a centre of activity is the print then not a centre? Derrida in *Structure, Sign, and Play*, described the 'non-centre otherwise than as a loss of centre.'[8] Does the existence of multiple impressions of the same image also point to the print as a non-centre? The absence of the matrix in the visible artwork seems to point to a loss, an absence which serves to decentre attention from the art object. In modern printing technology and terminology, lithography was reinvented as offset – a term which implies a compensating equivalent, that is, compensation for a loss incurred by distancing the art object further from the matrix. If an art object acts as a presence signifying also the absence of the artist, is there a doubling of absence in a printed art object? Does this recognised absence alone account for the fanatical concentration on media and matrix in virtually every printmaking history? Is it this absent matrix which causes viewers (patrons and practitioners alike) to peer so closely at the surface of the print that the complete image cannot be seen in focus and to ask the perennial question, 'How is this done?'

Given the intense curiosity about the matrix and technical practice, it is possible to construct the matrix as a psychosexual object and the making of prints as a psychosexual, reproductive act. The actual printing then, in a twist of Freudian theory, is a primal scene, a 'fantasy of sexual activity.'[9] Public demonstrations of printmaking technique and the act of printing satisfy the curiosity about the reproductive act and allow a vicarious participation in it. Otherwise the absent matrix causes anxiety for the viewer who experiences a kind of frustration and in some cases an inability to see the image. In print exhibitions, didactic information and displays of matrices and tools often are shown as surrogates which substitute for the primal scene.

That we increasingly describe printmaking as a matrix-based form of image-making begs us to ask further what is encoded or encrypted here. Questions concerning coding, especially identity and gendered code, have been dealt with extensively in theory and in other media or disciplines. The most significant question that can be asked is: why have we chosen 'matrix' as an identifier? Matrix seems, on the face of it, an apt word to describe the models or forms from which images are pulled or produced, particularly when 'plate', 'block', or 'stone' can't describe the proliferation of current technological possibilities. But, matrix is not simply model or form, not simply that which gives origin or form to a thing, but, literally matrix is 'womb.'

The word matrix is omnipresent in contemporary humanities, arts, and sciences. Found in metallurgy, polymer theory, literature, engineering, genetics, poetics, robotics, and virtually every discipline (it has even found its way recently into popular cinema), matrix is a most useful word, a Jack-of-all-trades, except that this Jack is really a Jane. The matrilineage of the word should be clear. Though the meaning of the word has been partially cloaked in modern times, the etymology of matrix is easily traced. In Late Latin, matrix meant womb. From the Latin, it was incorporated intact and unchanged into the English language. In 16th century literature, metaphoric parallels were drawn between the matrix and the earth as Mother Earth, the great womb. By the early 17th century the word was used in printing to describe moulds for casting type.[10] In the 1850s, three mathematicians appropriated the word to describe a rectangular numeric array and hyper-complex numbers. Since then, every scientific discipline has found a use for the word. While abbreviated dictionaries of the early 19th century often listed womb as the sole definition of the word, some contemporary counterparts of those heavily abridged dictionaries omit the original definition of the word altogether. According to linguistic models, the proliferation of scientific and scholarly redefinition of matrix might be considered as a process of amelioration or elevation, but it seems rather a change of a different sort. Still, the matrilineage of matrix resonates and the link between matrix, reproduction, and printing is unmistakable.

Old art history surveys have described printmaking as one of the minor arts and even as the 'handmaiden of the fine arts' because of its reproductive capabilities. It is also identified as a labour-intensive art form. Matrix, reproduction, labour. From those points, it doesn't take an expert cryptographer to crack the code: printmaking is and has historically been gender-coded 'feminine.'

We know that gendered codes have been assigned to various art forms throughout history. Michelangelo gender-coded Flemish painting feminine (and simultaneously coded Italian painting as its opposite). Michelangelo is said to have characterised Flemish art as that which 'will appeal to women, especially to the very old and the very young, and also to monks and nuns...' because it is 'done without reason or art...without skillful choice or boldness...without substance or vigour.'[11] In a painting, it is understood that the ground has been gendered female. Mira Schor reminds us that 'painting in the high Italian Renaissance increasingly became a system for ordering and subduing nature, laying a grid on chaos (femininity), which in the 20th century became a process of razing and asphalting.'[12] A coded project of modernist painting, and particularly that of the Abstract Expressionists, was to reconstruct painting, which had become associated with the effeminate, as a masculine enterprise, 'as an expression of virile passion'.[13] In the United States, this recoding of art in the 1950s marked the end of a period of gender equality in the arts and the end of the intense activity in graphic arts funded by the WPA and the FAP (Work Projects Administration and Federal Arts Project) in the 1930s.[14] We know that printmaking was in danger of disappearing in postwar America and that time period coincided with the gendered reconstruction of painting.

Whether one believes that a gendered code resides within or without, that is, inside or outside the coded subject is less significant than the fact that the code exists and operates actively, though covertly. By choosing not to consciously recognise the coding of our discipline (and I think that many of us felt rather than knew the code, and preferred to silence the discussion), by choosing to remain cloaked, even from ourselves, we missed a critical juncture in the 1980s in the Postmodern debate where issues of originality, post-structuralism, deconstruction, and critique of patriarchy intersected. While many writers at that time rightly questioned if Postmodernism was a masculine invention, a final ploy of patriarchy to leave the canon intact by declaring it obsolete, print artists missed that debate also. Photography was there, printmaking wasn't.

The gendered code of printmaking explains much in relation to issues of marginalisation, reproduction, and originality. If print images spring from a matrix/womb, they are ordinary mortals. The genius, who is never gendered female, produces something different. The offspring of genius has been likened to the birth of Zeus' daughter, the goddess Athena, patroness of art. Athena was not born from a goddess' womb, but instead sprang directly from the head of Zeus the father. Creation is constructed thus, and not as reproduction; it occurs without labour and without the matrix/womb. The destruction and cancellation of the matrix in the service of creating the uniqueness and 'originality' of a limited edition multiple and the production of an evidential 'proof' of the dead mother are fascinating practices. This modern printmaking practice, forming an equation between destruction of the matrix and the creation of originality, embraces outmoded concepts of opposition. And though concepts of genius and originality have been thoroughly debunked in theory,[15] in practice, they still hold considerable power. Recently in an opinion contrary to Benjamin's prediction, Michael Kimmelman posited that 'the allure of the original will increase, not decline, and in direct proportion to the availability of reproductions.'[16] Nevertheless, clinging to notions of genius, hierarchy and originality is not to the advantage of those who have been coded as other.

The issue of gendered codes approached from another direction sheds more light on the problem. Histories of printmaking, as previously noted, are largely chronicles of technical practice arranged along a linear time line. Science and technology are traditionally coded as masculine enterprises, and are highly prized in both Western and Eastern cultures. Therefore, any field strongly associated with technology ought to be coded as masculine and, in the hierarchical structure of any patriarchal culture, ought to occupy the highest tier. That printmaking, arguably the most technical of all art forms, does not occupy this tier suggests that it has not been coded as masculine and that a different code is operative. Interestingly, recent technological shifts towards electronic digital imaging seem to cause printmakers to unconsciously reach for a masculine gendered code and refigure the field as printmaKING. Witness the recently adopted use in North America of the French word *giclée*[17] to describe ink-jet prints. Clinton Adams, Emeritus Professor of the University of New Mexico and the Tamarind Institute of Lithography, suggests that the use of this term shows that American printmakers do not know colloquial French. However, *giclée* makes an obvious reference to the masculine and at the same time reinforces the notion of all printmaking as a reproductive function. Printmaking, it would seem, is always reduced to a sort of biological determinism. Attempts to reconstruct printmaking as masculine in order to reposition its rank in the art world is to accept patriarchy, hierarchy and opposition as the natural order of things. It also ignores the central features of Postmodern thought related to 'the redefinition of the nature of authority…the re-working of traditional gender roles,' and the understanding of gender 'as an artefact of social structures.'[18] What must occur is not a recoding, but a challenge to existing notions and a reconsideration of gender. The outmoded framework of division and opposition must be dismantled.

Within this Postmodern or post-Postmodern era and within the context of a persistently patriarchal world, the 'master printer' is a curiously archaic construction. This trope is unquestionably offensive on so many levels in so many cultures, and is yet seemingly perfectly acceptable to printmakers. Does the use of this term mean there are no feminists among printmakers nor men and women of goodwill who would avoid using exclusionary, colonialist language? I know that neither of those is entirely true. Yet this figure would seem to be a contradiction to the understanding of gendered encryption in printmaking. But it must be remembered that the master printer functions as a servant in collaborative printing. And, if considered as a masculine gendered figure, the master printer has a necessary role in conjunction with the matrix in a reproductive process, and thus serves to reinforce the gendered code of printmaking as feminine. At the same time, another equally complex function operates in printmaking and to understand it we must look to our habitual reversal – the printmaker's understanding of the mirror image. Beyond the reproductive function, the function of reversal explains the largely unquestioned use of the term 'master printer'. Printmakers have the capability to see the dual nature of all images/texts/identities which exist always as themselves and always as their mirror images. But this experience of reversal is not shared with the rest of the art world nor with society; this experience further marks the printmaker and printmaking as other, as 'eccentrics,' described by Linda Hutcheon as those who do not occupy the centre, the traditionally marginalised groups.[19]

What are the other implications of the mirror image? Carl Zigrosser referred to the 'potential duality' of prints as a characteristic that distinguished prints from other art forms, but he referred only to aesthetics and utility.[20] While the mirror has been explored in psychoanalysis, especially in Freudian theory,[21] and has been used in literature as a metaphor for reflection of truth, reality, or states of being, it has not been considered as a process of reversal. Printmaking's particular duality of the mirror image, this capability of dual perception and reversal, has been little explored in imagistic, conceptual, or theoretical terms by printmakers. When left becomes right, right becomes left, and up becomes down, anything is possible in a curiouser and curiouser through-the-looking-glass world. In Postmodernity it is understood that history, language, and signs do not have fixed meanings, and the mirror offers a powerful tool for exploring this. Is this the site of 'more than one identity'[22] in the body of printmaking?

Recognising that not all print media involve a mirror reversal, is there yet another site that involves a relationship of a different kind – a site shared by all printmaking, photography and digital imaging? Printmaking and printing have historically occupied a crossroads, now shared with photography and digital media, through which all cultural and scientific information passes. That constitutes another site, but it too has more than one identity. Perhaps the greatest challenge that must be faced is the recognition of the nature of that shared site, the recognition that these media are fundamentally based on binary opposition. Pairs of oppositions are the conceptual and technical basis for printmaking: black and white, high and low in relief and intaglio, grease and water in lithography, open and closed in serigraphy. Photography has been constructed as a medium which images with light, but it equally depends on darkness. The digital image is formed with off/on technology, the zero/one of computer programming. The computer never allows maybe, only yes or no. Perhaps it is absurd to ask civilisation, which is itself formed on sets of oppositions such as good/evil, strength/weakness, left/right, right/wrong, to conceptualise its information delivery systems in any other way. How could the emissaries of civilisation be conceived of otherwise? Even so, it is necessary that binary opposition, the model of polar thinking that has characterised patriarchal Western philosophy and culture, should be addressed in contemporary printmaking, and here also there must be a reconsideration and critique of existing notions of opposition as the natural order of things.

Printmaking is often described as a mediated art form, referring only in part to technical practice and the role of the matrix as mediator standing between the artist and the art work. Mediation also suggests the possibility and perhaps the necessity of interpolating, interposing, interceding, interfering, and intervening in aesthetic, theoretic, philosophic, social, and economic ways. Can we now theorise a space for printmaking practice that, quoting Foucault, 'is one in which space takes for us the form of relations among sites'?[23] The great challenge for printmakers will be to determine the sites with which to engage and what form the relations among sites will take.

Print artists must negotiate with theory, location, identity, and multiple subjectivities. 'Printmaking proper'[24] must engage with new technologies, reversals and oppositions, and with reproduction modes that include neither the pain nor the pleasure of touching materials. Artists who chose to work with print media and with print thought must resist the conceptual framework of binary opposition and try to bridge the huge spaces between polar opposites. We must, as Ruth Weisberg suggested, not be unwilling to 'construct a framework of ideas and concepts that would locate our practice in relation to the larger intellectual paradigms of our time.'[25] Will print artists successfully avoid the formation of new hierarchy, hegemony, and a grand narrative as we re-vision printmaking and negotiate with theory? Linda Hutcheon wrote, we must engage in 'a more general questioning of *any* totalising or homogenising system ... from the decentred perspective, the "marginal" takes on a new significance'.[26] Heterogeneity, mutability, and provisionality must become part of our theoretical and visual vocabularies. An understanding must be gained that theory and practice are not oppositional positions, nor is gender. Theory when carefully and fully considered, has the capacity to make art and practice more interesting, to empower artists, to open spaces, and to deepen experience. As print artists revisit the primal scene of creation again and again, it must be remembered that the margins and other spaces, the matrix, and the conceptual challenges that await us are among the most interesting parts.

Notes

1 This title was first suggested by Steve Murakishi of the Cranbrook Academy of Art, Bloomfield Hills, Michigan, USA. Murakishi organised a panel discussion

at the Mid America Print Council Conference in 1998. All panel participants, including this author, were asked to give papers on *The Re-Vision of Printmaking*. Murakishi's own re-vision redefines printmaking as design.

2 Mitchell, S. A. and Black, M. J. *Freud and Beyond: A History of Modern Psychoanalytic Thought* (New York, 1995), p. 226.

3 Kramer, K. guest editor *The Journal of the Mid America Print Council*, Vol. 5, Issue 2, 2.

4 Clifford, J. 'Notes on Travel and Theory', in: James Clifford and Vivek Dhareshwar (eds), *Inscriptions 5. Traveling Theories, Traveling Theorists* (Santa Cruz: University of California at Santa Cruz, 1989), p. 177.

5 Bhabha, H. K. interviewed by W. J. T. Mitchell, in 'Translator Translated', *Artforum*, March 1995, p. 83.

6 Rich, A. *Notes Towards a Politics of Location, Blood, Bread, Poetry: Selected Prose 1979–1985* (New York and London: W. W. Norton, & Company 1984), p. 212.

7 Shepheard, C. 'The Territorial Divide: Critical Issues in Contemporary Print', *State of International Printmaking* panel, College Art Association Conference, Boston, Massachusetts, USA, 1996, manuscript, p. 2, and again, p. 1.

8 Derrida, J. *Structure, Sign, and Play, Writing and Difference*, translated by Alan Bass (Chicago: University of Chicago Press, 1978), p. 292.

9 Schneider Adams, L. *The Methodologies of Art* (Boulder and Oxford: Westview Press, 1996), p. 194.

10 *The Compact Edition of the Oxford English Dictionary* (Oxford: Oxford University Press, 1971), p. 238.

11 Michelangelo, as quoted in Svetlana Alpers, *The Art of Describing: Dutch Art in the Seventeenth Century* (Chicago: University of Chicago Press, 1983), p. xxiii, and again, p. 223.

12 Schor, M. *Figure and Ground, Wet: On Painting, Feminism, and Art Culture* (Durham and London: Duke University Press, 1997), p. 152.

13 Langa, H. 'Egalitarian Vision, Gendered Experience: Women Printmakers and the WPA/FAP Graphic Arts Project' in: Norma Broude and Mary D. Garrard (eds), *The Expanding Discourse, Feminism and Art History* (New York: Harper Collins, 1991), p. 421.

14 Ibid., p. 420.

15 Krauss, R. E. *The Originality of the Avant Garde and Other Modernist Myths* (Cambridge, MA: MIT Press, c.1985) on painting and sculpture as reproduction/repetition. See also Michel Foucault, *The Order of Things: An Archaeology of Human Sciences* (New York, Pantheon, c.1970) on origins and originals.

16 Kimmelman, M. 'Art View: No Substitute for the Real Thing', *NY Times*, Feb. 22, 1998.

17 'Giclée' translates literally as 'squirt', 'spurt', or 'spray'.

18 Mitchell and Black, op. cit., p. 169, and again, p. 222.

19 Hutcheon, L. *A Poetics of Postmodernism* (New York: Routledge, 1988), p. 12.

20 Zigrosser, C. *The Book of Fine Prints* (New York: Crown Publishers, 1937, rev. ed. 1948), p. 10.

21 See Sigmund Freud, Jacques Lacan, and others for discussions on the mirror stage in infant development and mirroring in psychoanalysis.

22 Rich, loc. cit.
23 Foucault, M. 'Of Other Spaces', translated by Jay Miskowiec, *diacritics*, Vol. 16, No. 1, Spring, 1986, p. 23.
24 'Printmaking proper' is a term used to describe the traditional area of printmaking practice.
25 Ruth Weisberg, as quoted by Carole Shepheard, op. cit., p. 1.
26 Hutcheon, loc. cit.

Andrzej Bednarczyk

The shape of graphic art*

Reasons

Today, we are discussing graphic art. Before we do that, we have to state clearly our motivations and aims, because the soundness of raising questions about graphic art is not obvious nowadays.

Among opponents to this question, there are essentially three distinct positions. First of all, there are claims that the question is redundant since everyone knows what graphic art is. It is not a new occurrence and many studies and analyses have been devoted to it, so its essence has already been thoroughly investigated. Secondly, there are claims that the question is redundant since it is not relevant. Discussing art as such is important, but without delving into its disciplines and techniques. Thirdly, the question is redundant since artistic categories in the post-industrial world have disappeared, liberating us from the necessity to categorize. But despite these doubts, we feel a pressing need to discuss the identity of graphic art.

Since this centuries-old discipline of art is demanding a re-examination of these issues, we have to acknowledge that we have ceased to know what graphic art is, and what we do know has proved to be insufficient. Indeed, following the phenomenon of graphic art makes it clear that the current

* Andrzrej Bednarczyk. 2010. 'The Shape of Graphic Art'. In: *im:print 2010: zustandsprotokolle aktueller druckgrafik / journal for the state of current printmaking*. Edited by Schneider, Michael, Maurer, Philipp and Lebzelter, Georg. Vienna: Springer Verlag, pp. 97–109. Reproduced by kind permission of the author and Springer Verlag. Translated from Polish to English by Urszula Humienik-Dworakowska (edited for publication).

Note from the editor of the original publication: Andrzej Bednarczyk does make use of a differentiation between the Polish word 'matrica' = English 'matrix' and the Polish word 'macierz' = English 'matrix'. The different forms of the plural of matrix (matrix – pl. matrices, matrixes) still give a hint to the different meanings that are expressed by this differentiation. Michael Schneider.

measures and models do not correspond to the described occurrence. Graphic art in its subsequent unveilings eludes them like a slippery fish.

I will describe the reasons for this state of affairs using the architectural structure of Krakow, where I live and work, as an example. The building of the Jan Matejko Academy of Fine Arts is adjacent to the Barbican and city walls with their St. Florian's Gate. These are medieval fortified constructions that outline city boundaries. What is so notable about these constructions? These fortifications, surrounding the city by design, are now located in its very center. Could it be the result of a former disaster of turning the city space onto the wrong side, so that the outskirts of the city converged in its center and the center scattered towards the periphery? The truth is not so colorful: the city simply passed its former borders. Krakow's suburban villages have been incorporated into it and something that never 'was' Krakow is now a part of its identity. No sane person will claim today that Krakow starts behind Florian's Gate. The need for the constant adjustment of borders and redefinition of identity is a sign of its life and development.

The same is true for graphic art, which in the course of its dynamic transformations has already passed its old borders. Our loss of knowledge about its identity is not a problem of graphic art itself, but rather a problem of describing it with inadequate or too arbitrarily adopted models. These problems can be easily avoided by complying with the modern model – experimental cognitive paradigm – which has been obeyed since Karl Popper's era, with the requirement of falsifiability. In it, a created model of reality is considered correct if it is consistent with the experiment's results. However, if the examined occurrence reveals something that does not fit or denies the model, this model is rejected as defective. Unfortunately during the study of culture, we often meet with dogmatic attitudes in which the model is defended rather than the facts.

The second attitude – the question of graphic art being unnecessary, because it is art *per se* that is important – is logically unsound. Art is a multi-dimensional occurrence, and like all occurrences and similar kinds of entities, it is subject to both synthetic examination and component analysis. Moreover, to achieve a synthesis, it is necessary to know its components. One cannot determine the identity of a three-dimensional block without distinguishing, analyzing and understanding what are width, length and height. No one will claim that for reaching knowledge about the human body as a whole it would be unnecessary to ask what is a hand? Of course, we know that man and art are important. However, we ask what is a hand, what is graphic art – as their components. We need this knowledge to understand the essence of things, especially today, when many artists in search of adequate means of expression go beyond media identity boundaries, compiling them, merging them into an indistinguishable whole or denying the established rules. We do not postulate a return to practicing art in its pure form. The thing is to exceed and not ignore, ensuring that our wonderful artistic freedom is not based on ignorance and lack of understanding.

The third claim for a disappearance of categories in the post-industrial world seems to be the result of a misunderstanding of the *construction – deconstruction – reconstruction* principle, which is one of the cornerstones of postmodern thought. It constitutes an equivalent in the history of European philosophy to the revolution in physics achieved by Albert Einstein's general theory of relativity, taking away the peremptoriness from the dimensions of the space–time continuum. Also in this case, the categories – dimensions – do not disappear, only their understanding changes, and the conclusions obtained on the basis of reasoning and measurement depend on the contextual mutual influence between them as well as on the researcher. In the specific case of exploration of identity of an occurrence, the above method would take the following form: *definition – de-definition – redefinition*. In a collision with the artistic world, post-modernity experienced a misfortune similar to the vicissitudes of the achievements of psychoanalysis and depth psychology pervading into art. Both in the first and in the second case, the great discoveries and ideas provided an invigorating impetus and new perspectives for European culture. At the same time, they opened the gate for gibberish, intellectual laziness and spiritual languor. To creatively use these achievements, we must remember that the resignation from category kills the power of postmodern thought, and, following the words of Professor Barbara Skarga, deconstruction changes into destruction.

So we discuss graphic art to redefine its identity in the contemporary hypostasis.

Searching for a method

Setting about to determine the definition of graphic art, we should begin with formulating a new method of research. It seems that the hitherto utilized methods have ceased to adequately describe and explain this occurrence. I find essentially three reasons why we are encountering difficulties in our reflection on the identity of graphic art. The first is the creation of the image of identity as a list of characteristics essential for a given work or creation to be deemed as graphic. This, however, makes it difficult to distinguish factors indispensably making up the identity of the form from individual features. Just as in a sequence of statements like: *John is a human. John is blond*. Although the two sentences may be true for John, they are not true for every human, ergo – hair color is not a determinant of the identity of the human species.

The second reason could be a not concise enough differentiation of the graphic technique from graphic art, which prevents us from determining their interrelationship. In the case of this discipline this seems to be extremely important, following Marshall McLuhan's statement: *the medium is the message*. We are moving in an expanse between technique and art, where we are stating that not every composition made using the graphic technique is a work of art and not every work of art is graphic art. Modeling the identity of graphic art exclusively on the basis of technique causes constant difficulties for emerging new techniques, and their dynamic development makes the method outright useless.

This last sentence leads us to the third reason, which seems to be the utilization of models that are too stationary, namely those that do not contain the factor of time and the changes in the subsequent hypostases of identity. The issue of time in contemporary graphic art is an indispensable factor. The emergence of new techniques and related forms of artistic articulation formerly took place within the rhythm of many generations, and now, especially since computers have entered into the graphic studio, this has accelerated to single years or even months. Sometimes I joke that I love my computer, it is the only thing in my house that ages faster than me. This dizzying pace of technological change makes the graphic art situation specific and different from the other disciplines of art. Above all, it is necessary to examine the identity of evolving occurrences by studying its states in a dynamic continuum of changes. Statements about unchangeability should be placed in the archives of history of human thought along with the Ptolemaic cosmological model of a stationary world.

Our intention is to unearth the geometry of the bubbling magma of graphic art.

Method

In thinking over the identity of graphic arts, we will use three methods hoping that they will let us avoid the above-mentioned imperfections. These are: (1) spatial modeling, in which factors are treated as dimensions; (2) examining the attained factors in relation to the graphic technique, graphic art and graphic work; and (3) examining the attained results in the perspective of time.

Customarily, a description of a studied occurrence or thing is presented in the form of a list of constitutive characteristics arranged 'side by side', heeding to include what is indispensable and sufficient. In the case of a description of identity, the better method seems to be spatial modeling, since the interrelationships that occur among factors/dimensions are significant. This is because identity is a nonlinear structure. It is thus a whole, which isn't a mere sum of its parts, but forms a value exceeding this sum. This value is not present in any individual part but is everywhere.

To outline the principles of this method, we will use an example from geometry. To determine the state of a changing point in time in three-dimensional space (3D + T), we need six spatial points of reference and two temporal. To describe any freely moving or changing object, we need to know its height, width, length, speed and type of changes between the boundary conditions of the experiment. This method, taken from the field of science, has demonstrated its usefulness not only in determining the shape and location, but it also enables one to interpolate the past and the future of an object with good accuracy depending on the degree of its determination. When dealing with a dynamic entity (occurrence), which is naturally open to the influence of an external action, we find it to be subject to fluctuation. In this case, only an exact distinction between individual and arbitrary characteristics from the constitutive characteristics of type enables outlining the shape of its identity, even though it appears in different hypostases. This is particularly important if we want our model of identity of a dynamically evolving art discipline to keep its merits regardless of the passage of time.

In spatial modeling of identity, the examined object is treated as a block in space with the number of dimensions equal to the number of indispensable and sufficient constitutive factors. If we manage to achieve this compliance, we can acquire knowledge about the identity of an object, what it is, how it looked in the past and how it will appear in the next hypostases, as well as its functioning. If this compatibility does not occur, we cannot say anything meaningful about the object, just as we cannot meaningfully talk about the essence and nature of a cube while excluding one of the three dimensions. The action and hypostasis of the object carry within themselves all the features of its identity.

Graphic art, as one of the disciplines of art, has been differentiated on the basis of technique, but graphic art is not identical with its technique. Firstly, because as I mentioned previously, not every composition realized using its means is a work of art. Secondly, because their common characteristics, considered from the perspective of technique and art, reveal or acquire a different meaning, which I will demonstrate later on. Graphic art and graphic technique are connected through the aspect ratio, which means that they are interconnected and form a plane where graphic artistic objects take place. Outside of this plane, the object is neither artistic nor graphic.

In this plane, we will now build a six-dimensional block of graphic art and we will examine its individual constitutive characteristics/dimensions from three perspectives: technical, artistic discipline, and graphic work.

Matrix

The matrix is an idea more encompassing than graphic art, so let's first consider what the matrix is in general. We can speak of a mathematical matrix, a genetic matrix, a sound matrix, an algorithmic matrix, a mold matrix, a graphic matrix and others. The identity of the matrix is revealed in three factors. These are: the function of the trace carrier, the function of the intermediate form, and the automatism of marking. Everything that has the features indispensable for potential marking in the receiving area can be the medium of the trace. The material from which the matrix is made is negligible, as long as its structure permits making an impression. Moreover, the matrix does not have to be material; it may be a mathematical or a conceptual structure. The carrier of the trace can be anything that has a fixed shape/order not subject to essential or accidental changes during marking. The method of making the matrix or whether it was made at all is irrelevant. I can find an item bearing the features necessary to mark, and by my decision it becomes a matrix. If, for example, I was to strike sheets of paper with a slab of fatty beef so that they leave a trace or mark, then at this point it functions as a matrix. I'm not postulating the creation of *beefography*, I just want to show that neither materiality, nor the type of shape, nor how it is made or if it was made at all have an effect on whether a matrix is a matrix.

The matrix functions as an intermediate form. It is not a final product or a tool enabling its creation. What distinguishes it from a tool is the final content inscribed in it and the passive giving of the content to the original. A tool, on the other hand, although its structure affects the product is beyond the content and active by its nature. What connects the tool with the matrix is involvement in the process and the requirement of adequacy of their use for the intended purposes. Therefore, even the most sophisticated waving of a piece of printing block in the air will not create a graphic print.

This leads us to the third factor of the identity of the matrix – automatic marking. This means that the order contained within the matrix can be reproduced. In this case, the matrix is related to a vessel. Loose or liquid material automatically takes its shape without the conscious interference of the person doing the filling. Also in the case of the matrix, the compatibility of the end result with the pattern stems from the characteristics contained within it and the person only has to retain the adequacy of the procedure.

Each type of matrix is characterized by a specific set of features, distinguishing it from the others. So for example, an audio matrix allows tracing a sound recording at the area of a sound wave, and a sculptural matrix enables creating a trace in three-dimensional space.

The graphic matrix, which is of particular interest to us presently, functions as a medium enabling imprinting the trace of a visual recording on the surface. It contains all the features of the broadly defined matrix, and what distinguishes it from others is an inseparable combination: the visuality of the recording and a surface receiving the imprint (the screen), with the reservation that this surface is not necessarily flat.

In traditional graphic art, the matrix existed exclusively in the form of a surface material mechanically or chemically treated. The advent of digital recording, light-sensitive and electrostatic matrices did not introduce any significant changes in the understanding of the identity of the matrix. From the perspective of a graphic technique, the matrix is one of the fundamental determinants of its identity.

In graphic art, the matrix has not yet been performed, in other words it has not been a work of art. In modern practice, it is sometimes directly or indirectly present in a work by inclusion in the scope of artistic expression of the act of marking, such as in the work by Zbigniew Salaj entitled *Translator* (2002), in which a brayer coated with a pattern imprints a paper tape in front of the viewer. Its presence may therefore be one of the characteristics of a work, but is not required and, as such, it is often an individual characteristic, but does not fall within the characteristics of graphic art.

Automatic recording methods

Using a matrix means that the record made with it is an automatic process, in which external interference is unnecessary and unacceptable. The mechanical method of recording, in its essence, is a faithful transfer of the order contained within the matrix to the target area. However, this transfer must take the form of a translation from the language of the matrix into the language of the final product. If there was no translation, the result would be an identical clone of the matrix. Then the matrix would be multiplied rather than giving birth to the trace, so it would lose the status of a matrix. The term 'translation' is etymologically equal to transfer (Latin: *translatio* stemming from *transferre*, where *trans* means 'to the other side', and *ferre* means 'to carry', 'to rearrange'). Translation occurs when the target product retains the order of the original, but differs in at least one of the factors. For example, in mathematics an isometric translation in expanse changes the position of the figure in relation to the other figures; in genetics it is an ultimate translation of information for a specific protein structure; this text, originally written in Polish was translated into a different language; and the raised surfaces of the wood block are transformed into a set of printing ink stains on the surface.

The final product of an automatic recording method is shaped by a set of three components of the process: the type of matrix, the recording method and the type of area of the recording, and it is possible by the mutual relevance of the three.

Graphic work is created by using automated methods of visual recording and it is the basic factor of the identity of the graphic technique. These methods fall within the scope of graphic art's identity in that they limit the spectrum of artistic articulation to automatically recordable procedures and languages, and since the medium is the message, they strongly affect its shape. The printing process of traditional graphic art, let's call it 'pressura', occurred by physical and mechanical transfer of printing ink from the matrix onto paper under pressure. Just as in the discussion of the identity of the matrix, we find that the emergence of digital, light and electrostatic mediums made no significant changes in the nature of the imprinting process, but expanded it so that it passes into the broadly defined projection, which also contains pressura as its special case. The Latin etymology of the term 'projection': *proicere – throw in front*, used to describe the process of transferring the image onto the surface receiving it empowers us to integrate all of its methods into a single category.

The printing process in traditional graphic art was not present in the work; we only saw it *post factum* through its physical effects. Currently, in the case of graphic art that is not in material form and is intended solely for projection before our eyes, the process of projection falls within the scope of graphic artwork.

Two-dimensionality of the composition

The prerequisite to making a projection of a matrix is the existence of a receiving area, and in the specific case of graphic projection, the surface receiving it. Such a surface becomes a screen. The essence of the surface being the screen is its function and a set of features enabling its reception. The screen is a barrier located in the path of a projection so that it stops on itself the order of the matrix. For this to happen, the screen cannot be parallel to the direction of the projection and must possess a structure enabling its visualization and retention in the time necessary for the reception, adequate to the nature of the matrix and the projection process. Therefore, passing a CD with digitally recorded graphics through a printing press with the intention of imprinting it on spilled water does not make sense.

What the screen is made of is irrelevant. It may be a sheet of paper, a pane of glass, the wall of a building, as in the case of the projection on the facade of the Whitney Museum of American Art by Krzysztof Wodiczko (1989), or even a cloud of water vapor like in the work of Ksawery Kaliski titled *against nothingness – entirety and infinity* (2005/6). This last example shows that the surface of the screen does neither have to be homogeneous nor in one plane. A pane of glass used as a screen is an interesting case, which demonstrates the essence of compliance, required for the existence of the projection. The projection of printing ink on a pane of glass makes recording possible due to the ability to hold paint. The projection of light does not give the ability of stopping the image as the light needs screen clarity below one hundred percent.

A specific and necessary case to discuss at this point is holography. Regardless of the many techniques of creation, we must divide them into two groups. Those that give the illusion of a three-dimensional image on the collective of closely located surfaces with a phase flow satisfy the requirement for a screen, and as such could be included in graphic art. By contrast, a hologram, in which a three-dimensional image is formed by an interference of light on the diffraction grid, is a method of spatial modeling and is a kind of light sculpture.

From the above findings, we come to the obvious conclusion that the graphic screen is always two-dimensional. So we could jump to the conclusion that a constitutive feature of the graphic work is its flatness. But there is no logically legitimate reason why the surface should be flat. Mathematical spatial modeling treats the flat surface as one specific case out of a great number of possibilities. This truth also applies to graphic work. The factor of its identity is two-dimensionality, and flatness is one of the possible cases, and as such is an individual characteristic. However, if we agree with the postulate of distinguishing two-dimensionality from flatness, we must remember that the surface can be bent in such a way that we obtain a finite surface without edges. An excellent example of such a surface is a sphere, which has a finite area, but we cannot determine any boundary point on it. When this happens in graphic art, we obtain a three-dimensional object. It remains a work of graphic art, while its surface maintains the function of a screen subordinate to the projection.

The end result of the projection process is always the resultant of the features of the matrix, the projection and the screen. A sheet of paper acting as a screen, as well as a computer monitor, is neutral in content. Although their type has some influence on the final expression of the graphic work, the difference is negligible in this context. However, there are cases where the screen is semantically important and enters rightfully within the scope of artistic expression. Such a case occurs when the bend of the surface takes on significant shapes. This happened, for example, in the work of Zbigniew Bajek titled: *Tattoo – Face* (1998), and *Tattoo – Female and Male* (1998), in which the artist produces a slide projection on his own face and models' bodies. In the case of a graphic composition projection onto a non-graphic composition, for example a picture, sculpture or architectural structure, we are dealing with interdisciplinary work, in which the graphic art is one of the factors of a broader identity. Belonging to one of the disciplines is still possible, as long as one of its components is the dominant expression.

Potential multipliability

Potential multipliability results from a fusion of the constitutive characteristics of the matrix and any automated recording procedures as well as the medium receiving the projection. Two types of collectives may occur in the process of projection while maintaining these characteristics: the series* and the edition.

In the case of the series, individual pieces that are a part of it differ from each other in individual characteristics and the place occupied in the physical or conceptual space, and the exhibited features integrate them into a collective provided that the differences do not exceed the principles of type similarities. A series is formed when between the constitutive characteristics of the three process components there is some kind of 'algorithm of the variation'. Thus the projection process can affect the transformation of the matrix so that each subsequent time it will project slightly differently. An algorithm of transformation can be inscribed into the process of projection regardless of the constancy of the matrix and the receiving medium may be subject to fluctuations in quality, so that each successive projection will lead to a slightly different, but not random, change in accordance with an algorithm.

In the case of the edition, the units are similar and differ only in the place occupied in space, and other differences between them are negligible. Of course, the condition of creation of the edition is the absolute stability of the three components of the projection process.

Potential series and edition quantities are the matter of wear on the material matrix. When we are dealing with intangible matrices (mathematical and conceptual), this figure is potentially infinite.

All of the above rules apply in graphic art and technique. A graphic work of art is potentially duplicable, that is, it may exist as an original in more than one copy, which while they are not identical remain identical as a unit or a type. The number of prints actually made is of no importance. We must remember that graphic art made in only one copy for any reason is still graphic art. What is more, most of the time we present and see it as an individual, and the edition is an assumption. We can therefore conclude that the actual multiplicity of impressions does not fall within the scope of the identity of a graphic work of art. However, although not required, the fact of repetition might enter the scope of a work's means of expression. This happens when the same composition uses repetition of a motif, and this repetition is semantically significant.

Let's take the example of verbal language. In the phrase: *I'm walking, I'm walking, I'm walking, I'm walking*, repetition can express the length and the arduousness of the hike, and in Shakespeare's famous phrase: *words, words, words*, repetition can be interpreted as an emphasis of the

* Editor's note: The translation from Polish uses 'population' – 'series' appears to be the more appropriate term in this context.

shallowness of chatter versus actions. The same may occur in a graphic work of art; although the reasons for the use of repetition are different, it is consistent with the nature of the medium. Importantly, the possibility of mechanical repetition, belonging to the matrix-based techniques, distinguishes the repetitive disciplines from those based on the use of tools. Indeed, regardless of whether the potential repeatability shall be indicated in the work, the technical feasibility of the marks determines the spectrum of the available means of expression of the discipline.

As in the discussion of the issues of two-dimensionality and flatness of a graphic work and the use of semantically significant screens, we are saying that in the case of combining techniques and graphic means of expression within other work, it is the fact of superiority that decides to which discipline such a work of art belongs. In the absence of a distinguishing feature, meaning that all the means are equivalent, we have an interdisciplinary work.

The potential to create an edition or series of visual records on the surface is a constitutive characteristic of graphic art. It can be shown – but does not need to be – in a graphic composition and sometimes is an individual characteristic of the works. As such, it is not a factor of the identity of graphic art.

The original

The potential multipliability discussed above, resulting from the nature of the matrix and the automatic method of visual recording, makes it necessary to consider the issue of originality of the graphic work of art. We place this question in the context of works which were created with the use of tools and exist as originals in only one unit, and all, even the most faithful, must be regarded as a copy of the original. In this case, originality is synonymous with the existing artifact individually, and uniqueness is one of the factors of their identity. In graphic art these rules do not apply, since here the equivalence of originality with the individual existence of the work is suspended. But what is the original? It etymologically stems from the Latin *originalis* – the original, and this term from *origio* – the beginning, *oriri* – to be born. So, original is what has no predecessor, the source. It is the opposite of a copy or replica, which are understood as the exact repetition of a previously created work of art. Then, we have a prototype and a replica created in its likeness. However, the first copy of an edition of graphic images is not the prototype for the next. Their identity or similarity is derived from the fact that they are created as a result of an automatic projection process of an order stored within the matrix, and as such have the status of equivalence. An original of a graphic art is the edition with all the prints actually realized as a part of it. The potential quantity is limited by the capacity of the matrix, which, however, in the case of digital matrices, which do not wear down, loses any importance. In the latter case quantity is actually the result of a social contract.

The question of originality is somewhat more complicated in the case of graphic art that does not have a material form and exists only in virtual space, such as works intended for light projection as well as works existing on the Internet. Such work does not exist permanently in physical space and its realization is equivalent to every presentation. According to the property law understood as an unlimited right of use, the data carrier is the original. But from the perspective of the identity of graphic art, the original is the act of projection. Also in this case, between multiple projections of the same composition, there is an equivalence relation. Then, the edition size is flexible and may be subject to similar limiting social agreements.

Finally, it should be noted that regardless of whether we have an existing material graphic work of art or virtual, it is a visual composition of the surface and multiplied as an original.

The graphic character of the composition

Graphic art, like any artistic discipline and the related techniques and tools, utilizes the scope of its means of expression. These, in turn, determine the possible methods of conduct and shape, but do not ultimately determine the verbal layer of a work of art. Knowing these dependencies, we use terms such as graphic, painterly, sculptural, in order to verbally describe the nature of the composition. To achieve our goal, we use them metaphorically, because if used literally they describe the method of creation and not the nature of the composition. Interestingly, in the description of the work of one discipline, we use terms drawn from the others. We do not talk about the picturesque of a painting, the sculptural quality of a sculpture, the graphic quality of a print, the pastel quality of a pastel, the photographic likeness of a photograph, or the drawing quality of a drawing. That would sound nonsensical. However, we often discuss the painterly mark in lithography, the sculptural character of a drawing, the graphic quality of a painting, the pastel-like tones of a photograph, and the photographic precision of details. Although very useful in describing artwork, these metaphors are not suitable for the determination of boundaries of identity of graphic art and graphic technique, because they are a description of individual characteristics and not the discipline.

The only determinant of the nature of the graphic composition is the spectrum of means of expression available within the triad: matrix – projection – screen, with all the above-described conditions.

Dimensions

As I mentioned in the introduction, the factors of the identity of graphic art: the matrix, the projection, the screen, the repetitiveness and originality, are subject to fluctuation over time, and are treated as dimensions. So, in this model, it is a six-dimensional complex considered from three perspectives of study as a technique, as an artistic discipline and as a work of art. This means that each of the constitutive characteristics is inextricably linked with the others, and only makes sense in this combination. The resignation from even one dimension makes it impossible to know and determine the shape and boundaries of the identity of graphic art.

Definition

Graphic art is a repeatable technique as an original visual projection of a matrix on a surface. It is a discipline of expression of artistic content through a repetitive visual projection of a matrix on a surface as an original. It is repeatable as an original work of art in the form of a visual projection of a matrix on a surface.

Quod erat demonstrandum.

José Roca

The graphic unconscious or the how and why of a print triennial[1]*

No one would deny the privileged – and indeed central – role that biennials and other large-scale art events play in the diffusion of contemporary art practices today. And yet critics have contested the biennial model on the basis of the following allegations: biennials trivialize contemporary art, establish a homogenous field that lacks sensitivity to specific contexts, reiterate the same artists, and neutralize even the most critical art practices by embedding them within a format that favours large-scale spectacle over individual substance. In short, biennials have become ubiquitous, generic, and repetitive.

With so many biennials sprouting up across the globe, how can each one maintain a distinct profile? Should biennials simply address their local contexts and thus abandon any pretence of attracting an international audience? If so, should they opt instead to respond to a self-selected group of interested arts professionals, to their natural constituents (i.e., printmakers themselves, along with historians and collectors of print), and to the public at large? Under current conditions, how can one even define an audience? Is the format itself flawed by definition, or is it simply a matter of identifying appropriate contexts in which to stage these exhibitions? If the former is true, then is it possible to reinvent the biennial format? Can this genre be re-thought while maintaining its central tenets, or has the biennial form become obsolete? Put otherwise, is today's art world in need of an entirely new model?[2] These were some of the basic questions that informed our decisions as we defined the format and goals for *Philagrafika 2010*. The first incarnation of what was designed to become a regular, Philadelphia-based art festival, *Philagrafika 2010* needed not only to show innovative

* José Roca. 2011. 'The Graphic Unconscious or the How and Why of a Print Triennial'. In: Moore et al. (eds), *The Graphic Unconscious*. Philadelphia, PA: Philagrafika, 21–9. Shortened. Reproduced by kind permission of the author and Philagrafika.

and inspiring artwork but also to declare a coherent set of curatorial principles.[3] One of the exhibition's givens was medium-specificity since the consortium of individuals and institutions that spearheaded this initiative was deeply involved with and invested in the efficacy of print.[4] Rather than being a liability, this medium-specificity established one of the traits that we believe distinguished *Philagrafika 2010* from the more than 200 temporary art events currently in place on five continents, a list that continues to grow daily as cultural administrators and politicians come to realize the potential of biennials and other massive art events for boosting local economies through cultural tourism, thus increasing the appeal of a given site for the so-called 'creative class.'[5]

As we embarked on this project, we wanted to avoid a narrowly defined, thematic approach – a tactic more appropriate for future incarnations of the festival – and opted instead for a conceptual framework broad enough to accommodate diverse artistic practices and strong enough to articulate a wide range of work in an intelligent manner. Biennials, after all, are not tightly curated shows that function within the orthodoxy of art history. Rather, they offer a glimpse of current practices in the form of a cross-section. As such, they are arguably fictional constructs prone to failure due to the inherent instability that accompanies the uncertainty surrounding what will (and will not) be produced and shown. And, unless circumscribed to a specific region or country, they are likewise vulnerable to unavoidable gaps in terms of geographic diversity, given the complexity of the global art scene. Thus, any attempt to narrow the field produces a more manageable universe to navigate. Most biennials choose a theme through which to read contemporary artistic production, and many work within a defined geographic territory. But we did not subscribe to either of these strategies. Instead of establishing a topical framework for the art, we opted for medium-specificity and set out to problematize print as a category.

Philagrafika 2010 aimed to bring together work hailing from across the globe and produced in a variety of media, including sculpture, performance, video, and installation as well as, of course, diverse approaches to print as traditionally defined. We envisioned *The Graphic Unconscious* not as a proper theme *per se* but as a *theoretical device* to mobilize the imprint, along with its implied characteristics, seriality, and dissemination, and to re-read – indeed re-imagine – critically the field of contemporary artistic production.

The Graphic Unconscious refers to the unconscious invocation of print – or its characteristics, including seriality, multiplicity, and dissemination – in contemporary art, quite often by artists who either do not consider themselves printmakers or shy away from being associated with a single medium. In order to give this curatorial concept some historical depth, we tried to define the term 'imprint' in its crudest terms: as an at times unconscious will to communicate knowledge more efficiently through the reproduction of a message. We then focused on the resemblance by contact that derives from the artistic trilogy matrix-ink-support characteristic of most print processes.

The first 'conscious' print was probably the imprint left by a hand on the wall of a cave – think of Lascaux or Altamira – executed with the intention of communicating something to others or to posterity. And the archetypal *imprint* occurs in Daniel Defoe's novel *Robinson Crusoe* (1719), in which Man Friday's footprint left in the sand signalled an encounter with a savage Other that called into question the European conception of the world.[6] In both cases, the matrix was the body, and the imprint, the indexical trace of its presence. These gestures could – at least potentially – be repeated indefinitely, enabling them to reach a wider audience. In the realm of art, where individuality (in the form of a single, original masterpiece) is often the norm, prints permit at once the existence of the individual mark and the possibility of its reproduction, and thus expand their insertion into the collective domain. Walter Benjamin proposed an interesting analogy in *A Small History of Photography*: 'it is through photography that we first discover the existence of this optical unconscious, just as we discover the instinctual unconscious through psychoanalysis.'[7] This gives rise to a provocative question: Is there a *print* unconscious? If so, where does it lie? Just as printed materials have become so pervasive in our daily visual culture that they pass by unnoticed, so too have print processes taken on an increasingly central role in artmaking without being acknowledged. As Judith Hecker, Assistant Curator of Prints at MoMA, has remarked:

> Installation, performance, and video art, photography, and new-media technology (including digitization, virtual reality, and the internet) have expanded artistic vocabularies, and artists are increasingly drawn back to the printed series because it enables further exploration into the multiple, developmental, and spatial structures of these other mediums.[8]

Can the *ethos* of printmaking serve as a framework through which to understand contemporary artistic production? And, by extension, can a close reading of contemporary art from the perspective of the printed image productively illuminate our understanding of the world?

Let's start by defining what is meant by printmaking. There are three instances of artistic activity involved: the actual imprint, its multiplication, and the implied dissemination that ensues. Uruguayan artist and curator Luis Camnitzer, referring to works done in the 1970s, suggests that by emphasizing the dissemination of works over their creation, there was a significant paradigm shift, a trend equally valid for digital images, which can likewise be printed indefinitely, with no progressive loss in the 'matrix' whatsoever.[9]

The focus was on infinite distribution, not on craftsmanship. That quest for infinity, rather than the lack of craftsmanship, probably insured that not many of those pages were kept by collectors eager to increase the value of their assets. However, that quest for infinity came closer to some essential, perhaps Kantian idea of the print. We thus reached one of the many blurry areas with which we are plagued in printmaking jargon: while print refers more to a form of dissemination of information than to the result of a craft, printmaking is only an action, and the resulting object we call print then, is a proof of that action, but not really concerned with dissemination.[10]

This conundrum returns us to the act of leaving an imprint as the ontological focus of printmaking, and the resulting print as the testimony of that primeval urge, that fundamental question: Why leave an imprint? This seems like a rhetorical question, but it remains one seldom asked by print practitioners. Printmaking, for many, remains concerned with technique, a medium focused on the *how* and not the *what*. Stressing the craft aspect of print has often obscured the fact that print is but one of the tools that art has at its disposal for achieving an end. Historically, the craft aspect of printmaking has been championed by many artistic printmakers, who defined themselves *through the medium* as if a creative endeavor could be achieved solely by mastering its means of production.[11] This brings us to yet another conundrum: artistic printmaking betrayed even the promise of accessibility that the multiple image purports to allow. As Cuban curator and critic Gerardo Mosquera has remarked, 'Our "artistic" print posits a contradiction: it is a reproductive medium that self-limits its reproductive possibilities.'[12] Preoccupied with defining the realm of printmaking exclusively from a technical standpoint, printmakers have indeed printed themselves into a proverbial corner.

Media are means that are too often mistaken for ends, and this rings especially true in the realm of print. Printmaking is a tool, and a powerful one at that. But only by acknowledging that its intrinsic qualities make it ideal for saying something that cannot be said equally well in other media can print be reclaimed from technique-as-content and be understood as content *through* technique. But what can be gained from territorializing technique? Self-isolation can be traced to the medieval guilds' definition of standards and commercial territory, craftsmanship as a commodity that had to be defended. In a way, printmakers created islands within the sea of artistic practice, colonies of like-minded individuals working together within indifferent or hostile realms.[13] 'In Printmaking: A Colony of the Arts', Camnitzer declared:

> When I refer to a colony I mean it quite literally: as a territory taken over by another power where identity is maimed and slowly forgotten, values are shifted and the will for independence becomes ritualized into an increasingly empty and hopeless vow.[14]

Camnitzer is referring to many printmakers' tendency to entrench themselves within the intricacies of their craft and the specifics of technique, rather than to allow the processes of print to be merely the means by which to achieve conceptual goals. And he adds:

> The clear and focused wish to package and circulate information, added to a detachment from art, gave industrial printing its apparent freedom of action. The actual printing part has only been a temporary and eventually dispensable solution to the problems posed by the circulation of information. It was, nearly, a technical accident. Printmakers, however, seduced by and attached to this accident while pursuing artistic ambitions, tend to work under the presumption that they have to print in order to produce art. Once they print, or know how to, the hope arises that something with artistic merit will automatically follow. Making prints is the task. Art seems to be a miraculous byproduct.[15]

Such provocative remarks by an avowed printmaker bring to the fore a key question: How can one break down the frontiers that define so narrowly the territory of printmaking? How can one reclaim printmaking as a means and not as a goal in and of itself? And, most importantly, how can one make visible the various forms of print that sit at the very core of contemporary artistic practice?

The Graphic Unconscious intended to show the pervasiveness of printed matter in contemporary art. But this exhibition also had a larger purpose: to show how these practices inscribe themselves in culture and society writ large. Thus, when we speak of the manifestation of an unconscious drive, we are not only referring to the artist as an individual, but rather to what could be termed 'a society of reproduction', where culture is experienced mainly, at times even solely, through its virtual or actual surrogates. In an essay on *The Graphic Unconscious*, the critic Avi Alpert asserts:

> To speak of a 'graphic unconscious' here is not to speak of what is revealed in the psychoanalytic slips of personality, but rather in what the social matrix itself obscures in the very move to print culture. The conceptual formulation of the show thus owes as much to Fredric Jameson's *The Political Unconscious* as it does to Benjamin. The question here is not the psychoanalytic moment of individual psychology, but rather the functional repressions, disavowals and slippages of society at large. Indeed, this does not remove the individual, it only forces us to confront the personal psyche as a worm in the blood of a vast (and often prosthetic) social organism.[16]

The motivation to mount an international print event of this magnitude does not stem from a will to reclaim a space for 'printmakers' within the realm of contemporary art but rather from a desire to show the centrality of a *will to print* in contemporary practice, broadly defined. Indeed, events like *Philagrafika 2010*, the *Poly/graphic Triennial* in San Juan, Puerto Rico (2004 and 2009), or the *Mostra de Gravura de Curitiba* in Brazil under Paulo Herkenhoff's direction (1992 and 2000), have been criticized by printmaking circles as spaces that have been taken away from them and granted instead to artists who are not strictly defined printmakers. But in making this claim, these artists (and critics) lose sight of these exhibitions' goal – and this is particularly true in the case of *Philagrafika 2010* – not to claim a new stake for print in the realm of contemporary art, but rather to uncover aspects of print's impact that have already, indeed always, been in place, even if unrecognized and obscured. Brazilian curator Paulo Herkenhoff has spoken of his reluctance to allow a 'return of the repressed' in printmaking to manifest itself in the print biennials that he curated for Curitiba, opting instead to present the print as an integral dimension of contemporary art. Instead of reclaiming printmaking for printers themselves, he preferred to show the importance of print in the larger scheme of current art production within projects of all, and even mixed, media. In this sense, Philagrafika has followed his lead, conducting a deeper artistic excavation and implementing a much broader definition of print. Herkenhoff contended that the anxiety lurking within print practitioners – of not being adequately recognized – can be traced back to printmaking's status as 'a technique that demands that the intelligence focus on the consummate skill necessary to the technique [itself], one that prefers being a victim to acting critically. Something that functions between hysteria and sterility.'[17] But when print processes are mobilized, even if inadvertently or unconsciously, by artists working in various media, the term *print* can be reclaimed, referring once again to a series of actions rather than to a stable substantive, to a process instead of a product. Relieved of its technical imperative and fundamentalist overtones, the printmaking found within artmaking can then be connected back to the possibilities that various print media allow, some of which cannot be achieved otherwise. Herein lies the political potential, the subversive quality, the urgency, and the currency of print today.

But there remains a related aspect of graphic art that should not be overlooked: the ubiquity of the digitally printed image, which has been instrumental in not only democratizing the printing act but also naturalizing the term *print*. For centuries after the advent of the press in the fifteenth century, printing was done almost exclusively by trained printers; today, however, nearly everyone hits the 'print' key at least once a day. The digitally printed image flows seamlessly from the screen to the desktop, from the domestic realm to the public sphere. It is literally everywhere. This might explain why traditional print techniques have once again risen to the fore in current artistic practice: in the age of the ever-present, digitally reproduced image, their physicality can be understood as a kind of political reassertion of the artist's presence. Print implies a shift from the optical to the haptic, from a purely visual regime to the centrality of the physical act of transferring a trace by direct contact.[18] Printmaking shares photography's status as index of a physical referent. But unlike photography, which is literally 'an emanation from the referent', as Roland Barthes pointed out, an imprint acquires its indexical quality by contiguity: one surface is in physical contact with another.[19] French philosopher and art historian Georges Didi-Huberman posed a number of key questions in his essay published in conjunction with the exhibition *L'Empreinte* at the Pompidou Centre in 1997. In that show, and its resulting catalogue, Didi-Huberman exhibited an understanding of the heuristic quality of imprinting, stressing its process over its results. In a later work, he extended his inquiry into the medium, exploring the motivation behind the prevalence of print for modern and contemporary artists.[20]

In addition to signalling, like photography, that something *was* there, the imprint indicates: *something corporeal transferred the information by physical contact and rendered the image that you are witnessing*. If the imprint is the body of the print, might it also be its soul?[21] Are these tangible and intangible qualities that print embodies what ought to be called the *graphic unconscious*? The ontology of the graphic act is to leave an imprint on a support, one that can be reproduced at will. Thus *reproduction*, or the possibility thereof, becomes another essential characteristic of the print. The print ethos implies generosity through multiplication, accessibility, and collaboration; it presupposes a desire to disseminate knowledge in order to reach a wider audience. All these attributes that seem inherent to print have become major preoccupations that permeate the spectrum of artistic practice today, and not just in the field of what can be conventionally termed 'printmaking'. Our task as curators of *The Graphic Unconscious* was to expose and underscore the graphic component in contemporary artistic practice. Put otherwise, we set out to identify ways in which the graphic act manifests itself in a meaningful way in current artistic production. This is what was at stake in *Philagrafika 2010*. For the sake of consistency, we considered a print anything that had three components: a matrix, a transfer medium, and a receiving surface. This could be, for example, a plate, ink, and paper; a digital file, laser-cut vinyl, and the walls and floors of an exhibition space; a silk-screen, charcoal dust, and water. The matrix stores the necessary information to reproduce; the medium transfers that data, and the support, in turn, receives it. All kinds of contingencies can alter the outcome of the process and often enrich the results. These are just some examples of the expanded print, as we chose to understand this concept, that were included in *Philagrafika 2010*, with instances of the medium ranging from woodcut to video, sculpture to performance, with endless permutations in between.

[...]

Bringing to the fore the print component of sculptural, environmental, performance, pictorial, and video works, and highlighting the relevance of print's appearance within and to contemporary art was the goal of *The Graphic Unconscious*. We chose to work within the relatively narrow territory of print in order to expand standing definitions of it from within. Hence the exhibition as Trojan horse: medium-specificity provided an alibi that allowed us to commit the crime. Or, in more psychological terms, print took on the guise of a self-imposed straightjacket, which motivated us to think of creative ways of finding release. It was here, within this liberating effort, that our curatorial role resided. If there is a graphic unconscious in contemporary art, our task as curators was to bring it to the surface of public consciousness, to reclaim a space for the *return of the repressed* (imprint) lurking inside contemporary artistic practice.

Notes

1 This essay was formulated throughout the entire process of conceiving, executing, and evaluating *Philagrafika 2010*. As such, it has benefited from both hindsight and feedback. Moreover, the text includes modified versions of earlier texts, blog entries, and public presentations also conceived as part of *Philagrafika 2010*.

2 The unrealised *Manifesta 6* is an example of a radical rethinking of the model: the curatorial team had conceived their biennial as a temporary international arts academy and not as an art exhibition. Scheduled to occur in Nicosia, Cyprus in 2006, that biennial was cancelled due to political reasons.

3 Originally conceived in 2005 as a quadrennial event, *Philagrafika* has been reconfigured as a triennial and is expected to open again in 2013.

4 Philagrafika, the institution that organized *Philagrafika 2010* was formerly known as the Philadelphia Print Collaborative.

5 For further discussion Richard Florida, *The Rise of the Creative Class: And How It's Transforming Work, Leisure, Community and Everyday Life* (New York: Basic Books, 2002).

6 Daniel Defoe's *Robinson Crusoe* is considered by many to be the first English novel and, as such, one of the foundations of Western modern thought.

7 See Walter Benjamin, 'Little History of Photography,' in *Walter Benjamin: Selected Writings. Volume 2: 1927–1934*, eds Michael W. Jennings et al. (Cambridge, MA and London: Belknap Press of Harvard University Press, 1999), 510–12. Originally published as 'Kleine Geschichte der Photographie,' trans. Edmund Jephcott and Kingsley Shorter, *Die Literarische Welt* 38–40 (Sept.–Oct. 1931).

8 See Judith B. Hecker, 'One Thing After Another: Serial Print Projects,' in *Modern Contemporary: Art at MoMA Since 1980* (New York: The Museum of Modem Art, 2000), 516.

9 Camnitzer, 'Printmaking: A Colony of the Arts,' in *The Graphic Unconscious* (Philadelphia, PA: Philagrafika), 102–7. Also available at: www.philagrafika.org/pdf/WS/Printmakingacolony.pdf [Accessed 20 July 2016]. Camnitzer is referring to works by Dan Graham and Joseph Kosuth printed across the pages of *Artforum* in 1969, in a conscious attempt to bring fine art to the masses through industrial processes.

10 Ibid., 105–6.

11 I use the term 'artistic printmakers' to distinguish between these practitioners and commercial printers.

12 Mosquera, Gerardo. El diseño se definió en Octubre (Bogotá: Biblioteca Luis Angel Arango, 1991), 25. Translation mine.

13 'Prints' remain, at best, a second-rate category in the realm of artmaking, often not even acknowledged. For example, in a review of a ceramics show at the ICA in Philadelphia, a critic for a major art international magazine wrote: 'Clay seems to be the last of the "secondary" disciplines coming after photography, crafts, and, most recently, outsider art – to break into fine art circles.' The reviewer did not even consider print as a secondary or neglected art form, which shows that it is simply off the radar screen of the art world's consciousness. See Melissa E. Feldman, 'Dirt on Delight,' *Frieze* 124 (June–August 2009): 200.

14 Camnitzer, 'Printmaking: A Colony of the Arts,' in *The Graphic Unconscious*. Philadelphia, PA: Philagrafika, 102.

15 Ibid, 103.

16 See Avi Alpert, 'Untitled (Notes on *The Graphic Unconscious*),' accessed 15 September 2010, www.phiilagrafita.org/pdf/WS/notesonthegraphicunconscious.pdf.

17 See Paulo Herkenhoff, *Marcas do corpo, dobras da alma*, ex. cat. of the XII Mostra de Gravura de Curitiba (Curitiba: Mostra de Gravura de Curitiba, 2000), 294. Herkenhoff's biennials brought together works by artists such as Lygia Clark, Mira Schendel, Louise Bourgeois, Fred Wilson, and Glenn Ligon, to name a few.

18 'Resemblance by contact [George Didi-Huberman's exhibition and essay] sought to question the optical model of imitation by promoting the model, tactile and technical, of hands-on work.' See Susana Gallego Cuesta, 'Esthetique de l'empreinte,' *La Vie des idées*, last modified June 5, 2008, www.laviedesidees.fr/Esthetique-de-1-empreinte.html. Translation mine.

19 See Roland Barthes, *La Cámara lúcida. Notas sobre la fotografía*, 1980, trans. Joaquin Sala Sanahuja (Barcelona: Paidos, 1990), 142. The term index is taken from the semiotic theory of C. S. Peirce, who uses it to designate a sign that is connected to its object by a direct cause-and-effect relationship.

20 Georges Didi-Huberman, *La Ressemblance par contact. Archéologie, anachronisme et modernité de l'empreinte* (Paris: Editions de Minuit, Collection 'Paradoxe,' 2008).

21 '[George Didi-Huberman's] essay explains how the hand-print is a tactile form of representation that closes the gap between the mimetic reflection and its model, thereby avoiding the dominance of the eye and mind, imitation and idea.' See Johanna Walker, 'The Body is Present Even if in Disguise: Tracing the Trace in the Art Work of Nancy Spero and Ana Mendieta,' *Tate Papers*, accessed 15 September 2010, www.tate.org.uk/research/tateresearch/tatepapers/09spring/)joanna-walker.shtm.

Richard Harding

Print as other: the future is queer*

> The question is not whether we all have identities, but whether we are prepared to recognise them. (Younge 2010, 40)

My fascination with the notion of 'print as other' stems from the connections I see between printmaking and identity politics. Identifying who or what we are positions us within a particular demographic, arena or community. This is not a new practice. What is interesting in the context of printmaking is how different artists do this and why they do it.

So, who am I? I am a concept-driven, process-loving printmaker. I am also a queer-identified art practitioner. It is through these two modes of identification that I will discuss how artists do or do not identify with printmaking and the effect that this has on their work and practice. I will use artworks of several practitioners as examples to highlight analogies between various notions of 'otherness' and printmaking.

Position, proposition, protocol

Embedded in the many mediums of printmaking is the process of reproduction, a quality that can be considered essentially female. It is through the reproductive matrix that printmaking begins its alignment with otherness through notions of the feminine.[1] It is also through this reproductive method of repeated image making that printmaking activates another aspect of otherness: sameness and difference. This aspect can be aligned with the identity politics of gay, lesbian and queer. Within this framework 'queer'

* Richard Harding. 2013. 'Print as Other: The Future Is Queer'. In: Morgan, Luke (ed.), *Intersections and Counterpoints: IMPACT 7 International Multi-disciplinary Printmaking Conference Proceedings*. Clayton, Victoria: Monash University Publishing, pp. 205–11. Reproduced by kind permission of the author and Monash University Publishing.

is used to cover the identity politics of others that do not identify with the hetero-normative identity of 'straight'. To clarify this position it is important to revisit the general production manner and customs of printmaking.

The basis of all print media[2] is its facility to reproduce itself from an original matrix such as a plate, block or digital file. During the printing process the artist aims to produce an edition or set of prints that are the same. These are usually based on a *bon à tirer* or artist proof that all the other prints are measured against. Generally, an edition of prints is made to be identical, though through the production of multiples differences inevitably occur. The artist-printer is discerning towards any difference that is not predetermined. The difference within the traditional edition is usually rejected or used for another purpose.[3] It is this search for sameness in the print edition that I align with gender sameness and the scrutiny of difference with sexual orientation through the hetero/homo binary.

Some print practitioners may argue that print as 'other' is now an outmoded view, as the print is ubiquitous in global culture, especially if we are operating within a post-painting or, to refer to American theorist Rosalind Krauss (1999, 10), a 'post-medium' art world. I question this. Imbedded in the art community and art education systems is a historical hierarchy that attempts to maintain the status quo of 'painting as king'. For this discussion I have nominated one particular hierarchy for ease of identification rather than the many complex hierarchies that are at play simultaneously around us at any given time. It is from this perspective I position printmaking within a 'painting-normative' art community, local and global, thus aligning medium otherness to the hetero-normative world within which we all operate. This statement is not meant as a negative, its aim is to create a space for further exploration. With these concepts in mind, does otherness inhibit some art practitioners from identifying as a printmaker or labelling their work as a print?

There are various applications at work here. The 'painting-normative' art world operates in the realm of the 'original' that is authenticated via uniqueness, cultural significance and commercial value; or as Walter Benjamin (1936, 7) states 'the genuineness of a thing is the quintessence of everything about it since its creation that can be handed down, from its material duration to the historical witness it bears'. Printmaking challenges this through its reproductive technology by making many copies or impressions from one matrix; Benjamin (7) predicted printmaking's position in otherness by stating 'it substitutes for its unique incidence a multiplicity of incidences.'

This leads to the ongoing debate of original versus reproduction. Within this debate the modes of making, naming and classification are forever at the fore of why and how artists, dealers and collectors use particular definitions and protocols. 'For example the print historian Carl Zigrosser coined the neologism "serigraphy" to differentiate fine art applications of screen-printing from their commercial equivalents. The term "Giclée" has likewise been invented to distinguish fine art digital prints' (Saunders 2009, 38). The reasons for using one system of naming or labelling above or instead of another usually operate with a purpose as they do within many facets of life.

The importance of naming

The reproduced image has many names: impression, copy, replica, simulacrum, facsimile, duplicate, clone etc. It is the naming of the process or material that identifies the essence of original from reproduction. Stuart Purves (2006, 20) explains the difference between the original print and the reproduced copy as 'the artist's hand [being] directly involved in the printmaking process'. He goes on to state that 'printmaking as an original art form is still a largely misunderstood medium'. Purves recommends removing the generic banner of printmaking to avoid confusion, favouring specific medium names such as etching, lithograph or screenprint. Even though he aligns this suggestion with descriptive painting terms like, 'oil on canvas', Purves (21) adds, 'Printmaking and Painting are as different as land and sea'. It is this difference that again partners print with 'other'. This otherness does not reduce printmaking's preoccupation with the original. In fact, it is heightened through a system of authentication via the signing and archiving of 'limited' numbered editions.

According to Saff and Sacilo (1978, 396) the numbering and signing of editioned prints has been 'standard practice' since the 1930s. This standard print numbering system uses fractions to designate the print number over the edition number, telling discerning collectors the print number within the edition run. This system works in two ways: Firstly, it authenticates the print as an original and that it is limited in number. Secondly, it sets up a form of pricing via the number of the prints in the edition and the number available; basic economics of supply and demand.

Joel Gailer is a print-based artist who takes this 'standard practice' very seriously and uses it within his work. Moving back and forth from the limited edition and the multiple, Gailer caused a flurry within the Australian printmaking community by winning the prestigious Fremantle Print Award with his work, *hot process* (2008). As art theorist and critic Ted Snell (2008) wrote in the *Australian* online, the selection of Gailer for the Fremantle Print Award in 2008 was 'An audacious choice by the judges, it will undoubtedly raise the ire of many practitioners while encouraging others to continue Gailer's rethinking of the medium'.

Published in the August edition of the *Australian Art Almanac*, Gailer (2008, 89) used, 'mass production as a form of print-making' inserting a page of white text on a black background announcing that, 'printmaking is so hot right now'.

In an artist statement released with the work Gailer (2008) declared: 'I produce my own version of printmaking as mass produced unlimited print editions available at the cost of a magazine. The aesthetic is text and basic forms, commenting on print and popular culture simultaneously.' He goes on to say: 'I work outside the traditional concepts of unique object exclusivity, limited edition and gallery. My work is an attempt to democratise/inform/play/quote/humour and revitalise printmaking.'

Gailer's use of standard print hierarchies and assorted image production methods spans diverse genres of socio-political positioning and art posturing within general culture, while his use of ubiquitous everyday print processes coupled with a non-gender specific dialogue also positions Gailer's practice in the subcultural realm of other. His print-based sexually suggestive and ambiguous wordplay allows a variety of readings and brings to mind Neil Emmerson's (1992) discussion on the sexualised print in his paper 'Returning to Venusburg'.

In his paper presented at the Second Australian Print Symposium, Emmerson (1992, 1) states that 'Printmaking seems always to have fought to keep its boundaries squeaky clean. New technologies are formally courted before being ranked and assimilated into traditional formulas.' Emmerson (1) refers to printmaking as playing the 'reproductive whore', even though it 'has the face of "democratic media"'. This he says is 'negated due to limited edition marketing strategies'. In spite of all this cynical posturing Emmerson has an exceptional understanding of the paradox of the print original and has been overtly aware of the transgressive nature built into print and its production for decades. This is demonstrated through a history of exhibitions such as *Surrender and Penance* (1999) and *God (Made Me Do It ...)* (2009) that use alternative matrix surfaces, materials and modes of printing with constructions and various installation systems.

Similar to Gailer and Emmerson, my interest here relates to the first component of 'standard practice': authentication, or more precisely the notion of the authentic or real. Like many artists I use print mediums not only as a vehicle for my concept, but as an added component or a reiteration of my idea. According to Krauss (1999, 53) 'the specificity of mediums, even modernist ones, must be understood as differential, self-differing, and thus as a layering of conventions never simply collapsed into the physicality of their support'.

I refer to this as the 'conceptual vehicle' whether I am producing images in the conventional manner of editioning or the less rarefied mode of multiples. My choice of print-based processes is a purposeful strategy that locates my practice within a socio-political context. As Walter Benjamin (2008 [1936], 12) deliberates, 'its being reproducible by technological means frees the work of art from its existence as a parasite upon ritual. The reproduced work of art is to an ever-increasing extent the reproduction of art designed for reproducibility ... rather than being underpinned by ritual, it came to be underpinned by a different practice: politics.'

It is with Benjamin's statement that I connect my research in gender and sexual orientation through the making of print-based art works back to the politics of 'other'. With the repetitive production that fabricates sameness but delivers difference, what is the original? In print terms the original is based in the matrix the print comes from, whether it is a stencil, block, plate or screen. Within the work *Invisible Man* (2009) the dichotomy of the print original is played out as an analogy for masculine performance to highlight and reference the hetero/homo binary.

My premise here is that hetero-normative masculinity is positioned as alpha with all other forms of masculine performance situated beneath this mode of representation. This gender performance is played out and repeated over and over. With each social situation our gender performance changes and morphs creating nuances that are inevitable, similar to the editioning or production of various print mediums. The base matrix of *Invisible Man* (2009) is not a plate or block but a found magazine image, scanned, manipulated, collaged, digitally printed and silk-screened with a stencil. The production of the work incorporates electronic and hand-printed elements embedding the image with the inherent print concepts of sameness and difference, in a historic and contemporary sense. Even with the aim of sameness in printing, invariably differences occur. It is this variation through the ink, paper and printer that allows the notion of difference to enter the realm of sameness.

The paradox here is the confusion of the real with the impression, or the real with the constructed. A good example is the practice within the gay community of 'straight-acting' that is being used as a way of describing oneself as masculine. In this situation the gay male uses heteronormative masculine performance as 'the' guide to being masculine. The concern here is the more a gay male performs or simulates this mode of masculinity the more he is rendered invisible as 'other', thus building a closet around himself. Being gay and masculine creates a paradox that is imbedded in hetero-normative dominance, just as the original print creates a paradox within the painting-normative art world.

The future is queer

According to educator and activist Robert J. Hill (2004, 87) 'Queer is "living out" the notion that we can never adequately identify or codify identity; rather, it is about contingent knowledge whose meanings we must constantly re-evaluate and reinterpret'. Queer is many things that cannot

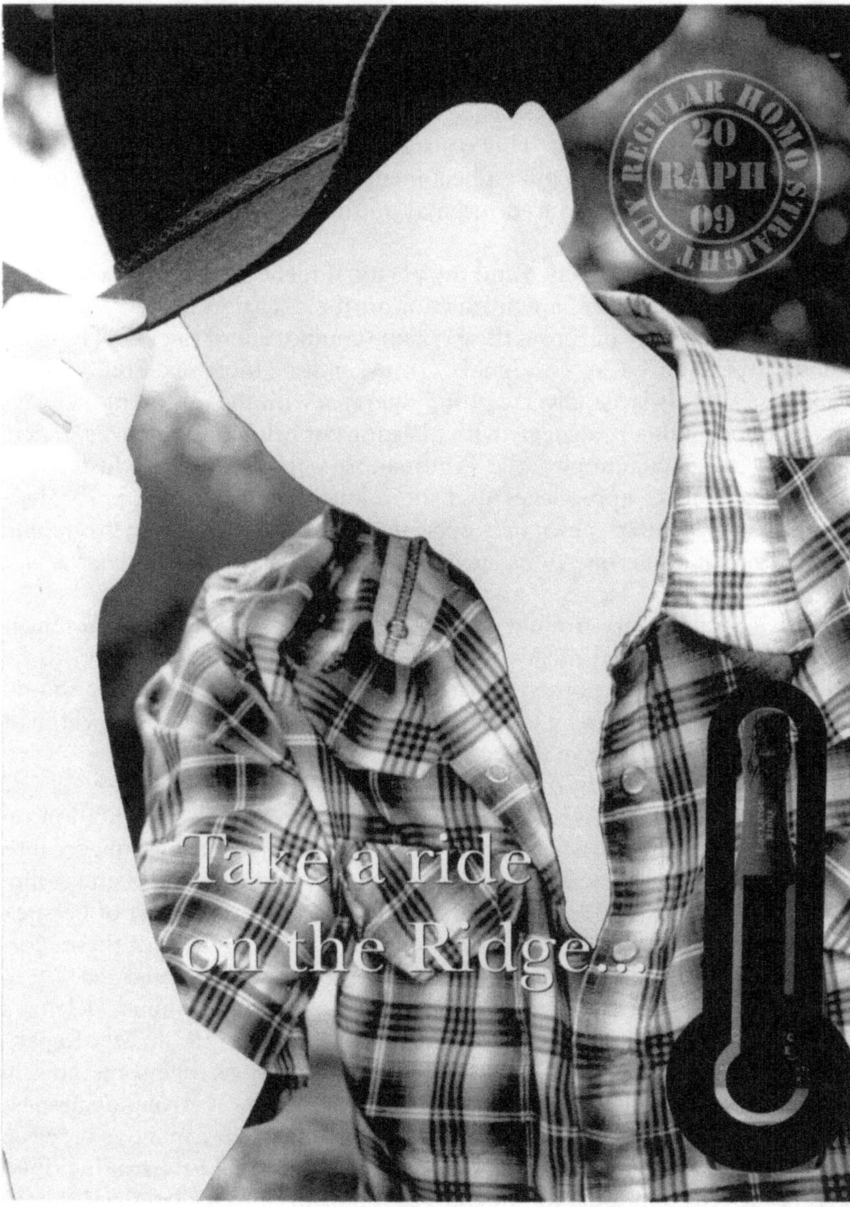

Richard Harding, *Invisible Man*, 2009. Digital inkjet print with screen-printed gouache. 42 × 29.7 cm.

be defined in any single realm, real or virtual; the inclusive and non-delineated notion of queer always avoids definition. It is an ongoing construct that morphs into something else just when you think you have the answer. This transformative essence of queer is the connection I align with the essence of printmaking. This constant reinterpreting and re-evaluating that Hill refers to is an ongoing phenomenon within print media due to the dichotomies of the reproduced original and the ever-growing processes of technology.

Through my print practice and my personal identity I activate a sense of otherness by aligning my art production to the assertion of queer marginalised groups, for my purposes the gay male component of the LGBTIQueermunity (Lesbian, Gay Bisexual, Transgender, Intra-sex and Queer community). This large, diverse group operates with the notion of inclusivity while continuing to struggle with questions of belonging and acceptance. Like the Queer community, the Printmaking community is inclusive and multifaceted in its approaches and intentions. The multiple approaches, mediums and demographics that operate within its sphere trigger ongoing debates surrounding questions such as '*what is a print?*' and '*what is not a print?*'

British author Gary Younge (2010, 78) states: 'No identity is homogeneous. But for a social identity (as opposed to a personal identity) to be viable it cannot be so porous that large numbers of those whom it should include fail to recognise it as meaningful while large numbers whom it should not include believe they are part of it.'

In 2007 Neil Emmerson exhibited a work titled, *Are We There Yet …?* In relation to print practice and queer politics, this is still the question on everyone's lips. *Are We There Yet …?* is played out on a television, set into the gallery wall with a looped colour segment from the musical fantasy film *The Wizard of Oz* (1939). Over the television is an opaque sheet of Perspex distorting the image into moving swatches of colour. In front of these morphing colours is a plinth with a single cast brogue shoe painted red.

The repetitive loop of *Are We There Yet …?* brings to mind Deleuze's *Difference and Repetition* when he quotes D. A. Hume (1978, 70), 'Repetition changes nothing in the object repeated, but does change something in the mind which contemplates it'. This work indicates a strong awareness of being 'print informed' within a particular practice that can move between disciplines and mediums utilising the inherent qualities of printmaking. Film offers the perfect antidote to sameness as it morphs into something different frame by frame. Through the repeated and looped image Emmerson plays two parts; while he indicates with his opening question that the journey is not over yet, he is also the frustrated parent responding with 'nearly there' using a silent yet blurred portrayal of Judy Garland travelling down the yellow brick road, over and over again. While the red brogue shoe masculinises Dorothy (Garland's screen character) it also suggests a reframing of

Cinderella into '*Cinderfella*'. In his exhibition response, *Act Natural*, Emmerson (2007, 26) continues to ask questions: 'Can we, do we, construct ourselves through our practices or can we construct our practice through ourselves?' From my position, print practice and the self are intertwined. They inform each other to construct a creative space for production that is distinctly queer and thus transformative in the process of making.

While Emmerson ironically calls for us to 'act natural' to avoid detection, the works of Lesley Duxbury require the viewer to look closely to reveal surprising effects or hidden elements within. From a traditional printmaking background, Duxbury has navigated her practice through many guises to its present point of print-based mixed media works. Her images are based on photographs and notations of atmospheric phenomena, weather patterns, or cloud formations, at times coupled with text or text as image.

David Bromfield (2002, 3) in his catalogue essay for Duxbury's exhibition *Zoom* (2002) poetically discusses her works through 'the democracy of the sky' and how they have an 'inborn certainty that they must change'. It is this democracy and certainty of change in the work, which is amplified through the artist's print-based practice, that allows the space for queer to really enter the work in a transformative sense. Bromfield (3) goes on to state, 'They [the works] merely mirror our sense of being, caught between destiny and desire, which is more than enough'. Again Bromfield identifies within Duxbury's work the notion of queer through a 'sense of being'.

These connections of 'other, queer and printmaking' are exemplified through the digital work, *Then & Now* (2004). Within this diptych Duxbury highlights printmaking's inherent qualities of sameness and difference by stating 'I used a photograph that I had taken of the sky of Hampstead Heath in London on the same day of the year and time that John Constable had 180 years previously. Curiously I found the cloud formations to be extraordinarily similar' (Grishin 2010, 17). Duxbury's intermixing of concept and process moves the work through memory, temporal and natural phenomena in a romantic yet scientific manner. The queerness of this work operates within difference yet what is looked for is sameness. It is this subversion of sameness through difference that continually aligns print practices with queer.

Final thoughts

Embedded within the production of prints and print-based works will always be the notion of other through the matrix 'mother'. It is through this production that the offspring of the matrix can be transformative, allowing the printed form to move easily between copy and original, multiple and unique, dependent only on the artist's intention. In *Simulations* Jean Baudrillard (1983, 94) muses 'Being and appearance are melted into a common substance of production and work'. It is this coming together of production and work, or in this context, image through print production, that continues to fascinate print-based artists. Like the queer community, it is by constantly moving through unknown territories and revisiting old ones that have or have not changed that we can position ourselves within the current art world without concerns for apology or a victim role of 'other'. It is Baudrillard (1983, 96) who again tells us that it is through the reversal of production and reproduction that 'we leave behind the counterfeit to enter (re)production'.

Notes

1 For further discussion on the feminisation of the print medium through the matrix see: Pelzer-Montada, Ruth. 2001. 'Authenticity in Printmaking – A Red Herring?' In *IMPACT 2 Conference Proceedings*, 5.
2 In this context print media includes photography.
3 This process of rejection could also be aligned with acts of prejudice or homophobia within a larger discussion.

References

Baudrillard, J. 1983/1994. *Simulation*. Cambridge, MA: MIT Press.
Benjamin, W. 2008 [1936]. *The Work of Art in the Age of Mechanical Reproduction*. London: Penguin Books – Great Ideas.
Bromfield, D. 2002. *The Sky Is for All: The Work of Lesley Duxbury:* Exhibition catalogue. Sale, Victoria, Australia: Gippsland Art Gallery.
Deleuze, G. 1978. *Difference and Repetition*. Trans. Patton, Paul. New York: Columbia University Press.
Emmerson, N. 2007. 'Act Natural'. Proceedings from *(are we there yet …?)*. Otago, Dunedin, New Zealand: Scope Art. School of Art, Otago Polytechnic/Te Kura Matatini. Available as a PDF from: www.thescopes.org/art/issues.php?issue=2&title=art.
Emmerson, N. 1992. 'Returning to Venusburg'. Presented at the 2nd Australian Print Symposium 9–11 October. Australian National Gallery, Canberra, Australia. Available from: www.printsandprintmaking.gov.au/catalogues/bibliography/138199/emmerson-neil-returning-to-venusburg.aspx.
Gailer, J. 2008. 'Saatchi Online: Joel Gailer'. [Accessed 23 December 2010.] Available from: www.saatchionline.com/joelgailer.
Grishin, S. 2010. 'Editorial: Death of Digital Printmaking?' *Imprint* 45 (4) Melbourne: Australia.
Hill, R. J. 2004. 'Activism as Practice: Some Queer Considerations'. *New Directions for Adult Education and Continuing Education* 102 (Summer). Wiley Periodicals Inc. USA.

Krauss, R. E. 1999. *'A Voyage on the North Sea': Art in the Age of the Post-Medium Condition*. New York: Thames & Hudson.

Pelzer-Montada, R. 2001. 'Authenticity in Printmaking – A Red Herring?' Presented at *IMPACT 2 International Printmaking Conference*; University of Art and Design, Helsinki, Finland. Available from: www.uiah.fi/conferences/nummeracad/impact/preface.html.

Purves, S. 2006. 'Original Versus Reproduction: Why Definitions in Printmaking Matter'. *Imprint* 41 (1).

Saff, D. and Sacilo, D. 1978. *Printmaking: History and Process*. Orlando, Florida: Harcourt Brace Jovanovich College Publishers.

Saunders, G. 2009. 'Lasting Impressions? A Museum Perspective on Digital Fine Art Printmaking'. In P. Coldwell, B. Rauch (eds), *The Personalised Surface: New Approaches to Digital Printmaking*. London: FADE. University of the Arts: 37–44.

Snell, T. 2008. 'Fremantle Hails the New Prints of Pop'. *The Australian*, 28 August. [Accessed 23 December 2010.] Available from: www.theaustralian.com.au/news/arts/fremantle-hails-the-new-prints-of-pop/story-e6frg8n6-1111117318935.

Younge, G. 2010. *Who Are We – and Should it Matter in the 21st Century?* London: Viking.

Barbara Balfour

The what and the why of print[1]*

I have already written this essay. Or else I have a strange sense of *déjà vu*, more precisely *déjà écrit*, that I've already written it. I've returned to many of these thoughts concerning print media over a number of years, in discussion with students and fellow artists or in the form of statements, reviews, and conference papers. I know I will risk repeating myself here; however, this in itself is inherently printerly.

I am taking as my starting point the set of core questions established in classical Greek philosophy, further applied in medieval legal questioning, and later adopted in twentieth-century journalism – namely *who*, *what*, *when*, *where*, and *why*. For this text, I will concentrate my attention on two particular questions in relation to print: the *what* and the *why*. Within the context of the overall publication, other key questions will be addressed by others elsewhere: the *who* (Open Studio and all the artists who have had connections to it), the *when* (the past four decades of this organization), and the *where* (Toronto, within Open Studio's national and international network). Furthermore, I would like to acknowledge my intentional avoidance of the '*H*' often appended to the five *Ws*, namely the *how*. Examinations guided by this category of question so often derail discussions of print-based work by an inordinate focus on technique. Furthermore, a wide range of publications, from educational manuals to ostensibly critical texts, have amply covered this territory.

My reflections on the *what* of print will entail an ontological and material consideration of what can be construed as the medium specificity of this already multiple set of media, while my contemplation of the *why* of print will address the possible sets of reasons behind one's adoption of print as an artistic practice and mode of production. I will strive to eschew two

* Barbara Balfour. 2016. 'The What and the Why of Print'. In: Cooper, Tara and Law, Jenn (eds), *Printopolis*. Toronto: Open Studio, pp. 142–57. Reproduced by kind permission of the author and Open Studio.

extremes – neither assuming a defensive stance in relation to anticipated critics nor staging a 'love-in' for devoted print practitioners. My ideal audience would comprise people who are attracted to print and all its potential, particularly those who have a close relationship to it yet retain a somewhat guarded skepticism about print's conventions and parochialisms.

In writing, neither to defend nor extol print, I nonetheless want to propose a series of observations about what print is and why one employs it as a medium. Instead of referencing theory, specifically print-related theory connected to principles underlying this practice, I want to turn to a more empirical approach based on my experience over the years as a student, instructor, professional printer, curator, writer, and artist. I've had to confront assumptions, misconceptions, and paradoxes relating to print-based practices that, in crucial ways, have both perturbed and expanded my notion of what print can be.

I don't want to deny the importance of theory in relation to print, although I can say that it is arguably more difficult to locate the key texts of what might be called 'print theory' as opposed to theory which deals with, for example, painting or photography. In keeping with print media's relatively low status in the historical hierarchy of art media, its typically misunderstood and often devalued status as copy, as well as its somewhat elusive and malleable characteristics and qualities, the existence of an easily identifiable canon of theoretical texts devoted to the consideration of print is, unsurprisingly, not at all self-evident. By tracking down a few far-flung references and texts pertaining to print, or gathering together books and articles not expressly concerned with print, yet where it's possible to read fruitfully between the lines, one can extrapolate towards a deeper understanding of print media.

In developing what I had intended as a print theory course in the Critical Issues stream of the Department of Visual Art and Art History at York University in Toronto, I ultimately mobilized some key concepts coming out of print practice to devise a reading list of theoretical texts germane to a range of media. Entitled 'Repetition, Reproduction, and Reproducibility,' the course considered these modes of production in relation to issues including originality and the copy, forgery, moulds, multiples, mechanical reproduction, seriality, and infinity. In this way, the course content was not only a reflection of my own background and practice in and out of print media, but also of interest to students working in print and/or other media.

'First of all, I must acknowledge publicly that I don't like prints.'[2] I can't resist quoting this rather provocative opening sentence of José Roca's address to an audience attending the SGCI (Southern Graphics) Conference in Philadelphia. It's not the knee-jerk response of someone who might not know a lot about print (yet would profess all the same to know what he or she does like), but rather a statement spoken by the Artistic Director and Chief Curator of *Philagrafika 2010*. Roca knew this statement would get

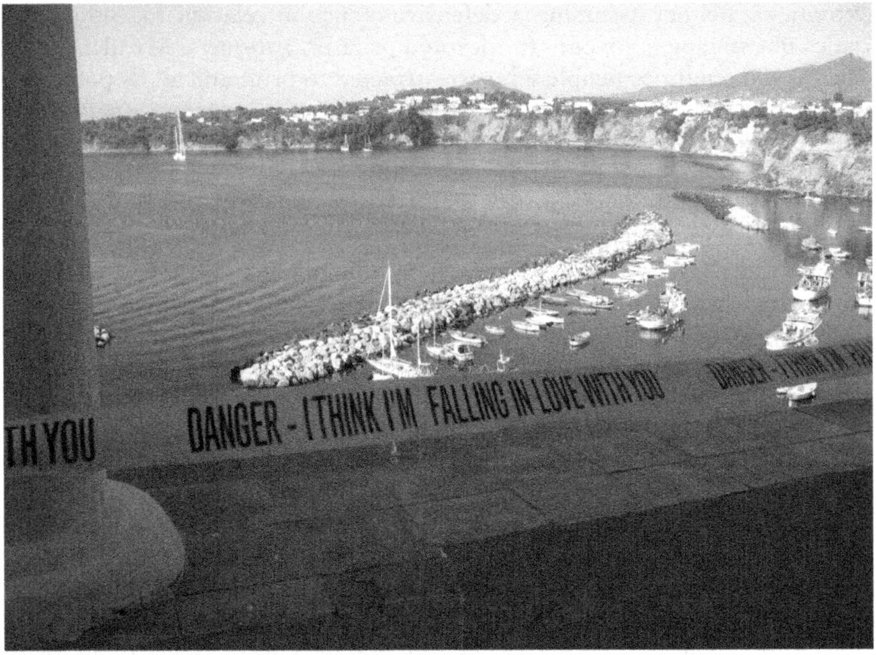

Barbara Balfour, *DANGER (I Think I'm Falling in Love With You)*, 2004. Printed text on biodegradable caution tape. Dimensions variable.

the immediate attention of this particular assembly. Implicit in much of his following argument was a resistance to medium specificity in general as well as a refusal to maintain an unquestioning emphasis on the technical nature of printmaking, arguably the prevalent approach in print discourse and print-related curatorial practices. The majority of the work in both the main and ancillary Philagrafika exhibitions and events tended toward breadth and diversity in terms of what might constitute print-based practice, with stress on the inclusion of cross-disciplinary production with a print connection. I can easily identify with Roca's initial confession and subsequent retraction: 'I will backtrack a little. Let me acknowledge publicly that I like print.'[3] I have often found myself in this somewhat equivocal position, supportive and critical of print in turn. I've felt like a kind of double agent, yet one with sincere loyalty to both sides.

What is print? I should say that I love definitions; some of my favourite books are dictionaries. However, in attempting to define print, I am faced with the enormity of all that this could entail. I could remove incidental marks produced outside of the field of art, such as fingerprints or tire tracks, or avoid so-called commercial or industrial manifestations of print, such as newspapers, books, or billboards – but I could just as easily see any of these forms incorporated into print-based art practice. I'd prefer to avoid a limiting, exclusionary definition. Yet even if I restrict myself, for the sake of argument, to the types of print media most commonly used in art practice – their individual histories, material characteristics, and modes of production are so varied that any serious articulation of these phenomena would necessitate a complex diagram or flow chart. In place of an all-encompassing description of what print is and can be, I will offer various suggestions that are in no way exhaustive.

But first, I will make a brief detour into the realm of the *how*, not in terms of specifics but rather the broad mechanics of print. This entails the following:

- *matrix* made of wood, copper, lead, limestone, linoleum, aluminum, or polymer (with tires, erasers, pumpkins, and embossed cookies as a few unconventional alternatives);
- *mark-making* or the affixing of imagery (drawn, painted, photographic, or digital, etc.) onto the matrix;
- *ink* as the seemingly indispensable material of the printing process (yet blind or non-inked impressions are possible, as well as prints produced through the use of organic or synthetically produced substitutes, by themselves or in combination with a vehicle approximating the consistency of ink, such as pureed fruit or Pepto-Bismol);
- *pressure* to transfer (or create an imprint or rubbing) by hand, press, or other implements (baren, rolling pin, stencil, or steamroller) imagery from matrix to substrate;
- *substrate*, with paper being the most consistently used substance for millennia, although alternatives are numerous (such as fabric, wood veneer, plastic, metal, a wall, a sidewalk, Silly Putty, skin).

This discussion of the *how* of print acknowledges print as a verb, ranging from clearly formed, non-cursive hand-lettering, to imagery or text produced through the use of the hand, printing presses, or computer printers. The various modes of production range from individual, artisanal, and handmade to mechanical and large-scale industrial, from low-tech to high-tech. Furthermore, the term 'printing' can be used to describe any number of different kinds of mark-making, embossing, indentation, or impression, taking place either literally (onto paper, fabric, skin, etc.) or figuratively (as in making a strong impression on someone or something), or both. This activity leads us to consider print as a noun, the print or printed object or printed matter that is the end result and residue of printing.

What is it? Several years ago, an art historian walking into the gallery of the Department of Visual Art and Art History at York University was unable at first to identify which medium-specific area a particular undergraduate student exhibition represented. I was actually delighted that the work, made by Print Media students – involving books, stuffed fabric objects, paper replicas of indulgences, and multiples made of soap, wood, and other materials – departed from what one might expect from an exhibition of prints. What I consider to be print's all-embracing, chameleon-like nature – that it can look like or mimic as well as actually incorporate other perhaps more identifiable media – is part of why this is so.

Although pleased that this student exhibition defied immediate categorization, I have been bemused, in other situations, where the multiplicity of manifestations of print can lead to work not being recognized as such. When objects as diverse as the Shroud of Turin or Andy Warhol's 'paintings' are not discussed, expressly, in terms of their printed qualities, I long for clarification to be made – not to claim their inclusion in some definitive list of printed works or for the sake of bringing them into the print fold, but to acknowledge that part of what makes certain work interesting is connected to its printed nature. Deep down, these situations make me want to call out, 'but it's a print!' Such acknowledgements might lead to print's inclusion in a broader discussion of art and culture. This seems to be a conundrum peculiar to print – that it can be at once ubiquitous and obscure. This paradoxically invisible presence often occurs where print enters the world, hidden in plain sight yet not completely identifiable.

Returning to the printed work that has come into being, I will begin to describe what it is, although this definition in the abstract will gain in complexity according to all the possible permutations. The printed work could be produced by an individual medium or the combined use of media such as drawing, painting, digital software, installation, photography, sculpture, or video. In its end result, it could be an instance of a particular print medium or combination of various print media involving etching, letterpress, lithography, relief, screen-printing, print installation, or artists' books. (Although I can attest to the fact that if someone asks 'What is it?' and the response is 'a lithograph,' one will quickly return to the topic of *how*).

Broadly speaking, printed work can materialize in various forms, going something like this: a unique example (monoprint or monotype) or a copy or multiple (virtually identical or with repeated elements, appearing as part of a series or varied edition, in a fixed or unlimited number). In the multiple form of an edition, the printed work would have the capacity to be a simultaneously and geographically dispersed series of copies, thereby potentially entering a mode of circulation made possible by publishing, literally the making public of work (which is not to say that the singular print can't circulate in the world as well).

This discussion of the *what* of print, acknowledging print as a noun, leads us to its connotation with the printed word and brings to mind newspapers, magazines, or books. However, it could also include marks such as fingerprints or footprints, and various forms of print reproductions involving inexpensive examples such as photocopies or so-called fine art prints and photographs. Once a printed art work is made public, it could appear as a sheet of paper within a portfolio or as a framed work, perhaps the most common means of presentation within print and art settings – yet innumerable manifestations of its paradoxical ubiquity and invisibility outside the realm and context of art persist. I once gave a class of undergraduate students twenty minutes to search out examples of 'everyday prints' – examples of quotidian printed matter in their immediate environs. They produced items such as subway transfers, candy wrappers, bookmarks, birth certificates, dollar bills, credit cards, invoices marked 'PAID' with a rubber stamp, a concert ticket, a takeout menu, an exhibition invitation, and patterned clothing. In addition to discussing these examples in terms of their individual merits and print-based commonality, we were led to wonder why it tends to be more difficult to identify and explain what a print is, as opposed to a painting, photograph, or sculpture.

I'm attracted to the notion of print as a particularly porous range of media, yet I have to admit that print's capacity to incorporate other media, in combination with its shape-shifting nature, remains both a strength and a liability. As a metaphor for print's porosity, rather than choosing the passive and accepting sponge, I would turn to the membrane of human skin: both a receptive and protective membrane. I strive for that healthy balance, in which print is inclusive of and amenable to incorporating other

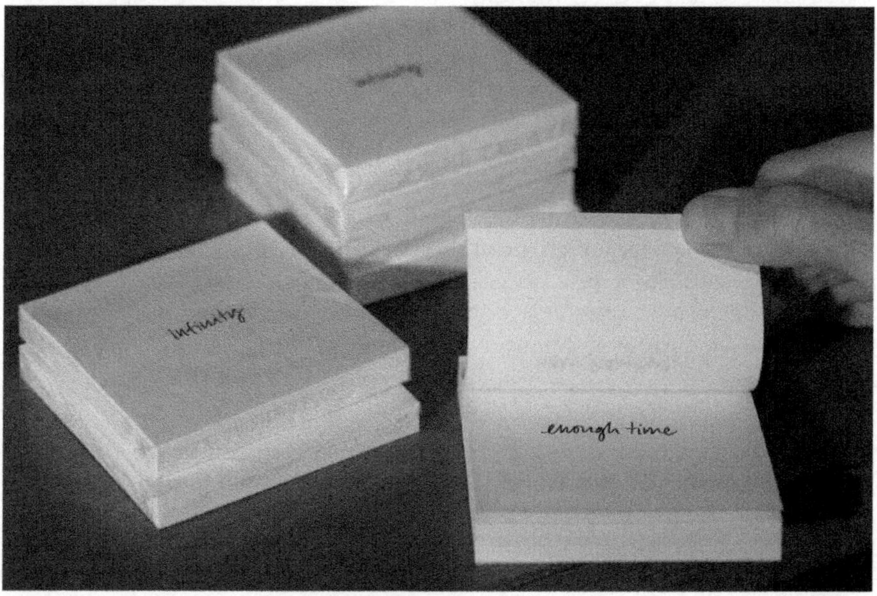

Barbara Balfour, *100 Things That Make me Happy* (stack version), 2007. Screenprint, edition of thirty reconstituted stacks of Post-it notes, wrapped in cellophane. 3.25″ × 0.5″.

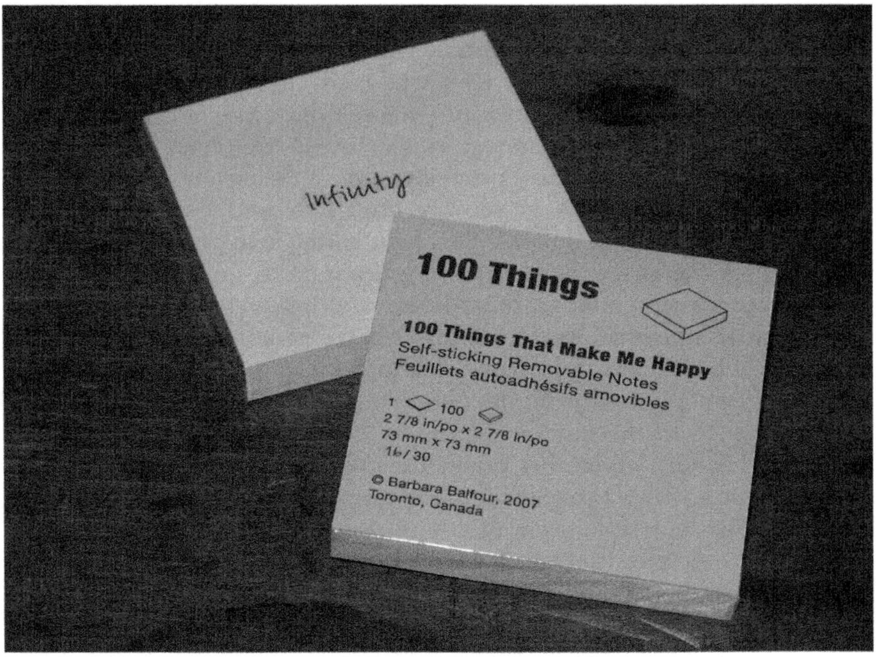

Barbara Balfour *100 Things That Make Me Happy* (stack version), detail, 2007. Screen-print, edition of thirty reconstituted stacks of Post-it notes, wrapped in cellophane. 3.25″ × 0.5″.

media, yet retains the integrity of what could be called its 'printness.' While having nothing against blended and cross-pollinated media, I feel that it is worthwhile resisting, as a long-term strategy, print's co-optation by other more commonly accepted media. There have been too many progressive curatorial projects in which print's incorporation or, at times, apparent sublimation into other practices seems to be upheld, paradoxically, as its salvation. Even the catalogue accompanying the excellent *Print/Out* exhibition includes a curious prediction concerning print, by curator Christophe Cherix:

> While printmaking might very well lose its distinctiveness as a traditional artistic medium, many of its key characteristics – its reproducibility, capacity for distribution, and even its collaborative nature – remain essential for art-making. Looking at the vast range of extraordinary projects produced during the past two decades, it is perhaps not the disappearance of the print medium that we are witnessing, but rather the advent of a time in which prints will simply be called 'art.'[4]

I would be hard pressed, if you forgive the expression, to think of the practitioners of any other medium embracing a chain of events in which they would willingly sacrifice its specificity in order for it to be subsumed under the general rubric of 'art.' Who would want to strip a medium of its historicity or its distinct qualities? Furthermore, I was under the impression that prints were always already 'art.'

At a gathering of what I would call print-based artists, or at least a group of artists brought together by a museum exhibition of prints and a print portfolio, an artist I have come to know and respect addressed me by adamantly stating, 'You're not a real printmaker.' I bristled at the suggestion I wasn't perhaps being taken seriously in terms of my print-based practice, and yet realized that 'printmaker' is not a term I tend to use. It might be akin to how being called a water-colourist often has a pejorative association, linked perhaps unjustly to its more conservative manifestations.

I view my own practice as both print-based and hybrid, both committed to print in its many manifestations (most often lithography, artists' books, multiples, and installation) and also open to employing different media on a project-to-project basis (extending to 3D animation, photography, sculpture, and video, for example). So when I arrived in a new position as Head of Printmaking in the Department of Visual Art and Art History at York University, after a number of years without a dedicated full-time faculty member in this area, I was surprised at first when the students greeted me as a 'real printmaker.' As part of the area's revitalization, I soon changed its name to 'Print Media,' as a way of acknowledging how print is not only about the making of prints, but also printed books and ephemera, print installation, and any number of permutations of printed objects or forms.

In response to the question 'What do you do?' – often followed by 'What kind of artist?' – one might fall into the habit of self-identifying in terms of the medium or media one uses. It's this tendency toward conflating artist and medium, or the foregrounding of one's medium, that seems to eclipse all else, such as the nature of one's projects, concerns, or politics. Yet it might be possible to reclaim the notion of medium-specificity in our current era of interdisciplinarity, what might even be considered the post-medium era. Although defining one's practice as interdisciplinary might very well reflect the actual state of one's practices, it has also come to suggest that 'inter' is somehow more advanced, more evolved, more sophisticated – and that it's a bit retrograde or anachronistic to focus on merely one medium. In terms of print, it is so multifarious and multitudinous that ideally we can take advantage of the great diversity of individual print forms as well as unifying and shared qualities. In so many ways, rather than being misunderstood and summarily dismissed, print could just as easily be championed as one of the least medium-specific set of media.

With print as well as other media, it seems more empowering to think less in terms of a set of defining forms and attributes and more in terms of capacity and mobility, such as what one can accomplish by using certain media. Although I don't believe in psychic mediums – i.e. people who claim to be able to serve as a conduit between the living and the dead – the notion of a medium as an enabling agency rather than an ossified form is appealing, perhaps even allowing for a happy medium. If we think of media in terms of means and intervention, as forms of communication linking two things, then we allow the notion of medium to regain its sense of agency. Part of the problem arising from discussions of medium-specificity is that distinctions and subsequent assessments often lead to the inevitability of value judgments that work against a productive plurality of media. I am less interested in preserving a hierarchical or adversarial framework of media and more interested in working toward a relational understanding of print *vis-à-vis* other media.

Common to the diverse array of print media, there is one unifying aspect that bridges the *what*, *when*, *where*, and even the *how*: its reproducibility. If we set aside the oft-misquoted title of Walter Benjamin's essay, 'The Work of Art in the Age of Mechanical Reproduction' and look to the more accurately translated title now commonly in usage: 'The Work of Art in the Age of Its Technological Reproducibility,' we can envision a more edifying and exciting way of envisioning print. Print media's capacity to make multiples stems from its matrix/transfer mode of production, thereby enabling its 'original copies' (in the words of Martha Buskirk)[5] or its 'singular multiples' (to borrow from the title of the Peter Blum publication) to go out into circulation and exist simultaneously in various sites.[6] Accordingly, we could bridge discussions concerning print and digital media by focusing on the commonalities between websites, print on demand (POD) publishing and print media, and making use of their inherent multiplicity.

What's up with print? This informal query about the current state of print carries the connotation of something being wrong or amiss. I'm actually less concerned with print's rising and falling status, spanning centuries of this evolving, persistent, and multi-faceted set of media. It does, however, interest me that print encompasses so-called traditional as well as new media, often at the same time and even in the same artwork. Print's technological advances can be plotted along a teleological trajectory charting innovations as well as incorporating resurgences of certain forms that become fashionable once again after periods of relative obscurity (letterpress being a recent case in point). Although the speed and efficiency of one medium might at a certain point in history eclipse another (intaglio with respect to woodblock printing, for example), it tends to be more of a factor within commercial applications (such as the optimum mode for printing sheet music) than with artmaking. Any number of print media developed over the past centuries can be employed today, separately or in combination with each other. I don't really ascribe to a belief in the obsolescence of art; I was tempted to use holography as a counter-example, but it seems to be resurfacing in art practices. As I once stated in the title of a conference paper I delivered, 'reports of the death of print are greatly exaggerated.' To say we are living in a post-print era makes as much sense as saying we are living in a paperless era, a situation that home and office computing has prevented more than facilitated. Setting aside a larger discussion about e-books, I prefer to envision the coexistence of print and digital forms of publishing rather than the need for one to eclipse the other.

What's up with print? (reprise) If posed this question I might be able to distinguish, by the interlocutor's tone, whether it was intended as skeptically provocative or genuinely inquisitive; as in 'why this medium in particular?' Moving from what print is or can be, now that I have put forward the notion that it isn't dead, I would like to address the possible rationales, or set of reasons, behind one's adoption of print as a mode of production and artistic practice – to go from what you do when you print to why you print.

In the university setting, especially at the introductory level of undergraduate studies, students tend not to be familiar with printmaking as a medium (or they might have had one brief experience with something like lino-cut, perhaps involving a slight injury). They might have enrolled in a print course not exactly knowing what was involved, or on the recommendation of a fellow student or instructor who told them that if they like drawing, or painting, or photography, or digital imaging, then they might like printmaking, as all have print applications. In addition, at York University as well as at other institutions, there is often a print/sculpture crossover with students working in both areas, perhaps due to the range of materials and physically involved methods found in each. And then sometimes you just stumble onto print.

I'll now make a shift and address the unknown reader, surmising that you have some relationship to print and might be a print practitioner. In addressing the *whys* and *wherefores* of print practice, I'll suggest numerous aspects of print that you might find as compelling as I do, and that might be behind your decision to work in print media. First of all, you might respond to the communal atmosphere and lively dynamic of a print studio or print shop, whether in a university, a centre such as Open Studio, or any other professional setting. Print studios tend to accommodate the gregarious as well as the introverted, working side by side. Print studios are also the site of collaborative art practices: between one artist and another, between artist and printer, and/or between artist and writer (to name a few possibilities).

Whether you are drawn to print immediately or you learn to love it, any number of aspects of this range of media is appealing. You might enjoy the mark-making (carving, inscribing, stamping, etc.) and image-making (with stencil, photography, and various digital media) as well as the particular possibilities of layering in print (leading to successive state proofs, variations on an image, creative approaches to colour separation, a density of superimposed images, or individual layers generating other prints in turn).

You have probably come to terms with, and maybe even learned to enjoy, the inevitable labour of print: the technical steps and procedures, physical and chemical (almost alchemical), involved in the preparing, processing, proofing, revising, and printing of your work. You are probably familiar with the cycles and reversals of making marks, leaving or erasing traces, making messes, and cleaning up afterwards (as well as filing, polishing, applying grounds and emulsions, with various states of inkiness along the way).

Above all, you have to enjoy the activity of printing – its craft, in the best and original sense of the word. This might involve the familiar return to tacitly embodied aspects of labour, the mental alertness that enables one to detect a problem arising in the proofing stage – inevitably leading to the need for trouble-shooting – and the flexibility to change one's direction and work with the unexpected, arising through an engagement with process.

It is a virtue to have patience, or to acquire a taste for it, when encountering the stages and processes of printing, often involving waiting periods for etching, curing, drying, etc. in addition to what is, in the beginning, often an admittedly slow learning curve. You have probably come to understand that certain aspects of print require the investment of time, often defying instant gratification.

You might appreciate the peculiar logic of printing, related to an ethos of efficiency. This is, in part, borrowed from the commercial print realm's imperative to manufacture economically viable products as well as a practical outcome of the labour involved in printing. Or, despite all this, you might want to take advantage of embracing a decidedly illogical approach to printing, where aesthetics and conceptual intentions trump well-reasoned and systematic approaches to production.

You may have taken note of the curious separation that exists in print between imagery and colour. Mark-making, photography, or any other kind of imagery, once part of a printing matrix, can be altered by the hue and intensity of the colours of ink with which it is printed. This malleable and dynamic characteristic is familiar to anyone working in digital imaging.

Once attuned to print, you will probably respond to the particular aesthetic of ink on paper (or any of its substitutes or alternatives), whether it be the most subtle and refined lithographic tusche wash on rag paper, an exquisitely hand-inked, multi-hued *bokashi* on deceptively thin Japanese washi, handprints that have endured thousands of years on cave walls, or a totally DIY and non-archival newsprint proof. Or you might be fascinated by that weird remove one becomes aware of, when the image is transferred from matrix to substrate.

All at once, it is a mirroring, a separation, and a repetition. Beyond this, there is the possibility of additional repeats and recurrences.

All of this inescapably physical activity tends to result in a surprisingly thin layer of ink on a sheet of pristine paper, often with no apparent signs of the labour involved. I have often likened this and other curious print processes that demand repeated effort to that of housework, in which success ultimately lies in the lack of evidence of any mess or work involved. You might also be sensitive to the insistent flatness that remains, even if your print takes on three-dimensional aspects. And although the tactility of print media may be something only a practitioner is aware of, or someone who actually handles prints, it does exist. Various forms of print media, from those with aspects of incision, deep biting, and low relief on one end, to the more smooth and planographic on the other, allow for a range of haptic as well as visually perceptible phenomena, both in the process of making as well as in the final product.

You might be drawn to the play between a given material's receptive nature and transformative potential as well as its sometimes obdurate nature; something to be reckoned with more than defeated by. This strange oscillation between constraints and possibilities, with self-imposed guidelines and strictures not unlike those deployed in Conceptual Art practices, allows nonetheless for various kinds of agency.

You might be attracted to print's capacity for reproduction, its inherent reproducibility, dating back to the multiple copies of the Chinese Diamond Sutra printed in 868, and the later innovations of moveable type in Gutenberg's 1455 Bible – continuing in our current digital age, with computer software emulating so many print processes. Print's reproducibility, leading to multiplicity and proliferation, allows work to exit simultaneously in different places (similar to sculptural multiples and digital copies). You can choose whether to strive for a faithful edition of prints or to pursue aspects of difference and repetition through permutations. Reproducibility's potential can be either an interesting byproduct of the print process and/or an integral and well considered aspect of your project. Nevertheless, it allows you to experience the distribution, consumption, and reception of prints in modes that circumvent certain site-based exhibition systems. You might also come to realize that the tension between original and copy, with the copy often demonized in discussions of reproductions versus so-called fine art prints, is not the case here with original work existing in multiple form in the deployment of equal exemplars.[7]

In addition to all the physical aspects of printmaking and print-based work, you might be attracted to the literal and figurative language of print: the resonance of technical terms, the complexity of metaphors (often body-related), and even *double entendres* (while trying to avoid the most obvious puns, of course). I am assuming you know something about both sides of the equation, the material processes that constitute the making of printmaking, as well as its 'printness' – the look, feel, and nature of something that's been printed. I am well aware that, to those either familiar or unfamiliar with print-based work and practice, this range of media can be by turns appealing, frustrating, and mystifying. And yet in trying, despite myself, to rationalize why one (including myself) would want to work in print, I have come to realize that I am answering the wrong question. Rationalizing why one would like print is like rationalizing an attraction to any number of things: soap operas, stand up paddle-boarding, champagne, or even falling in love. It is less a case of arguing one's interest or enjoyment – and more a case of claiming and acknowledging just that. There is no need to establish the aetiology of such a predilection.

The *why* of print has now led me back to the *what* of print: its peculiarities, its distinctiveness, its quiddity. I find myself endlessly fascinated by the *whatness* of print – its shape-shifting qualities that make it so like other media, inescapably hybrid, and the persistence, nonetheless, of a printerly *je ne sais quoi*.

Notes

1 Dedicated to my students, who inspire me to articulate what it is about print that makes it so interesting.
2 Roca, José. 'Prints, or Contemporary Art?', lecture given at the SGCI Conference in Philadelphia, March 27, 2010. A modified version of this talk is accessible through *Working States*, the online publication program of *Philagrafika*, at www.philagrafika.org/workingstates1.html.
3 Roca, 'Prints, or Contemporary Art?'
4 Cherix, Christophe. 'Print/Out', in *Print/Out: 20 Years in Print*, Christophe Cherix with Kim Conaty and Sarah Suzuki (New York: The Museum of Modern Art, 2012), 26.
5 Buskirk, Martha. *The Contingent Object of Contemporary Art* (Cambridge MA: The MIT Press, 2003).
6 Walker, Barry with contributions by Faye Hirsch, et. al., *Singular Multiples: The Peter Blum Edition Archive*, 1980–1994 (Houston: The Museum of Fine Arts; New Haven: Yale University Press, 2006).
7 For an intelligent and wide-ranging discussion on the nature of the copy and notions of copiousness, see Marcus Boon, *In Praise of Copying* (Cambridge, MA: Harvard University Press, 2010).

Part II Further reading

Abell, Catharine. 2015. 'Printmaking as an Art'. *The Journal of Aesthetics and Art Criticism* 73 (1): 23–30.

Alpert, Avi. 2010. 'Untitled (Notes on the Graphic Unconscious)'. In: Working States. *Philagrafika*, 1–2. www.philagrafika.org/pdf/WS/notesonthegraphic unconscious.pdf [Accessed 27 February 2017].

Box, Rowland (ed.), 2001. *In-Print: Evolution in Contemporary Printmaking: A Radical Look at the Evolution in Contemporary Printmaking*. Kingston upon Hull: Hull Museums & Art Gallery.

Camnitzer, Luis. 2006. 'Printmaking: A Colony of the Arts'. Re-printed in: Philagrafika et al. 2011. *The Graphic Unconscious*. Philadelphia, PA: Philagrafika, 1–4. www.philagrafika.org/pdf/WS/Printmakingacolony.pdf [Accessed 25 January 2018].

Cornwell, Graeme. 1992. 'The Techno-Fetish in Printmaking'. 2nd Australian Print Symposium. www.printsandprintmaking.gov.au/references/4852/ [Accessed 19 January 2017].

Goddard, Stephen. 2001. 'Printmaking: Will the Center Hold?' In: Box, Rowland (ed.), *In-Print, Evolution in Contemporary Printmaking: A Radical Look at the Evolution in Contemporary Printmaking*. Hull: Hull Museums and Art Gallery, 10–14.

Green, Charles. 1992. 'Art as Printmaking: The Deterritorialized Print'. Second Australian Print Symposium, National Gallery of Australia, Canberra. www.printsandprintmaking.gov.au/references/3927/ [Accessed 5 March 2015].

Jameson, Kathleen V. 2005. 'A New State Reassessing Prints'. *Art Lies* 46: 14–28. https://texashistory.unt.edu/ark:/67531/metapth228011/m1/16/ [Accessed 2 October 2016].

Knofler, Monika, Russegger, Georg, Schneider, Michael. 2011. 'Druck am Limit – Print Unlimited? Zwei Veranstaltungen, ein Thema. Two Events, One Topic'. In: *im:print 2011. zustandsprotokolle aktueller druckgrafik / journal for the state of current printmaking*. Edited by Schneider, Michael and Maurer, Philipp. Vienna/New York: Springer, 21–48.

Lyons, Beauvais. 1999. 'In Praise of Neglected Print Histories'. In: Parraman, Carinna and Brewer, Emmeline (eds), *IMPACT International Multi-disciplinary Printmaking Conference Proceedings*. Bristol: Impact Press, 17–24.

Merrill, Hugh J. 1994. 'American Dialogue Defining Printmaking in the 1990s'. *Printmaking Today* 3 (2): 2–3.

Merrill, Hugh. 1993. 'Post Print, Staking Claim'. *Contemporary Impressions*, 1 (1), Spring: 7–9.

Morgan, Luke (ed.), 2013. *Intersections and Counterpoints: IMPACT 7 International Multi-disciplinary Printmaking Conference Proceedings*. Clayton, Victoria: Monash University Publishing.

Murphy-Price, Althea. 2008. 'Printing the Edges: Defining Print within Contemporary Installation'. *Contemporary Impressions*, 16 (1): 24–7.

Nelson, Adele. 2012. 'Sensitive and Nondiscursive Things: Lygia Pape and the Reconception of Printmaking'. *Art Journal* 71 (3): 26–45.

Nelson, Robert S. 'Why Printmakers Can't Talk'. 2nd Australian Print Symposium, 1992.

Norton, Judith. 2010. 'Print Is Dead! Long Live Print!' *OLA Quarterly*. 16 (1): 3–4.

Olynyk, Patricia. 2002. 'Making Marks Beyond the Print Studio: Mapping an Interdisciplinary Terrain'. *Contemporary Impressions*, 10, Fall: 20–5.

Parry, Janis Eugenia. 1991. 'Deviation and its Imperatives: The Plight of "the Unique Print"'. *Print Collector's Newsletter* 21 (6) (Jan.–Feb.): 211–31.

Pelzer-Montada, Ruth. 2008. 'The Discursivity of Print: Damien Hirst's Series *The Last Supper* (1999)'. *Visual Culture in Britain* 9 (1): 81–100.

Pelzer-Montada, Ruth. 2004. 'Technology Versus Concept, or the Site of Practice Versus the Bite of Theory'. *Contemporary Impressions*, 12 (2): 21–5.

Petr, Mark. 1995. 'Prints, Politics, Polemics'. In: Tyler, Linda and Berry, Walter (eds), *Hot Off the Press: Prints and Politics*. Tamarind Institute, Albuquerque: The University of New Mexico Press, 87–93.

Philagrafika et al. (2011) *The Graphic Unconscious*. Philadelphia, PA: Philagrafika.

Piercy, Sioban. 2001. 'Centre/Periphery – The Predicament of Fine Art Printing'. In: *IMPACT 2 International Printmaking Conference Proceedings*. Helsinki: University of Art and Design UIAH. www.uiah.fi/conferences/impact/piercy/Piercy.pdf [Accessed 15 February 2017].

Pulin, Carol. 1994. 'Postmodern Printmaking: A Key'. *Contemporary Impressions* 2 (1): 11–13.

Suzuki, Sarah. 2011. 'Print People: A Brief Taxonomy of Contemporary Printmaking'. *Art Journal* 70 (4): 7–25.

Walker, Sam. 2000. 'Printmaking as Syntax of Contemporary Art'. *Contemporary Impressions* 8 (1): 2–5.

Weisberg, Ruth. 1990. 'The Absent Discourse: Critical Theories and Printmaking'. *The Tamarind Papers*, 13: 8–10.

Weisberg, Ruth. 1993. 'Critical Theory and the Print: New Criteria for Print Qualities in the Expanded Field'. *Contemporary Impressions* 1 (1): 10–12.

PART III

Keywords

Introduction to Part III

As the title suggests, the texts in Part III put the spotlight on recurring key terms that function as points in the discursive network about prints and printmaking, chief among them: reproduction, seriality, aura, the edition, the multiple, the matrix, the imprint. As in botany, where from such nodal points further 'branches' or directions emerge, often such key terms intersect. Seen from the perspective of today – in the context of digital technologies' prevalence – older reflections and insights become invested with new emphasis or urgency.

The dates of writing vary from the 1980s through to the 2000s, with the majority of texts published between 2000 and 2016. Authored by art historians, a philosopher and artists, they encompass diverse curatorial, art historical, philosophical and playfully creative methods. Also included are texts that adopt different approaches to specific forms and aspects of the materiality of prints as objects and their production. These comprise their literal as well as metaphorical or associative features.

In the brief preamble to his short history of printmaking, German art historian Ernst Rebel notes that printmaking has gained attention among scholars of new media. The rapid development of image technologies, especially digital media, has revived an interest in prints and printmaking. They are now recognised as having provided the basis for the 'technical image' and therefore crucial to a genealogy of new media.

Within an expanded art context for print, it seems expedient to consider the recurring, if changing, parameters of printmaking, as signalled by some of its basic terms. Rebel highlights etymological and anthropological, as well as semantic and historiographic, aspects of the basic terms that pertain to 'print' and 'printmaking'. These allusions are relevant to thinking about prints and printmaking although they may be more apparent in some European languages such as German, in which the designation of print and its variants contains the word 'graphic'.[1] The German 'Druckgrafik' (literally: 'press-graphic'), for example, encompasses the dual nature that has been typical of the medium for centuries, namely the incising or marking on the one hand, and the technical transfer on the other.

In the shortened but otherwise unchanged chapter from her book *The Image Multiplied*, published in 1987, art historian and curator Susan Lambert provides an invaluable insight into the historical relationship between prints as reproductions and the question of the 'original' print. She demonstrates that, historically, not only were these notions and attendant practices considered less important than more recently, but they were also less clearly defined. Moreover, works that might have been regarded as 'original' latterly, were, historically, often created expressly for reproduction. The emergence of the notion of the 'original' print in the more familiar sense – including the attendant practices of the limited edition, the numbering of prints in an edition and the conventions around the artist's signature – are traced back to the nineteenth century. The 'original' print's codification, Lambert reminds us, occurred as late as the 1960s. The crux of printmaking – as espoused by these definitions and categorisations – promotes its reduction to techniques, a factor remarked upon by other authors in this volume. Lambert ends her chapter with a succinct and dry statement that still rings true: 'The "original" print still has its adherents, but the concept is outmoded' (152). Her historical contextualisation complicates any vestiges of the notion of the 'original' print and reveals its multiple ironies. It thereby exposes it as a primarily market-driven device that exploits and reinforces wider cultural values.

Unfortunately, it is not possible to reproduce the full original text here with its many excellent illustrations, which are supported by detailed text commentaries. The reader is encouraged to seek out the original text and/or search the images mentioned online.

If Lambert's text gives historical insight into changes as to the practices and values attributed to reproduction, Clare Humphries' recent conference presentation provides a timely re-examination of Walter Benjamin's famous text on reproduction – or more accurately, 'reproducibility' – especially his often-misrepresented notion of 'aura'. It is also an excellent example of rigorously executed research motivated and informed by practice, as the author explains.[2] Noting Benjamin's own inconsistencies, Humphries arrives at the conclusion that aura arises within reproductive media themselves. This is contrary to the common misunderstanding of Benjamin's essay, which holds that reproductive media obliterate aura. Humphries then explores the shifting nature and auratisation of reproductive media such as print. She also pinpoints the need to examine the 'naturalisation' of art and image-making that has occurred, especially through digital reproducibility. Print, as a reproductive medium itself, is beautifully positioned to query this seeming naturalness of images in the digital age. This insight is what makes her text so valuable to contemporary printmakers. Humphries' analysis can be fruitfully read in conjunction with Didi-Huberman's nuanced analysis of Benjamin's text further on in this section.

In 2015 the *Journal of Aesthetics and Art Criticism*, on the initiative of philosopher Christy Mag Uidhir, devoted a whole issue to printmaking. The chosen essay by philosopher K. E. Gover sets out to consider the limited edition from an ontological perspective. Even if much printmaking today subscribes to an 'expanded' practice that frequently eschews the limited edition, the latter is still a sufficiently prevalent aspect of print practice to warrant special consideration. It could even be argued that the explicit or implicit distancing from the limited edition, that is characteristic of expanded print practice today, relies to some extent on the format of the limited edition as its invisible sub-text.

While ontological approaches have taken a back seat in art theory, such a method brings to the fore questions that can fruitfully inform and expand contemporary practice. Another value of the essay is that it concedes the often unacknowledged economic considerations at play in the persistence of the limited edition, but also provides a more artist-centred analysis for its continuing deployment.

Examining the positions of Nelson Goodman, Nigel Warburton and Christy Mag Uidhir, Gover's main question is whether the relationship between a print's matrix and the resulting edition can be ontologically compared to a musical score and its performances. This comparison yields certain insights, but remains unsatisfactory. Writing on the ontology of the print so far has failed to make a differentiation between what makes a print an artwork and what makes a print 'a genuine and authentic artwork'. Existing analyses have thus increased the confusion.

Gover concludes her intriguing analysis by ascribing to prints an ontologically 'unusual' status. They occupy an 'intermediate position' between 'pure multiples' – which can exist in unlimited numbers – and singular artworks of which only one physical object exists. In the final instance, she regards the edition as the (authentic) artwork. Each individual print in an edition then becomes a particular instance of the artwork, defined by its provenance and the artist's intention.

One of the earliest computer artists, German Frieder Nake, reflects on the differences between two different types of print matrix, both frequently used by contemporary printmakers – often in the same work of art. These are the physical plate or screen that serve as matrix on the one hand and the digital 'pixel' matrix on the other. He considers in particular the role of the plate and the pixel matrix in relation to memory. All forms of the 'materialisation of living processes' extinguish such processes' specific features. Think, for example, of any representation, be it a painting or a photograph, in comparison to the reality to which it refers. In the digital matrix, this reduction takes on a special form: Everything that is semiotically, socially interpretable is converted into mere calculable signals. These then need to be interpreted, or made semiotically meaningful again. This 'doubling' is usually hidden within the software and seldom reflected upon. It is recognisable in the conventions adopted by programmes such as Photoshop, with their deployment of familiar procedures and specific features that draw on cultural precedents, for example the design and naming of the workspace as 'canvas'.

Nake highlights the analogy between the printing plate and human memory – it 'wears out', it 'forgets'. However, this is not the case with the digital matrix. If the printing plate is 'one and no other', the pixel matrix gives rise to a peculiar 'volatisation' or evaporation: the pixel matrix – enabled by the programme – can produce an infinite variety of 'structurally similar, but visually different graphics'. Printmakers might argue that this propensity for variation of the digital matrix is already inherent in the non-digital matrix, as print artists from Rembrandt onwards have demonstrated. However, Nake's text alerts print artists to the quantitatively new level of almost infinite variability that is facilitated by the pixel matrix.

The next text is the initial section, musically titled 'Ouverture', of the eminent French art historian Georges Didi-Huberman's book, which is dedicated to the cast or cast object and other forms of imprints or impressions (French: *empreinte*) in art. The text originally appeared in the catalogue for Didi-Huberman's exhibition of the same title in 1997. An unaltered reprint appeared in 2008 (Editions Minuit, Paris) and this is its first English translation.

The connotations of the French word *empreinte*, especially the terms 'imprint' or 'impression', have attracted writers on print to Didi-Huberman's text, but it has sometimes been cited inaccurately. Hence this translation is intended to set the record straight and to make one chapter of this important text – with its many reference points for a critical thinking on print – available in English.

Didi-Huberman attributes art historical negligence of the cast object or imprint and latterly the ready-made, to the obsession with a (wrongly understood) notion of 'origin' that shuns the seemingly mere mechanical reproduction of reality. He finds evidence of this attitude in recent art historical positions that are otherwise quite opposed to each other, such as the postmodern ethos of Rosalind Krauss and the anti-postmodern stance of Jean Clair. The roots for both attitudes can be traced to the Renaissance. They are echoed in the misunderstanding of Benjamin's seminal text on reproducibility.

Even if prints are the result of more complex processes than either the cast or the ready-made, they share the fundamental qualities of the 'imprint'. Hence, they can be argued to be not unaffected by attitudes towards either of these. (In fact, one could explain the establishing of excessive regulations and definitions to determine the 'original print', as discussed by Lambert, as an almost desperate attempt to counteract the very same lurking apprehensions.) It is these often hidden or unacknowledged cultural assumptions attached to prints and printmaking that give Didi-Huberman's text resonance for printmakers, not any straight equivalence between prints and the cast.

Australian artist and educator Deidre Brollo explores and problematises the frequent and powerful metaphor of 'imprint' and 'impression' – since antiquity – in relation to memory. Drawing on recent neuroscientific theories, she counters the assumption of a static and passive notion of memory storage with current, 'dynamic' and 'distributed' models of memory. She then discusses the work of two artists who use processes closely tied to the notion of memory as imprint, namely photography and printmaking, in order to question photography's indexical connotations as a guarantor of memory. According to Brollo, print processes can function as 'guerrilla' forces by 'infiltrating' the seeming 'integrity' of a photograph as container for memory. The notion and activity of forgetting attains a more positive role than is conventionally the case. Contrary to the usual conception of forgetting as destructive – as an act of 'erasure' – it is shown, in the work of the artists, as a 'latency'. This implies that forgetting and the material forms of imprint and impression, become open to new possibilities.

The next text uses a non-artistic mode of printing to ask profound questions about the sensory and 'spiritual' properties of technologies, even the most pithy ones. The issue of the joyfully eclectic journal *Cabinet* in which this text appeared was dedicated to the theme of 'Learning'. The text, billed as the autobiographical work of a Brazilian poet and graphic artist called Yara Flores,[3] compares vividly, poetically and with ironic detachment as well as some nostalgia the 'spiritual' power – or the sensory and metaphorical potency – of a now outdated technical mode of reproduction with its successor, the Xerox machine. The latter is found lacking in the former's redolent qualities. (Aptly) called 'spirit duplicator', in this seemingly autobiographical account it served to disseminate the Catholic doctrines of 1970s theological school teachings before being replaced by the Xerox machine.[4] Ultimately, the text argues for the importance of a 'semiotics of technology' in relation to 'thinking about pedagogy'. More generally, it illuminates 'the shifting use of concrete referents for our inner life' and memories.

The introduction, by the three founders – Amze Emmons, R. L. Tillman and Jason Urban – of the now sadly defunct web resource *Printeresting*, to their (edited) manual is at once playful as well as serious. Fittingly, it adopts the format of a manual itself, yet constitutes a deconstruction of this prevalent written source category on printmaking. This critical attitude starts with the authors that have been included in the collection. Contrary to the masculine ethos of traditional manuals, half the represented authors – judging by their first names – appear to be female. Published with a limited distribution, in the spirit of artistic self-publishing and the tradition of fanzines, *The Manual* adopts the latter's DIY aesthetic as well as its eclectic content. Its mix of visual and textual source materials include the following:

- a critical account and analysis of international printing manuals (Josh McPhee);
- texts that are entirely in keeping with the conventional manual, such as the 'processing of a lithographic stone', in the form of matter-of-fact, detailed class instructions (Brian Garner);
- all manner of ironic visual and verbal send-ups of the main methods of manuals, such as instructions, demonstrations, graphs, tables and technical illustrations. Some of these are specific to printmaking, others purposely not: for example, there is the appropriated, reproduced copy of historical embroidery instructions; a matter-of-fact recipe for 'How to Make Scones'; as well as the sardonic 'Screen-Printing Trouble Shooter Slide Chart Diagnosis Aid'.

In their introduction the editors contemplate the attraction of manuals in general and print manuals in particular. The socio-cultural role of manuals was, of course, made possible by print itself. They permitted the representation and multiplication of both professional and – in more recent history – amateur expertise. Ultimately, following Ivins, they entailed a democratisation of learning and knowledge. Noting that expert knowledge is now often being distributed digitally, rather than via print, the authors emphasise the difference between information and knowledge, while stressing the intertwining of hand and mind that manuals demand. In this way, they highlight the possibilities as well as the limitations of manuals.

Catherine Brooks' text is an excerpt from the aforementioned *Manual*. Her short autobiographical account meditates on the close – and often surprising – interconnections between human and material, culinary and artistic relationships in the context of her work at Crown Point Press in San Francisco and Atelier René Tazé in Paris. True to the title, the colour yellow is the binding agent in the tale. Brooks' theme is made palpable by, firstly, the inclusion of detailed instructions for mixing and printing a particular shade of black ink, Noir Coloré, which – unexpectedly for the non-artistic reader – incorporates yellow; secondly, by similar instructions for the use of an egg yolk to make, serve and 'enjoy' mayonnaise; finally, by a recipe for 'Goat Ocher'. This was a yellow ink made with goat butter on the insistence of artist Richard Tuttle at Crown Point Press, although both the artist and the press ultimately shied away from using it. Brooks' quirky account draws parallels between life experience, specific locales, natural and manmade materials, human relationships and passions and the making (and the leaning about making) of art.

The notion of a 'printmare' – in analogy to a nightmare – is the pretext and theme for the artist and tutor at London's Royal College of Art, Nicky Coutts.[5] In a poetically conceived and intricately argued reflection, she considers the multiple nature and mutual enfolding of prints and humans, humans and animals, reality and imagination, past and future print and other technologies. Ingeniously linking French suicidal vets, Saint Anthony, Padre Pio – a twentieth-century Catholic saint – and Hillary Clinton, as well as citing such diverse thinkers as Hélène Cixous, Elias Canetti, Walter Benjamin, Gustave Flaubert and Hito Steyerl, Coutts diagnoses our loss – through reproductive technologies – of a fixed and stable physical location as a point of orientation. Instead, our constantly shifting real and metaphorical 'horizon line' acts as a 'catalyst for addressing where we stand physically and metaphorically in a world of multiples' (222). Concurrently, our multiple – and increasingly even 3D-printed – selves posit fundamental questions as to who we are.

Notes

1 It derives from the Greek 'graphein' – to incise, but also to write and to draw.

2 For another re-examination of Benjamin's influential text which is less print-specific – although it appeared within the context of a print-event, namely the 27th Ljubljana Biennial of Graphic Arts – see Komelj (2007). On artistic research, see also Thomson's essay (2014) in Part IV.

3 'Yara Flores' is one of a number of 'pseudonymous alter-egos' of US historian of science D. Graham Burnett. This authorial doubling (and multiplication) seems particularly fitting in the context of a publication on print with its double nature of matrix and (multiple) imprints as well as its otherwise multiple identities.

4 The 'spirit duplicator' is also known as a 'Ditto machine' in the US, 'mimeograph' in Canada, 'Banda machine' in the UK or 'Roneo' in France and Australia.

5 *Printmare* was the title of a small self-publishing venture by staff and students in Print at the Royal College of Art (RCA), London, in which this text originally appeared.

Reference

Komelj, Miklavž. 2007. 'Reproducibility and its Aura'. In: *Catalogue of the 27th Biennial of Graphic Arts: Exhibitions of Reproducible Art*, edited by mglc International Centre of Graphic Arts. Ljubljana: International Centre of Graphic Arts, 68–81.

Ernst Rebel

Coordinates of a history of the technical image*

Today, print is gaining renewed attention. Over and above purely historical interest, it has become a field of research for questions as to the technical conditions of images in general. As the dizzying expansion of digital media raises more and more questions as to their historical development, the old, graphic world of the technical image appears in a new light. Technically and artistically it reveals itself more and more as the pre-history in which many of the coordinates and building blocks of modern visual culture have their origins. Therefore my use of the term 'technical image' is broad. In addition to various systems of print, it also encompasses those of photography, industrial image print production and digital image generation. Nevertheless, the narrower field of printmaking – as the manually printed artistic image – constitutes the focus of this account. Proceeding from this main focus, the book aims to show the interconnectedness of old and new, artistic as well as extra-artistic image worlds. The thesis is that this

* Ernst Rebel. 2003. *Druckgrafik. Geschichte, Fachbegriffe* [*Printmaking. History, Terminology*]. Ditzingen: Reclam. Shortened excerpt, pp. 9–13. Reproduced by kind permission of the author and Reclam Verlag. Translated by Hugh Keith and Ruth Pelzer-Montada.

Editor's note: Links to keywords in the Appendix of the original text have been removed.

Translators' note: The German word for printmaking and print as an overarching category is 'Druckgrafik'. The noun 'Druck' means 'pressure' or 'print' and the verbs 'drücken'/'drucken' mean 'to press' and 'to print' respectively. The noun 'Grafik' and the adjective 'grafisch' correspond to the English 'graphics' and 'graphic'. The German word for printmaking and print as an overarching artistic category is a compound of these two words, namely 'Druckgrafik'. To differentiate artistic printmaking or 'Druckgrafik' from graphic design, German uses 'Gebrauchsgrafik' (applied graphics) for the latter. In English, the adjective 'graphic' tends to veer towards the notion and practices of design – graphic design – more frequently than it does to artistic print. The same is not the case in German – and other European languages – to the same degree.

interconnectedness can be located in 'trace elements' within the graphic elements themselves.

But all these claims describe, as it were, only the distant horizon. First of all, this book aims to provide detailed information about facts and keywords. What is the printed image? What kinds of changes, in terms of its technical processes, has it undergone historically? What kinds of exchanges does it have with the different genres of art? How did it change perception and aesthetic conventions? And above all the book aims to identify the artistic independence achieved by systems of graphic production before they were transmedialised in the 19th century. All of these constitute its specific themes.

[...]

The history of printmaking is considered to be part of art history. At the same time, it should be understood as the archaeology of the history of our modern media.

'Typical' basic terms

Print and graphics

According to its two linguistic components the term 'Druckgrafik' [printmaking] encompasses a technical and a trace-like dimension. It is in this combination that printmaking's peculiar double-character as an aesthetic system and as a medium of image and text reproduction lies. The Greek root '*graphein*' points to the process of incising, carving, scoring of a shape into its material support. Printmaking seen in this way is (at least until around 1800 when the planographic method of lithography was invented) the collective name for the fashioning of specific reliefs, into which ink was rubbed for the purpose of image-making. The other part of the word 'Druck' [pressure] designates the ensuing, primarily technical process which consists of the ink being transferred from the graphically treated print matrix onto the supporting material, usually paper. The transfer can occur by means of the weight of the human body or by using technical equipment.

Regardless of the individual processes of creation or inking, throughout the centuries of printmaking's development, it never loses its double-character. It characterises all its artistic, religious, scientific, political and commercial achievements. This occurs partly through differentiation from older, existing media, such as writing and image-making (drawing, painting), partly in exchange with them. From today's perspective, the elements and components of printed reproduction can be systematised by looking at art. This is because from the outset these elements entail a strong, primordial expressive and metaphorical value which is interesting – from an anthropological perspective (Belting, 2001: 41). Footprints in soil, sand and snow are to be understood as both *trace* and *imprint*. Seen from this viewpoint, they not only represent basic bodily forms of sign-making in general, they also, more specifically, embody pre-graphic (or print) forms. They possess certain particular qualities that can be 'read' or 'deciphered', at the same time as more general traits that permit typological classification. The Greek word *typos* (the mark of a stroke, blow, print) in its original sense may be derived from practical-aesthetic actions. In the graphic context the typological can be understood as the repeatable general appearance of all elements of a trace, as the *standardisation* of the unique. This raises the question of authenticity. Trace and imprint prove their authenticity even when they permit its detachment from their uniqueness, even when they transfer it into intentional multiplicity. In this sense, the imprints of seals are typical 'graphic' objects. They combine standardised signification with reliable repeatability. Even more reliable, as far as bodily uniqueness is concerned, are fingerprints. One could refer to them, hyperbolically, as 'skin imprints' that are usually left by chance and whose formations, as is well known, serve modern criminal investigation.

Whatever functions both as testimony and confirmation in the imprint and trace can be used productively in picture making. An example closer to the sphere of art history would be stamping or textile printing. This can be understood as the primitive multiplication of ornaments by means of wooden blocks (that is stamps) on cloth, animal skins or plant-based fibrous tissue. In textile printing one can already find a realisation of an artistic principle of this early form of printmaking: namely the standardisation of beauty. For example, in order to avoid having to paint the same flower design multiple times by hand, a relief stamp with the flower design is imprinted or rubbed onto the cloth instead. In this manner, saving time and effort, decorative beauty can be more or less exactly repeated in a crafted, yet standardised way. Such artefacts lead to us to the threshold of graphic picture making.

References

Belting, Hans. 2001. *Bild-Anthropologie. Entwürfe für eine Bildwissenschaft.* München: Wilhelm Fink Verlag.

Susan Lambert

The status of the reproduction*

Original or reproduction?

Today everything is 'original' from the junk shop's bygones to the local butcher's sausages. The word is frequently used in place of 'genuine', a living reflection of the value our culture attaches to the idea of the original. In this light, it is ironical to reflect that works of art achieve the status of original only through reproduction. Equally, the idea of the reproduction is most easily defined as the opposite of some kind of 'original'. Yet the cachet attached to the concept of originality is a relatively recent phenomenon. What we now consider as the most characteristic works of the great masters were usually preceded by full-size cartoons and painted *modelli*, which might bear more of the master's own hand than the 'finished' works. These were followed by copies or variations, painted sometimes by the artist himself and often, as it were, under licence within his milieu. In such a sequence of collective effort the idea of a single 'original' is hardly relevant, and even if we decide to privilege a particular part of it, the relationship between the original and the 'reproduction' is far from as simple or mechanical as Man Ray proposed.

'An original is a creation motivated by desire. Any reproduction of an original is motivated by necessity. The original is the result of an automatic mental process, the reproduction of a mechanical process. In other words: inspiration then information: each validates the other.'[1] The mechanism of creativity is itself complex, continuous and collaborative, and the significance we attach to it is a variable qualified by its every manifestation and 'reproduction'.

* Susan Lambert. 1988. 'The Status of the Reproduction'. In: Lambert, Susan. *The Image Multiplied: Five Centuries of Printed Reproductions of Paintings and Drawings*. New York: Abaris Books, pp. 12–35. Edited and reproduced by permission of the author.

Editor's note: Lambert's text was published in 1988. When the author refers to 'our own' or 'the present' century, she means the twentieth century.

The radical change in the attitude to originality which has taken place during the centuries covered by this study has greatly influenced the respect in which reproductive prints are held. In 1480, the artist, whether painter or engraver, saw his job as one of furthering a tradition. His aim was to develop and refine treatments of subjects handed down to him and to pass them on in an improved form to posterity rather than to create new ways of seeing. There was little premium attached to inventiveness and pictures were not meant to be an expression of the artist's personality; any image was likely to reflect an earlier composition and to provide a basis for a later one. Reproductive prints took their place in this chain; they were, like all works of art, more or less close to their sources and not, therefore, basically different in the way they were conceived from the majority of paintings.

Cristofano Robetta, the son of a Florentine hosier who came to engraving through work as a goldsmith relatively late in his development, approached the problem of composition in a way that was typical of artists of ordinary talent at the turn of the 15th and 16th centuries. The overall arrangement of the figures was often derived more or less closely from a known masterpiece but the background was supplied from another source or from the artist's imagination. The extent to which the work deviates from its source largely determines our perception of it as an interpretation; only the respectability conferred by time stops us describing it as plagiaristic, or as a reproduction.

Many subjects had rigidly established conventions for their depiction. This was so for the *Annunciation*. The angel was shown as having entered from the left, kneeling in such a way as to provide a dynamic diagonal suggestive of recent movement. The Virgin, more or less static, was normally placed to the right, the point of culmination of the image. The action had the narrative movement of a frieze, and was arranged on a narrow stage, parallel to the onlooker, as in Filippo Lippi's altarpiece for the church of San Lorenzo in Florence which shows, nevertheless, an advanced understanding of the recently discovered principles of perspective. But these Lippi shows off in the background to the scene rather than by re-designing the whole representation of the subject on a deep stage. That the anonymous engraver used Lippi's painting as his model is clear, not so much because of the similarity of composition but rather because of the faithfulness with which such details as the form of the lectern are followed.

In certain genres it was accepted that an image should be adapted in reproduction to accord with the accepted pattern for that kind of print. This was true of portraiture in the 17th century when the fashion for 'heads' engraved in the form of a bust looking out through a border led, on occasion, to the presentation of three-quarter and even full-length portrait 'originals' in this format. The borders, usually specifically designed for the engraved version, gave the reproductive engraver great scope for form invention and for additions to the iconography often of the greatest importance, far beyond anything conceived of by the 'original' painter. Thus the engravers who promoted the image of the English monarchy in the early 17th century endowed James I with the attributes of Solomon or Augustus Caesar, and even the simplest classical ornament applied as a border to a bust portrait endowed its subject with a similar air of authority. The iconographic language of the engraved border was adopted back into the practice of painters late in the 17th and 18th centuries, so that painted images by artists from Lely to Gainsborough seem to allow a priority to the portrait engraving. Indeed the border became a feature of such splendid elaboration that it was taken up by some portrait painters themselves as decoration for their original compositions.[2]

Even reproductions which acknowledge the source of the image through inscription often show unexpected changes when compared with the so-called original. Wenceslaus Hollar came to England in the retinue of the Earl of Arundel in 1637 and must have been involved with any plans that the Earl had on the lines recorded by Vertue 'to make a large volume of prints of all his pictures, drawings and other rarities'.[3] However when his circumstances changed and Hollar found himself exiled to Antwerp without a patron and in need of money, the etchings he published of the Leonardo drawings from the Arundel collection show the heads grouped in combinations of his own invention. A particularly fine head, for example, is presented as a single study whereas three slighter sketches are merged into one composition.

As late as the 18th century the artist's creation was not sacrosanct. J. G. Huquier, better known as the publisher of sets of ornamental patterns, acquired the plates for Watteau's *Figures de Différents Caractères* between 1739 and 1745, some fifteen years after their original issue by Jean de Jullienne. Accustomed to providing images as patterns for craftsmen, he valued these plates only as reproductions of the unique conceptions of a master so far as this enhanced their value as useful types which could be adapted to many uses. To help them appeal to the current decorative taste he added backgrounds which elaborated the mood of the figures and replaced their distinguished isolation with an up-to-date prettiness. Although printed from the same plates as Jullienne's 'original' reproductions they no longer reproduce Watteau's drawings. The embellishments affect the images so that they have little more in common with Watteau's conception than his own figures had with the genre of single figures he had inherited from the previous generation.[4]

Additional work to the plate can, when the painter and engraver is the same person, transform what starts as a reproduction into the artist's latest statement on the subject making it, in a sense, the prime version. Hogarth's paintings are on the one hand independent works of art yet at the same time carefully worked preparatory studies for the engravings. Equally the engravings, which in their early states reproduce the paintings closely, have an independent life. Never obsessed with reproducing the painting exactly – he did not work from a mirror image and his prints are therefore usually in reverse of the paintings – once work on the copper had begun Hogarth worked from pulls from the plate as much as from the painting. As time passed radical changes could occur clarifying or adding to the message. About twelve years intervened between the initial publication of *A Rake's Progress* and the reworking of its fourth plate. The earlier version shows the Rake on the point of arrest for debt, with his forsaken mistress, whom in an earlier plate he had been shown buying off, offering to bail him out. The later version introduces the idea of gambling as the source of his ruin: the sign of White's, a notorious gambling house, makes its appearance on one side of the street and on the other, a group of boys gamble with cards at the Rake's feet.

The interpretative nature of the hand-formed reproduction at least cannot be denied. Even where reproductions seem intended to present the image faithfully it is surprising how much can be put in or left out. The success of the image in its new form depends unexpectedly on its handling by its conveyor. A comparison between two lithographic reproductions of Ostade's *Artist's Studio* made in the same country at approximately the same date and likely, therefore, to be prone to the same influences, shows how much one individual's version of an original can differ from another's. Forms which are suggested rather than delineated in the tonality and texture of paint are drawn out with considerable variety and discrepancy. In Sir Hubert Herkomer's words 'To interpret other men's work – to render a coloured work in black and white – is a difficult art. To find the black and white that, as it were, underlies the colour, needs a fine sensitive eye.... The interpretation of pictures is an art in itself and should be judged and valued accordingly.'[5]

The nature of reproduction is not however as simply imitative as Herkomer's praise for it suggests. However well or badly a reproduction captures the character of the original, it contributes to our reading of the original. The process of reproduction has the effect of removing the image from its 'original' context, usually reducing its size, and providing it with unforeseen juxtapositions. The result for the onlooker is not only a different experience from that undergone in the presence of the original but an irreversibly changed relationship with the original. This factor shows up most clearly when considered in relation to large decorative schemes like the Sistine Ceiling. Once a composition on a scale that calls for panning the eye, perhaps even also craning the neck, has been comprehended as an image that can be held in the hand or as part of a series of framed pictures on a wall, the struggle to grasp the composition in its larger and less accessible form takes on a different character. Response to the original is tempered by considerations, perhaps only in the subconscious, of how the image lives up to our vision of it in reproduction. The place of discovery is taken by a search for the anticipated.[6]

Designing for the reproductive market

The definition of a reproduction as an image made in emulation of an original is further complicated by the fact that many originals owe their very existence to the demands of the reproductive trade and are, therefore, designs which have a reproduction as their end product.

It is not customary to discuss such images of high status as Dürer's woodcuts in a context of reproduction. Critical attention, however, concentrated on his engravings in the later 16th and 17th centuries, by which time woodcut was often regarded as a utilitarian technique, lacking a direct relationship between the cutter's action and the printed mark. Rather than creating the surface that holds the ink, the cutter creates the voids; the block is pared away on either side of the desired line in such a way as to reproduce it as faithfully as possible. Hans Sachs's verse, which accompanies Jost Amman's illustration of a woodcutter in the *Ständebuch*, described a woodcutter's simple ambitions at the time of its publication in 1568:

> I am a wood-cutter good,
> And all designs on blocks of wood
> I with my graver cut so neat,
> That when they're printed on a sheet
> Of paper white, you'll plainly view
> The very forms the artist drew:
> His drawing, whether coarse or fine
> Is truly copied line for line.[7]

Woodcuts were, as this jingle suggests, most often cut by professional cutters rather than by the originator of a design. Whether Dürer cut at least some of his earlier blocks himself has been much discussed but any cutters he employed would have operated so closely to his instructions, probably following lines drawn by him actually on the wood, as to make any distinction between hands at least marginal. Examination of the cutter's work in Dürer's woodcuts shows, however, the technique developing from a predominantly linear to a basically tonal one. The encasing outlines of the early prints, easily rendered in relief on wood, give way increasingly to the vocabulary of hatchings, flicks and dots executed more easily on metal plates worked in intaglio with a burin.[8] Had Dürer selected woodcutting as the technique most in sympathy with the graphic idea he wished to realise, rather than as the most practical technique in which to mass-produce the desired 'picture' at a price the market would afford, would he have pushed an inherently crude technique to such limits of subtlety?

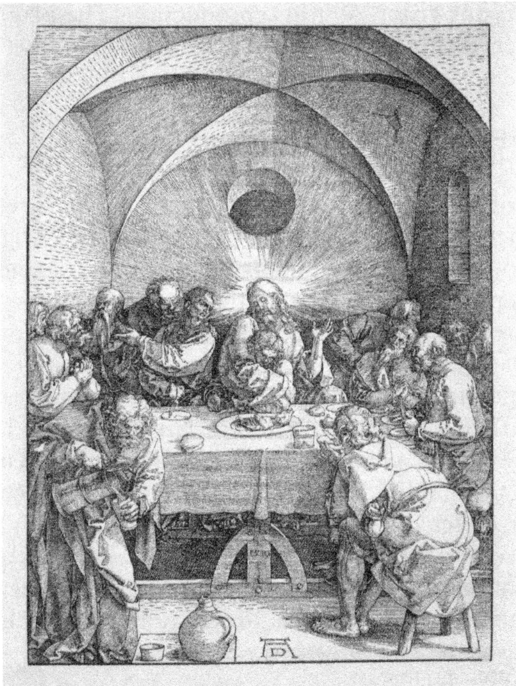

Albrecht Dürer, *The Last Supper*. No 2 of the set of twelve cuts illustrating the Passion of Jesus Christ, known as *The Greater Passion*, published in book form in 1511. Signed with monogram AD and dated 1510. Woodcut. 39.7 × 28.5 cm.

At least in their genesis Dürer's woodcuts should not seem so different from, for example, the lithographs of Thomas Shotter Boys whose plates in *Picturesque Architecture in Paris, Ghent, Antwerp, Rouen, etc.* are acknowledged in the introduction as 'Pictures drawn on stone, and reproduced by printing with colours'. The text makes it clear that the medium of lithography was selected not for any distinctive quality it would bestow on the image but precisely for its capacity to simulate a greater variety of 'original' techniques. We are told that 'The view of the Abbaye St. Amand, Rouen, is intended to present the appearance of a crayon sketch heightened with colour; that of Ste. Chapelle, Paris, a sepia drawing, with touches of colour; the Fish-Market, Antwerp, a slight sketch in water-colours; St. Laurent, a finished water-colour drawing; the Cour of the Hôtel Cluny, an oil-painting'[9] and so on. While the differences are not so apparent to our eyes, the stated intention leaves us in no doubt that the artist was providing what are in essence, if not quite literally, reproductions of his work in unique media for the wider market.

This market was well-established at least by the middle of the 16th century and a very large number of the prints that we now think of as reproductive were made not after independent masterpieces but from drawings made especially for the purpose. Much of Goltzius's work was of this kind. Beginning as the engraver of ornamental frames for the prints of his master, Dirck Volckertsz-Coornhert, he quickly became established independently, acting as his own publisher by 1582 and in time publishing the work of others. His early prints consist largely of reproductions of drawings by contemporaries and although, after a trip to Italy, he turned to the ancient and modern classics as subjects for his own burin, he also provided large numbers of drawings of his own invention for his assistants to engrave. That his drawing of *Lot and his Daughters* was made with reproduction in mind is suggested not only by the existence of a print by Jan Saenredam dated the same year but also because the protagonists in the drawing are all shown as left-handed. With the reversal of the image, which the process of engraving naturally produced, this anomaly was corrected.

Oil paintings were also made for the engraving trade. In England, John Boydell, an engraver turned print publisher who became Lord Mayor of London in 1790, even claimed an attempt to create a British school of painting through the commissioning of paintings specifically for reproduction. He argued that the failure of history painting, the most highly regarded form of art at the time, to flourish in Britain was due to a lack of patronage rather than to a lack of native talent and conceived a business venture to remedy the situation.[10] Shakespeare was chosen as a source of suitably patriotic and dramatic subject matter and paintings were commissioned for an ambitious new edition illustrated with engravings. Profits from the sale of the edition and from large engravings sold separately from the text were intended to finance the painters' fees and the reproduction costs. To start with the venture was a success. Gillray, bitter that his services as an engraver had been turned down, was able with a ring of truth to pillory Boydell as a sorcerer who sacrificed Shakespeare for gain. But fluctuations of commerce were such that Boydell's bankruptcy was avoided eventually only through disposal of the project's assets through a lottery.

Most of the paintings designed for the reproductive trade were not as elevated in subject matter as those that formed the Shakespeare Gallery. More typical were Wheatley's *Cries of London*, a subject well-known in the history of engraving. Fourteen of the paintings were exhibited at the Royal Academy between 1792 and 1795 but before the exhibition of any of them a newspaper 'puff' announced that they were 'intended for the engraver and Schiavonetti, a very ingenious Italian artist, has already began upon those which are finished in a very promising style'.[11] The prints were published by Colnaghi but whether they initiated the project or Wheatley painted them as a speculation to be sold to a print publisher is not clear. Only two of the paintings survive, one a subject that was not engraved until this century and the other a variant on the design engraved as *Gingerbread*. But the stretcher of the latter bears the address of Colnaghi's,[12] suggesting that they were involved at least with that version when it was a blank canvas.

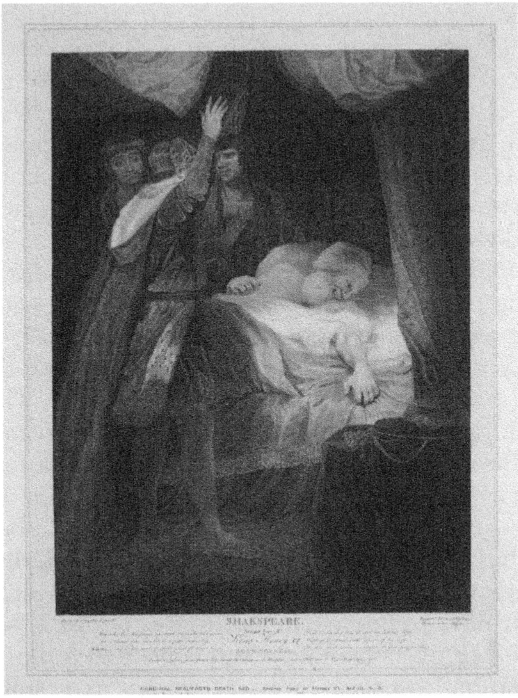

Caroline Watson, *Cardinal Beaufort's Death Bed from the Second Part of Henry VI, Act II, Scene iii*, 1792. Stipple engraving after Sir Joshua Reynolds (PRA), 1792. 56.9 × 40.5 cm.

The second half of the 18th century saw the rise of a large group of artists who made their living by providing designs for the reproductive market. The resulting prints are indubitably what we think of as reproductions but what they produce is of little consequence in terms of Art. The images were desired as something outside the realm of art or as little luxuries for their own sake rather than as a reproduction of a great 'original'. In our own century Margaret Tarrant's name is familiar as an artist, not because her paintings can be seen in our public art galleries but because reproductions of her fairy-filled fantasies have decorated the bedrooms of small children and her images of blessedness have been used as prizes for Sunday School classes for over fifty years.

The 'original' print versus the reproduction

Artists have made what we now consider to be 'original' prints almost since the invention of printmaking but the concept did not gain currency until the 19th century and was not defined until the present century. At a time when printmaking from blocks, plates and stones worked by hand was the only means available to mass-produce a visual image, prints with any relationship with the 'fine' arts were greatly in the minority, for the same means were used to fulfil a multitude of utilitarian functions in the day-to-day life of civilisation. Printmaking as a technique contributed to the economy in a manner analogous to other techniques of manufacture.

The development of photography in the middle of the 19th century had a subversive effect on the engraving trade for it became split into two distinctive and somewhat hostile camps, one 'fine' art and the other 'commercial'. The engravers who aspired to the status of artist had long-standing reasons for wishing to dissociate themselves from reproductive work. Their relatively low standing had been highlighted in England by the attitude of the Royal Academy, which on its foundation in 1768 admitted no engravers as such, Francesco Bartolozzi being described as a painter. Shortly afterwards six engravers were elected as associates but without the right to vote or to teach engraving in the Academy Schools. When in 1812 a committee was set up to investigate the inferior position held by engravers in the Academy, it reported that engraving was wholly devoid of 'those intellectual qualities of invention and composition which painting, sculpture and architecture so eminently possess ... its greatest praise consisting in translating with as little loss as possible the original arts of design'. The committee concluded 'that with such an important difference in their intellectual pretensions as artists, it appeared to the framers of the Society that to admit engravers into the first class of their members would be incompatible with justice and due regard to the dignity of the Academy'.[13] The growth of photomechanical processes gave engravers an opportunity to distinguish not only the subject matter of their work from that of the more commercial end of the trade but the technique also, a development which must have contributed to the Academy's eventual acceptance of engravers on an equal basis as painters and sculptors in 1928.

A pamphlet by Seymour Haden, president of the British Society of Painter-Etchers and Engravers[14] on *The Relative Claims of Etching and Engraving to Rank as Fine Arts*, issued in 1883, shows the ideas with which this kind of printmaker became preoccupied. In it he put forward the biased but prevailing opinion that etching (which among printmaking techniques had been the preferred medium of painters in the past), 'depending on brain impulse is personal' and thus ranks as fine art whereas engraving, tainted by its earlier use as primarily a reproductive medium, is 'without personality and all the attributes which attend the exercise of the creative faculty' and is, therefore, merely a craft.[15] Societies founded to infuse 'creative' printmaking with vitality stressed how the prints they promoted differed from images that used the new technology. For example Théophile Gautier, the critic, appealed to the public in the first portfolio issued by the influential

Société des Aquafortistes founded in Paris in 1861 thus: 'In these times, when photography fascinates the vulgar by the mechanical fidelity of its reproductions, it is necessary to assert an artistic tendency in favour of free fancy and picturesque mood' and subscribers were assured that each impression of the prints sold was an original work of art.[16] A fetish was made out of the variety of effect achieved by different inking of the plate or the use of papers of different absorbency, denying the basic multiple nature of the print. These prints were often issued in an artificial number of states with a large number of proof impressions, first creating the market for something ratified and precious, and then pandering to the collector who saw himself as possessing a particular kind of aesthetic sensitivity in his appreciation of them.

Formal definitions of the 'original' print were not promulgated until the 1960s and then ostensibly to help tax inspectors and customs and trading standards officers to distinguish original work from reproductions so that the former could receive privileged treatment and to protect the public from reproductive work which masqueraded as original.[17] But the importance that the regulations attached to a particular kind of manual involvement with the making of the printing surface on the part of the artist makes it appear in retrospect that they were framed also as a counter-movement by the old guard against a new generation of artists who were finding a powerful and personal means of expression in the photomechanical techniques of popular visual communication, shunned by artists since their invention.

The definition agreed at the Third International Congress of Artists in Vienna in 1960 formed the basis of the definitions adopted in many countries. It focussed largely on technique, stipulating that only prints 'for which the artist made the original plate, cut the wood block, worked on the stone or any other material' could be considered 'originals'. Any loophole of interpretation that this wording provided was tightened up in national definitions. Thus the United Kingdom National Committee of the International Association of Painters, Sculptors and Engravers in 1963 stressed that a print must be pulled from a surface 'predominantly executed by the hand of the artist, either from his own design or interpreting the work of another artist or as a result of collaboration'.[18] This implied that the choice of technique was more important even than the originality of the image which could, if the 'hand' of the printmaker was evident enough, be inherently reproductive. The definition issued by the French National Committee of Engraving in 1965 was even stricter for it excluded 'any and all mechanical or photomechanical processes'.[19] The debate captured the attention of a wide range of artists and became itself a subject for their art.

The definitions also concentrated on such peripheral matters as far as the essential character of any image is concerned, as the size of the edition and the obligatory presence of the artist's signature. Yet as early as the 18th

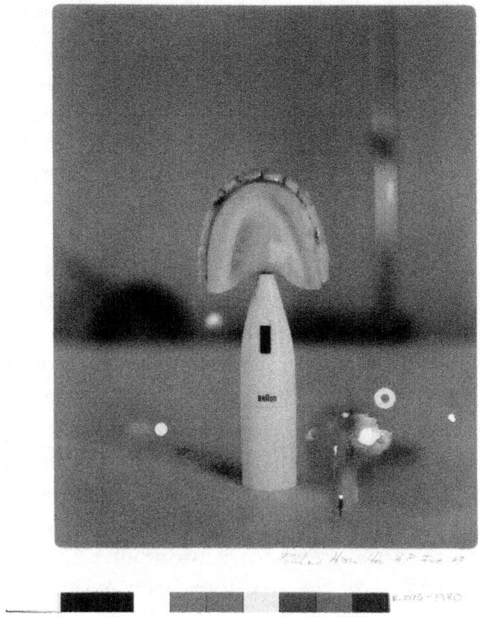

Richard Hamilton, *The Critic Laughs*, 1968. Offset lithograph, laminated and retouched with enamel paint, and screen-print. 59.5 × 56.5 cm.

century publishers of reproductive prints had used the exclusivity of the limited edition to fuel the demand that rarity creates. In France Jean de Jullienne, for example, limited the edition of his 1735 edition of the collected volumes after Watteau to one hundred copies[20] to try to stimulate a market which was already glutted. In England the very real fragility of the mezzotint plate provided a pretext for the sale of 'proof' impressions. It was indeed the reproductive trade which began to rationalise the practice. The Printsellers' Association, founded in 1847 to control the quality of reproductions, issued *A few words on Art which are also words of advice and warning*[21] in the 1880s and distinguished four categories of impression: artist's proofs, proofs before letters, lettered proofs and prints. The artist's proofs were defined not as the term that is usually used today as proofs of 'original' prints outside the main edition reserved for the artist but as a first run of prints from the plate before any letters. The proofs before letters were described as proofs lettered with the names of the painter and engraver but without the title. Each impression of both sorts of proofs from an edition approved by the Association were marked with a unique combination of letters, the former on the lower right and the latter on the lower left corner. All the proofs were to be issued in limited editions although curiously the artist's proofs, which were to be the first to be run off, were often printed in the largest quantity.

In spite of these connections with the reproductive trade the limited edition has become closely associated with the original end of the market. But many editions of reproductive prints continue to be limited and many prints original in concept are now, like reproductions, printed in photomechanical techniques capable of printing any number of equally good impressions.

Both reproductive and original prints have been signed in order to convey approval of a particular impression. The presence of the signature of anyone involved in the production of a print inevitably contributes to a sense of it being the product of an individual rather than of a machine. The presence of the artist's signature suggests the artist's immediate involvement. But since Whistler, who charged double for individually signed impressions of his prints, the print trade has capitalised on the artist's signature to increase the value of the product. The cheaper end of the reproductive trade may append a facsimile signature, and even a genuine signature only proves that the artist actually touched the sheet for a moment.

Only in the last decade has the freedom been extended to printmakers that was won for painters and sculptors early this century by such statements as Duchamp's presentation of standard sanitary fittings and department store wine-racks as gallery exhibits. Duchamp aimed to 'reduce the aesthetic consideration to the choice of the mind, not to the ability or cleverness of the hand'.[22] The 'original' print still has its adherents, but the concept is outmoded. As in the past, original prints and reproductions have the same technology at their disposal. A print is what is claimed for it. How successful it is in relation to its pretensions, is a different issue.

Notes

1 Mundy, Jennifer. *Man Ray: Writings on Art*. N.p.: Getty Publications, 2016, p. 442.
2 For example *Portrait of a Young Boy* by Mary Beale (1632–1697), VAM P 38 – 1962.
3 Vertue, p. 47. For more information see Pennington, p. xxiii.
4 For example, by Claude Gillot and Bernard Picart. See Roland Michel p. 239.
5 Herkomer, Sir H., *Etching and Mezzotint Engraving* 1892, p. 92 and 102.
6 See Benjamin and Malraux for discussion of the symbiotic relationship of reproductions and originals.
7 English translation quoted from D. Rosand, 'Titian and the Woodcut alla Venezia', *Art News*, New York, 1976, p. 56.

8 David Landau pointed this out in a paper at the conference of the Association of Art Historians, 1987.
9 The publisher's descriptive notice is quoted in full in E. B. Chancellor, *Picturesque Architecture in Paris, Ghent, Antwerp, Rouen etc. Drawn from Nature on Stone by Thomas Shotter Boys, 1839*, 1928, pp. xv–xvi.
10 I am indebted to David Alexander who pointed out that 'Boydell's role has been exaggerated since he was a skilled publicist and had to plead patriotic motives when his business became shaky.'
11 I would like to thank David Alexander for bringing this quotation to my notice. It is quoted from Alexander and Godfrey 91 where W. Roberts, *The Cries of London*, 1924, p. 12 is given as the source.
12 The address is Colnaghi Sala & Co., Late Torre No 53 Cockspur Street facing Great Suffolk Street, London, cited from Webster 102. This address is puzzling. Torre gave up business in 1788 when the address was 132 Pall Mall. The firm moved to 23 Cockspur St. in 1799.
13 Royal Academy General Assembly Minutes, 1812, 3, 90–1. See Fox for more information.
14 Founded in 1880, the Society received a royal charter in 1889.
15 Quoted from Newton p. 15.
16 This portfolio is in the Department of Designs, Prints and Drawings, VAM E.1320 – 1624–1901.
17 See *Art/66*, International Association of Art, 1972, p. 7.
18 Quoted from U.K. National Committee of the International Association of Painters, Sculptors and Engravers, *The Definition of an Original Print Agreed at the Third International Congress of Artists, Vienna, September, 1960*, 1963. For more information on the concept of the 'original' print and the definition applied in the U.S.A. see C. Zigrosser, *A Guide to Collecting & Care of Original Prints*, 1966.
19 See O. Grandsire, 'Protection du Createur et de l'Amateur d'Estampes', *Nouvelles de l'Estampe*, 1979, pp. 7–15.
20 *Prospectus* November 1734. Repr. in Dacier & Vuaflart, pp. 40–2.
21 pp. 22–3.
22 d'Harnoncourt, A. and McShine, K. eds, *Marcel Duchamp*, Philadelphia, 1973, p. 275.

References

Alexander, D. and Godfrey, R. T. 1980. *Painters and Engraving. The Reproductive Print from Hogarth to Wilkie*, exhibition catalogue, New Haven.

Benjamin, W. 1970. 'The Work of Art in the Age of Mechanical Reproduction', *Illuminations*, 219–23.

Dacier, E. and Vuaflart, A. 1929. *Jean de Jullienne et les graveurs de Watteau au XVIIIe siècle*, Paris.

Fox, C. 1976. 'The Engravers' Battle for Professional Recognition in Early Nineteenth-Century London', *London Journal*, 2:1, pp. 3–31.

Malraux, A. 1949. *The Psychology of Art, Museum without Walls*, trans. S. Gilbert. New York.

Newton, C. 1979. *Photography in Printmaking*. London: Victoria & Albert Museum.
Pennington, R. 1982. *A Descriptive Catalogue of the Etched Work of Wenceslaus Hollar 1607–1677*, Cambridge.
Roland Michel, M. 1984. *Watteau, an Artist of the Eighteenth Century*, London.
Vertue, G. 1930–55. 'Vertue Notebooks', *Walpole Society Annual Volumes*, 18, 20, 22, 24, 26, 29, 30.
Webster, M. 1970. *Francis Wheatley*, London.

Clare Humphries

Benjamin's blindspot: aura and reproduction in the post-print age*

I. Breaking up with Benjamin

In 2009 I began a doctoral project that set me on a collision course with Walter Benjamin's aura. The project germinated as I handled personal objects passed down from my deceased family and was struck by their potency. Often personal objects are understood as representations of the past, or narrative repositories, but it was my aim to consider what other work objects perform in the present. I began with a 'hunch' (Gray and Malins 2004: 30), that objects have an aura. Not that they possess a physical property, but that an auratic experience can arise when a subject encounters them. I thought of aura as being more than great value, and departed from the widely held understanding of Benjamin's (2007b) aura – that is, the aura of an original work ripe for deconstruction.

Not only did I perceive that objects have an aura, I chose to examine their aura through printmaking, a reproductive practice. This was despite Benjamin's well-known claims that reproduction opposes aura. My decision was impelled by my fascination for how the viewer may recover the sensuous activity of print-based imaging, and also emerged from my belief that printmaking is locked in a permanent conversation with aura that has endured for centuries.

Although I do not identify with the conventional reading of Benjamin, it was difficult to study the notion of aura without addressing his seminal contribution. By proposing a relation between aura and reproduction Benjamin wrote himself and the notion of aura into the history of printmaking. However, as an artist using print media I found his work to be a bone in the throat, something I could neither spit out nor swallow whole. Benjamin's

* Clare Humphries. 2015. 'Benjamin's Blindspot: Aura and Reproduction in the Post-Print Age'. In: *Academic Papers, Illustrated Talks, Themed Panels: IMPACT 9 International Printmaking Conference Proceedings*. China: China Academy of Art Press, pp. 34–9. Reproduced by permission of the author and *IMPACT* Conference.

thoughts on aura seemed impossible to expel given how deeply they are embedded in the history of printmaking. Equally though, I was not able to accept them. Ultimately, I found Benjamin's theory productively irritating, and in this paper I attempt to account for the understanding that I established with his thinking.

Whilst Benjamin's formulation of aura features prominently in printmaking discourse, Kathryn Reeves makes the astute observation that his work is 'often cited, often misunderstood' (1999: 69). Discussions of Benjamin's work tend to rehearse a narrow interpretation of aura that focuses almost exclusively on 'The Work of Art in the Age of Mechanical Reproduction' essay, and simplifies his position to a conflict between aura and reproduction. A far-reaching debate has ensued which questions whether reproduction has led to a loss of aura that Benjamin forecast. In the midst of this debate little attention has been paid to the lesser-known essays in which Benjamin addresses aura, including 'Little History of Photography' (2005), and 'On Some Notes in Baudelaire' (2007a). A close reading of these texts suggests that many aspects of Benjamin's thought – arguably the most productive ones for printmaking – are overlooked in favour of the aura-reproduction opposition. Little is said, for example, about his paradoxical idea that the aura is 'the unique appearance or semblance of distance, no matter how close it may be' (Benjamin 2007b: 518), despite the importance of distance to print-informed discourse (Weisberg 1986: 58) and the fact that '"paradox" can be seen to be a fundamental characteristic of printmaking' (Kirker 2009: 156). Similarly scant attention is given to Benjamin's discussion of early portrait photography in which he conceptualises aura as an inter-subjective encounter (Benjamin, 2005).

Although Benjamin's writings may be misunderstood, his analysis of aura also presents its own complications. Benjamin's writings on the topic are 'ambiguous' (Duttlinger 2008: 81), 'ambivalent' (Benjamin 1991: 141), 'opaque' (Elkins 2003: 97) and 'elusive' (Haxthausen 2004: 50). There is also a 'lack of consistency' (Benjamin 1991: 141) between his various writings as to whether the loss of aura is to be celebrated or mourned.

Another significant complication arises from the fact that Benjamin's utopian model against the aura has failed to materialise. His proposition that reproduction opposes aura has been widely criticised to the point where 'further critique of Benjamin's hypothesis seems unnecessary' (Areford, 2010: 9). Furthermore, reproduction has fallen short of producing the promised critical distance in audiences (Balsom 2013; Sigurdsson 2011), whilst reproductions have actually intensified and elevated the status of their originals, promoted authorship and helped to construct the canon (Mattick 1993). In Sydney Tillim's words, 'far from eliminating the aura and devaluing original artworks, reproduction just as readily creates an appetite for them' (1983: 67). Latour and Lowe (2011) similarly suggest that when an original is copiously reproduced it does not become less auratic but rather more fertile than an original without copies. In fact, they call the copy 'proof of fecundity' (2011: 279).

Putting aside questions about the original and copy, a more substantial issue in applying Benjamin's thinking to printmaking lies in his understanding of reproduction. Put simply, he is concerned with reproduction as the photographic copying of existing paintings and sculptures, not with the multiple as a fine art practice. Benjamin's view of reproduction is therefore far removed from contemporary notions of the multiple-original, and represents a 'simplified and even distorted' (Verhoogt 2007: 19) view of reproductive media. Benjamin fails to acknowledge that copying technologies can produce 'endless ... [and] exquisite variations' (Davis 1995: 381). He also overlooks the potential for different reproductive methods to produce 'completely different objects – a fact which changes their character and function and the way they are consumed' (Tillim 1983: 68). As a result, Tillim (1983) argues, whilst it is possible to use the umbrella term reproduction for processes that have technical similarities, every reproductive process results in a distinctive outcome. In fact, a reproduction 'often develops an "aura" of its own' that 'derives from the transparency of the reproductive process itself' (Tillim 1983: 68).

Although Benjamin overlooks pivotal ideas in reproductive art practice, the problems I have raised with his theory have more to do with how we locate his contribution in contemporary practice. It is important to be mindful that Benjamin's objective is not to provide a theory for art practices that use reproductive methods, and problems arise when we to try to make his ideas perform in this context. In my opinion, Benjamin's key contribution is to draw our attention to the moment of transition between two technologies, 'the transition from one set of representation practices to another' (Bolter et al., 2006: 31). In 'The Work of Art in the Age of Mechanical Reproduction,' for example, he addresses the move from printmaking to photography and then film, whilst in 'Little History of Photography' he deals with the shift from portrait painting to the daguerreotype and then commercialised portrait photography. These movements instigate shifts in the way collective audiences engage with cultural representations that, in turn, change the way aura is experienced. This sheds light on why Benjamin writes in *The Arcades Project* (1999: 365) that different cultural epochs experience aura in different ways. In other words, Benjamin's aura originates by virtue of mechanical reproduction, specifically when shifts in technology bring about change in cultural production.

II. Aura's emergence

A clear example of Benjamin's interest in the transition between technologies appears in his examination of the daguerreotype in 'Little History of

Photography'. Writing ninety years after Louis Daguerre's invention, Benjamin nostalgically laments: 'There was an aura about them, a medium that lent fullness and security to their gaze even as it penetrated that medium' (Benjamin 2005: 516–17). He attributes the mystical aura of the daguerreotype to its characteristic dark tonality and its long exposure that fixed the melancholy gaze of the sitter. The aura of photography was lost, he claims, with the rise of 'commercial, conventional portrait photography' (Benjamin 2005: 519) and its capacity for speed and portability. He concludes the essay with a final tribute to the daguerreotype that emphasises its historical distance: 'the first photographs emerge, beautiful and unapproachable, from the darkness of our grandfathers' day' (Benjamin 2005: 527).

On the surface it may appear that Benjamin holds contradictory views about the relationship between photography and aura. In 'Little History of Photography' he suggests photographs can be the site of aura, whilst in 'The Work of Art in the Age of Mechanical Reproduction' he claims photography can destroy it. However, his perceptions of aura vary depending on whether he is discussing a superseded technology or the latest innovation. Benjamin maintained that the obsolete daguerreotype exudes aura and that commercialised photography destroys it. The daguerreotype is auratic in retrospect because it is irretrievable, or in Benjamin's words it has become 'unapproachable' (Benjamin 2005: 527). What Benjamin failed to anticipate was that, eventually, early twentieth-century photography would also become auratic when compared with its digital counterparts. For a contemporary audience obsolescence now 'endows the film print with the very aura it was once said to destroy' (Balsom 2013: 24).

Benjamin's idea that a photographic aura inheres in redundant technology suggests that aura is associated with a desire for something that is on the verge of loss or appears unrecoverable. When a technology is supplanted we lose hold of one way of representing the world. However, often the superseded technology continues to bring traces of the past into the present, and we may develop new understandings of how it functions. In fact, once a media ceases to operate as the dominant paradigm it may become 'othered, different,' even 'desirable' (Luckman 2013: 251). The digital revolution in the twenty-first century, for example, has been accompanied by a 'renewed aura of the analogue' (Luckman 2013: 251), encompassing vinyl records, letterpress printing and the Polaroid photograph. In our digital world it is the analogue that produces a compelling sense of being close to, yet distant from, earlier modes of representation. Analogue imaging now calls to mind Laura Marks' idea that 'aura is the sense an object can give that it can speak to us of the past without ever letting us completely decipher it' (2000: 81). Objects with aura, Marks says, function like a fetish; that is, they have a power to represent something that is not present by virtue of prior contact with it, and they therefore accrue a social value that is not reducible to commodification (Marks 2000: 80). The aura of an object or media 'inheres in ... the discursive layers that take material form in them' (Marks 2000: 80). It manifests as trajectories through time that are embedded in their materiality.

By maintaining traces of the past in the present, outmoded media evoke Benjamin's more flexible conception of aura as a distance brought close. However, obsolescence is not the only means by which reproductive media produce a perception of a near-distance. The very semiotic structure of reproductive representation engages an interchange between presence and absence. The photograph or the printed impression can never bring an audience into contact with the reality that produced it, and thus the work is always incomplete, pointing beyond itself to something that is missing. Reproductive media operate within the paradox that they perform the presence of an absence.

III. Conclusion

Although it has become 'common theoretical currency' (Duttlinger 2008: 79) to define Benjamin's notion of aura in opposition to mechanical reproduction, in this paper I have attempted to come to a more nuanced understanding of his work. I suggest that Benjamin highlights how reproductive practice changes the relations between audience and image, which in turn, alters the nature of auratic experience. In contemporary culture this has involved the proliferation of aura, rather than its decline. Aura persists in copies and originals, in photographs, film and out-dated technologies. As Douglas Davis writes, 'the aura, supple and elastic, has stretched far beyond the boundaries of Benjamin's prophecy into the rich realm of reproduction itself' (1995: 381).

Perhaps, then, Benjamin's greatest error is to underestimate the capacity of the aura to surface anew, to come forth in new milieus. Had he recognised this he might have seen, as Latour and Lowe (2011) did, that the aura can migrate from originals to copies, and can proliferate in the media he thought would destroy it. He may also have predicted a day when reproductive practices could take on heightened significance and appear as sites of auratic contemplation. If we consider how aura arises (rather than how it declines) a more flexible conceptualisation can emerge which accounts for aura's persistence in reproductive media.

References

Areford, D. S. 2010. *The Viewer and the Printed Image in Late Medieval Europe*. Ashgate Publishing, Farnham, England.

Balsom, E. 2013. *Exhibiting Cinema in Contemporary Art*. Amsterdam University Press, Amsterdam.

Benjamin, A. 1991. *The Decline of Art: Benjamin's Aura, in Art Mimesis and the Avant-Garde*. Routledge, London, 138–49.

Benjamin, W. 1999 [1982]. *The Arcades Project*, ed. Rolf Tiedemann, trans. Howard Eiland and Kevin McLaughlin. Harvard University Press, Cambridge.

Benjamin, W. 2005 (1931). 'Little History of Photography,' in M. Y. V. Jennings (ed.), *Walter Benjamin: Selected Writings*, vol. 2 1931–1934. Belknap Press of Harvard University Press, Cambridge, MASS. 507–230.

Benjamin, W. 2006 (1972). *On Hashish*, edited by Howard Eiland. Belknap Press of Harvard University Press, Cambridge MASS.

Benjamin, W. 2007a (1939). 'On Some Motifs in Baudelaire,' in H. Arendt (ed.), *Illuminations*. Schocken, New York, 50–89.

Benjamin, W. 2007b (1936). 'The Work of Art in the Age of Mechanical Reproduction,' in H. Arendt (ed.), *Illuminations*. Schocken, New York, 40–68.

Bolter, J. D., MacIntyre, B., Gandy, M. and Schweitzer, P. 2006. 'New Media and the Permanent Crisis of Aura,' *Convergence: The International Journal of Research into New Media Technologies* 12 (1), 21–39.

Carvajal R. (ed.), 2007. *Tacita Dean: Film Works*. Miami Art Central and Edizioni Charta, Miami.

Cuttlinger, C. 2008. 'Imaginary Encounters: Walter Benjamin and the Aura of Photography,' *Poetics Today* 29 (1), 79–101.

Davis, D. 1995. 'The Work of Art in the Age of Digital Reproduction: An Evoking Thesis, 1991–1995,' *Leonardo* 28 (5), 381–6.

Duttlinger, C. 2008. 'Imaginary Encounters: Walter Benjamin and the Aura of Photography,' *Poetics Today* 29 (1), 79–101.

Elkins, J. 2003. 'Ten Ways to Make Visual Studies More Difficult,' in *Visual Studies: A Skeptical Introduction*. Routledge, New York, 63–124.

Fischer, N. and El Sani, M. 2013. 'Selected Works: Aura Research'. Website of Nina Fischer and Maroan el Sani, accessed 10 July 2013, www.fischerelsani.net/selected/aura.html.

Gray, C. and Malins, J. 2004. *Visualizing Research: A Guide to the Research Process in Art and Design*. Ashgate Publishing, Hampshire, UK.

Haxthausen, C. W. 2004. 'Reproduction/Repetition: Walter Benjamin/Carl Einstein,' *October* 107, 47–74.

Hughes, A. and Ranfft, E. (eds), 1997. *Sculpture and its Reproductions*. Reaktion Books, London.

Ivins, W. I. 1969. *Prints and Visual Communication*. MIT Press, Cambridge.

Kirker, M. A. 2009. *Printmaking as an Expanding Field in Contemporary Art Practice: A Case Study of Japan, Australia and Thailand*, PhD diss., Queensland University of Technology.

Latour, B. and Lowe, A. 2011. 'The Migration of the Aura: Or How to Explore the Original through its Facsimiles,' in T. Bartscherer and R. Coover (eds), *Switching Codes: Thinking Through Digital Technology in the Humanities and the Arts*. University of Chicago Press, Chicago, 275–98.

Luckman, S. 2013. 'The Aura of the Analogue in a Digital Age: Women's Crafts, Creative Markets and Home-Based Labour After Etsy,' *Cultural Studies Review* 19 (1), 249–70.

Marks, L. U. 2000. *The Skin of the Film: Intercultural Cinema, Embodiment, and the Senses*. Duke University Press, Durham.

Mattick, P. Jr. 1993. 'Mechanical Reproduction in the Age of Art,' *Theory Culture Society* 10 (127), 128–47.

McShine, K. (ed.), 1999. *The Museum as Muse: Artists Reflect*. The Museum of Modern Art, New York.

Morton, C. and Warr, T. (eds), 2012. *Christian Thompson: We Bury Our Own*, exhibition catalogue. Gallery Gabrielle Pizzi, Melbourne.

Reeves, K. 1999. 'The Re-Vision of Printmaking'. In: Parraman, Carinna and Brewer, Emmeline (eds), *IMPACT International Multi-disciplinary Printmaking Conference Proceedings*. Bristol: Impact Press, 22–35. www.uwe.ac.uk/sca/research/cfpr/dissemination/conferences/IMPACT%20PROCEEDINGS%20copy.pdf [Accessed 25 January 2018].

Sigurdsson, G. 2011. 'Towards the Work of Art in the Age of Digital Simulation: Walter Benjamin Revisited,' *Literature and Aesthetics* 11, 51–73.

Skadden, E. 2009. *Collapsing New Buildings*, Master's thesis, Rhode Island School of Design, Rhode Island.

Tillim, S. 1983. Benjamin 'Rediscovered: The Work of Art After the Age of Mechanical Reproduction,' *Artforum International* 25 (1), 65–73.

Verhoogt, R. 2007. *Art in Reproduction: Nineteenth-Century Prints after Lawrence Alma-Tadema, Jozef Israëls and Ary Scheffer*. University of Amsterdam Press, Amsterdam.

Weisberg, R. 1986. 'The Syntax of the Print: In Search of an Aesthetic Context,' *The Tamarind Papers: A Journal of the Fine Print* 9 (2), 52–60.

Weisberg, R. 1990. 'The Absent Discourse: Critical Theories and Printmaking,' *The Tamarind Papers: A Journal of the Fine Print* 13, 8–10.

K. E. Gover

Are all multiples the same? The problematic nature of the limited edition*

I

In Spring 2003, sibling artists Jake and Dinos Chapman exhibited an artwork that they made by defacing a rare set of Goya prints that they had purchased for £25,000. The scenes of violence and brutality depicted in the prints were inspired by Goya's experiences in the Peninsular War between Spain and the Napoleonic Empire. The series is widely regarded as a masterpiece. The Chapman brothers altered the prints by drawing puppy and clown heads on the faces of the war victims. The defaced work is fittingly titled *Insult to Injury*.

Insofar as they intended to outrage the public with their violation of such a rare and important artwork, the Chapman brothers certainly succeeded. But the provocation was tempered by the fact that the artwork destroyed was a multiple. Other, unmolested copies of the same series by Goya still exist; hence, they destroyed an instance of Goya's work, but they did not eliminate all of its instances. Aside from the ethical question of whether the Chapman brothers were justified in destroying the Goya prints, this case also raises some ontological questions: did the Chapmans destroy an artwork, or just the instance of an artwork (treating the set as one unit)? Does the fact that the prints were pulled in 1937, over a century after Goya's death, count against their authenticity as Goya prints, or does his authorship of the work reside wholly in his etching of the plates?

The ontological structure of fine art prints is often understood as a type-token relation. This puts prints in the same category as other art forms in which the work is instantiated by its tokens, such as music, dance, film, and literature. The reason why prints are understood as tokens is that each

* K. E. Gover. 2015. 'Are All Multiples the Same? The Problematic Nature of the Limited Edition'. *The Journal of Aesthetics and Art Criticism* (JAAC) 73 (1): 69–80. Edited by the author. Reproduced by kind permission of *JAAC* and Wiley.

impression within an edition counts equally as an instantiation of the work. Because multiply instantiable art forms have no single object that can be pointed to as *the* artwork, the ontological questions multiply in kind. We wonder what, exactly, constitutes the artwork, and how we can determine which instances count as successful iterations of the work. We might wonder whether it is even appropriate to understand multiples as ultimately pointing back to one single abstract object, the 'type,' that counts as the artwork proper.

Fine art prints are importantly different from other kinds of multiples because their production is tied to a physical process involving a production artifact (the template) and a detailed and highly technical process involving paper, ink, and press.[1] This raises the question of what 'the artwork itself' consists in when we consider the case of the limited edition fine art print. Is it the matrix prepared by the hand of the artist, the print pulled from it, the relation between print and plate, or the edition? Or is 'the artwork itself' an abstract object, the type of which the impressions are the tokens? This leads us to the counterintuitive notion that fine art prints give us access to, but are not themselves *the* artwork. Nicholas Wolterstorff endorses this view when he remarks that 'In looking at a print one sees two things at once, the print and an impression thereof. In listening to a symphony one hears two things at once, the symphony and a performance thereof.'[2] Printmaking and the non-physical arts thus have a common problem when it comes to determining just where, exactly, the artwork is, and what it consists in when there is no single physical object to point to as the work.

The aim of this inquiry is to determine whether printmaking is best understood ontologically as analogous to a work-performance relation. Are prints the visual analogue of symphonies? My motivation for pursuing the comparison of printmaking to music is twofold. First, because relatively little has been written on the ontology of fine art prints, our use of an already developed body of scholarship will help us to gain some traction on the question. Second, within the existing literature on the ontology of prints, there seems to be a persistent confusion about the difference between what makes a print an artwork, and what makes it a genuine or authentic artwork, signed or in some other way ratified by a given artist.

And yet it is not at all obvious that we can simply apply the insights on the work–performance relation in music to such a profoundly different medium as printmaking. For example, an important difference between prints and performances is that prints within an edition are (usually) expected to be identical in look and in status. There is no hierarchy of prints within the edition. Performances, on the other hand, are viewed as creative, interpretive acts. Variation is expected and even valued, so long as it occurs within the parameters of the score.

Both Nelson Goodman and Nigel Warburton raise the comparison between prints and performances only to reject it.[3] I begin by assessing their arguments against understanding prints as analogous to musical performances. Then I turn to the contrasting view offered by Mag Uidhir in one of the few recent contributions to the literature devoted to the ontology of printmaking. I point to some problems with his argument that illicit and accidentally pulled prints can still be instances of the work in question if they are sufficiently similar to the authorized impressions. Here I appeal to David Davies's distinction between P-instances and E-instances in order to understand the conflict between Warburton's overly restrictive print ontology and Mag Uidhir's self-described 'permissive print ontology.'[4] I conclude by suggesting that prints are indeed ontologically unusual insofar as they occupy an intermediate position between pure multiples, of which there can be an unlimited number of tokens, and singular artworks, which consist of one physical object.

II

Once we look past the bias of ordinary usage, it appears that the structure of the relation between a plate and the resulting print does indeed share some important common characteristics with that of a musical work and the performances thereof. First, the printmaking process seems to mirror in certain respects the composer–performer model. Artists very often rely on master printers to execute their editions. This is true even of artists who identify themselves primarily as print artists. The production of the template can be seen as akin to the composition of the score. The master printer is like the musician who interprets the score and instantiates the work.

Second, with the exception of monotyping, prints are inherently multiple. One plate can generate many instantiations of the work. Third, in both cases there is a 'robust causal relation' between the artist's creation and the final product. Whether it be a musical composition or a copper plate, the resulting aesthetic object is shaped and determined by the artist's work, which is not encountered directly by the audience, but only indirectly through its performed instantiations.

There is widespread agreement that in order for a performance to count as an instantiation of the work, the intentions of the artist must be fulfilled, intentionally so, and more or less accurately. However, in the case of music, no one requires that the composer personally ratify or authenticate any given performance in order for it to count as a genuine instantiation of the work. But the conventions surrounding printed artworks are different. Whereas anyone competent enough, and with the proper intention to do so, can play Rachmaninoff's *Prélude in C Minor*, prints are more difficult to instantiate: not only does one have to gain access to the artist's template and the requisite tools and skills for pulling a print from it, but even if one has a print, it is not clear if one also has a genuine instance of the work, or just a derivative exemplar thereof. Not only the artworld, with its venal concerns about provenance and market value, but also artists and theorists expect prints to be approved by the artist in order for them to count as genuine. Usually the artist's signature is the marker of this certification. This widespread practice seems to speak against the status of prints as analogous to musical performances because they require an extra level of oversight from the artist: she or he has a direct hand not only in determining the causal process, but the final product as well.

But simply pointing to the fact that the customs surrounding prints and musical performances are different in our culture is not yet enough reason to reject the comparison. It may be that our cultural practices are inconsistent from a philosophical point of view. And yet theorists differ on the question of why, exactly, we should not consider prints as ontologically analogous to performances. Goodman admits that there is a surface similarity between prints and musical performances, insofar as both are inherently multiple.[5] However, he denies that they are, in fact, analogous. What is decisive for Goodman is that a musical composition is inherently abstract, and is embodied by notation. Well-established conventions establish what counts as a correct translation of that notation into sound. A genuine instance of a composition can be determined simply by comparing the sonic event to the score to check that they correspond. A print, on the other hand, is genuine for Goodman by virtue of the history of its production: it is an authentic print if and only if it has been created through contact with a particular physical template.

On the printmaking side of the equation, Warburton has criticized Goodman's assertion that having the right history is sufficient for ensuring that something be a genuine print. He points out that Goodman's definition would permit smudged or otherwise defective prints taken from the original matrix to be counted as instances of the work. And yet, Warburton points out, 'This is implausible. Even with print-making, history alone does not determine authenticity: there are some minimum standards of print-making quality which have to be met for any print to count as a token for the particular type in question.'[6] Goodman found it impossible to demand that there be standards of correct correspondence between a print and its plate in the same way that we can judge the accuracy of a performance to the score. This is presumably because musical notation functions as a symbolic system with a highly developed set of conventions governing correctness. An artist's prepared template, on the other hand, is a material object. When we ask whether a print is actually a 'Rembrandt,' we want to know, at the very least, whether it was pulled from the plate Rembrandt prepared, and not an imposter. And yet Goodman's understanding of the causal connection between plate and print seems crude. He seems unconcerned with the look of the print, despite the fact that this is ultimately the embodiment of the artist's intended artwork. Just because a template is a physical object, and not a linguistic one, does not mean that we cannot apply 'minimum standards of print-making quality' to putative instances of a printed artwork. A wrinkled Rembrandt should not make the cut simply because of its source.

Even with this correction to Goodman, however, Warburton is unwilling to regard prints as analogous to musical performances. Whereas Goodman was too permissive in his standards for what counts as a genuine print, Warburton's rejection of prints as performances comes from the opposite direction. For him, no set of established conventions could ever be accurate enough to ensure that a print (he is concerned specifically with photographic prints) is a genuine instance of the artist's work. In every case, he says, the artist must approve the print, even if the print is visually indistinguishable from an already-approved print.[7] While the cynic might claim that such narrow standards for certification are motivated by the desire to restrict edition size and to thereby ensure higher prices, for Warburton it is a matter of the artist's moral rights:

> There are never any guidelines for distinguishing the contingent from the constitutive in photographic printmaking. Consequently only the photographer can determine that a print is of sufficient quality for it to count as an authentic print. Anyone else can only hazard a guess, and may in the process seriously damage our understanding of a photographer's style, and thus his or her possibility of creative expression.[8]

For Warburton, what makes a print genuine is not simply its source, but its certification by the artist. This is particularly important because not only photography, but the production of prints generally, is a mechanized process, often accomplished by technicians and not the artist himself or herself. The artist's approval of the prints is a way to compensate for this mechanization and distance from the artist's hand. For Warburton, the artist's authentication of the print is an epistemic, not an economic, issue: only the artist is in the position to know whether a given print satisfies his or her intentions for the finished artwork.

Warburton's account lends theoretical support to standard artworld practices surrounding prints by living artists. Yet his insistence that 'even if two prints were virtually (or even actually) indistinguishable, only the one certified by the photographer would count as genuine or authentic,' seems implausible on epistemic and ontological grounds.[9] To claim that the artist has the unique ability to determine whether a given print is authentic, even if the print shares the same causal history and looks exactly the same as others in the edition, enters dangerously into the realm of mystification. It is as if each print requires the special blessing of the artist in order to transform it into an authentic work of art. While it is certainly accepted practice nowadays for artists to restrict the size of their editions, even in the age of digital prints where no special darkroom manipulation is used and identical prints can be made at the touch of a button, it is also fairly obvious that this kind of manufactured rarity is in place because it helps to keep the prices up and enables artists to make a living.

But the question is whether such a practice is defensible on purely ontological grounds. On the one hand, Warburton is right to note that prints pulled from the same plate can vary widely in appearance. Many variables are involved in the process, and the production of fine art prints is not a matter of simply dropping off a prepared matrix at the shop to be processed just as we used to drop off rolls of film to be developed in the days before digital cameras. At the same time, however, there is something about Warburton's principled insistence on the necessity of the artist's sanction that seems disingenuous. If two prints are visually indistinguishable and share the same history of production, what difference should it make to their ontological status as a genuine iteration of the work whether one has the artist's official approval and the other does not? While the economic motivations for this practice are obvious, from an ontological point of view it seems arbitrary and threatens to violate the nature of printmaking as an inherently multiple medium – an attempt to turn prints into the equivalent of unique paintings.

III

In one of the only recent essay-length considerations of print ontology, Mag Uidhir offers a striking account that stakes out a third path apart from Goodman and Warburton's approaches.[10] It attempts to preserve the inherently multiple nature of printed artwork while at the same time respecting the importance of artists' intentions in the execution of the work. Best of all, he avoids the mystification and preciousness that threatens Warburton's demand for artist authentication of each print. Mag Uidhir's argument is striking not only because of its extended and imaginative treatment of an overlooked subject matter, but because his conclusion contravenes standard artworld practices and assumptions governing genuine prints.

Mag Uidhir's argument hinges on his definition of 'relevant similarity,' by which he means that the prints in question 'share all constitutive appreciable properties in common in virtue of sharing a causal history. Two prints share a causal history if and only if they are printed from the same template (e.g., a particular etched copper plate), by the same process (e.g., intaglio), onto the same support (e.g., paper).'[11] Mag Uidhir argues that prints mistakenly included in the edition, or made after the artist's death, or made illicitly without the artist's permission, are nevertheless artworks so long as they have the correct causal history. While prints pulled from forged, degraded, or altered plates are one thing, correctly executed prints from authentic, intact plates are artworks, even if the artist has not authenticated them. Mag Uidhir provocatively dismisses the significance of the artist's final oversight and approval by arguing that 'relevant similarity' is 'exhaustive' in determining the artwork-status of the print. This is not to deny the importance of the artist's intention in creating an artwork and determining its disposition. The upshot of his argument is that those intentions can be fixed ahead of time by the artist in her preparation of the matrix and stipulation of the 'right sort of way' to pull the print. No extra layer of ratification by the artist of any particular print is necessary in order to guarantee its status as an artwork – if it has the same constitutive appreciable properties as the prints that have been approved. Once the artist determines the conditions for 'relevant similarity,' and so long as those are followed, any print is an artwork because the artist's intentions have indeed been respected. While he does not belabor the comparison, we can see that Mag Uidhir, perhaps alone among theorists, treats the relation of a print to its matrix much as we understand the relation of a performance to a musical composition. So long as the performance is faithful (or faithful enough) to the score as set by the composer, then the performance counts as an instance of the work. No further ratification by the artist is needed.

But before I pursue the question of whether or not prints should be regarded as ontologically analogous to performances, I must point out two problems with Mag Uidhir's argument. The first is that his definition of 'relevant similarity' does not ensure that the artist's intentions will necessarily be fulfilled. Mag Uidhir defines 'relevantly similar' prints as those that 'share all constitutive appreciable properties in common in virtue of sharing a causal history.' He further explains that by 'constitutive appreciable properties' he means those 'relevant descriptive physical (internal) features of the print (for example, color, shape, size) as well as those relevant descriptive nonphysical (relational) features (for example, aesthetic, semantic, representational features) supervening on (in part determined by) those relevant descriptive physical (internal) features of the print.'[12] What is confusing about this definition of 'relevant similarity' is that the term 'relevant' is employed three times, which seems to beg the question of what is and is not relevant when considering the ontological status of a print as art. But it seems clear enough from this definition, as well as from the hypothetical examples of accidental and illicit prints that Mag Uidhir provides, that for him the 'constitutive appreciable properties' are fixed by the physical features of a print and its causal history: it has to have been pulled from the right matrix in the right sort of way. This is what enables his imaginary thieves and bunglers to make prints that lack the artist's authentication but nevertheless share in the same ontological status as those in the edition: they were made in the same exact way and look exactly the same as the signed prints.

Against Mag Uidhir, let us imagine that a certain contemporary artist with an affinity for conceptual art decides to make an edition of prints called *Only on Tuesday*. The concept behind this piece is that only prints produced on Tuesdays are eligible for inclusion in the edition. Suppose the trial proofs were produced on a Friday, and various colors were tested until the artist found just the right combination. Once the artist found that one of the proof prints had the right look for the edition, it was signed by the artist and labeled 'B.A.T.,' which signifies that all of the prints in the edition should match it. And yet, because the B.A.T. proof was not pulled on a Tuesday, it does not fulfill all of the artist's intentions for the edition, which is that they not only be visually identical to the B.A.T. proof but that they be pulled on a Tuesday. According to Mag Uidhir's stated definition of 'relevant similarity,' a print pulled on Monday or Wednesday could just as well be included in the edition with no loss to the fulfillment of the artist's intentions for its constitutive appreciable properties. Would the prints pulled on a day other than Tuesday be artworks? Sure, in one sense they are. But they are not genuine instances of *the* artwork *Only on Tuesday*. It seems that Mag Uidhir would either have to reject those sorts of avenues for artistic expression, or he would have to revise his definition of 'relevant similarity' to provide for the particularities of artists' intentions. In this case, he would have to say that being pulled on a Tuesday is part of the requirement for 'relevant similarity.' But this is not how he defines 'relevant similarity.' Being pulled on a Tuesday is a nonphysical feature of the print that does not supervene on its relevant physical features. If Mag Uidhir wants to add to his definition of constitutive appreciable properties 'and any other special requirements that the artist has for the print,' then we seem to be on a slippery slope that leads right back to Warburton, for an artist could stipulate (as many in fact do, or at least assume) that only those prints that he or she authenticates count as genuine instances of the work. Many artists would balk at the idea that they have to accept as equally genuine prints that have been pulled illicitly or accidentally from their plates, unless the concept of the work involved precisely such an open approach to the edition. Mag Uidhir is of course aware of this; the implication of his argument is that these artists are being irrational.

Perhaps they are. But I would reply that an artist does not have the power to confer or withhold the status of 'artwork' to a print with his signature, but rather the status of 'member of the edition,' which means the artwork intended for publication. This leads us to the other problem with Mag Uidhir's argument, which is that it commits the fallacy of equivocation. He trades on the ambiguous use of the designation 'artwork,' which in some cases refers only to signed or otherwise certified authentic artworks of a certain artist, and in other cases can mean the simple ontological designation of something as an artwork as opposed to, say, a credit card statement, passport photo, or notebook doodle. For example, when discussing the status of prints that may be 'relevantly similar' but are not included in a given edition, Mag Uidhir articulates a version of the standard view:

> Whether or not a print is an artist proof or a trial proof or part of an open or limited edition is largely intention-determined, that is, what purpose the print was intended to serve, especially whether or not the print was intended for public reception. Surely such distinctions must be preserved *when considering prints as artworks* [emphasis mine].[13]

Contrary to this view, Mag Uidhir claims that the conditions of 'relevant similarity' are sufficient to guarantee that a print is an artwork, even if the print lacks the artist's sanction. He argues that the artist's intention that it be included in the official set of prints to be published – the limited edition – is irrelevant to the print's status as an artwork: 'An artist's intention that a print be an artist proof is no more relevant to that print being an artwork than is the artist's intention that a print be used as a napkin to absorb a spill.'[14] And yet the phrase 'considering prints as artworks' exploits the ambiguity in our understanding of that term. Indeed, if we are talking about the descriptive designation 'is an artwork' in the deflationary sense of simple ontological designations, then the artist's proof is doubtless an artwork. But then so are the smudged, discarded prints and the pristine proofs tucked away into master printers' archives. The question of whether something is an artwork in this most basic sense does not satisfy the further question of whether it is an artwork in the other, more restricted sense of that term. After all, artists sometimes make artworks that they detest and reject as 'their' artworks. While certainly the hated creation is still an artwork, and a genuine one in the sense that it did issue from that artist, insofar as it falls short of the artist's desired intentions, for whatever reason, we usually do not consider it to be a work of that artist. And yet that is the issue: we are not concerned with the status of the artifact qua artwork, but whether it is an authentic instance of the artwork as intended by the artist. In other words, there is a difference between claiming that an unsanctioned print is *an* artwork, and claiming that it is *the* artwork, that is, an authentic instance of the artwork, no different than the ones the artist intended to publish. Mag Uidhir argues that, all other things being equal, the artist's intention that this print and not that one be included in the edition is irrelevant to their ontological status as art.[15] But we can easily grant their art status in the more general sense while still withholding our assent that such unauthorized prints are necessarily part of the artwork as conceived by the artist. And it seems to be this latter, stronger claim that Mag Uidhir wants to assert.

Mag Uidhir's permissive print ontology has the undeniable appeal of avoiding the mystification that surrounds our cultural obsession with authenticity and provenance. It respects the inherently multiple nature of the printed artwork. But it does so at the expense of ensuring that the artist's intentions actually will be fulfilled in the finished print. The assertion that a 'relevantly similar' yet unintentional, illicit, or posthumous print is nevertheless an 'artwork' begs the question, because it fails to tell us whether it is a *legitimate instance* of the artwork in question.

One way to understand the difference between Mag Uidhir and Warburton is to say that they are operating with different conceptions of what constitutes an instance of an artwork. Davies argues that the philosophical discussions surrounding multiples tend to conflate two distinct senses of the term 'instance.'[16] Sometimes we understand an instance of a work to be one that gives the audience epistemic access to the work: 'E-instances' offer an adequate experience of the work. On the other hand, we also speak of instances – as opposed to mere copies – as having a certain history of production, a provenance. Davies calls these 'P-instances.' Using Davies's distinction, we can see that Warburton and Mag Uidhir are employing different standards for what counts as an instance. Mag Uidhir emphasizes that even illicitly or accidentally produced impressions of a print will be adequate E-instances. Warburton, on the other hand, counts only as legitimate those impressions that are ratified P-instances, even if the unsigned impressions are perfectly adequate E-instances.

This conflict is particularly salient in the case of limited edition fine art prints because, unlike symphonies or novels, they do not have indefinitely many instances. What makes limited edition prints problematic but also so interesting is that they are multiples, but not pure multiples. Mag Uidhir is right if he means to suggest that prints do not undergo some mystical transfiguration from nonartwork to artwork simply because the artist deigns to affix her signature to it. However, the question whether unsigned impressions are authentic instances of the work is a different issue.

It seems to me that one of the artist's tasks when creating an edition of prints is to set the size of the edition. While the prints within an edition are each authentic instances of the artwork, the edition as a whole is also, in an important sense, *the* artwork, that is, the one that the artist intended to publish. While edition size may seem arbitrary and irrelevant when interpreting fine art prints, a couple of considerations may remind us of its salience: first, from the perspective of the viewer, the membership of a print to an edition is visually reinforced on the print itself, when it is signed and numbered as, say, five out of an edition of fifteen. Thus when we look at a print, we are constantly reminded that it is one instance of the work out of a larger number of (possibly) extant instances. Moreover, from the perspective of the artist, the completed edition is the end result of the creative process that generated the prints. The entire set of prints is the finished 'work.'

The limited edition places prints in a middle position along a continuum between the singular work of painting or sculpture, on the one hand, and the infinitely repeatable tokens of performables. It may seem that membership of one print rather than another within an edition is arbitrary and irrelevant if the print was pulled in exactly the same way and looks exactly the same. Would it really alter the artwork if one more print were added or excluded from the authorized set? Perhaps not. But art making in any medium consists of numerous decisions by the artist that affect the final disposition of the work. Some of these decisions may indeed be arbitrary. And yet that is what makes the work *the work*: the artist's intention that it be so, and his or her ratification of those decisions as the ones that form the work's constitutive appreciable properties.

IV

The phenomenon of the limited edition is an awkward case for the philosopher, who must confront an art form that is inherently multiple but not purely so. There are times, however, when this ontological uniqueness can be gainfully exploited, as the Chapman brothers did with *Insult to Injury*. The Chapman brothers' decision to use a set of rare, mint-condition Goya prints as the fodder for their vandalism was precisely calculated to obtain its intended effect. By defacing a multiple, they were able to elicit the public's horror at the intentionally vulgar destruction of a treasured masterpiece, while at the same time avoiding the condemnation that would have ensued had they violated the only existing instance of Goya's artwork. If they had targeted a unique painting by Goya, or the only remaining set of prints, the destruction would have been so great that it would have made it difficult if not impossible to appreciate the defacement as having any artistic merit. On the other hand, if the Chapman brothers had chosen to deface facsimile copies of the Goya etchings, or had used some other common, mass-produced set of images rather than a relatively precious object, their act of violence would have been stripped of its power. And that is precisely what is so compelling about *Insult to Injury*: what seems initially to be a crass, gratuitous act of violence against an artwork turns out to be just the point. The images of senseless suffering and needless brutality depicted in *The Disasters of War* are made viscerally real for us again by the Chapmans' defacement of those rare, precious prints. By exploiting the properties of the limited edition, the Chapmans made art lovers feel the impact of their violent gesture, while ensuring that their 'insult' was not insurmountable.

Notes

1 Wolterstorff, Nicholas. *Works and Worlds of Art* (Oxford University Press, 1980), p. 95.
2 Wolterstorff, p. 41.

3 Goodman, Nelson. *Languages of Art* (Indianapolis: Bobbs-Merill, 1986), pp. 118–19; Nigel Warburton, 'Authentic Photographs,' *British Journal of Aesthetics* 37 (1997): 129–37.
4 Uidhir, Christy Mag. 'Unlimited Additions to Limited Editions,' *Contemporary Aesthetics* 7 (2009), www.contempaesthetics.org/newvolume/pages/article.php?articleID=527 [Accessed 25 April 2017].
5 Goodman, pp. 118–19.
6 Warburton, p. 133.
7 Warburton, pp. 133–4.
8 Ibid.
9 Warburton, p. 134.
10 Mag Uidhir, 2009.
11 Ibid.
12 Ibid.
13 Ibid.
14 Ibid.
15 Ibid.
16 Davies, David. 'Multiple Instances and Multiple "Instances",' *British Journal of Aesthetics* 50 (2010): 411–26.

Frieder Nake

Printing plates and pixel matrix: the mechanisation of memory*

It is really no more than a trivial observation, something of a truism: cultural progress – if we are looking for it – would most likely be found in the outward manifestations of people's physical skills and abilities. To put it coarsely, but no doubt correctly: such progress lies in the mechanisation of the capacity for work. What presents itself to us as technology, is congealed, preserved, dead labour,[1] labour in a zombified state.[2] At the push of a button, it can be set in motion and stopped again. In between, it sometimes achieves tremendous effects.

[…]

Our topic is the image. What is more, our topic is the memory that can be taken on by a printing plate, a piece of material. More specifically, my topic is the dissolution and volatilisation of the printing plate into symbols that have become weightless, which it would indeed be impossible to weigh: the *pixel.*

[…]

When contemporary artists choose lithography or etching as their expressive medium, they still face the task of producing a 'printing plate', i.e., preparing a wood block, metal plate or polished stone so that it can be used to print (in comparatively small print runs). We will briefly discuss how memory is relevant to this process.

Other people these days produce prints digitally. We will also discuss this process, drawing attention to the transition from the printing plate to the pixel matrix[3] under the aspect of material memory. Our question will be:

* Frieder Nake. 2010. 'Printing Plates and Pixel Matrix: The Mechanisation of Memory'. In: *im:print 2010: zustandsprotokolle aktueller druckgrafik / journal for the state of current printmaking.* Reproduced by kind permission of the author, *im:print* and Springer Verlag. Edited by Schneider, Michael, Maurer, Philipp and Lebzelter, Georg, Vienna: Springer Verlag, pp. 124–35. Translated into English by Brainstorm, Vienna.

what can 'material memory' be and what will become of it (memory) in the course of the algorithmic revolution?

Memory

We possess the ability to commit actions and experiences to memory, as shown by the obvious fact that we remember the actions and experiences lived through in the past. That ability to remember is what we call memory. Memory is the basis of our constant efforts to give meaning to our lives and to life in general. Memory is nothing other than *lived-through life*.

Today, the comparison between memory and a *storage unit* stands to reason. Every book is a storage unit. We can describe this storage function quite precisely. On their pages, books store printer's ink in certain shapes. We call these shapes 'letters, numbers, punctuation marks'. Our ability to remember helps us determine the meanings of the various shapes. The meanings are not intrinsic but rather assigned to these shapes by the social collective. The process of identifying such assigned meanings is called reading.

Books store shaped and organised printer's ink from which we create meaning with the help of our memories. We do not always succeed in doing so, which suggests that our memory has gaps. It is obviously a gross oversimplification to compare human memory with a storage unit. If we insist on doing so, then it must be a type of storage unit in which the stored substances change, are lost, grow or shrink. Not so with the book, the analogue storage based on printer's ink, and even less so with the digital storage unit of a computer.

In fact, human memory has a great capacity to forget. Since the actions and experiences that become components of our memory come from our lived-through life, memory is also bound up with life in progress. All the insights offered by neurobiology and the cognitive sciences concerning the structures and functions of the brain and memory are merely foisted upon them based on theory and empiricism. It may be justifiable, useful and practical for a while, in a certain context – but it will never provide the final explanation. What is offered to us there may be a way of speaking on how we communicate, but (unfortunately) no more.[4]

André Leroi-Gourhan speaks of memory as a basis of intelligence 'in which chains of actions are recorded.' He fails to describe, however, what that basis might be or how it does the recording.[5]

Memory and social memory

Memory is primarily a human attribute. We are not interested, here, in whether animals also have memory. They no doubt do, but the extent to which their memories are comparable need not concern us here.

In writing, we possess an important technique of creating an external memory function. As creator of culture, mankind creates many such material forms of memory. To cite just one similar prominent example: the clock, which represents the materialisation of the image of time.[6]

We experience time or, better put, we create it by living. Our time is nothing other than our life. Time is what forces its way from our life into our memory, what remains of our life there and leaves a trace. As with any materialisation of an individual living process – no matter how similarly it may take place in other individuals – all of its specific, unmistakable, unique distinguishing features are extinguished in its materialisation. The materialisation always resorts to a general scheme, procedure or process.

The clock adopts, in mechanical form, the uniformity that lived-through time is assumed to have, an incessant flow in an infinitely uniform stream moving forward. The repetition of what is apparently always identical is shown by the clock's circular dial and rotating hands. Brilliant. Our image of time is shaped by the mechanical clock.

This is a characteristic of material memories: the mode and form of materialisation is reversed in the course of history and, from the externalisation of one aspect, it becomes the core and essence of the phenomenon.

One powerful materialisation of social memory was the project of the French Encyclopaedists. Under the leadership of Denis Diderot and Jean Le Rond d'Alembert, seventeen volumes of texts and eleven volumes of illustrations (copperplate engravings) appeared between 1751 and 1781, followed by four supplementary volumes, another volume of plates and, finally, two index volumes.[7] That formidable undertaking relied on the assistance of 178 contributors, some of them noted intellectual giants of the French Enlightenment. The 'entire knowledge of humanity' was to be presented 'in a well-thought-through anthology and critical presentation'.[8] The century was to be permanently recorded with all of its science, technology and art: an externalised expression of a society's intrinsic nature.

Each individual is familiar not only with the ability to remember but also with the often embarrassing failure of memory in specific instances. Often these are gaps in the memory of the individual: particular facts, figures, data. We try to avoid them by recording the individual memory in layers of social storage and through technical storage in documents and computer technology. 'Building machines that can remember everything' is a dream of the material memory divorced from the individual.[9]

This precisely, we can say without hesitation, has very little chance of ever coming true. 'Remembering everything' would presuppose that everything is stored. The very thought smacks of imperialistic if not outright fascistoid musings.[10] Of course, machines can be set up and integrated into an organisation of slaves that record and store a great deal. It may be so much that it seems like 'everything' to us in test questions. This 'everything', however, would just be 'the great deal' that only appears to be 'everything' because of the mechanical setup.

What can be memorised in a storage unit of an (electronic) machine is always limited to the calculable; the situation and context of chains of action are taken into account only to the extent that they are calculable, if at all.

It is true that the programmability of the trans-classical machine raises it above the single-purpose machinery of classical mechanics. Nonetheless, everything that can be gained from the computer is implicit in the notion of the *semiotic engine*.[11] The material that is processed by computers is *a priori* of a semiotic nature. Yet the sign processes must necessarily be reduced to signal processes on computers, thereby stripping signs of their *essential* characteristic: their interpretability.[12]

Historically, Leroi-Gourhan distinguishes between five different stages of development of the social (i.e., collective) memory: oral tradition, written tradition, communication through index cards, mechanical recordings and electronic recordings.[13]

The sequence of these five stages simultaneously expresses the formidable acceleration and reproduction of knowledge (or better put: of data[14]) that has accrued to the collective memory. In the 19th century, at the latest, it had become so extensive that an individual memory was no longer capable of absorbing it. As a result of the extent it had attained and the continued acceleration of its growth, it was no longer possible to create order within the documents of collective memory themselves. Rather, order had to be created outside of them using tools such as directories, anthologies, lists, tables and indexes, which form a meta-layer supporting social memory. This is the stage that Leroi-Gourhan calls the index card stage.[15]

With such cards, the hand-operated machine was first established in collective memory, giving rise to media to manage access to content-bearing media. Punch cards made mechanical processing possible. The electronic storage of the data encoded and recorded on punch cards led to the current stage of digital processing. Such storage requires algorithmic description of the processes of searching, finding and representation, paving the way to our current stage of the global digital, algorithmic collective memory that has now become interactive and networked, to boot.

Printing plate

Now it is time to turn back from our excursus on externalised memory to our more restricted subject: the printing plate that became a pixel matrix.

In our excursus, we set the scene for this transformation, which happened not so long ago.

A printing plate is an object made of a material, such as wood or metal, that is set up to stain a sufficiently large piece of paper with ink when pressed down in close contact with the paper. The printing plate must first be coated with ink, which it then transfers to the paper when it is pressed down onto it. This process can be repeated as many as several hundred times, depending on the mechanical properties of the materials used.

In this sense, the printing plate has a material memory – indeed, it is such a memory. The graphic-iconic and textual-symbolic forms that are engraved into the printing plate are reproduced in the act of making close contact with the paper. It is a perfect 1:1 analogy, a faithful representation, including the lateral reversal.

Viewed from the angle of memory, we are dealing here, as could be expected, with a form of mechanical storage, a simple if not to say primitive side of memory. We do not know the extent to which such storage is involved in the motivation- and interest-driven human memory. It is true that brain researchers assume that we have cerebral neuronal networks in order to perform such storage, and it is hard for us to imagine that memory could exist at all without some form or 'storage' or 'filing'. All the same, the biochemical or other nature of the engrams that could be hypostasised as the contents of human memory remains a matter of speculation.[16]

While the individual human memory owes its current state entirely to the living body's processes of practical experience, mechanical memory – if we decide to call it that – is produced by working people, as the result of their work, i.e., an artefact.

Regardless of how a printing plate is produced and regardless of how experience is deposited in the human brain through encoding: the 'recall' of a memory in the case of the printing plate is based on the mechanical process we described above, whereas human memory relies on processes that are almost completely beyond our conscious control. In such processes, the essential factor is often an event, a keyword, a minor detail that stands in practical connection with the recalled content but generally concerns it rather indirectly. The most important thing, however, is that the contents of a memory are generally recalled differently by different people and triggered by different clues. They depend on the situation and context.

The printing plate does have one remote similarity with human memory, however: it wears out materially through use, precisely because it is mechanical in nature. In a manner of speaking, longterm use makes the printing plate 'forget' (the impressions fade). The iconic form of the printing plate memory, its analogous character, is quickly worn away and can efface the memory of form almost completely. Form is what the material memory of the printing plate 'remembers'.

Pixel matrix

The material memory of the printing plate, which is virtually one with it, corresponds to the stage of handicraft activities. It is true that the division of labour has already become established throughout such activities, yet Horst Janssen and his printer Rudolf Frielinghaus – and other such teams – are deeply dependent on one another. There is a certain melancholy about wear through long-term use that, no doubt, makes an essential contribution to the aura of printed works produced using traditional techniques. Great craftsmanship and expertise are required of both participants: the graphic artist and the printer.

It is precisely this relationship that is blown away in the digital age. The analogue model of the printing plate etched, cut or engraved with direct artistic skill is replaced by the digital model of the *pixel matrix* designed, implemented and encoded with indirect algorithmic care. Gone are the lines which convey the delicate harmony of will, eye and hand, gone is the inking that let a worried yet confident creation of tension shine through; expressive impetus and quivering directness have become a thing of the past, replaced by the pixel and series and arrays of tiny picture elements.

We have grown accustomed to thinking of images as composed of picture elements. We overlook the fact that we invented them in order to control images mechanically, generate them automatically, set them algorithmically into motion that we ourselves can physically control. So much loss and pain – so much gain and joy!

It is true that if only picture elements are to be used, if pixel matrices are to replace images, then pixels must be products of thought with systematically encoded locations with x and y coordinates as well as an encoded tristimulus value of red, green and blue components. The intractability, inexorability and standardisation of this analysis may send shivers down our spine, but we must admit that the resulting demolition leads to a doubling of the image that opens up radical new inroads to the image and makes a new way of thinking about imagery both possible and necessary.

Thought no longer guides a hand armed with a tool over the printing plate material to reshape it through its partial destruction, so that it finally helps produce something surprising. These days, it is the hand that helps thought to find its *algorithmic* formulation. The formulation is not a formula, but it compels thought to be much more precisely formulated than before. The graphic idea must be thought through in detail and perfected in the mind far more than ever before. The removal of the hand from the direct production of the work has led to a rapprochement and penetration into the class of drawings, to which one but many others too belong.

An individual work, which is present in the 'here and now', becomes less interesting. It is being replaced by the class of works that tends to be infinitely extensive and in which the works are similar to one another in a certain precisely definable manner. This is true even if the similarity is not visible but rather notional.

What is to be printed no longer comes from a skilful hand, guided by thought, in a confrontation with resistant matter. It comes instead from the execution of the programme written and tested in advance, which was assigned or interactively supplied with input data – a process that, once the intense intellectual efforts of encoding have been completed, is displayed automatically at dizzying speed by an algorithm.

In our topic of material memory, which can no doubt claim the pixel matrix as one of its own, an interesting shift has come about. The printing plate was always one and no other. Its memory consisted of an essentially unchanging but replicated print, No. 17 out of 100, for example. The pixel matrix, however, gives rise to doubling. The image that we are just contemplating is merely the result of the programme run. The programme can then be run a second, third and fourth time, with slightly or radically different input data, perhaps with different probabilities[17] for the selection of random numbers. With clever programming, one and the same programme is without further ado capable of generating a wide variety of structurally similar but visually strikingly different graphics.

Even if the configuration of the pixel matrix is held constant, its appearance can still be transformed through various interpretations of its tristimulus codes.

The removal of the shaping hand from the printing plate to be engraved enhances the mental, conceptual level. A concept is described rather than work being performed. In contrast to conceptual art, the concept is described algorithmically. This means that it has become an *executable* concept, a concept that can produce the coded form (pixel matrix) of a work through interpretation by the machine's processors.

Do we not intuitively perceive that what is happening here is a bit more like memory? Here, too, there is an absence of forgetting, that important faculty of human memory which computers, with their merciless storage units, can only dream of (if they were capable of dreaming). Yet the faculties of the mechanical – and thus material – memory are far less trivial than those of printing plates. We will suggest the reason for this in our final section.

Volatilisation and doubling

Knowledge and information congeal into data in the storage units and processors of the semiotic engine of the computer. Freed from all contexts and interpretations, data are merely what is left over of knowledge and information when also deprived of all context. In technical terms: signals.

In semiotic terms: data. From the economic and political point of view, the historical task of the computer is the *mechanisation of brainwork*. Brainwork has always been socially defined, however. It belongs to a stage in the development of the forces of production in which all work is performed in a socially mediated form.

The causes and objectives of brainwork may be tangible in socially occurring processes and situations, even in things. Yet they can only become objects of brainwork if the actual processes are represented by models, i.e., signs. All brainwork becomes signs and real processes can be manipulated only in the form of signs and sign processes. Moreover: to ensure their mechanisation, the sign processes must be reduced to syntactic and then to calculable processes. It is therefore indispensable for a process of mechanisation of brainwork to begin with a reduction to calculable signal or data processes.

It is in this form that the context-laden sign processes appear at the periphery of the computer, as soon as they are channelled through the computer's input ports. The results then appear at the output ports in such extremely reduced form. As soon as they are made perceptible to human senses as signals in texts, images or sounds, as a simulation or computer animation, the signals that we observe once again shoot out semantics (information) and pragmatics (knowledge). We are unable to resist. But if we think about it carefully: meanings are directed at the signals only through us, through our constructions and interpretations.

The signs, reduced to signals, so that they can be processed by algorithms, the signs and their processes are what all people have to deal with when they programme computers or use programmes. Since we cannot help but interpret the sign processes and sign bodies that present themselves to us, the signs immediately regain their full scope through our senses. Yet they do so, as I would like to put it, in a *doubled form*: because *we* interpret the signals simultaneously and interlocked with one another, as the processors do in parallel with us. The sign becomes an *algorithmic sign*: a sign in a permanently doubled interpretation: by man and by machine.

It goes without saying that the computer's powers of interpretation have no freedom. In diametrical opposition to people, who are free in their interpretations, the processor defines the one and only meaning that may be possessed by the programme code. The computer's interpretation proves to be a determination, a definition. If everything is defined correctly, the code is simply executed. The algorithmic sign therefore possesses, besides the signal in the form of which it first appears and besides the object that is represented by the signal, two interpretants: the intuitive interpretant of humans and the determined interpretant of the processor.[18]

The doubling of objects and processes on the computer into computer objects and external objects goes hand in hand with the fluidisation and volatilisation of objects and processes. For in their semiotic form, which is the only one that counts here, they are generally in a constant flow. Individual works are only instances of the class they belong to and stand for. As instances, they are replaceable at any time by others. The algorithmic sign constructed inside the computer is a signal from the computer's internal point of view.

I am in the habit of speaking of the 'subface' of images. This is intended to remind us of the following: when the image is displayed on the monitor of the periphery, our immediate interpretation of the (calculable) 'subface' merges with a (perceptible) 'surface'. Printing or any other method of making things perceptible generates this sensory counterpart. The digital image is a unit composed of the 'subface' and surface. The surface is for us, which is why it is perceptible. The 'subface' is for the processor, which is why it is calculable. Perception generates unending processes of interpretation. Calculation generates a single process of determination.

The pixel matrix is therefore a calculable and volatile form of mechanical-material memory. Congealed in the corresponding algorithm is the mental work, which had required living labour when printing with the old printing plates. In the process of their mechanisation, the relationships are turned topsy-turvy. They are so topsy-turvy that people keep talking about mechanical intelligence, the creativity of machines, and so on. In reality, however, it is all just like with the printing plate, only a hundred years later.

Notes

1 As Karl Marx called it in an apt metaphor.
2 In other words dead, but in such a way it (the work) can be shaken awake without returning to life.
3 Which amounts to the same thing as 'from analogue to digital'.
4 Recommendable in this regard is Daniel L. Schacter, *Searching for Memory. The Brain, the Mind, and the Past*. New York: Basic Books 1996.
5 Leroi-Gourhan, Andre. *Hand und Wort. Die Evolution von Technik, Sprache und Kunst*. Frankfurt: Suhrkamp 1980, p. 276.
6 Leroi-Gourhan, op. cit, p. 312.
7 Manegold, Karl-Heinz (publisher). *Die Encyclopédie des Denis Diderot. Eine Auswahl*. Dortmund: Harenberg 1983, p. 253.
8 Manegold, op. cit. p. 255.
9 Leroi-Gourhan, op. cit., p. 331.
10 Quasi the biological variation of data retention, which has run aground a bit in the Federal Republic of Germany.
11 Nadin, Mihai. 'Semiotic machine'. In *Semiotic Encyclopedia Online*, www.semioticon.com/seo/S/semiotic_machine.html (March 3, 2010).
12 Nake, Frieder. 'The Semiotic Engine. Notes on the History of Algorithmic Images in Europe'. *Art Journal* 68, 1 (Spring 2009), pp. 76–89.
13 Leroi-Gourhan, op. cit., p. 323.

14 I associate knowledge with the pragmatic dimension of the fully revealed sign. In the case of machines, however, we are merely in the syntactic dimension, where we encounter signs in the form of data and signals.

15 Leroi-Gourhan, op. cit., p. 329.

16 According to a book by Daniel Schacter (1966), the German biologist Richard Seman (1859–1918), who met with a tragic death, introduced the terms *engram* (permanent change in the nervous system as the result of practical everyday experience over time), *engraphy* (inscription of information into the memory) and *ecphony* (activation of the memory) in his book entitled *Die Mneme*, which was published in 1904.

17 To put it more precisely: with a different distribution function.

18 For the processor, two of the components of the sign coincide: the object and interpretant of the sign. The determined interpretant is none other than the object, i.e., the thing that is designated by the sign.

Georges Didi-Huberman

Opening up an anachronistic point of view (1997)*

> As always, current artistic developments *(ein aktuelles Kunstgeschehen)* led to a construction of an appropriate history. [...] What had seemed meaningless up to now acquired significance from the latest efforts of contemporary artists; [...] since what is effective in history *(das geschichtlich Wirkende)* is always a consequence of the immediate present.
> Carl Einstein, *Negro Sculpture*[1]

Empreintes precede or follow us, wherever we go. Many escape us, many fade away, sometimes even under our very eyes. Some merely glimmer, others dazzle us with their brightness. Others still are long gone, but something tells us that they remain, deeply buried, and could still be discovered if either interest or methodology impels us to do the right archaeological digging. Some, on occasion, even seem to follow us. Many will survive us. Given that *empreintes* are many and varied and differ so greatly one from the other, can they really be said to constitute a genre? Indeed, we tend to

* Georges Didi-Huberman. 2008. 'Ouverture sur un point de vue anachronique'. In: *La ressemblance par contact – archéologie, anachronisme et modernité de l'empreinte*. Les Éditions de Minuit: Paris, pp. 9–23. © Les Editions de Minuit. Reproduced by permission. Translated by Miranda Stewart, PhD.

Editor's note: A limited selection of footnotes and references has been provided. For full references, please consult the original chapter.

Translator's note: The title of the book from which this chapter derives (*La ressemblance par contact – archéologie, anachronisme et modernité de l'empreinte*) can be translated as: *Resemblance Through Contact – Archaeology, Anachronism and Modernity of the Imprint*. However, the word *empreinte*, the subject of Didi-Huberman's book, can mean variously 'print', 'imprint', 'impression', 'trace' or 'mark'. While Didi-Huberman uses this term predominantly to denote sculptural casts and cast objects, he also extends its use to cover associated procedures and other forms of impression. There is no single English term that encompasses the denotative range of the French word *empreinte* in terms of the material objects it covers, or its potential metaphorical connotations. Hence the translation retains the original French *empreinte*.

refer to *empreintes* in the plural, precisely because each one appears only to exist as an *individual instance*: because each source for an *empreinte*, each object that imprints itself is different, each location in which an *empreinte* is made (depending on materials, texture, malleability of the substrate) is different, because each action, gesture, procedure whereby *empreintes* are created is different.

In these circumstances, can we really talk about *empreintes in general*? It would be impossible, even absurd, to try and compile an inventory. We could, albeit in vain, try to identify certain categories. However, they would spawn infinite subcategories, and, in any case, offer just too many individual features, 'one-off' *empreintes*. In that case, all I could do in this essay would be to identify some particularly striking or '*problematic*' isolated examples, so to speak. These would offer evidence of regularities and particularities, of 'symptoms' of what might, I would hope, prove to be an emerging issue, an incipient '*problematic*' development, provided we keep an open mind and are not constrained by any predetermined criteria. In any case, it would clearly be a mistake to banish *empreintes* to the realms of a tidy past as a *prehistoric condition* of images (whether this condition is perceived as rooted in the dark ages or alternatively in some Arcadian past). It would be no less a mistake to 'anchor' them in a falsely specific, falsely definitive present moment of a *modern,* or even post-modern condition in the visual arts.

We must, so to speak, play with both these timeframes if we want to think the *empreinte*. Let us call this the anachronistic point of view. It does not seek to deny history, quite to the contrary. However, we should be well aware that no history of *empreintes* exists as such. No history exists for this specific *process*, essentially an expertise built up over the ages, that can be applied to an extremely wide range of materials and techniques; no history exists for this theoretical paradigm that underpins so much abstract thinking, particularly in relation to such basic notions as the sign, trace, image, resemblance or genealogy; no history exists for this practical and theoretical procedure which has governed the formal and operational decisions of so many artists, particularly in the twentieth century.

When no such history exists, our only option is to take an anachronistic point of view which is essentially a moment, an *experience* of anachronism. Not so much to replace history but rather to create a history for a moment that it had neglected hitherto. Carl Einstein adopted this particular approach when he introduced African sculpture into art history as a new object. He made an appeal to the anachronistic moment of statuary art proper to Cubism at that time – i.e. 'contemporary' to 1915 – an art which had hitherto been reduced to the mere status of an ethnographic or functional object.[2] Walter Benjamin coined the expression 'dialectical image' to refer to his important hypothesis about the anachronistic nature of works of art that have not acquired the 'readability' of history. In these works, he said,

'Past meets present in a flash [...]: it is not something that happens, but an image that flashes up' – images in which past and present shift, transform, mutually challenge each other to create something that Benjamin called a *constellation*, a dialectical configuration of disparate elements.[3]

However, Aby Warburg's work clearly offers the first compelling analysis of this anachronistic juncture of disparate elements that come together at the precise moment when a visual object raises the issue of its place within the history of art. In a famous essay on fifteenth-century Florentine portraiture, Warburg made so bold as to introduce into the notion of Renaissance (a term still misinterpreted as meaning some kind of return to the 'purity' of ancient times), a fundamental element of impurity. This impurity related precisely to the procedures for creating *empreintes* (in the sense of making moulds). An impurity of this nature requires historians to turn their hand to anthropology and problematise, to some considerable degree, their own models of the development, of tradition and 'progress' of the arts. This impurity became suddenly apparent in the expressive *modern* beauty of the faces painted by Ghirlandaio, the cold plaster of *Roman* funerary masks, *Etruscan* terracotta and *mediaeval* wax votives. Different times jostled for place, warred with each other in these images – the signs and symptoms of impurity. This allowed Warburg to go beyond the all-too comfortable 'tradition of iconology', for which he is customarily known, and forge a new model of temporality, a contemporary model akin to Freud's – a complex model of what he called 'survival' or 'afterlife' (Nachleben).[4]

Empreintes now appear in their own right, at very least, as anachronistic 'things' – they are clearly a visual and tactile 'evocative present'[5] of a past that continues to 'work' and transform the substrate in which it has left its mark. When procedures for making *empreintes* are employed by artists, they are bound to create temporal complexity, and this must be explored anew on each occasion. An anachronistic point of view – over and above traditional historicism – should seek to reveal this very complexity; reveal the dynamics of the 'afterlives' involved; describe how, in a work produced by casting, the *ancient* nature of a particular expertise meets *current* practice to produce, as in a flash, a constellation, the 'dialectical image' of an anachronistic object, or to use a more Nietzschean term, an *untimely* object. We should be attentive to Carl Einstein's proposition: start from the 'current situation' and analyse how 'the contemporary artistic process has created', from its own excursions into anachronism, a 'history', a potential history of the *empreinte*.

Consequently, our starting point has to be the 'current situation'. But what precisely is this situation? Everyone would appear to agree that it is in 'crisis', some cynically harping on about the end of values as we know them, others lamenting a decadence, the loss of everything we know, and using this to call for a 'return to the real values' of yesteryear. An utterly tedious and somewhat distasteful discussion. If, indeed, it is true, as Georges Bataille has said somewhere, that all issues essentially come down to the 'question of the division in time', then we should examine, in discussions such as these, the particular *temporal models* which sanction the use of words such as 'crisis', 'death', 'loss' and 'decadence'. Leaving aside value judgements, a *particular notion of origin* is what, in my view, effectively structures that dualism whereby the anti-modernism and post-modernism of our 'current situation' are placed, with striking symmetry, in opposition to each other.[6]

A salient example of this symmetry, and one which, indeed, takes us right to the heart of the problem of *empreintes*, can be seen in the universal interpretation of Walter Benjamin's famous text on the 'The Work of Art in the Age of Its Technical Reproducibility', which first appeared in 1936.[7] This is, without doubt, an outstanding, but exceedingly complex, disturbing and contradictory text; it reflects a tension typical of Benjaminian thought that can only be grasped by constantly confronting it with itself. However, this text is most frequently reduced to a very trivial (and indeed historically incorrect) argument: the technical reproducibility of images, particularly their photographic reproducibility, is argued to attack the very core of art as a notion, namely its uniqueness; and to have eliminated all the qualities of the 'original', all its aura, all its cultural value ... Reproducibility – according to this argument – becomes a *mechanical* sign, the 'sign of the times' of twentieth-century art.

This summary alone simply juxtaposes the two antithetical positions that I mentioned above. The first consists of extrapolating a *loss of origins* from Benjamin's 'decline of the original', and consequently of meaning in general. This requires us to superimpose a metaphysical notion, namely that of origin, in the traditional sense as criticised by Derrida, onto the technical reality presupposed by the original.

This assumption of a loss of origins – even though this loss is said to start with Rodin – is intended to support a *post-modernist position* which seeks to silence all discourse about 'meaning', 'value', 'humanity' and 'form' in general.[8] The second point of view makes the same extrapolation but negatively, this time *to lament a loss of origin*, and consequently of 'meaning', 'value', 'humanity' and 'form' in general (hence its obsession with the supposed 'anything-goes' attitude and particular hatred of Derrida's works in all shapes and forms). This nostalgia for origins encapsulates an *anti-modernist* perspective designed to reduce all the modern 'inauthenticity' of inhuman 'technical reproducibility' to silence.[9]

The distinction between these alternative positions is too symmetrical – insufficiently dialectical – to be truly relevant. It is partly the fruit of trivial theorising, philosophical truisms and factional cherry picking. It is in striking contrast, it should be said, to Benjamin's own view. When he advanced his hypothesis of a 'decline of aura', he also argued that aura would survive within reproducible images themselves.[10] Indeed Benjamin had, in 1928, suggested *rethinking the concept of origin* along lines which were totally different to those he is assumed to have held. A metaphysical origin to be deconstructed, an origin which, according to post-modernist critics had been lost, an origin to which an uptight anti-modernism constantly harked back – it is all one and the same origin, and every jot as trivial: it is the same *origin-as-source* that Benjamin lambasted in the neo-Kantianism of Hermann Cohen, that Marc Bloch, in turn, would go on to lambast in the methodological framework of *The Historian's Craft*.[11]

Benjamin, however, was not averse to entitling his 1928 work *The Origin of German Tragic Drama*. Origin-as-source had been replaced meanwhile by another, differently relevant notion, for which Benjamin had used the image of an 'eddy-as-origin', as a sort of fluid sign, an internal catastrophe within the development of the future: a leap, a *crisis of time* which happens in the rhythms of destruction and survival, of a Now and a Then. This is the *eddy-origin* postulated by Walter Benjamin in all his work.[12] It is not unrelated to what later would be defined by the author of the *Arcades-Project* as a 'dialectical image'.[13] In short, in this definition, an origin is not a 'thing' from which everything derives: it is more an anachronism, a process of dialectical departure, an interruption of history itself, an *opening up* which is both wounding (disfiguring) and revealing (truth-bearing).[14]

We should therefore, urgently, redress the manic or depressive effects wrought on art history by a fairly rudimentary reading of Benjamin's work on the technical reproducibility of images. By seeking to 'open up' an anachronistic point of view – one that is neither archetypal nor modernist, nor even post-modern or anti-modernist – I am simply refusing the current avenues offered by art criticism. Indeed, for our very subject we can do no less: is the process of the *empreinte* one of *contact with an origin* or one of *loss of origin*? Does it demonstrate the authenticity of presence (as in direct physical contact) or does it, on the contrary, demonstrate a loss of uniqueness contingent on the possibility of its reproduction? Does it generate uniqueness or mass production? Is it characterised by having an aura or by being one of a series? Resemblance or dissimilarity? Identity or anonymity? Is it deliberate or random? Does it signal desire or mourning? Does it possess form or is it formless? Is it the same or different? Familiar or strange? Does it entail contact or distance? ... I would say that an *empreinte* is a 'dialectical image', an explosion of all the above: something that is as related to *contact* (a foot sinking into the sand) as it is to *loss* (the absence of the foot in its impression); it is as related to contact with loss as it is to loss of contact. This explosion forces us to rethink certain temporal models in the case of *empreintes*. The, often unreflective, use of these models has led to particularly hardened positions in debates about aesthetics in what we might call the 'current situation'.

However, if we 'start from the current situation', we must take account not only of a certain discourse but also confront it with the objects that it claims to portray. Indeed, there is one which, from all points of view, acts as a common denominator, a cardinal point on which all main lines of friction converge. It is to be found in Marcel Duchamp's work which is studied and cited even more extensively than Benjamin's on the technical reproducibility of the work of art.[15] It is felt even more powerfully to be at the crux of the debate, not only about twentieth-century art, but also about the work of art in general.

Can we still view – can we still exhibit – *Female Fig Leaf*? This small galvanised plaster object, made by Duchamp in 1950, is now extremely familiar to modern art specialists. It has become undeniably polyvalent, and capable of being shown by turns as a sexual, paradigmatically erotic, form,[16] and as an example of a 'frozen paradigm', in other words, something 'much more fatal than anti-form' itself.[17] It is said to be the negative imprint of female genitalia. However, the merest glimpse would tell you that it bears so little resemblance to these parts that any prurient viewer – ever keen to see every detail, the actual thing it represents – would not give it a sideways glance. In the eyes of the historian, on the other hand, this object is simply an example of the well-known erotic component of Duchamp's work; as an *empreinte*, as a direct imprint of reality, it is not unrelated to what is most fascinating, and yet exasperating, in Duchamp's work, namely the *readymade*.

From this moment – the minute that the very word passes one's lips – this small plaster object is immediately caught in the vice of a new symmetry, similar to the one I have already described: a dualism juxtaposing two values customarily taken from current knowledge about Duchamp, two interpretations from that twentieth-century moment that is assumed to be the *origin of the loss of origin*, namely the moment of the *readymade*. The first point of view consists of *positing the loss of origin* which Duchamp is argued to have consummated in his 'killing' of 'traditional skills', namely the age-old conditions of artistic labour: *the object* is replaced by the *phrase* – a phrase which confers artistic status on 'anything'. *Doing* is replaced by the *uttering* of a kind of law – a 'law of modernity [which] says only one thing: anything goes',[18] thereby opening up a disconcerting, highly paradoxical field for aesthetic reflection.[19] The second point of view consists not only of *lamenting the loss of origin* supposedly initiated by Duchamp, but also of holding his 'non-work', his 'disastrous legacy' up to obloquy.[20] The *anything-goes* attitude, seemingly proffered as a 'law of modernity', becomes, in circumstances such as these, a justification for condemning a work as 'invalid', for an outburst of aggressive disgust, for a rejection tinged with resentment.[21]

Here again, the very shape of the debate – revolving, as it does, around the notion of 'anything goes' – becomes an epistemological barrier. It prevents us from taking the debate any further. Worse still, it prevents us from seeing clearly, and almost obliges us *not to look* at this *Fig Leaf* which, nonetheless, has not yet revealed either the substance of which it is made, nor, indeed, how it has been made. Whether implicitly or explicitly, this reduction of Duchamp's work to a single idea – a ratifying phrase, a conceptual 'intention' – relieves us of the need to look.[22] When this same work is reduced to the 'stuff and nonsense' of 'anything goes', we are compelled not to look, and an object such as *Female Fig Leaf*, for example, is rendered utterly *un-viewable*: aesthetically invalid and morally obscene. However, the obstacle to viewing, in both these cases, is not unrelated to the issue at hand, *the empreinte*. There is nothing to view because there is no formal invention, and there is no formal invention because the object is merely a borrowing, a reproduction, a simple imprinting of reality. There is nothing to view because there is no skill, no artistic work, and there is no artistic labour because there is only a simple *empreinte*, a mechanically reproducible imprinting of reality. There is no work of art to be considered, because there is merely an *empreinte* – a non-work par excellence.

If we are to view this supposed 'non-work', namely *the empreinte*, and try and accord it the consideration it intrinsically deserves, we must also 'set off from the current situation', but proceed in a different direction. Set off, namely depart, leave, in the sense of that perpetual motion that Benjamin saw in all true historical thinking: 'Brush history against the grain'.[23] By this he meant to construct history within the ever-changing perspective of an anachronistic point of view. It is striking to see to what extent the 'current situation', in the history of contemporary art, is still shackled to a particular methodological isolationism, which admits of very few exceptions, despite the work of Meyer Schapiro and Leo Steinberg. On the one hand, the history of contemporary art is kept at arm's length by a strand of conservatism that is terrified of the anachronistic ability of a present moment that is capable – as Carl Einstein and Walter Benjamin have both shown – of making objects emerge from 'eddies', objects which have their true origins in the past. On the other hand, contemporary art history and criticism remain at arm's length from an enduring past, clinging to reductionism, terrified of the anachronistic ability of a past that is capable – as Aby Warburg has shown – of presenting objects originating in the present as having an afterlife.

In current critiques of modernism, such as the 'loss of origin' consequent on the development of technical reproduction, and the 'loss of origin' due to Duchamp's legacy, scholars are clearly unaware that they are perpetuating a time-honoured, strictly *academic* tradition. *Modernism*, before it was associated with Greenberg and discussed by art critics, was associated with Vasari. Vasari was effectively the first to have systematised, in the sixteenth century, the concept of *moderno*, and elevated it to the driving force behind a governing aesthetic, a historical discipline (namely art history itself) created for this particular purpose, and art institutions (namely academies of fine art), also created to give social coherence to all the foregoing.[24]

Broadly speaking, the issue is to assess to what extent *serially producing an object* can be seen as tantamount to destroying its authenticity and aura. This question is at least as old as Vasari himself, a man who blithely overlooked the role of techniques of reproduction in the emergence of authentically 'modern' sculpture.[25] Also as old as Vasari is the question of knowing to what extent '*producing*' or *exhibiting a serially produced object*, as Duchamp did, can be seen as tantamount to destroying artistic skills as such. Indeed, Vasari failed to mention the serially produced nature of Ghirlandaio's work or the *readymade* veil used by Donatello to cast the bronze for his *Judith*.[26] Both share the same, very old, dividing line that underlies all such issues: the distinction between *the liberal and the mechanical arts*, the first of which guarantee authenticity, uniqueness and aesthetic qualities and the second, which – after a radical shift in mediaeval thinking – is rejected by Vasari's humanism on the grounds of serial production, multiplicity and a lack of aesthetic qualities.

More specifically, this distinction involved differentiating between two types of technical procedure: *imitation* procedures – where *imitazione* is, as argued by Vasari, a portmanteau word for the artist's entire 'métier', alongside the notion of *invenzione*, and certain *reproductive* procedures which are 'mechanical', outside artistic 'knowledge' and 'métier' in the modern (Renaissance) sense of the word. It should now be clear why no history of the *empreinte* exists in the visual arts. Vasari had to reject techniques for making *empreintes* in the area of non-artistic reproduction, of artisanal non-intervention. Current norms, which do not permit classification of objects produced by moulds as 'intellectual works', where objects such as *Female Fig Leaf* fail to enjoy the *copyright* or legal protection afforded to 'art works',[27] are merely a throwback to the Italian *academic* debates of the sixteenth century.

Consequently, any history of *empreintes* must be read against this backdrop of five centuries of censorship of our history of art, understood as a 'humanist discipline'. It is hardly surprising that the finest analyses of procedures for creating *empreintes* come from anthropology and prehistory, two disciplines well acquainted with anachronism which makes them better placed to 'read history against the grain'. We effectively need to juggle two timeframes – the historical past and the present moment. We need to ask 'recent works by sculptors', starting with Marcel Duchamp himself, *to open up the Past* to the anachronism of objects that have been neglected by the history of art; and to ask the historical past, starting with prehistory itself, *to open up the Present Moment* to the anachronism of objects that have been neglected by art criticism. These objects are the result of sedimentation, of an anthropological 'depth' into which we must try, albeit arbitrarily and on a small scale, to probe.

Notes

1 Einstein, Carl. 1915, translated by Charles W. Haxthausen and Sebastian Zeidler, 'Carl Einstein' in: *October*, Vol. 107 (Winter, 2004), pp. 124–5.
2 Ibid. See also Didi-Huberman, G., 1993b, pp. 23–5; Loraux, N., 1993, pp. 23–39; Rancière, J., 1996, pp. 53–68.
3 Benjamin, W., 1927–1940/1989, pp. 478, 479. Cf. Didi-Huberman, G., 1992, pp. 125–52.
4 Warburg, A., 1902/2003, pp. 101–35. Cf. Didi-Huberman, G., 1994a, pp. 383–432. Id., 1996d, pp. 145–63.
5 Cf. Fédida, P., 1985, pp. 23–45, and Id., 1995, pp. 7–16, and passim.
6 Cf. Baudrillard, J., 1996, p. 4.
7 Benjamin, W., 1936/1991, pp. 140–71. This work was translated from German (1935) by Mr de Gandillac. Cf. Benjamin, W. 1935/1974, pp. 137–81. [Translator's note: Gandillac's translation with the title 'L'œuvre d'art à l'époque de sa reproductibilité technique', which is used here by Didi-Huberman, corresponds closely to the German original: 'Das Kunstwerk im Zeitalter seiner technischen Reproduzierbarkeit'. However, the English translation was for many years wrongly rendered as 'The Work of Art in the Age of Mechanical Reproduction'. This was later corrected by Michael W. Jennings et al.'s new edition of 2008.]
8 Cf. Krauss, R. E., 1986, pp. 152 and 170.
9 Cf. Clair, J., 1983/1996, p. 24.
10 Benjamin. W., 1936/1991, pp. 149–50 and 182. See also Didi-Huberman, G., 1996e, pp. 48–63.
11 Benjamin. W., 1928/1985, pp. 43–4. Bloch, M. and Bloch, E., 1949/1993, pp. 85–9.
12 Benjamin, W., 1928/1985, pp. 43–4. Didi-Huberman, G., 1996a, pp. 138–50.
13 See Benjamin, W. 1927–1940/1989, pp. 473–507. Id., 1928/1985, pp. 23–56. Buck-Morss, S., 1989, pp. 221–52.
14 Derrida, J., 1962, p. 60.
15 Benjamin, W., 1936/1991, pp. 179–80.
16 See Bernadac, M-L. and Marcadé, B., 1995, p. 26.
17 Bois, Y-A. and Krauss, R. E., 1996, pp. 202–7.
18 de Duve, T., 1989, p. 118.
19 See in particular Danto, A. C. C., 1981, pp. 22–5 and 159–61. Bourdieu, P., 1992, pp. 339, 345 and 399–401. Genette, G., 1994, pp. 154–76.
20 Le Bot, M., 1992, p. 15.
21 See Gaillard, T., 1992, pp. 51–7; Didi-Huberman, G., 1993a, pp. 102–18.
22 See Danto, A. C. C., 1981, pp. 159–61.
23 Benjamin, W., 1940/1991, p. 343.
24 See Rossi, S., 1980, *passim*. Didi-Huberman, G., 1990a, pp. 65–103.
25 See Didi-Huberman, G., 1994a, pp. 383–432.
26 See *infra*, pp. 100–7.
27 Châtelain, J., 1988, pp. 49–54.

Select bibliography

Please note: the English version, if available, appears in square brackets.

Baudrillard, J. (1996) 'Le Complot de l'Art', *Libération* (May), p. 4.

Benjamin, W., Muller, S. and Wohlfarth, I. (1928/1985) *Origine du drame baroque allemand*. Paris: Flammarion.

[Benjamin, W. (1963/2003) *The Origin of German Tragic Drama*, trans. John Osborne, London: Verso Books.]

Benjamin, W. and de Gandillac, M. (1935/1974) 'L'œuvre d'art à l'époque de sa reproductibilité technique', in: *L'Homme, le langage et la culture: Essais*. Paris: Denoël, 137–81.

Benjamin, W. (1936/1991) 'L'oeuvre d'art à l'époque de sa reproduction mécanisée'. Trad. W. Benjamin et P. Klossowski, *Écrits français*, Jean-Maurice Monnoyer, Paris: Gallimard, 140–92.

[Benjamin, W. (1968) 'The Work of Art in the Age of Technical Reproduction', in H. Arendt (ed.), *Illuminations*. New York: Houghton Mifflin Harcourt, 217–51.]

[Benjamin, W. (2008) *The Work of Art in the Age of Its Technological Reproducibility, and Other Writings on Media*. ed. Michael W. Jennings, Brigid Doherty and Thomas Y. Levin, trans. Edmund Jephcott et al., Cambridge, MA: Harvard University Press, 19–55.]

Benjamin, W., 1927–1940/1989. *Paris, Capitale du XIXe Siècle: Le Livre des passages*. Trad. J. Lacoste et R. Tiedemann (1989) Paris: Editions du Cerf.

[Benjamin, W. and Jephcott, E. (2006) *Walter Benjamin: Selected Writings, Volume 3: Paris, Capital of the Nineteenth Century, Writings 1935–1938*, ed. Howard Eiland and Michael W. Jennings, Cambridge, MA; London: Harvard University Press.]

Benjamin, W. (1940/1991) 'Sur le concept d'histoire', in Monnoyer, J. M. (ed.), *Ecrits français*. Paris: Gallimard, 339–47.

[Benjamin, W. and Jephcott, E. (2006) 'On the Concept of History' in *Walter Benjamin: Selected Writings*, volume 4, 1938–1940, ed. Howard Eiland and Michael W. Jennings, Cambridge, MA; London: The Belknap Press of Harvard University Press, 389–400.]

Bernadac, M.-L. (1995) *Féminimasculin – Le sexe de l'art*, ed. Bernard Marcade, Paris: Centre National d'Art et de Culture Georges Pompidou/Gallimard/Electa.

Bloch, M. and Bloch, E. (1949/1993) *Apologie pour l'histoire, ou, métier d'historien* (French edition). Paris: A. Colin.

Bois, Y.-A., Krauss, R. E. and Pompidou, C. G. (1996) *L'informe: Mode d'emploi*. Paris: Centre Georges Pompidou Service Commercial.

[Bois, Y.-A. and Krauss, R. E. (2000) *Formless: A user's guide*. 2nd edn. New York: Zone Books.]

Bourdieu, P. (1992) *Les règles de l'art: Genèse et structure du champ littéraire*. Paris: Seuil.

[Bourdieu, P. and Emanuel, S. (1996) *The Rules of Art: Genesis and Structure of the Literary Field*. Stanford, CA, United States: Stanford University Press.]

Buck-Morss, S. (1989) *The Dialectics of Seeing: Walter Benjamin and the Arcades Project*. Cambridge, MA: MIT Press.

Châtelain, J. (1988) 'Les problèmes juridiques du moulage', Paris: La Documentation française, 49–54.

Clair, J. (1983/1996) *Considérations sur l'état des beaux-arts: Critique de la modernité*. Paris: Gallimard.

Danto, A. C. C. (1981) *The Transfiguration of the Commonplace: A Philosophy of Art*. 7th edn. Cambridge, MA: Harvard University Press.

Danto, A., Hary-Schaeffer, C. and Schaeffer, J-M. (1989) *La Transfiguration du banal: Une philosophie de l'art*. Paris: Ed. du Seuil.]

Derrida, J. (1962) 'Introduction', in Edmund Husserl *L'Origine de la Géométrie*. Paris: PUF.

Derrida, J. (1967) *De la grammatologie*. Paris: Éditions de Minuit.

[Derrida, J., Spivak, G. C. (1977) *Of Grammatology*. Baltimore, MD: Johns Hopkins University Press.]

Didi-Huberman, G. (1990a) *Devant l'image: Question posée aux fins d'une histoire de l'art*. Paris: Editions de Minuit.

[Didi-Huberman, G. and Goodman, J. (2005) *Confronting Images: Questioning the Ends of a Certain History of Art*. United States: Pennsylvania State University Press.]

Didi-Huberman, G. (1992) *Ce que nous voyons, ce qui nous regarde*. Paris: Editions de Minuit.

Didi-Huberman, G. (1993a) 'D'un ressentiment en mal d'esthétique', *Les Cahiers du Musée national d'art moderne*, 43 (printemps), 102–18.

Didi-Huberman, G. (1993b) 'La leçon d'anachronie', *Art Press*, No 183, 23–5.

Didi-Huberman, G. (1994a) 'Ressemblance mythifiée et ressemblance oubliée chez Vasari: la légende du portrait sur le vif', *Mélanges de l'Ecole française de Rome – Italie et Méditerranée*, CVI(2), 383–432.

Didi-Huberman, G. (1996a) '"Imaginum pictura ... in totum exoleuit" Début de l'histoire de l'art et fin de l'époque de l'image', *Critique*, 586, 138–50.

Didi-Huberman, G. (1996d) 'Pour une anthropologie des singularités formelles. Remarques sur l'invention warburgienne', *Genèses. Sciences sociales et histoire*, No 26, 145–63.

Didi-Huberman, G. (1996e) 'The Supposition of Aura. On the Once, the Now, and the Modernity', in Francis, R. (ed.), *Negotiating Rapture: The Power of Art to Transform Lives* [published in conjunction with the exhibition of the same title at the museum of contemporary art, Chicago, 21 June–20 October 1996]. Chicago: Museum of Contemporary Art, Chicago, 48–63.

de Duve, T. (1989) *Au nom de l'art: Pour une archéologie de la modernité*. Paris: Editions de Minuit.

Einstein, C. (1915/2004) 'Negro Sculpture', trans. Charles W. Haxthausen and Sebastian Zeidler, 'Carl Einstein' in *October*, Vol. 107 (Winter), 122–38.

Fédida, P. (1995) *Site de l'étranger*. Paris: Presses universitaires de France.

Fédida, P. (1985) 'Passé anachronique et présent réminiscent. Épos et puissance mémoriale du langage', *L'Écrit du temps*, 10, 23–45.

Gaillard, F. (1992) 'Fais n'importe quoi', *Esprit*, 179, 51–7.

Genette, G. (1994) *L'oeuvre de l'art*. Paris: Éditions du Seuil.

[Genette, G., Trans. Goshgarian, G. M. (1997) *The Work of Art: Immanence and Transcendence*. Baltimore, MD, United States: Cornell University Press.]

Krauss, R. E. (1986) *The Originality of the Avant-Garde and Other Modernist Myths*. Cambridge, MA: MIT Press.

Krauss, R. (1993) *L'originalité de l'avant-garde et autres mythes modernistes*. 3rd edn. Paris: Macula.

Le Bot, M. (1992) 'Marcel Duchamp et ses "célibataires mêmes"', *Esprit*, 179, 6–15.

Loraux, N. (1993) 'Éloge de l'anachronisme en histoire', *Le Genre humain*, 27, 23–39.

Rancière, J. (1996) 'Le concept d'anachronisme et la vérité de l'historien', *L'Inactuel*, 6, 53–68.

[Rancière, Jacques (2015) 'The Concept of Anachronism and the Historian's Truth (English translation)', *InPrint*: Vol. 3: Iss. 1, Article 3. Available at: http://arrow.dit.ie/inp/vol3/iss1/3.]

Rossi, S. (1980) *Dalle botteghe aile acca- demie: realtà sociale teorie artistiche a Firenze dal XIV al XVI secolo*. Milan: Feltrinelli.

Warburg, A. (1902/2003) 'L'art du portrait et la bourgeoisie florentine', in *Essais florentins*. Paris: Klincksieck.

[Warburg, A. (1999) 'The Art of Portraiture and the Florentine Bourgeoisie', in *The Renewal of Pagan Antiquity: Contributions to The Cultural History of the European Renaissance*. Trans. David Britt and Kurt W. Foster. Los Angeles: Getty Research Institute for the History of Art and the Humanities, 184–221.]

Deidre Brollo

Untying the knot: memory and forgetting in contemporary print work*

In attempting to understand and articulate the complexities of memory, we often turn to metaphorical language. Words such as 'imprint' and 'impression', terms reminiscent of the fundamental language of printmaking, create a sense of the past remaining visible in traces left behind, of experience literally leaving its mark upon us. The pervasiveness of this motif of the impression is not coincidental or recent – it is part of the intellectual inheritance passed to us from the classical world. It has continued to inform and direct thinking on memory to the present day, but its cultural influence extends much further, as is evident in the privileging of those objects, such as the photograph, which appear to embody this metaphor. As seductive as it is, the motif of memory-as-imprint is not unproblematic, but neither is it unchallenged. Tacita Dean and Paul Ogier are two artists who employ print and photographic media – forms with a familial relationship to this metaphor of the impression – to both undermine it and to offer alternative conceptualisations of memory and forgetting.

The sense of the mind as a receptive surface upon which experience is imprinted is an expression of early and enduring metaphors of memory that have their roots buried deep in the Socratic dialogues of Plato, where memory is conceptualised as a print made upon the soul. Socrates explains:

> Now I want you to suppose, for the sake of the argument that we have in our souls a block of wax ... We make impressions upon this of everything we wish to remember [mnēmoneusai] among the things we have seen or heard or thought of ourselves; we hold the wax under our perceptions and thoughts and take a stamp from them, in the way in which we take the imprints [marks, sēemeia] of signet rings.[1] (Ricoeur 2004, 9)

* Deidre Brollo. 2013. 'Untying the Knot: Memory and Forgetting in Contemporary Print Work'. In: Morgan, Luke (ed.), *Intersections and Counterpoints: IMPACT 7 International Multi-disciplinary Printmaking Conference Proceedings*. Clayton, Victoria: Monash University Publishing, pp. 81–7. Edited and reproduced by permission of the author and Monash University Publishing.

This metaphor of the wax tablet is varied and persistent; it is revisited by Aristotle in *De Memoria et Reminiscentia*, and appears in the *Ad Herennium*, Cicero's *De Oralore*, and in Quintillian among many others.[2]

In this foundational classical metaphor, the original perception is stamped into memory as a ring into wax, leaving both an imprint or physical mark (or *tupos*), along with an impression (or *eikōn*), which is the recognition of the now absent ring (Ricoeur 2004, 13, 14, 51, 507n). The *tupos* represents the storage of memory, the *eikōn* the recollected memory image – the 'present representation of an absent thing' (7). The implication of this metaphor is that without the imprint, no recollection is possible: 'whatever is obliterated or cannot be impressed, we forget [*epilelēsthai*] and do not know' (9).[3]

Imprint and impression, trace and recollection, are deemed inseparable: without the corresponding physical trace, no memory is possible. Paul Ricoeur has noted that 'the entire modern problematic of "mnemonic traces" is, in fact, heir to this ancient alliance between *eikōn* and *tupos*' (Ricoeur 2004, 51). This defining principle, evident throughout the historical literature on memory, from Hooke and Descartes (Sutton 2003) to Freud (Whitehead 2009, 93–100), continues into contemporary research. Though it takes various forms, John Sutton (2003) writes that 'this idea that a "trace" acquired in past experience somehow "represents" that experience, or carries information about it ... has been the dominant view of memory in modern philosophy of mind, and it is assumed in much work on memory in cognitive science.'[4]

Though theories of memory still tend to favour the notion of some form of engram or memory trace in the brain (Sutton 2003), contemporary research has moved towards dynamic, distributed models which emphasise the plasticity of memory, where traces are neither static nor deterministic, but responsive and flexible (Sutton 2003). Daniel Schacter has argued that these fragments do not constitute memory itself, but rather form 'a new, emergent entity – the recollective experience' when they combine with a memory cue (1996, 69–70; Rose 2003, 104), which suggests that memory is an active process rather than one of passive storage. Indeed, the act of remembering is now seen as a creative not reproductive process (Sutton 2003). Jacques Chevalier has emphasised the incomplete and malleable nature of memory, remarking that 'things we remember and the way we remember them are shaped by evolving frames of cognitive and emotional reference' (2002, 31).

So rather than a static relationship of imprint and impression, we have instead a distributed model of memory, where traces are dispersed and fragmentary, and recollection is literally a re-membering, an active putting-together that weaves manifold threads into a process of remembrance that is inflected too by the habits, needs, perceptions and state of mind of the present. Through our interactions with them, the myriad places and things we encounter also provide us with suggestive cues that further activate and enliven the processes of remembering, as connections are formed and dissolved in response to our interaction with the world. The functioning of memory, then, cannot be considered in isolation from the interaction between body, mind and the world itself.

What then are we to make of those things that we deem to be objects or carriers of memory in the world around us? Just as the metaphor of the wax tablet has informed conceptions of memory within the mind or brain, so too has it influenced the way we memorialise, encouraging us to entrust our memory to objects, assuming that they can carry the past for us, that they will form the architecture of our own personal memory theatres (Forty 1999, 2; Melion and Küchler 1991, 3). More than any other object, it is the photograph which is so prized as an object of memory, appearing as it does to capture and hold fleeting moments of the past for us. It is our safety net, our memory knot, the object which most reassures us that the past is not lost. The alchemical receptiveness of photography relies on the existence of a referent to form its apparition of the real. As Roland Barthes explained, the connection made between the subject, the lens and the photograph goes beyond that of sight; it is of the order of touch (Barthes 1981, 80–1; Sontag 1979, 154; Batchen 2004, 31).

This sense of touch, of an image having been physically imprinted upon the photographic surface by contact with the subject, defines the photograph as an index (Batchen 2003, 193). The privileged position of the photograph, both as evidence and as memory, is related to this indexical nature (193–4, Batchen 2004, 31; Barthes 1981, 87–89): the photograph becomes a correlate of the world itself, and verifies through this verisimilitude. Blind to the object, we see only the referent, a seemingly direct glimpse of the past generated from the photograph's physical contact with the past moment which inspires a sort of belief in the viewer. We are encouraged to trust photographs: swayed by the evidence, the sense of authenticity which arises from a physical connection, a moment of contiguity with the world they depict.

Though it is seen to be analogous to memory, in fact the photograph is akin not to memory itself, but rather the metaphorical wax tablet of memory, resembling both the recollected memory-image, or impression, and its site of storage, or wax imprint. Unlike the vagaries of personal memory, the photograph, in itself, does not 'forget'. To repeat Barthes: 'in it nothing can be refused or transformed' (1981, 91). It presents a moment permanently 'fixed' and it is precisely this quality of stasis which allows it to perform a preservative function.

It is because of these characteristics of fixity and stasis that the photograph presents such a challenge to the integrity of memory. When confronted with a photograph of our past – an imprint taken of a moment, held captive from time – the exactitude of the copy speaks to its truthfulness, while its unchanging nature draws our own recollection of the event into question, and our own memory can appear hopelessly flawed, fallible and untrustworthy. The effect of the collision between the inherently malleable nature of personal memory and the resolutely fixed form of the photograph can result in 'photography quietly replac[ing] your memories with its own' (Batchen 2004, 15).[5] While we entrust the photograph to guard against forgetting, it is itself complicit, threatening to overwhelm and displace our own memory; 'not only is the Photograph never, in essence, a memory', argues Barthes 'but it actually blocks memory, quickly becomes counter-memory' (1981, 91).

While contemporary art practice has shown considerable interest in memory as a subject, such interest often manifests as metaphorical representations of memory, of imprint or impression. In seeking to evoke a sense of trace or touch, it presupposes that this physical proximity, the evidence of this closeness, represents an authentic record or 'memory'. But not all artists use photography in such a way, and I would like now to turn to a discussion of two artists who work against the grain of the photograph, who undermine these traits that can so easily lead to the displacement of memory. Tacita Dean and Paul Ogier are both artists whose work inhabits the interstice between print and photography, who circumvent metaphorical ideas of memory to instead engage with memory as evocation – with all the uncertainty that that entails – and forgetting as more than a mere absence.

In choosing these artists, my intention was to uncover ways in which it is possible to re-imagine a relationship between photography, print and memory that was not bound by this Platonic notion, and to examine how these forms might work to be evocative of memory rather than merely illustrative. In various ways, these artists undermine the troublesome assumption of photography as memory trace, while also discovering new ways to spark personal remembering. In some cases, print processes emerge as a sort of guerilla aspect in the work – a means of infiltrating and undermining the integrity of the photograph. Using various strategies, they cause us to doubt the photograph: its verisimilitude, its claim to truthfulness and its stasis. In doing so, we see the photograph less as a replica of memory, than as a provocation towards it.

Tacita Dean

In her use of the found photograph, British artist Tacita Dean resists the dogmatic nature of these objects as evidence, and instead coaxes out the more unruly, associative qualities they contain. In the 2002 series *The Russian Ending* Dean took a collection of early twentieth-century postcards sourced from flea markets (Dietrich 2002, 49) and re-imagined them as stills from unmade films. Dean has referenced the marketing techniques of early Danish cinema, in which different endings would be added to appeal to various audiences – typically, bleak and catastrophic for Russian audiences, or cheerful for Americans for example (Godfrey 2005, 100; Dietrich 2002, 51–2). To these dramatic depictions of funerals, shipwrecks and disaster, Dean has added a white chalky scrawl of instructions, directions to a non-existent film-maker, which draws attention to the artifice of photography, the choices, framing and individual viewpoint that inflect every instant stolen from the flow of time. They undermine any naturalistic or documentary sensibility the original images might have had: they now appear staged, and everything within the frame is *mise en scène*. Nothing seems incidental or without purpose within the 'scene' before us, and as such any sense of truthfulness has been dismantled. In playing up the staged qualities, Dean encourages us to look for clues, to follow these directorial interventions to blind alleys and dead ends. With the purposefully ambiguous and open-ended use of text, Dean provides the viewer with an abundance of material, but no firm narrative architecture, and there is never any one finalised form for the viewer to strive towards.

If Dean works to undermine stasis, a sense of touch or contiguity with the referent is also dismantled. The printmaker's hand intrudes to swell the distance between imprint and impression, as photogravure adds the rogue element of process to weaken any sense of indexicality. The image no longer has the illusion of pure impression, augmented now by the laying of the ground, the action of the mordant, the hand which wiped back the ink, the processes which add, subtract and alter; and most significantly, which meddle with a sense of photographic veracity. These print techniques are combined with photography, subverting the viewer's assumptions about the latter's verisimilitude, and undermining the very notion of a truthful impression, which threatens always to overpower the memory work of the individual.[6]

The artist's book *Floh* (German for 'flea') contains the reproductions of 163 photographs Dean collected from flea markets throughout America and Europe (Godfrey 2005, 91). Though carefully reproduced, these photographs maintain the haphazard randomness so much a part of the flea market. They are a mix of colour and black-and-white, images dating from various periods in time and clearly from many different places. They appear to exhibit no narrative ordering, and are not supplemented by any explanatory text – keeping, as Dean has said, 'the silence of the flea market, the silence of when I found them, the silence of the found object' (Godfrey 2005, 92). In her selection of images, Dean provides the viewer with no specific narrative direction: a family playing with a frisbee beside the sea, two nineteenth-century sepia-toned portraits, two identical cars parked side-by-side in the snow, their proud owners posing beside them. There is no didactic path to follow here, but rather an openness to potential, to multiple narratives: they suggest a known ordinariness, a recognisable oddness, a sense of stirring recognition.

Mark Godfrey (2005, 104) has commented that in their random anonymity, these found photographs bring a familiarity that does not challenge the viewer's own fragile recollections. Dean herself says that she has 'always believed that art works best when it responds to the autobiography of the viewer' (115) and Godfrey contends that *Floh*, with its motley assortment of everyday images, works in just such a way: 'found photographs emerge as magical in their appearance and in their fate, as superstitious, as charming – as democratic – because they are cherished like precious objects. Layered with time, they trigger memories not of the people they show, but from the people who look at them' (119).

Like Barthes, Geoffrey Batchen has argued that 'contrary to popular opinion, photography does not enhance memory – involuntary, physically embracing and immediate memory – but rather replaces it with images – images that are historical, coherent, informational' (2004, 94). However, if we can avoid seeing through the photograph to the referent, ignoring its mimicry of the past, but instead see the materiality of the photograph itself, Batchen argues, there exists the possibility for true involuntary recollection (94). Such a focus on materiality is an intrinsic part of *Floh*. Many of the photographs that Dean has selected reveal their material nature, prising apart the photographic object from the scene it depicts, and giving back to the photograph an existence other than the one it replicates. The moment of taking the photograph, the click of the shutter, is revealed in the blurriness of some images, in the overexposure of others; the possible evidence of chemical spills reveals the processing in the darkness of the lab; the trace of fingerprints on one surface (over the face of a young boy) hints at the affectionate use of the photograph; two scrawled-out faces in another suggest a much less warm encounter. Finally, no longer having enough meaning to those whom they belonged or those who had acquired them, their appearance at the flea market shows us their disposal.[7] These rich histories, suggested by the many material residues which they show evidence of, add to the mnemonic potential of these objects, by asserting the photographs' way of being, as well as their way of being used. These objects are thus seen to embody traces of their own history and, in revealing their material traces, they thicken their possible resonances.

Paul Ogier

Forgetting is generally conceived of as memory's opposite: where memory is seen to be positive, marked by presence (albeit of an absent thing), forgetting is aligned with the negative, with emptiness, with true absence. As Ricoeur has noted: 'forgetting is experienced as an attack on the reliability of memory. An attack, a weakness, a lacuna' (2004, 413). Here we are inevitably drawn back to Plato once again: if memory is deemed the preservation of the past in a material form, whether in an object, or memory trace within the brain, by extension forgetting is associated with the decay of that material form (Forty 1999, 4; Ricoeur 2004, 9, 51). This notion of forgetting, as the decay or erasure of a materially stored memory, inevitably works towards the establishment of a binary in which memory is characterised by presence and forgetting by absence. But there is a paradox at the heart of this dichotomy: if forgetting entails a true erasure, how can we be aware that we have forgotten?

An alternative conception of memory and forgetting may be found within the work of Henri Bergson. The model of recollection which Bergson proposes is one where forgetting is not characterised by erasure, or absence, but rather latency. As Ricoeur explains: 'forgetting then designates the unperceived character of the perseverance of memories, their removal from the vigilance of consciousness' (2004, 440). From this then we can derive a second conceptualisation of forgetting. In addition to the notion of forgetting as the negative or antithesis of memory we can also discern a positive

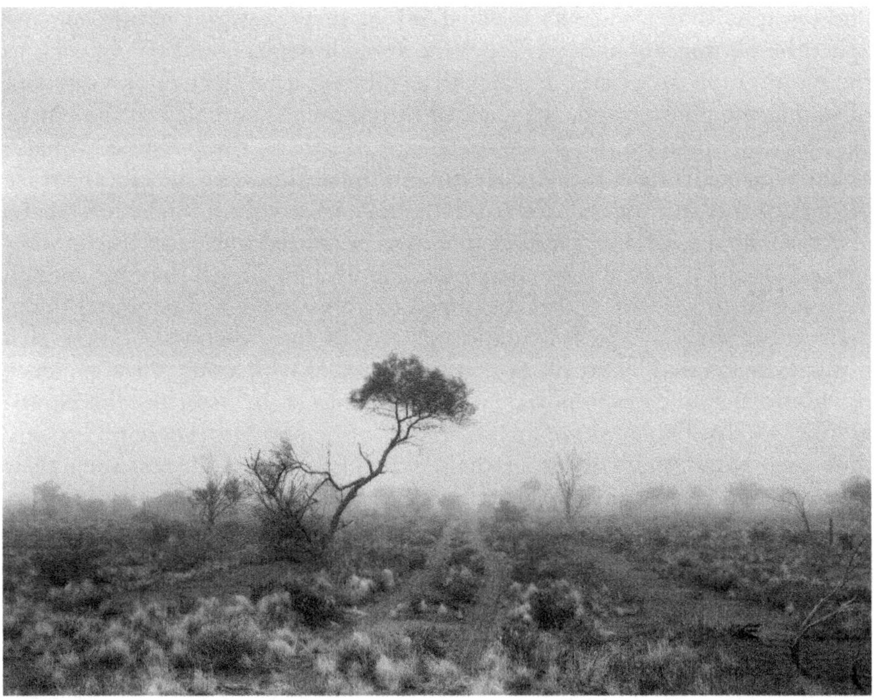

Paul Ogier, *One Tree (Former Emu Field Atomic Test Site) South Australia*, 2010. Carbon pigment print. 72 × 90 cm.

form, a 'reserve of forgetting' that is part of the work of memory (417). In drawing attention to absence, we become aware of the thing forgotten, latent memory is made active, and erasure is made incomplete. Both conceptions of forgetting are evident within the work of Paul Ogier, who uses this conception of forgetting as latent memory to draw attention to and problematise the notion of forgetting as erasure.

Ogier[8] displays a somewhat hybrid approach to his work, photographing with vintage lenses on large-format film cameras, and digitally printing the work using carbon-based pigments. For his series *10 Miles* Ogier photographed the residual traces of British atomic tests in Australia. Using historical research and declassified documents, the artist equipped himself with an understanding of the conditions, locations and background of the tests. Underneath the resulting images is an awareness of the fact of colonisation: the hidden knowledge that Australia represented a dark surrogate, offering for the tests an equivalent distance as that from London to the Russian Front, and a wilderness that was, to the colonial mind, isolated, secret and empty.

Both *One Tree* and *Kittens* (named after the esoteric British name given to that series of tests)[9] were taken at Emu Field in South Australia in 2010. Knowledge infuses these works, but they are not part of a documentary or historical tradition. They shun the impartial view, steeped in both the then and the now they are thick with after-effects and repercussions. Using early modernist lenses, his images visually quote the season and timing of the original detonations. The photographs reverberate with echoes of the other observers, those charged with documenting the blast on film, all from a 'safe' distance from ground zero: the road visible in *One Tree* was built for the original test photographers.[10] The low horizon and wide sky force our view upwards towards what is no longer there but is still everywhere: the blast and the fallout.

But if we look closer, what do we see? Whatever it is we expect, it is not there. *One Tree* hints at the detonation itself, and the 'black cloud' which subsequently drifted over Aboriginal settlements. The foliage is dispersed upward into the air, a fog is hugging the ground like falling dust, but the land itself seems strangely busy. This is a not a post-apocalyptic wasteland. While the tree itself was probably witness to the event, holding within its fibrous cells a molecular record, there seems to be much that is new clinging to life below it, huddled around a dirt road. Similarly, *Kittens* shows a gently ridged soil dotted abundantly with vegetation, all ballooning outward and upward from their lowly stations. These images raise questions in us. What am I not seeing? What did I expect to see?

It's in asking these questions that we begin to intuit the parts of the story we do not know. Objects and equipment were removed, holes dug to bury things. The land was scoured. Contaminated soil was tilled, topsoil laid over it and sown with seed. Roads and paths were erased or disrupted;

there are tracks that now lead nowhere. Ogier draws attention to the systematic and deliberate effacement of traces within the landscape – an erasure that was intended to remove evidence more than toxicity. While they hold knowledge of the event, these images also draw out the bitterness, showing us absence to confirm that we are right to think we are not seeing everything. When we are attuned to the sight of erasure, we sense forgetting as latency, as a potent and compelling knowledge that means the removal of trace, which constitutes a profound forgetting, has failed. This knowledge – this reserve of forgetting outlined by Ricoeur – draws attention towards the acts of erasure, and thereby nullifies them. An act of erasure cannot achieve its end – oblivion – if we are made aware of the act itself. Ogier shows us nothing where we expect something, and something where we expect nothing.

In summary, then, the Platonic metaphor that compares memory to an imprint left in wax is both seductive and enduring, and that metaphor finds an analogue in assumptions about the memory-value of photography. In fact, however, photography resembles the metaphor more than it does memory itself. Subverting such assumptions about photography and memory, Tacita Dean and Paul Ogier work with both print and photographic techniques to engage with memory as evocation – as a re-membering which involves the viewer rather than an imprint which the past leaves upon the work. Further to this, for Ogier, memory as re-membering also involves asking questions about forgetting, a notion that represents not mere erasure (as the metaphor of the wax tablet would imply), but something much more complex, productive and potent.

Acknowledgements

The author is grateful to Paul Ogier for his assistance.

Notes

1 Ricoeur's translation has been used here for its attention to resonances of imprint and impression in the original. See also Plato 1961, 897.
2 For more on this metaphor in Aristotle see Draaisma 2000, 25–7; Ricoeur 2004, 16–17, 20; Sorabji 2004, 50–1, 80–2; Whitehead 2009, 29–30. In the *Ad Herennium*, Yates 1992, 20–3; Whitehead 2009, 29. In *Cicero*, Whitehead 2009, 31; Yates 1992, 34. In *Quintillian*, Whitehead 2009, 31–2.
3 cf. Plato 1961, p. 897.
4 For a full discussion of the diversity of views on the subject, see Sutton 2003; Senor 2005. For Henri Bergson's refutation of the theory, see Bergson 1991, 117–18.
5 See also Barthes 1981, 91; Batchen, 2003.

6 For a discussion on the mnemonic possibilities of *The Russian Ending*, see Brollo 2007, 161–2.
7 cf. Godfrey 2005, 105–10.
8 Based on conversations with the artist (2010–11).
9 This series of 'smaller bomb tests' took place at Emu Field, and were continued subsequently at Maralinga.
10 Ogier observes that 'safe' distances were (and are) disputed, and that the distances involved varied significantly. His working title '10 Miles' refers to one such measure, but at Emu Field, the observation teams were four miles from ground zero.

References

Barthes, R. 1981. *Camera Lucida: Reflections on Photography*. Trans. Howard, R. New York: Hill & Wang.

Batchen. G. 2003. 'Short Memory/Thin Skin'. *The Australian and New Zealand Journal of Art*, 2 (2) and 3 (1) (double issue): 191–206.

Batchen, G. 2004. *Forget Me Not: Photography and Remembrance*. New York: Princeton Architectural Press.

Bergson, H. 1991. *Matter and Memory*. Trans. Paul, N. M. and Palmer, W. S. New York: Zone.

Brollo, D. 2007. 'Memory, Perception, & the Art of Seeing Double'. PhD thesis, Sydney: University of Sydney.

Chevalier, J. M. 2002. *Scorpions and the Anatomy of Time*. Montreal and Kingston: McGill-Queen's University Press.

Dietrich, D. 2002. 'The Space in Between: Tacita Dean's "Russian Ending"'. *Art on Paper*. 6 (5) (May/June): 48–53.

Draaisma, D. 2000. *Metaphors of Memory: A History of Ideas about the Mind*. Trans. Vincent, P. Cambridge: Cambridge University Press.

Forty, A. 1999. 'Introduction'. In A. Forty and S. Küchler (eds), *The Art of Forgetting*. Oxford and New York: Berg.

Godfrey, M. 2005. 'Photography Found and Lost: On Tacita Dean's "Floh"'. *October*. 114 (Fall): 90–119.

Melion, W. and Küchler, S. 1991. 'Introduction: Memory, Cognition and Image Production'. In S. Küchler and W. Melion (eds), *Images of Memory: On Remembering and Representation*. Washington and London; Smithsonian Institution Press: 1–46.

Plato. 1961. 'Theaetetus'. In E. Hamilton and H. Cairns (eds), *The Collected Dialogues of Plato, Including the Letters*. New York: Pantheon: 845–919.

Ricoeur, P. 2004. *Memory, History, Forgetting*. Trans. Blarney, K. and Pellauer, D. Chicago and London: University of Chicago Press.

Rose, S. 2003. *The Making of Memory: From Molecules to Mind*. Rev. edn. London: Vintage.

Schacter, D. L. 1996. *Searching for Memory: The Brain, the Mind and the Past*. New York: Basic.

Senor, T. D. 2005. 'Epistemological Problems of Memory'. In E. N. Zalta (ed.), *The Stanford Encyclopedia of Philosophy*, First published 3 January 2005.

Substantive revision 4 September, 2009. [Accessed 10 December 2010.] Available from: http://plato.stanford.edu/entries/memory-episprob.

Sontag, S. 1979. *On Photography*. Harmondsworth: Penguin.

Sorabji, R. 2004. *Aristotle on Memory*. 2nd edn. London: Duckworth.

Sutton, J. 2003. 'Memory'. In E. N. Zalta (ed.), *The Stanford Encyclopedia of Philosophy*. First published 11 March 2003. Substantive revision 3 February 2010. [Accessed 10 December 2010.] Available from: http://plato.stanford.edu/entries/memory.

Whitehead, A. 2009. *Memory, the New Critical Idiom*, Oxon: Routledge.

Yates, F. A. 1992. *The Art of Memory*. London: Pimlico.

Yara Flores

Spirit duplication*

Every technology is a metaphor. That much is clear. The difficult matter is to sort out whether this is a primary or secondary function. Which is to say, did we initially make this universe of instruments, machines, tools, and devices *as a way of talking about our condition*, only then to discover, *post hoc*, that all the amassed hardware also proved useful for solving various practical problems (washing dishes, killing neighbors, etc.)? Or did it work the other way around? Did we set out to kill our neighbors, say, and then notice that the sword was a lovely way to say 'violence'?

At first glance, the latter may seem much more likely. But presumably the sword said 'violence' before it was swung. If the question feels abstruse, remember that the stakes are high: Are we apes who learned to talk, or angels who learned to kill?

But let me be absolutely concrete. In the late 1970s, at the hands of a small, wiry, and inflexible nun, I received two years of formal catechism at an archaically traditional Catholic school. This meant that every Monday morning we received, each of us in the class, a single sheet of metaphysical dogma laid out in a simple question–answer format. For instance:

Q. Who made the world?
A. God made the world.
Q. Where is God?
A. God is everywhere.
Q. What is despair?
A. Despair is the loss of hope in God's Mercy.

Every Friday we were tested on our mastery of this material, and the tests took the *form of precisely the same sheet of paper we had received on*

* Yara Flores. 2010. 'Spirit Duplication'. *Cabinet Learning* (39). www.cabinetmagazine.org/issues/39/flores.php. [Accessed 22 December 2016.] Reproduced by permission of the author and *Cabinet*.

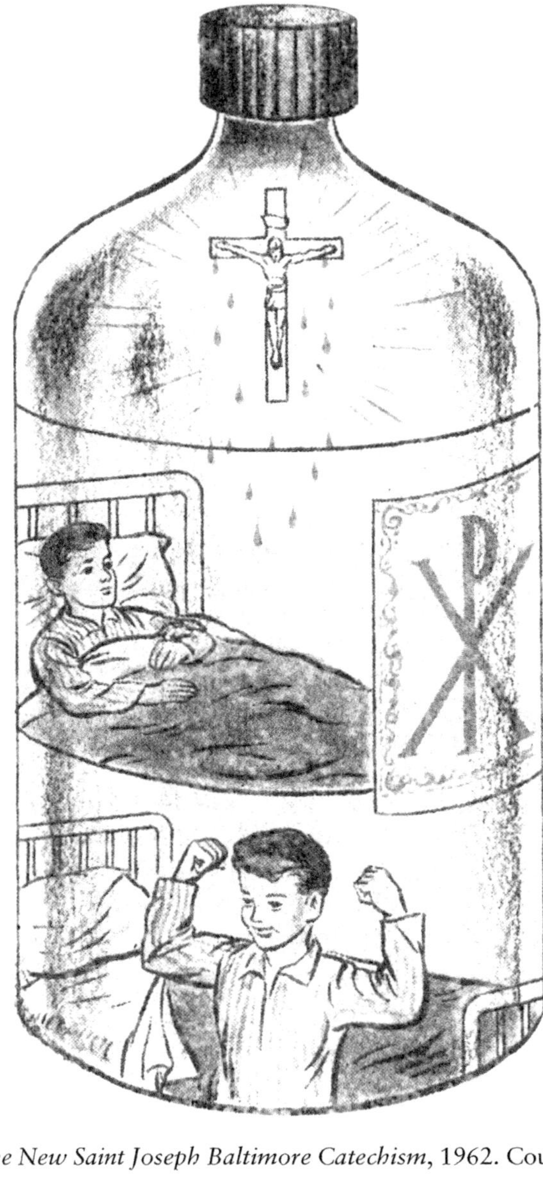

Image from *The New Saint Joseph Baltimore Catechism*, 1962. Courtesy of *Cabinet* magazine.

Monday from which the 'answers' had been erased. We filled them in, writing in blue pen.

Being disciplined, pious, and blessed with a good memory, I received uniformly perfect marks in this exercise, and grew in the satisfactions of tightly defined wisdom.

However, as it happens, between my first and second years of this training my school acquired a new 'Xerox' machine, which replaced the old ditto device upon which sister William had long relied. The technologies are very different.

The ditto machine, or 'spirit duplicator' as it is more properly known, was a manually ranked drum-printing device originally developed in the 1920s. It worked from a special 'master' that looked a little like a piece of carbon paper. This was in fact a sandwich of acetate and a thin tablet of deep purple wax. When you typed or wrote on the master, the wax stuck to the back of the cover page, producing a waxy negative of your original. This was then fixed, wax side out, to the revolving drum. As the machine went to work, the sheets of paper to be printed were individually wetted with a highly volatile mixture of isopropyl alcohol and methanol. Touching the roller, this combustible and intoxicating broth instantly dissolved the colored wax from the master, leaving a purple trace of every word.

Xerographic duplication, by contrast, is an electrostatic process, and makes use of bright light to recreate the original in a pattern of negatively and positively charged regions. A positively charged powder adheres to the negative bits of this pattern, which correspond to the dark parts of the original. Heat cooks this black dust onto the blank page, creating the copy.

I did not like the new copies. There was the disconcerting matter of the powdery toner. One of my first sheets, incompletely fused, vanished at the touch of my finger. Not encouraging, from a catechistical perspective.

But even worse was the dryness. Sheets fresh from the ditto machine came doused with their intoxicating vehicle. They were limp and delicate and heady. One breathed deeply, and felt a lightness of the spirit. Like the page, one was softened to receive the purple words.

By contrast, these strange new handouts were made of static ash, of a nervous kind of soot. They felt brittle, dusty, lifeless. Without the penetrating aroma of naphtha, the dialogic doctrines felt strangely inert. Absent the lurid aniline purple – redolent of both Tyrian splendor and cruel wounds – the blackletter teachings took on a dour formality.

It is very disorienting to go from theology as *Eros* to theology as *Thanatos* over a short summer vacation. And I am not sure I ever really recovered.

Which brings us back to the semiotics of technology. In an important book published in English as *Metaphors of Memory* (2001), the Dutch historian Douwe Draaisma traced the shifting use of concrete referents for our inner life. How does the mind work? Like a *block of wax*, suggested

Plato. Which is to say, it *takes an impression*. Or, later, the mind was said to be more like a *library*. Which is to say, *you fill it with books*. Each of these tropes had significant implications for thinking about pedagogy.

Q. *Is the pupil to be molded, incised, or impressed?*
A. *I don't know.*
Q. *Does wisdom shape up in us as ash, fixed by a dry heat? Or do we, soused with an intoxicating liquor, lick it from the purple page?*
A. *I don't know.*

Catherine Brooks

Three ways to use yellow*

Last fall I returned to France to present my lecture *Etching: the Practice of Alchemy and the Art of Connection*, in which I share the tales and technical tips of my career working with the mystical processes of intaglio printmaking. While passing through Paris I caught up with my former etching teacher, Mâitre d'Art René Tazé, who over a decade ago showed me the ways of graphic-alchemy, transforming base metals of copper and zinc into precious objects of paper.

The alchemists of the past worked to create an elixir of immortality. The master artists and artisans that I have worked with at Atelier René Tazé and Crown Point Press have developed elixirs of life – cultures – through recipes that combine unlikely ingredients and blend human relationships.

At Atelier René Tazé artists, artisans and apprentices work in symbiotic relationship to each other, then commune at mid-day to enjoy *la goût de la vie*, the taste of life, through the sharing of food. As an innocent apprentice, thirteen years ago, I could not (and still don't) see a hierarchy of materials or a difference between the sensitivity when mixing ink or making a meal. All endeavors in the atelier were for the purpose of creating connections through chemistry.

At Crown Point Press, printers were compared to laboratory assistants, executing experiments for scientists (read: artists). The doctrine was to never say 'no' to an artist's idea or deny them your effort at realizing their concept. Of all the artists I worked with during my seven-year tenure there, Richard Tuttle brought the most audacious proposals, including his desire to make ink with goat butter.

Here is a collection of some of the elixirs I have concocted with masters of print. All of them contain gold (read: yellow); one of them is edible and

* Catherine Brooks. 2014. 'Three Ways to Use Yellow'. In: Emmons, Amze, Tillman, R. L. and Urban, Jason (eds), *Manual: An Anthology of the Manual*. Austin, Texas: Printeresting, pp. 50–3. Reproduced by permission of the author and Printeresting.

two of them are not; each one should be replicated and used or consumed in the ferment of the graphic-alchemist's laboratory, the print shop.

Noir coloré

I recently unearthed an embarrassing sketchbook from my time in Paris in 2001. Inside the book I found bad drawings of masterpieces from the Louvre museum, street sketches, dramatic ruminations and René Tazé's secret recipe for colored black ink. With the right proportions – when a warm yellow ink is mixed into a dense black ink – the printed effect is like chine collé. With noir coloré – if wiped and printed correctly – the marks of a deeply etched plate will print black, and light plate tone will create a subtle yellow hue in the background, warming the image.

You will need:

- 50–70% Charbonnel, Very Dense Black, #5598
- 30–50% Charbonnel, Permanent Yellow Lake

Mix:

- On your palette, using a flexible ink knife, lay out a portion of black #5598.
- Massage the ink with your knife to loosen it up.
- Begin to incorporate the yellow ink into the black, creating a dark olive green mixture.

Ink & print:

- Apply a layer of the ink mixture onto the surface of your plate.
- Rub the plate lightly in circular motions with a densely packed, kneaded, 1-yard-square piece of tarlatan.
- Repeat with a cleaner piece of tarlatan.
- Rub the surface of the plate almost clean with the palm of your hand.
- You should still see a very slight haze of plate tone on the plate surface.
- Clean the plate edges and print.

Studio mayonnaise

At Atelier René Tazé the workday starts with warming the inking stations, getting paper wet, then cleaning the plate and press bed. Once all the materials are ready for editioning and printing commences, the conversation about the day's lunch menu begins until it is time to *faire des courses*: a trip around the neighborhood to visit the market, the butcher, the baker, and the bar, before preparing the meal.

While I was René's apprentice, before even sharing his ink recipes, he taught me how to make salad dressing. In 2010, when visiting him in

France, we prepared lunch in his atelier, which included studio-made mayonnaise. In describing the procedure for manually blending egg, mustard and oil, René uses the same command as when teaching the techniques of *taille-douce*. '*Doucement*' he says. Make mixing your mayonnaise a sensual experience and add the oil slowly, *softly*.

You will need:
- *Un jaune d'oeuf: a yellow of egg*. An egg yolk
- *Moutarde forte*: Dijon mustard
- *Huile d'arachide*: A light, edible oil like peanut oil
- *D'ail*: Fresh pressed garlic
- *Sel et poivre au goût*: Salt & pepper to taste

Mix:
- In a bowl stir together raw egg yolk and mustard.
- Add oil until the mixture begins to emulsify.
- Quickly whisk as you slowly incorporate more oil.
- Add fresh garlic, salt and pepper to taste.
- Enjoy as a side with fish or vegetables.

Goat ocher

In 2009, René took me to the South of France to visit his newly opened studio in Coustellet, Provence, L'art des Taille-Douciers. After touring the atelier we spent the rest of our time experiencing the region by ingesting its odors, flavors and colors: aromatic wild thyme; red, white and rosé wines; vermillion poppy fields; and ochre earth from the Roussillon clay and pigment mines.

Four years before this trip, I worked with Richard Tuttle in the Crown Point Press studio on the project that became, *Deep, In the Snow*. As René and I had done in Provence, prior to arriving at the CPP studio, Tuttle immersed himself in the Bay Area environment, exploring the terrain and ingesting the abundance that comes from it. He brought a half-eaten package of goat butter to the studio and insisted we use it instead of plate oil to make ink with yellow ocher pigment. Although the substance was quite slippery, it worked as intaglio ink and we used it for proofing until the prints were approved. Eventually fears about the butter-base of the ink going rancid or being eaten by pests changed his mind and the ink for the edition was made with a conventional recipe.

You will need:
- Goat milk butter
- Yellow ocher pigment powder
- Dust mask

Mix:

- On your inking palette, let a small portion of butter soften to room temperature.
- Wearing a dust mask, use a flexible ink knife to begin adding the dry pigment powder to the butter.
- Use the flat side of the knife to press the particles against the palette, so there are no clumps.
- Add as much pigment as necessary to create a thick, creamy ink texture.
- Ink and print.
- Do not ingest.

Amze Emmons, R. L. Tillman and Jason Urban

On the manual (in the manual)*

Preface

When we started Printeresting, we felt that the discourse about print was excessively technical, especially online. So we made a conscious decision: put aside the how, and focus on the why.

Seven years later, we've softened a bit on technique. Instruction is inherent to print, and technique is inherent to instruction. Our community makes things, and teaches others to make things. All that 'shop talk' offers a critical way to connect with each other. And so we decided to tackle the technical.

What better lens could we choose than the manual?

Amze, R. L. & Jason

Introduction

> 'of the hands, done by hand, operated by hand.' 'requiring human effort or physical labor.' 'a book of instructions, easily held in the hand.'

Maybe you pulled your first manual from a bargain bin in a dusty bookstore. It was like a book of spells: obscure recipes for strange potions, pictures of disembodied hands engaged in mysterious tasks. You thought: 'with *this*, I can teach *myself*.' But after hours poring over the fine print, your excitement turned to confusion. Perhaps confusion turned to despair. You returned to the studio, like the scolded Sorcerer's Apprentice. Ultimately,

* Amze Emmons, R. L. Tillman and Jason Urban. 2014. 'Preface and Introduction'. In: Emmons, Amze, Tillman, R. L. and Urban, Jason (eds), *Manual: An Anthology of the Manual*. Austin, Texas: Printeresting, pp. 3–6. Reproduced by permission of the authors and Printeresting.

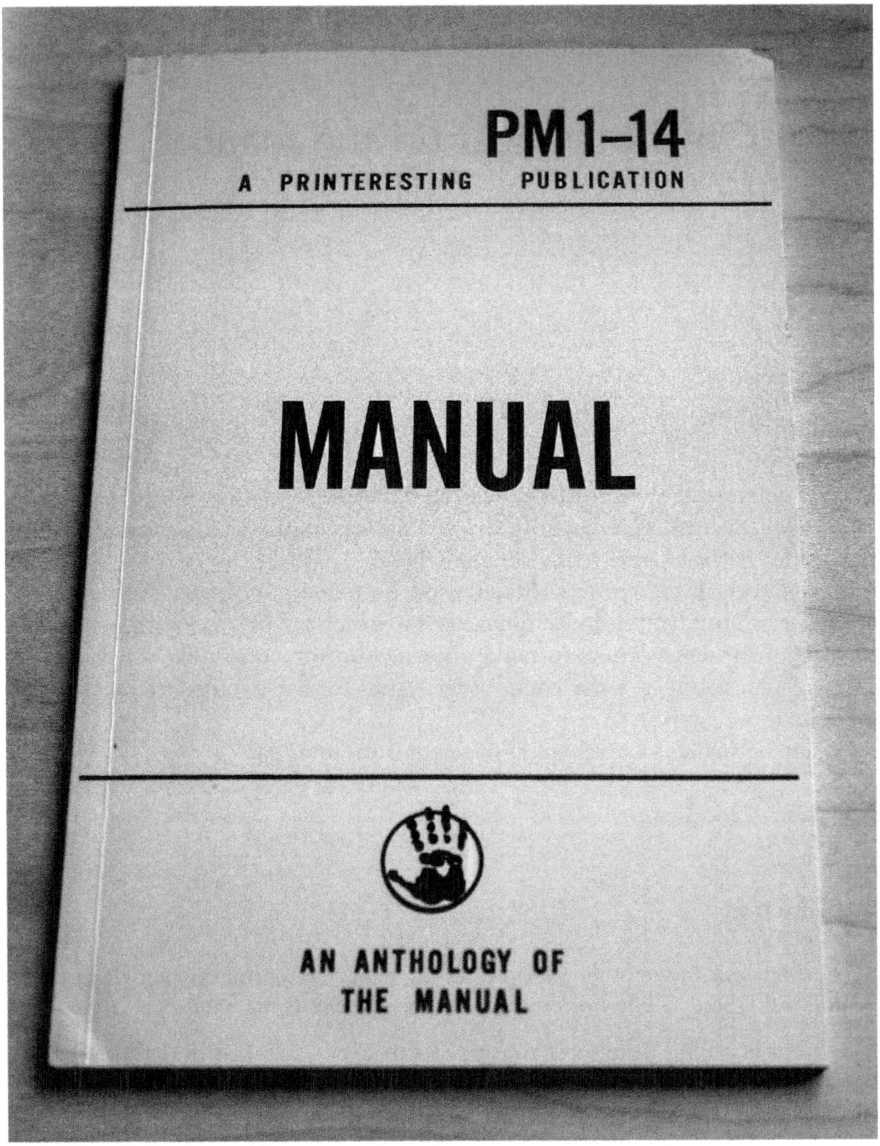

Cover page of *The Manual*, 2014. A4-size publication. Published by Printeresting.

though, your experience taught you something: the difference between information and knowledge.

Like a book of spells, the manual is in some ways a relic of the past.

In *Prints and Visual Communication*, William Ivins explained how the sharing of information through pictures and words shaped the modern world, even before the perfection of moveable type. In his 1994 'Sentences on Printed Art,' Richard S. Field put it succinctly: 'Prints represent the technology that made technology possible.' The fact that early printed didactic material like maps were fraught with inaccurate information does not invalidate the point. Correcting mistakes was the way the process worked.

Many of our trusted manuals have their origins in the latter part of the 19th and the early 20th centuries, including the *Chicago Manual of Style*, Robert's *Rules of Order*, and *The Boy Scout Handbook*. This era represented a moment of change not unlike the time we are in now: oral tradition and hands-on training might be replaced by the distant expertise of a disembodied author. In the past, the manual might prepare the anxious Webelo Scout for a weekend at a Jamboree. Boy Scouts may still carry a dog-eared copy of their Handbook, but they also have an app for it. Today, an anxious homeowner is less likely to pull out the *Time-Life Homeowner's Manual*, and more likely to pull out the smartphone (if only just to call the plumber).

Printmaking is not immune to this new status quo. These days an Internet technical forum is the most likely solution for a curious printer in need of a new lift-ground recipe, or guidance on the proper angles for CMYK separations. But long before the digital revolution, technology caused an even more radical disruption of the way printers pass on knowledge. Once upon a time, the print shop was like a cloister, with even trusted apprentices given information only when it was necessary. A better way to print a lithograph from a stone would have been a closely protected trade secret. But that was when stone lithography was an important technology. Eventually, like all print media, that technology was drained of its commercial vitality by newer approaches. When any technology becomes commercially obsolete, the few people who remain interested in it have much more to gain from sharing information than they do from keeping secrets.

And so it is that the cloistered environment of the ancient print shop presents a distinct contrast with the way people learn about prints today. The communal spirit of the current letterpress revival would have shocked the secretive, litigious printshops of 18th-century London. Sharing is now the best way for printers to protect their secrets – not from competitors, but from oblivion. This open culture has become a defining feature of the print community, leading naturally to the publication of some of our favorite printmaking manuals.

At their best, instructions are a gift, offering the possibility of understanding. But that possibility is not a substitute for real knowledge. Which is another reason why manuals are often such beloved tools for printmaking artists. As people who must use our hands, the multiple meanings of the word 'manual' are not incidental to us.

In his sometimes excellent, sometimes problematic book *Shop Class as Soulcraft*, Matthew B. Crawford argues broadly for the richness of 'the psychic satisfactions [and] cognitive demands of manual work.' An academic and a motorcycle mechanic, Crawford writes at length about the merits and limits of the automotive service manual. He notes that while modern diagnostic texts are produced by technical writers with only abstract knowledge, 'service manuals were once written by people who worked on and lived with the machines they wrote about.' Crawford describes a 'philosophic friendship' between the author of a well-crafted manual and its readers, a relationship that is akin to teacher and student, people bound together in 'a community of those who desire to know.'

But Crawford does not fetishize the manual as an object. In fact, he notes that real knowledge cannot derive from the mere possession of a rulebook, or even the ability to follow its instructions. Rather, he emphasizes practical experience, literal 'hands-on' engagement, as the only path to genuine understanding, citing Heidegger's case that one must use a hammer in order to know it. In his argument for the intellectual value of manual work, Crawford also cites the Greek philosopher Anaxagoras: 'It is by having hands that man is the most intelligent of animals.'

Throughout history, the significance of the hand in human development has been championed by philosophers and scientists alike, and not without reason. For it is through the hands as well as the mind that we learn. Thus the worth of the instructional manual lies not in the thing itself, but the manual and intellectual engagement required to explore its contents. That printed document that helped you learn your craft, then, is a bridge between information and understanding. And perhaps that is why you love it still.

Welcome to the Manual.

References

Crawford, Matthew B. 2010. *Shop Class as Soulcraft: An Inquiry into the Value of Work*. New York: Penguin Books.

Field, Richard S. 1994. 'Sentences on Printed Art.' *Print Collector's Newsletter* 25.5: 171.

Ivins, William M. 1969. *Prints and Visual Communication*. 9th ed. Cambridge, MA: M.I.T. Press.

Nicky Coutts

Animal print suicide*

Vets have a tendency towards suicide. Or so Hélène Cixous proposes recounting seven vets who took their own lives over just a three-year period in her local area.[1] In notebooks, not originally intended for distribution, she tells the story of how the dark hair of a 35-year-old vet turned to white overnight following the violent suicide of his colleague. To become a vet is to acquire a fatal illness, he told her. It begins with vocation, but nobody would become a vet if they truly knew what it entails. He then explains the multiple areas of expertise required of a single practitioner. The vet must be,

> … a doctor who has to be a surgeon, haematologist, pneumatologist, oncologist, general practitioner, psychiatrist, self-psychoanalyst, it's inhuman.[2]

For him the stresses of this particular profession groom the death drive. The animal is stressed, this stress is transferred to the human who absorbs it and in so doing the vet becomes the animal. Suicide becomes desirable as flight from the scenario, release from becoming animal and becoming double. Affirming the susceptibility of the vet to adopt the position of the animal he treats, the bereaved vet adds,

> Vets need to have a very close watch kept over them by loving masters.[3]

In the long tradition of the folding in of the animal into man, the vet houses the animal, and the animal houses the vet. They are connected by pain, and, through a mutual wish for release from it, can fatally assimilate.

Cixous' notes are part of a trajectory of thought on how we have evolved as inhabited beings, a set of ideas much visited in Elias Canetti's *Crowds and Power*, an extensive study of the human as multiple. Canetti stresses the importance of the Ancient Egyptian incorporation of animals within men and writes of the '…unchanging double figure of the totem,' an early

* Nicky Coutts. 2014. 'Animal Print Suicide'. In: Taylor, Finlay (ed.), *Against Nature – Print Mare I*, 18–27. Reproduced by permission of the author and RCA, Printmedia. Edited by the author.

prototype for the metamorphosis from man into animal and from animal into man.[4] Canetti considers not only the many routes of animal into human and vice versa, but also the way in which we inhabit each other, human within human. He describes the unique mobility of the human face, inherited from monkeys, reflecting our readiness to transform as social beings. We copy and imitate to communicate, to resemble temporarily those we address. Our companions are encouraged to recognize their own facial expressions in ours and to be at ease with a fluid mirroring. As with Cixous' vets, Canetti also recognises the extent to which this process of exchange is subject to pathologies. We can mirror to the extent that we fear, and risk losing, our own image. We can become locked behind the arranged faces, or masks, we present to others. We can start to believe in the faces we make and fail to shore up territory we previously recognised as our own.

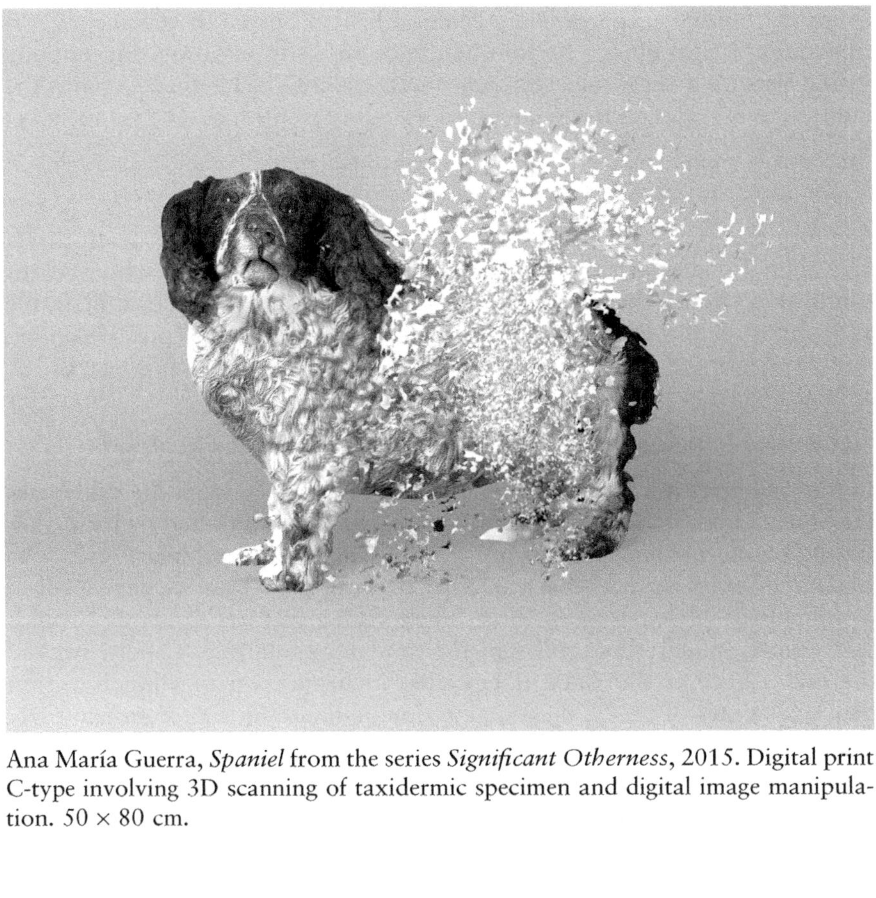

Ana María Guerra, *Spaniel* from the series *Significant Otherness*, 2015. Digital print C-type involving 3D scanning of taxidermic specimen and digital image manipulation. 50 × 80 cm.

The word 'Printmare' similarly evokes a darker side to ideas of multiplicity. A recent entry into language, it means,

> A terrifying or very unpleasant experience that is read about and haunts the reader long after they have stopped reading.[5]

As for the animal within the vet, print has lodged itself within the reader. As a result two separate, but simultaneous, places are occupied. The reader looks from their place in the physical world through the place that has invaded them via the medium of print. Walter Benjamin observed that the copy, the cast, the imitation, the replica were developed to reach a wider audience than could ever be possible for the original, in a single location.[6] Print as text and print as image multiply the possibilities, not only of the work of art itself, but also the places in which it can be encountered. Unlike a viewer of a painting, the viewer of a print would have been aware, from the early inception of the copy, that others elsewhere could be viewing this exact same image at the exact same time. The essential multiplicity of the print meets not only with the composite nature of its viewer who has evolved, which Canetti describes, as a doubled being, but also with a sharing crowd within multiple dimensions.

A forerunner of the idea of looking at a print while imagining others elsewhere viewing the same representation at the same time, was the idea of human copies appearing in more places than one during a single instant. Known as bilocation, Our Lady of the Pillar in 40 AD is believed the earliest proponent, with the more recent and better-known figure of Padre Pio, allegedly appearing simultaneously at several bedsides of the sick and dying until his death in 1968. Initially a practice intended to maximize the capacity of Christian saints or monks to attend as many in their flock as needed, more recently, during the presidential elections of 2008, Senator Hillary Clinton was also believed by some to co-exist in multiple locations giving speeches to crowds simultaneously in neighbouring states.

Whether or not we choose to trust in the idea of bilocation, the fact of its existence as a phenomenon stretching back historically indicates an early concern with the limitations of an individual bound to a single location at any one time. A cure for grounded existence exists in the act of copying. To print is also to free.

In *The Wretched of the Screen*, Hito Steyerl writes of a world consumed by multiplicity to the extent where we are not only inhabited, or capable of virtual bilocation through technologies such as Skype or FaceTime, but our ability to multiply, and be multiplied, is calling ever more into question the possibilities of our own viewing position. Steyerl suggests that a prevalent use of gaming and surveillance image use may be contributing to this anxiety. Having always navigated with a horizon to move towards, indicating which way is up or down, we now survey populations from the skies and through drone eyes from a range of coordinates and vantage points at once. In gaming too, we no longer have use for a horizon, viewing characters and combatants from a choice of many perspectives at any one time. Citing Walter Benjamin's views on Paul Klee's painting *Angelus Novus* (1920), Steyerl writes,

> Grappling with crumbling futures that propel us backward onto an agonizing present, we may realise that the place we are falling towards is no longer grounded, nor is it stable. It promises no community but a shifting formation.[7]

In Steyerl's analysis of Benjamin's writing on Klee, the subject falls backwards and doesn't know what is coming, other than the inevitability that the future lies at the back of the faller. It is we, all of us, who are falling. Yet soft flight, in the experience of most of us, ends in meeting a resistant surface in the end. Ultimately, soil, earth, ground are bound to arrest us. We expect an end to falling and in anticipating it spend less time and scope on the experience of falling itself.

Saint Anthony (c. 251–356), a figure much visited by artists, is celebrated for his visions, doubts and meetings with the devil.[8] He went to live in the desert to question his orientation in the spiritual world. Horizons in the desert can be misleading. Without their instruction on place and the location of the viewer within them, other possibilities for inquiry can take on more prominence. After seeing Pieter Bruegel the Elder's painting *The Temptation of St Anthony* (1557) Gustave Flaubert laboured for thirty years on a prose adaptation of the same name, constructing a paradigm shift in the concept of horizons similar to that observed by Steyerl. In an introductory essay to Flaubert's text Bisland writes,

> Flaubert's Lucifer has no relation to the jejeune Devil of man's early conception of material evil, nor does he resemble Goethe's Mephistopheles; embodiment of the Eighteenth Century's spirit of sneering disbeliefs and negation. He is rather our own tempter – Science. He is the spirit of Knowledge: Nature itself calling us to look into the immensities and readjust our dogmas by this new and terrible widening of our mental and moral horizons.[9]

While Steyerl's concerns stem from an interest in the impact of new optical technologies and cultures on perception, Flaubert's emanate from the impact of science on faith. St Anthony attempts blindness to the temptations of the physical world to increase sight or knowledge within. For both, the losing of the horizon line acts as catalyst for addressing where we stand both physically and metaphorically in a world of multiples. As Cixous shows with her suicidal vets and Canetti with his human and animal mirrors, each of us is already plural as we gaze on the copy.

The next form of inhabitation is predicted to arise from developments in print's link to technological innovation. Soon all of us will at some stage have the option of incorporating printed elements into our physical bodies. We already have the possibility of replacing defective blood vessels with 3D printed equivalents, grown in layers from the inside out. Printed titanium knee joints can be implanted to replace bone. It may be that the printmare ahead that we fall backwards towards, blasted by gales of progress, will require us to re-orientate again and question who or what is looking, acknowledging our printed selves.[10]

Notes

1 Cixous, H. (2004) *The Writing Notebooks*, ed. Sellers, S., London: Continuum, pp. 44–7.
2 Ibid., p. 47.
3 Ibid.
4 Canetti, E. (1984) *Crowds and Power*, New York: Farrar Straus Giroux, p. 374.
5 www.urbandictionary.com.
6 Benjamin, W. (1936) 'The Work of Art in the Age of Mechanical Reproduction', in *Illuminations*, ed. Arendt, H., trans. Zohn, H., Glasgow: Fontana/Collins, 1970.
7 Steyerl, H. (2012) *The Wretched of the Screen*, Berlin: Sternberg Press, p. 28.
8 Saint Anthony was also known as Anthony of Egypt, Anthony the Abbot, Anthony of the Desert, Anthony the Anchorite and Anthony of Thebes. His temptations have been represented by a range of artists, including Martin Schongauer, Hieronymous Bosch, Dorothea Tanning, Max Ernst, Leonora Carrington and Salvador Dalí.
9 Flaubert, G. (1874) *The Temptations of St Anthony*, Bisland, E., trans Hearn, L. (2001) Digireads, p. 8.
10 El-Showk, S. (21st October, 2013) *Science Focus – Science & Technology*, 'How to Rebuild your Body with 3D-Printed Parts'. www.sciencefocus.com/feature/tech/how-rebuild-your-body-3d-printed-parts.

Part III Further reading

Edition

Cohan, Charles. 1993. 'The Net of Irrationality: The Variant Matrix & the Tyranny of the Edition'. *Contemporary Impressions*. Fall: 9–11.

Salsbury, Britanny. 2012. 'The Serial Drama of the Serial Format: Tradition, Revision and the Print Portfolio in "Print/Out" and "Printin"'. *Art in Print* 2 (1): 10–16.

Tallman, Susan. 1991. 'The Ethos of the Edition: The Stacks of Felix Gonzalez-Torres'. *Arts* 61 (1), Sept.: 13–14.

Uidhir, Christy Mag. 2009. 'Unlimited Additions to Limited Editions'. *Contemporary Aesthetics*, 7. www.contempaesthetics.org/newvolume/pages/article.php?articleID=527 [Accessed 25 April 2017].

Reproduction/originality/authenticity

Barker, Chris. 2014. 'Mechanical Reproduction in an Age of High Art'. *Contemporary Aesthetics* 12. http://quod.lib.umich.edu/c/ca/7523862.0012.010/-mechanical-reproduction-in-an-age-of-high-art?rgn=main;view=fulltext#top [Accessed 28 February 2017].

Codell, Julie F. 2010. '"Second Hand Images": On Art's Surrogate Means and Media-Introduction'. *Visual Resources: An International Journal of Documentation*, 26 (3): 214–25.

Gilmour, Pat. 2008. 'On Originality'. *Print Quarterly*, 25 (1) (March): 36–50.

Gilmour, Pat. 1990. 'Originality Circa 1960: A Time for Thinking Caps'. *The Tamarind Papers*, 13: 28–33.

Haas, Kevin. 2011. 'Authentic Experience: Multiplicity and Dislocation in Printmaking and Contemporary Culture'. In: Hoskins, Stephen et al. (eds), *IMPACT 6 Multi-disciplinary Printmaking Conference Proceedings*. Bristol: Impact Press, 76–80.

Hendrickson, Julia V. 2013. 'Print and the Virtual, Authentic Image'. 1 March. *Ink: Notes on Contemporary Print, Art21 magazine*. http://magazine.art21.org/2013/03/01/print-and-the-virtual-authentic-image/#.WL1uanrUqzw [Accessed 12 February 2017].

Hopkins, Robert. 2015. 'Reproductive Prints as Aesthetic Surrogates'. *The Journal of Aesthetics and Art Criticism* 73 (1): 11–21.

Komelj, Miklavž. 2007. 'Reproducibility and its Aura'. In: *Catalogue of the 27th Biennial of Graphic Arts: Exhibitions of Reproducible Art*, ed. mglc International Centre of Graphic Arts. Ljubljana: International Centre of Graphic Arts, 68–81.

Latour, Bruno and Lowe, Adam. 2010. 'The Migration of the Aura or How to Explore the Original Through its Facsimiles'. In: Bartscherer, Thomas (ed.), *Switching Codes*. Chicago: University of Chicago Press, 275–97.

Pelzer-Montada, Ruth. 2001. 'Authenticity in Printmaking – A Red Herring?' In: *IMPACT 2 International Printmaking Conference Proceedings*. Helsinki: University of Art and Design UIAH. www.uiah.fi/conferences/impact/pelzer/pelzer2.html [Accessed 15 February 2017].

Purves, Stuart. 2006. 'Original Versus Reproduction: Why Definitions Matter in Printmaking'. In: *Imprint*, 41 (1), Autumn. http://imprint.org.au/flashback-friday/original-versus-reproduction-why-definitions-matter-in-printmaking/ [Accessed 12 February 2017].

Copy

Boon, Marcus. 2010. *In Praise of Copying*. Cambridge, MA: Harvard University Press. Also available: www.hup.harvard.edu/features/boon/In-Praise-of-Copying-by-Marcus-Boon-HUP-free-full-text.pdf [Accessed 8 February 2013].

Buskirk, Martha. 2003. 'Original Copies'. In: *The Contingent Object of Contemporary Art*. Cambridge, MA; London: MIT Press, 59–105.

Fiduccia, Joanna. 2009. 'Original Copies: Images in the Zero Dimension'. *Art on Paper* 13 (5) (May): 47–56.

Schwartz, Hillel. 1998. *The Culture of the Copy: Striking Likenesses Unreasonable Facsimiles*. Cambridge, MA: MIT Press.

Multiples

Cherix, Christophe, Suzuki, Sarah J. S. and Conaty, Kim. 2012. *Print/Out*. New York: The Museum of Modern Art.

Clintberg, Mark. 2012. 'Multiply/Divide: The Politics of the Multiple'. In: Dyment, Dave and Elgstrand, Gregory (eds), *One for Me and One to Share: Artist's Multiples by Multiple Artists*. Toronto: YYZ Books and Mercer Union, 114–23.

Cook, Roy T. and Meskin, Aaron. 2015. 'Comics, Prints, and Multiplicity'. *The Journal of Aesthetics and Art Criticism* 73 (1): 57–67.

Davies, David. 2015. 'Varying Impressions'. *The Journal of Aesthetics and Art Criticism* 73 (1): 81–92.

Delleaux, Océane. 2010. 'Free Prints and Multiples in Contemporary France'. *Print Quarterly* 27 (1) (March): 38–52.

Virtual

Coldwell, Paul and Rauch, Barbara. 2009. *The Personalised Surface: New Approaches to Digital Printmaking*. London: Fade Research.

Drucker, Johanna. 2009. 'Graphesis and Code'. *Digital Aesthetics and Projects in Speculative Computing*, 133–44.

Hall, Sean. 2001. 'Making it New: Transformations in the Grammar and Identity of Digital Printmaking'. *Digital Creativity*, 12 (1): 27–30.

Kushner, Marilyn S. 2001. *Digital Printmaking Now*. New York: Brooklyn Museum of Art.

Noble, Jim. 2002. 'Fatal Attraction: Print meets Computer'. In: Mealing, Stuart (ed.), *Computers and Art*. Bristol: Intellect, 77–93.

Thompson, Paul. 2011. 'The Digital Matrix and the Paperless Print'. In: Hoskins, Stephen et al. (eds), *IMPACT 6 Multi-disciplinary Printmaking Conference Proceedings*. Bristol: Impact Press, 44–8.

Thompson, Paul and Pengelly, Jon. 2014. 'Walking in the Garden of Forking Paths – Examining Notions of "Post-Physical" Printmaking in Digital Space'. In: Harrison, Paul, Shemilt, Elaine and Watson, Arthur (eds), *Borders & Crossings: The Artist as Explorer: IMPACT 8 International Printmaking Conference*. Dundee: Duncan of Jordanstone College of Art & Design, University of Dundee, 204–9.

Miscellaneous

Aarons, Philip, Roth, Andrew and Brand, Victor (eds), 2009. *In Numbers*. New York: PPP Editions.

Bate, David. 2001. 'Indexiphilia'. 12th Tallinn Print Triennial Conference. www.triennial.ee/15/web/tgtconference_bate.htm [Accessed 28 November 16].

Connor, Steven. 2001. 'Flat Life'. A paper given at the University of Glasgow in March 2001. www.stevenconnor.com/flat/ [Accessed 6 February 2013].

Darrieusseq, Marie. 2005. *White*. London: Faber and Faber, 118–19.

Derrida, Jacques. 2005. 'Paper or Me, You Know ... (New Speculations on a Luxury of the Poor)'. In: *Paper Machine*, trans. Rachel Bowlby. Stanford, CA: Stanford University Press, 41–65.

Emmons, Amze. 2015. 'Metaphor over Medium'. Blog: http://archive.printeresting.org/2015/02/24/metaphor-over-medium/ [Accessed 15 December 2016].

Falconer, Delia. 1997. *The Service of Clouds*. Sydney: Pan Macmillan, 64–78.

Gurney, Kim. 2003. 'Print as Metaphor'. *Artthrob*. Archive: Issue No. 73, September www.artthrob.co.za/03sept/reviews/impact1.html [Accessed 22 December 2016].

Harrison, Paul Liam, Shemilt, Elaine and Watson, Arthur (eds), 2014. *Borders & Crossings: The Artist as Explorer: IMPACT 8 International Printmaking Conference*. Dundee: Duncan of Jordanstone College of Art & Design, University of Dundee.

Hecker, Judith B. 2000. 'One Thing After Another: Serial Print Projects'. In: The Museum of Modern Art et al., eds Varnedoe, Kirk, Antonelli, Paola and Siegel, Joshua. *Modern Contemporary: Aspects of Art at MoMA Since 1980*. New York: The Museum of Modern Art, 516–19.

Hood, Mary. 2015. 'Appropriation in Post Digital Practices'. In: *Academic Papers, Illustrated Talks, Themed Panels: IMPACT 9 International Printmaking Conference Proceedings*. China: China Academy of Art Press, 9–14.

McMahon, Taryn. 2014. 'Print Synthesis'. *The Mid America Print Council Journal* 22 (1 + 2), Spring/Summer: 8–10.

Pelzer-Montada, Ruth. 2008. 'The Attraction of Print: Notes on the Surface of the (Art) Print'. *Art Journal* 67 (2): 74–91.

Ruth Pelzer-Montada (2011) 'Sensing Print: Reflections on the Materiality of the Contemporary Art Print'. In: Hoskins, Stephen et al. (eds), *IMPACT 6 Multidisciplinary Printmaking Conference Proceedings*. Bristol: Impact Press, 53–9.

Urban, Jason. 2014. 'Stagecraft: The Theater of Print in a Digital World'. *Art in Print* 4 (2): 1–4.

PART IV

The field

Introduction to Part IV

The texts in Part IV, as the title suggests, aim to circumscribe some of the major spheres of print activity. They are focused on the keywords of production, collecting, dissemination, education and research. Each of the keywords in this section refers to and comprises a wide range of activities that may complement but also at times compete with each other: for example, museum collecting operates differently from private collecting, even if there are also similarities. In other words, each keyword could merit a whole section by itself to cover the breadth of activities it encompasses. Furthermore, the texts that appear under a particular keyword – more often than not – could just as easily be linked to a different one. For example, the first text about an open-access workshop appears under the label of 'production', but it refers equally to 'collaboration' or 'dissemination'. It should also be stressed that all of the demarcated areas of activity that are highlighted in this part contribute to the discursive field, or the debates around the discipline, whether they do so explicitly or implicitly. Hence, it may seem artificial to separate discursive (Parts II and III) and seemingly operational matters (Part IV) into discrete parts. This division is simply for the purpose of easier analysis and should not be taken in any way as definitive.

In the following, keywords are set in bold.

Needless, to say, the making or **production** of prints is a decisive topic. More often than not, it is covered – as argued elsewhere in this book – through detailed technical instruction in the numerous manuals or specialist journal articles on printmaking. In addition, interviews with artists and other monographic writing on artists often yield insight into the making of works. These still constitute the majority of art criticism and a large proportion of the art historical investigation of prints. In the period covered by this anthology – which is marked by the increasing emergence of conferences and symposia dedicated to print and printmaking, as previously stated – the number of print artists who have provided a more comprehensive insight into their own working procedures has increased. Besides, since the late 1990s, the production or making of prints has gained an even higher level of critical investigation within the context of PhDs by artists in certain countries.[1]

The first selected text focuses on a model of **production** that is highly pertinent to printmaking and has been adopted in other fields, such as sculpture. Art historian and curator Daniel F. Herrmann reflects on Edinburgh Printmakers (EP) in Scotland on the occasion of its fortieth anniversary. Founded by artists, as the first open-access workshop in the UK, it functioned as a model for other, similar workshops. Open-access workshops in various configurations have been a vital feature of printmaking the world over (see, for example, London Print Studio; Hong Kong Open Print Shop; Trykkeriet-Center for Contemporary Printmaking, Bergen, Norway; Open Studio, Toronto, Canada – to name but a few). However, it should be stressed that this model does not exist in every country and moreover the levels of openness do vary across the world. The chosen Scottish example is exemplary in this respect.

Like private, purely commercial workshops, open-access workshops often collaborate with well-known artists to publish portfolios. They generally provide exhibition facilities for artists frequenting the workshop as well as presenting curated programmes of – often ambitious – exhibitions. They offer residency programmes of various types to further artistic development and training. Their public profile and funding are often closely tied to serving local communities through outreach and educational activities.

Herrmann traces EP's emergence in the context of the cultural and political ferment of the late 1960s in Western Europe and the US. His article touches on and echoes points made elsewhere in this anthology, such as the basic definition of the artistic print, its role in communication and its questioning of originality and uniqueness. If, historically, the all-too-mundane aspects of the craft of printmaking, the 'whiff' of the workshop, were suppressed in order to elevate print to an art form, this has changed thanks to, for example, important figures such as Stanley William Hayter (1901–88). The workshop as the material foundation for any printmaking activity encompasses not just technical equipment. It provides expertise and collaboration – of an artist working with a 'master' printer. Equally, it engenders sociality and commonality among the artists themselves. Herrmann highlights the importance of the open-access policy of an institution like EP – and its difference from the traditional studio.

As the previous entry indicates, production and **dissemination** are closely intertwined, especially for a private print publisher. Jeremy Lewinson's text – written in the 1990s – gives an insight into this important commercial model of print activity by focusing on the equally crucial format of the print portfolio.[2] It charts the establishment of British print publisher Charles Booth-Clibborn's Paragon Press. The essay touches on various print publishing models that inspired Booth-Clibborn but from which – as a commercial enterprise – he also sought to differentiate his own venture. At play are market considerations, the broader – in this case largely national – art-world context and personal ambition, even passion. Lewinson also discusses the format of the print portfolio in the twentieth century, especially its different narrative possibilities, through an in-depth focus on several artistic examples.

Today the range of print publishing activities has expanded immensely. In addition to the work of private publishers, artists' self-publishing – while not new – has become an important and rapidly growing feature of contemporary art.[3]

Many workshops, whether open-access or affiliated with art institutions and universities, combine print publishing with extensive research.[4] Unlike other research, the results are not always disseminated to the wider specialist field or the public. However, increasingly publications, as well as symposia and conferences with affiliated published proceedings, perform this important function.[5]

The text by Gillian Saunders, curator of prints and drawings at the Victoria & Albert Museum (or 'V&A') in London, gives insights into the broader parameters of museum **collecting** rather than private collecting. It uncovers the wider cultural and artistic ideologies – including the nature of the institution itself – that become apparent in the designation of objects worthy of collection by a national institution at a certain point in time. These involve an object's status within established hierarchies that are dependent on historically changing definitions of art and non-art, be it opposition between art and craft, or between art and everyday items. The examples discussed in the essay adhere to the concept of print as an aesthetic object but recent larger social, cultural and political values are mirrored in the focus on works that engage with and are made by women and artists of colour from the 1990s onwards.

A vital element as to the status of art and especially print is the question of technology. Saunders highlights the positive role that the V&A has played in its openness to new technologies throughout its history. Her main point – against overly dystopian views of the digital as subsuming older technologies – is the observation of a 'mix and match' approach between digital and older modes of printmaking. In the almost ten years since the essay was written, new challenges have emerged for museums' collecting strategies by multipart and distributed works, as, for example, discussed by the next two authors.

Sheryl Conkelton's text illuminates print's historic disseminating role in creating and sustaining public discourse. It was written for *Philagrafika*, the 2009/10 biennale in Philadelphia, USA (see essay by Roca in Part II). Conkelton also charts the changes to public discourse, especially in the twenty-first century: not only has it become global, but the public sphere is no longer conceived as the uniform, monolithic space of old. Instead, it encompasses different local, if overlapping experiences, by multiple publics. Nevertheless aspects of the 'old' public sphere still persist. Conkelton suggests that – in the context of the prevalence of digital mediatisation – the use of print media can function as a historical trope. This allows print to reflect critically on what the notion of the 'public' might actually mean today, especially when it is differently imagined from official, often exclusionary narratives. Conkelton's essay is an exposition of how some of the artists included in *Philagrafika* managed to fulfil this task of a differently imagined public sphere.

Print artist and cultural theorist Johanna Drucker's text was one of the keynote speeches at the *IMPACT 7* International Printmaking Conference 2011 in Melbourne. She considers the theoretical implications of emergent practices of production and **dissemination** that cross media and platforms, disregarding established notions of fixed objects. Recent theories of materiality have challenged the conventional assumption of objects as fixed and immutable. Drucker makes the important suggestion that all works of art ought to be considered as events rather than objects. In other words, new practices – such as the ones highlighted in her speech – with their emphasis on and potential for group authorship, collectivity and participation contribute to a questioning of the mere 'thingness' of objects. Drucker also reminds her audience that works that occupy multiple platforms do not necessarily rely on digital technologies, as is so often assumed today. By recounting historical practices or rituals which follow a 'distributed model' by leaving 'traces', she demonstrates that such historical practices foreshadow contemporary 'distributed' works.

Given that all art is political in the broadest sense, even if politics is an implicit rather than an explicit reference, it seemed important to draw attention to an area of print that has had vital importance for centuries, namely explicitly political or, even more specifically, **activist art**.

In his chapter from Josh McPhee's important exhibition and book *Paper Politics* (2009) about socially and politically engaged printmaking in the US, artist and activist Eric Triantafillou takes his cue from street art in San Francisco's Mission District and raises pertinent questions about the role of such art in a society that 'only claims to be democratic' (288). He asks what a truly political art might mean today, especially when such art is frequently appropriated by the system that it itself criticises. It then becomes a mere 'aesthetic commodity' (289).

He delivers a powerful argument and challenge, namely that activist printmakers' images frequently rely on the 'recycling' of familiar and binary 'visual tropes' and merely hold out 'the promise of universal emancipation' rather than contributing to true change (289). By critically analysing an earlier image of his own in this mode, he argues for a more radical approach and a more complex, 'systemic' view. Ultimately, he advocates a critical engagement with one's own (group's) values and visual practices and urges print artists to do so collectively in order to further social freedom for all.[6]

The text by curator and art historian Mari Carmen Ramírez constitutes an excellent general introduction to the function of **biennales.**[7] It also contextualises the Biennale of San Juan's distinctive location in Puerto Rico which is characterised as a 'hinge' between South and North America. Ramírez regards the specific sitedness of the biennale in terms of Bourdieu's concept of 'symbolic capital' – as a kind of operation that presents a crucial possibility for the survival of colonial peoples. At the same time, the 2004 biennale theme of 'trans/migration' encapsulates – in addition to regional and artistic challenges – the representation of, on the one hand, artists from Latin America and, on the other, Latino artists from across the world.

Ramírez further outlines the specific challenges to graphic art biennales or what she calls a 'fundamentalist' approach. The latter is based on a conservative model of both the definition of printmaking and the structure of an exhibition based on national artistic representation. Worldwide changes such as globalisation necessitated a rethinking along thematic or issue-based lines. Such a strategy is able to align itself with the malleability of contemporary art; furthermore, a curatorial model replaces the previous hierarchical apparatus.

Ramírez also traces the role of graphic art in Latin America at the time of the first biennale in 1970. She posits a disappearance of the matrix and suggests the notion of the 'imprint' instead. Nevertheless, she notes that 'classical printmaking' has not disappeared. Yet, expanded printmaking serves to challenge the 'values of the hegemonic centers' and ultimately can serve to foster change in the region.

Her analysis is relevant for printmaking in general. Although opposition to hegemonic values carries particular weight and traits that pertain to the region, this aspect of print is of relevance elsewhere, even if the specific features of such resistance will vary.

Critic Shang Hui diagnoses a resurgence of **Chinese printmaking** in the early part of the twenty-first century. Dominated by the woodcut since the 1930s, Chinese printmaking was subject to the demands of the ideology of the communist state until the beginning of reforms in the 1980s and so, in printmaking, this translated into the adoption of techniques other than the woodcut. National exhibitions and educational activities specifically addressed to children promoted prints of a broader variety to a growing audience. However, unlike other art forms, printmaking appeared to have missed the change to a resolutely contemporary art that occurred in China during the 1990s. Not unlike certain phases in the West, Chinese printmaking focused on mere technical proficiency without larger conceptual underpinnings and became ever more specialised. Art criticism ignored it, and its inclusion into the emerging contemporary art market of the 1990s was thus equally foregone. By contrast, Shang Hui grants printmaking in the new century 'a greater contemporary consciousness' and a 'humanistic concern with current social realities' (306). These realities are characterised by China's rapid transition to a consumer society.

Large national exhibitions are complemented by printmaking's firm placement in Chinese art academies, and a small number of workshops exist. Other promising ventures are the Guanlan Print Village residency programme and the Guanlan Print Biennale, as well as other biennales dedicated to print (Bejing 2003; Yunnan 2008). Shang Hui ultimately credits such international events with the important role of creating 'truly equal dialogues' and the promotion of Chinese printmakers' 'self-consciousness in a global context' as well as 'conceptual innovations, and experiments with new media' (309). These developments have been accompanied by a critical discourse on Chinese printmaking that – amongst other topics – is concerned with finding an indigenous language that is free from imitation of the West. Drawing on the concept of the 'imprint', the creative role of the artist is emphasised.[8]

In the context of an increasingly 'post-disciplinary' art context, Matthew Perkins asks as to the implications for a higher art **education** that has historically been structured according to medium-specific disciplines. He interrogates the notions of the terms 'discipline' as well as 'medium', both tied to the functioning of 'the studio'. In addition to creating specific knowledge/s, discipline-specific studios served to maintain boundaries between media. They further socialised individuals into such subject-specific knowledge/s and helped to create artistic identities ('I am a painter/printmaker/sculptor' etc). The studio then must be regarded as a locus for knowledge-creation within defined boundaries. Nevertheless, Perkins comes to the conclusion that in a post-disciplinary or hybrid art context, the practice of the studio should not necessarily be abolished. While 'knowledge of the specificities of disciplines and of their histories' is retained, post-disciplinary studios are characterised by an openness to dialogue across different areas/disciplines/media. At the same time they necessitate a questioning of disciplines or studio specialisms, all in order to make possible the emergence of the new (315).

Perkins draws his example from 'Photomedia' to indicate the crossover that is occurring through the adoption of similar digital means, across all areas of study. Comparable points can be made in regard to printmaking and, indeed, the changing scenario described by Perkins applies to many art departments and programmes. The question is how both subject-specific knowledge AND hybrid practices are made possible structurally, in terms of time-tabling, progress through a programme, access to materials, workshops, academic tutors and technicians. Models of best practice – which will, of course, be locally inflected – are in high demand.

As already indicated elsewhere, printmaking **research** takes many forms.[9] The steadily growing research focus of art schools and art education, – whether an institution is incorporated into a university or not – makes it important to feature a project that represents one possible approach to academic arts-based research in form of a PhD project.[10]

Amanda Thomson demonstrates the appropriateness and feasibility of a multi-modal, multi-disciplinary approach to research about conceptions of place and landscape in which print, especially book art, plays a significant role. Its aim – and contribution to knowledge – is to consider how art can augment and maybe even alter the insights of other disciplines, in this case, geography and anthropology. This short presentation gives a glimpse into the ways in which the project was informed by critical, theoretical, contextual and subject-specific writing, such as book art. Crucially, it also shows how textual research and the making of the artworks are intertwined and how both mutually enrich each other.

The final text is dedicated to an improbable sounding, yet real author. Written by R. L. Tillman, artist and educator and one of the founders of the inspiring web resource *Printeresting* (2008–15), it is a humorous yet serious reflection on the differences between art, craft and technique and on what may or may not distinguish expert and amateur knowledge. Ultimately, it pays homage to an expert amateur and draws attention to the fact that the boundaries between amateur and 'expert' knowledge are currently being re-thought.

Notes

1 The literature on arts-based research, including PhDs, is now substantial. See also Paul van der Lem (1999) for a broader contextualisation of PhDs in arts practice, written in the early days of such projects.
2 For different approaches to and analyses of the portfolio format, see Lyons (2011) and Coldwell (2013) in the further reading list.
3 See Drucker's text in this section. See also the further reading list for other references.
4 An early model was the Tamarind Studio, founded in 1960 in Los Angeles as the Tamarind Lithography Workshop. Now the Tamarind Institute, it has been affiliated with the University of New Mexico since 1970. In addition to the *Tamarind Papers*, published from 1974–92, three further volumes of the *Tamarind Papers* were published in book form between 1993 and 1998 in collaboration with the University of New Mexico Press. http://tamarind.unm.edu/pages/view/39-gallery-store-tamarind-papers [Accessed 25 February 2017]. In the UK, the Centre for Fine Print Research (CFPR), at the University of the West of England in Bristol, has created an exemplary model.
5 For one such publication, see Dellinger, Smith, Miller and Tampa Museum of Art (2014). See also Margaret Miller's presentation 'The Transgressive Mark' at the *Printmaking in the Expanded Field* symposium at the Oslo National Academy of the Arts in September 2015: http://pitef.khio.no/cr3ativspeaker/margaret-miller/ [Accessed 22 February 2017]. Miller is director of Graphic Studio at the University of South Florida (USF). See also Annis Fitzhugh's (2014) presentation at *IMPACT 8* in Dundee, Scotland. Fitzhugh is director of the open-access print studio in Dundee. The workshop shares its site – and

frequently collaborates – with Dundee Contemporary Arts (DCA), an exhibition venue that presents significant international exhibitions. The print studio is also in close proximity to Dundee University's School of Art research centre, further stimulating interesting research synergies.

6 For a lively discussion in response to this essay, see: https://justseeds.org/all-the-instruments-agree/ [Accessed 5 July 2017].

7 For discussions in the context of other biennales, see Roca (2011) in Part II; Škrjanec (2003).

8 On the notion of the 'imprint', see other discussions in this book, by Didi-Huberman (1997/2008) in Part III and Ramírez (2004) in Part IV.

9 Conference, symposia and biennale proceedings are excellent resources for an insight into the state of printmaking research.

10 See also endnote 1. Further sources can be found in the further reading list.

References

Coldwell, Paul. 2013. 'Just What is it that Makes an Artist's Folio So Special, So Appealing, So Important?' In: Morgan, Luke (ed.), *Intersections and Counterpoints: IMPACT 7 International Multi-disciplinary Printmaking Conference Proceedings*. Clayton, Victoria: Monash University Publishing, 7–11.

Dellinger, J., Smith, T., Miller, M. and Tampa Museum of Art. 2014. *Graphicstudio: Uncommon Practice at USF*. Tampa Museum of Art. London: Giles.

Fitzhugh, Annis. 2014. 'Numerical Manoeuvres: The Printer's Hand in a Post-Digital World'. In: Harrison, Paul, Shemilt, Elaine and Watson, Arthur (eds), *Borders & Crossings: The Artist as Explorer: IMPACT 8 International Printmaking Conference*. Dundee: Duncan of Jordanstone College of Art & Design, University of Dundee, 243.

van der Lem, Paul. 1999. 'Search and Research in Fine Print: Creating Practice-Based and Theoretical Research for the Discipline of Fine Print'. In: Parraman, Carinna and Brewer, Emmeline (eds), *IMPACT International Multi-disciplinary Printmaking Conference Proceedings*. Bristol: Impact Press, 115–24. www.uwe.ac.uk/sca/research/cfpr/dissemination/conferences/IMPACT%20PROCEEDINGS%20copy.pdf [Accessed 15 February 2017].

Lyons, Beauvais. 2011. 'Das Exchange-Portfolio als relationale Kunstform'. ['The Exchange Portfolio as a Relational Art Form'.] In *im:print 2011. zustandsprotokolle aktueller druckgrafik / journal for the state of current printmaking*. Edited by Schneider, Michael and Maurer, Philipp. Vienna/New York: Springer, 73–91.

Škrjanec, Breda. 2003. 'Fifty years of the International Biennal of Graphic Arts'. In *25th International Biennial of Graphic Arts Ljubljana*, eds Cherix, Christophe and Goodrich Noble, Madeleine. Ljubljana: mglc: International Centre of Graphic Arts. www.basis-wien.at/avdt/pdf/043/00061995.pdf [Accessed 12 May 2017].

Daniel F. Herrmann

Edinburgh Printmakers and the notion of the workshop*

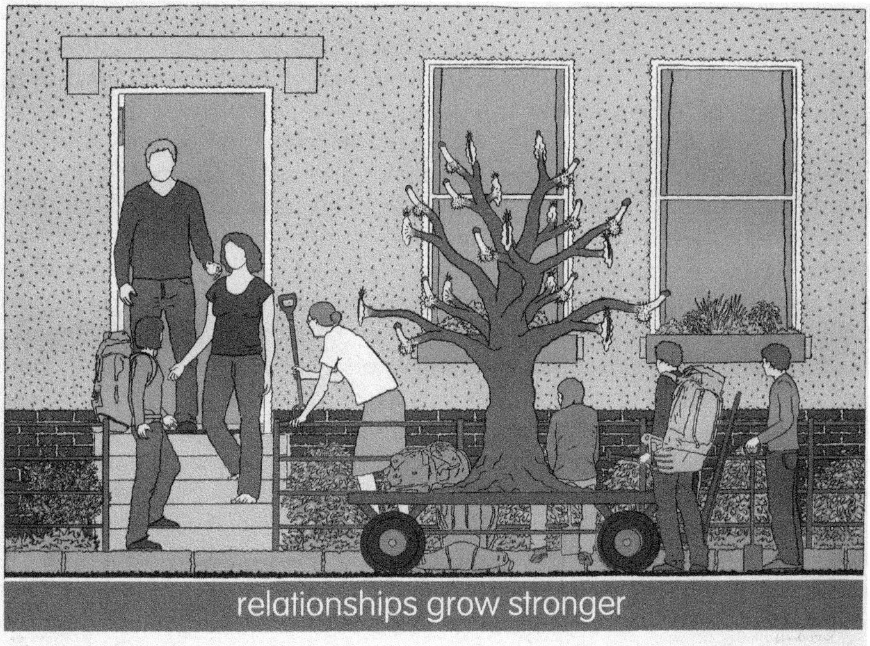

Chad McCail, *Relationships Grow Stronger*, 2007. Screen-print. Image 49 × 68 cm, paper 57 × 76 cm. Edition: 30, printed by Alastair Clark.

* Daniel F. Herrmann. 2007. 'Edinburgh Printmakers and the Notion of the Workshop'. In: *Edinburgh Printmakers: 40 Years of Original Prints*, Edinburgh: Edinburgh Printmakers, pp. 7–10. Reproduced by kind permission of the author and Edinburgh Printmakers.

Relationships grow stronger: Chad McCail's screen-print, the latest work to be made by Edinburgh Printmakers at the time of publishing, presents a scene of transition and adventure to the viewer. In front of what might be a communal dwelling, a man and a woman bid their farewells to a group of teenagers. Their backpacks filled to the brim for a long and exciting journey ahead, the four kids carry spades and planting tools. While the couple seem to give their blessings to one of the children, the others patiently wait, standing next to or sitting on a trolley that carries their fertile payload. The little tree reveals its fruit only at the second glance: the branches sprout male and female genitalia, deadpan and hilarious symbols of personal liberty and sexuality. These are not depicted in any lewd way; this sexuality is not meant to arouse cheap thrills. In the humorous reality of the print, in which even the grandmother peacefully hands over a pitchfork to the children in order to aid the planting of the tree, it much rather symbolises a spirit of independence, of self-exploration and freedom. In McCail's print, the viewer can witness an act of trust – one generation sending another one on the way.

With their abstracted colour schemes, the emphasis of lines and the anonymity of their protagonists, Chad McCail's artworks employ the aesthetics of former schoolbook illustrations. And indeed, the typeface used by McCail to letter his works is inspired by that of 'Ladybird' children's books. His works recall the feel of community education leaflets and other means of distributed pamphlets intended to educate a mass audience. Combining this with text messages that seem to come right from the hopeful time of the welfare state, McCail's works offer a utopian vision of a communal society that presents an alternative to contemporary life 'which is based on a system of exchange orchestrated by money, tasks and possessions.'[1] Devoid of either the doting nostalgia or the smug irony that so often goes hand in hand with artists' appropriation of past styles, such sincerity and commitment to the idea of the artist as an 'agent of social change'[2] is nothing but audacious. It is also most appropriate to the institution that is Edinburgh Printmakers.

When Robert Cox walked up to Philip Reeves in 1967 to outline the idea of the Printmakers Workshop, later to be realised by Roy Wood and Kim Kempshall, they conceived an audacious project indeed. Much more than just a production space, they created a true collaboration space – the first 'open access' printmaking studio of its kind in Britain. As such, Edinburgh Printmakers is not only a place of print production, but also one of social interaction, participation and education. It is a 'workshop' in the best possible sense: a place for mutual experimentation, analysis and debate, for teaching, learning, inspiration and communal involvement. It is, in this sense, a utopian space.

Printmaking is a curious medium. At its most basic, printmaking consists of the deliberate production of a matrix, used to transfer pigment onto a carrier – usually more than once. The matrix can take many forms: an etching plate, perhaps a woodblock, lithography stone or a mesh screen. The pigment may be applied by hand, roller or squeegee. The carrier will in most cases be paper, but can nowadays be almost anything, from fabric to foil. This simple definition already suffices to describe the medium's peculiarities: its facility for multiplying images and its dependency on mediating technology. A lot has been written on the possibility to multiply images. Printmaking's ability to create multiple images was used for both information and propaganda, was cause for praise and concern. It preceded photography in this and many other respects. More than 500 years after its inception, printmaking still succeeds in shaking up notions of what constitutes 'originality' and 'uniqueness' in art. This is a fascinating field and an important question for visual culture. But it is equally important to look at what material circumstances make this possible. Just as important and unique to the medium of printmaking are its specific tools, its specific equipment, its specific skills and the place in which these factors come together, the workshop.

In conversation with Gill Tyson, Philip Reeves said it best: 'You can paint pictures in a bedsit, but you can't print that easily.'[3] In order to make prints, you need equipment. Presses, lithography stones, tools – all of these are expensive and can hardly be afforded by a lone artist in his or her bedsit. More than anything, printmaking requires expert knowledge in how to operate the equipment and how to translate the artistic outcome envisaged in the artist's mind onto the final sheet. The economics and practicalities of the medium are thus conducive to a collaborative approach. Indeed, in contrast to drawing, which suggests immediacy between the artist's idea and its expression on the paper, printmaking has always had to deal with the many steps and processes in between the idea and the final work. The old inscriptions of *pinxit*, *delineavit*, *and sculpsit*[4] indicate the different steps in making a print and illustrate the long tradition of necessary collaboration between artists and craftsmen. For a long time, they also indicated a hierarchy. The *idea* was the noble realm of the lofty artist, the base execution that of the mere craftsman. This was perpetuated in the late eighteenth-century notion of the *peintre-graveur*, the 'artist-engraver', intended to elevate a specific printmaking process from a 'craft' to an 'art' by effectively suppressing most references to the workshop. It was only in the mid-twentieth century that the conditions of the printmaker's workshop were to come to be seen as an integral and even positive part of the medium. As late as 1953, William M. Ivins, founding curator of the department of Prints and Drawings at the Metropolitan Museum in New York, still described the material conditions of printmaking as 'omissions, distortions and subjective difficulties', which had to be overcome.[5] Thirteen years later, however, the art historian Herbert Read writes in the preface to Stanley William Hayter's seminal book *New Ways of Gravure* that Hayter had 'revived the workshop conception of the artist – not the artist as the lone wolf, howling on the fringes of an indifferent society, but as a member of a group of artists, working together, pooling their ideas, communicating to one another their discoveries and achievements.'[6] Here, we are witness to a radical change in attitude towards printmaking: Read's main criterion for the praise of the medium lies no longer in its propensity for verisimilitude, but much rather in its capacity as a conduit for aesthetic discourse. The value of the aesthetic product was now determined by its social production. This was a watershed. 'Hayter's studios were experimental; artists were on their own, exploring the techniques.' 'Hayter really was *the* person to come up with the notion of the printmaker's studio,' Alfons Bytautas, Senior Etching Technician at Edinburgh Printmakers rightly remarked in an interview.[7] In this respect, the 1967 founding of the Printmakers Workshop was following an important international trend, pioneered by Hayter's Studio 17 and proliferated by such important presses as Kelpra Studios in London, Tamarind in the USA and others.[8] In other respects, the Printmakers Workshop was perhaps more adventurous. Hayter's example of a print workshop, praised by Herbert Read in 1966, was shifting the focus from final outcome to its means of production. The Scottish workshop took this shift further. As an 'open access' space, it did not limit the aesthetic discourse, the 'communicating of discoveries and achievements', to an exclusive elite of invited artists alone, but institutionalised it as constitutional to an inclusive group of interested practitioners. Even if this might not have been an explicit goal at the incorporation of the Workshop in 1967, it was certainly a major factor once Ken Duffy was appointed managing secretary in September 1968: 'I remember [Kim] saying that this should not just be a workshop. This should be a place where people can meet and talk about prints, exchange ideas, and so on. There should be a kind of social side to it.'[9]

It is this workshop side of printmaking, the spirit of collaboration, accessibility, and social relationships that made the Printmakers Workshop significant. Forty years on, the generations changing, this still makes for the importance of Edinburgh Printmakers today. It is, in the best sense, a utopian project. Relationships grow stronger.

Notes

1 Chad McCail in an interview with Alice Strang, 8 April 2002, Scottish National Gallery of Modern Art registry files, GMA 4340.

2 Ibid.

3 Philip Reeves in conversation with Gill Tyson, [Edinburgh Printmakers, Part 1, 1967–1987, The Early Years, DVD].

4 Historically appended to the artist's name or initials on a painting, or engraved copy of a painting; Delineavit 'drawn by', Sculpsit 'carved (it)'; 'engraved (it)'.

5 Ivins, William, *Prints and Visual Communication*, Cambridge 1953, p. 122.
6 Read, Herbert, 'Preface', in S. W. Hayter, *New Ways of Gravure*, London et al. 1966.
7 Alfons Bytautas in conversation with Gill Tyson, [Edinburgh Printmakers, Part 1, 1967–1987, The Early Years, DVD].
8 For a more detailed overview of the historical development of open access printing presses in the English-speaking world, see Pat Gilmour, 'Artists' Workshops: An Historical Perspective', in Silvie Turner (ed.), *British Printmaking Studios*, London 1992.
9 Roy Wood, in conversation with Gill Tyson, [Edinburgh Printmakers, Part 1 1967–1987, The Early Years, DVD].

Jeremy Lewison

Projects and portfolios: narrative and structure*

Looking at the history of printmaking in the twentieth century it is striking the extent to which its peaks are defined by portfolios rather than by single prints. Although artists have always made superb individual sheets, particularly in the first half of the century, what stand out above all are the series. Picasso's *Vollard*, *347* and posthumously published *156* suites set markers for many of his contemporaries and successors in terms of scale, scope and coherence. The size of these suites seems not to have been predetermined; they were worked on intuitively and in intense bursts of creative activity. The *347 suite*, a series of 347 etchings, was executed from start to finish in just less than seven months, from 16 March to 5 October 1968.

Picasso was not the only artist of the earlier part of the twentieth century to create major series of prints. Dix's *War*, Matisse's *Jazz* (published as a book and a portfolio), Lissitzky's *Victory Over the Sun*, Beckmann's *Hell*, Kollwitz's *The Peasants' Revolt* and Dubuffet's *Walls* are among the exceptional productions of the first fifty years. Since the Second World War, however, there has been a sharper focus on this publishing format. Many truly remarkable portfolios spring to mind, among them Newman's *18 Cantos*, Rivers's and O'Hara's *Stones*, Johns's *First Etchings*, Marden's *Ten Days*, Motherwell's *A la Pintura* (a book of unbound sheets), Baselitz's *Eagles*, Warhol's *Marilyns* and LeWitt's *Forms Derived from a Cube*. As for the British contribution, Hockney's *A Rake's Progress*, Paolozzi's *As is When*, Hamilton's *Ulysses* project and Caulfield's *Laforgue* suite measure up to them all.

* Jeremy Lewison. 1995. 'Projects and Portfolios: Narrative and Structure'. In: Booth-Clibborn, Charles (ed.), *Contemporary British Art in Print*. London: Booth-Clibborn Editions, pp. 11–19. © Jeremy Lewison. Reproduced by kind permission of the author and Paragon Press. Edited and updated by the author for this publication.

It is not clear why the portfolio has been such a popular form during this period. Perhaps it is easier to market a group of works rather than an individual image. Given the unjustifiably low regard in which prints are held – museum print galleries are always separated from painting and sculpture galleries; painting and sculpture are often referred to as the primary media – it would not be surprising if commercial reasons formed part of the justification. There must be, however, more positive, aesthetic reasons for this flourishing. Perhaps it has to do with the publisher's and artist's ambition to make a great work, independent of other works, with an internal coherence and a unity, that provides its own context for display and contemplation and which has built-in momentum. Or maybe the effort to become familiar with a new medium, or to adapt working habits to a medium which requires a different approach, is so great that it hardly seems worthwhile to make a single image.

Historically some of the greatest prints have been published in groups. Goya, Callot and Hogarth are obvious examples of artists who have favoured this format, while other artists have made works which, while published separately, may be perceived as part of an ongoing group. Such is the coherence of Rembrandt's landscape etchings that had he been alive today, they would almost certainly have been released as a package. More recently, Georg Baselitz's *Neue Typen* prints and related works from 1965–66 exemplify the same tendency towards seriality in spite of their status as individually conceived works.

The nature of portfolios

Broadly speaking there are four different types of portfolio. The first is a set of prints which is essentially a literary narrative, such as Hockney's *A Rake's Progress*, where Hockney describes in images and words the experience of his first trip to New York as a young artist. His original intention had been to execute eight etchings based on Hogarth's tale of the same name, setting them in New York rather than London. What attracted him was the possibility of telling a story relying solely on visual means (although the incorporation of words contradicts this somewhat). Initially he set out to work towards its publication in book form. He attempted twenty-four plates but soon discovered that such a large number was technically too demanding and would dilute the story. He finally made sixteen. The book was never published but, after Hockney finished the plates, the project was bought by Editions Alecto and published as a portfolio in an edition of fifty.

The initial idea to publish the prints as a book rather than a portfolio indicates the essentially literary nature of this kind of project. Each image is numbered on the plate, thus determining the narrative sequence. In book form the experience of looking at the prints would have been more intimate and private. Furthermore only two plates at a time could have been viewed. As a portfolio the whole story can be seen at once, although the detail may only be understood print by print.

A second type of portfolio is one which sets up a technical rather than a literary narrative, one where the narrative consists of a sequence of technical moves or explorations, although not necessarily relational. In *Ten Days*, executed in 1971 but published in 1972, American abstract painter Brice Marden used his time in Kathan Brown's studio at Crown Point Press to experiment with different intaglio processes. He did not set out with the intention of making a portfolio. He had simply been commissioned by Bob Feldman of Parasol Press to make prints with Brown, Feldman having been so delighted with work he commissioned from Sol LeWitt on which she had collaborated. Marden already had some experience of etching, but Brown's technical mastery, learned during her time studying at the Slade School of Art in London, opened up new possibilities. He experimented with different approaches, using hardground etching, aquatint, burnishing, foul bite, overprinting with a second plate, handwiping (then rarely practised in the USA) and retroussage. He paid particular attention to the variable density of the ink, the ability to create light and shade through hatching, as well as through foul bite and plate tone. Marden had for a long time been familiar with Edward Hopper's *Evening Wind* with its densely hatched background creating subtle variations of light and shade. He employed Hopper's approach to depicting modulated shadow, not in the service of narrative, but to make a wholly abstract image. Indeed Marden was one of the first artists to make convincing and subtle non-referential images using intaglio techniques. But there is no particular order to their display and he worked on several plates at once. Packaged by Parasol Press as a portfolio, with this group of prints Marden familiarised himself with a medium of which he was to become a master over the next two decades. According to Marden the prints just evolved from one to the other so that the sequence of making each print became something of a narrative in itself.

The third kind of portfolio is characterised by a group of images which are linked thematically but which do not propose a linear narrative. Picasso's *347 suite* does not tell a story, but the group of images collectively depicts the fantasies of an artist in old age who, aware of his own declining sexual potency, casts himself in the role of voyeur. There are distinctive clusters of works within the portfolio, almost like discrete short stories, but they are contained within the binding of the central theme.

Finally, some portfolios assemble images by a variety of artists that have a thematic link but often it is of such a superficial nature that the portfolio is really a collection of unrelated works brought together under a group heading. A number of such portfolios were published in the USA during the heyday of Pop Art. While some individual images are engaging, the ensemble is generally disappointing because it lacks coherence. A European example of this is *Hommage à Picasso* that included one of the great prints of the last fifty years, Richard Hamilton's *Picasso's Meninas*. That Hamilton's print appears regularly on the market suggests many of the portfolios have been broken up, which in turn suggests a lack of internal coherence. Had the portfolio been an integral object the individual prints would not stand so well alone.

In his discussion of Coracle Press, a British publisher of artists' books and a gallery in the 1970s and 1980s, Thomas A. Clark described what he called 'book works' in terms which may readily be applied to the notion of the portfolio: 'The best book works show an understanding of book form as acute as the artist's awareness of gallery space. As in ill-conceived exhibitions, the least interesting artist's books treat the book as a portmanteau for the housing of separately conceived works. Where the form is handled well, the movement within the book and its integrity as an object are as satisfying as felicitous space in a gallery':[1] He goes on to equate the artist's 'book work' with an exhibition, distinguishing it from the latter by virtue of its portable nature. An artist's book 'is an exhibition which can be taken away', a permanent form in which the presence and order of exhibits is unalterable. Thus paradoxically, an exhibition of works of art such as paintings, however solidly constructed they may be, is ephemeral, whereas the artist's book, however poorly printed or thin the paper, if cared for, is permanent. The portfolio has some of the same characteristics: the artist may determine the order in which the prints should be seen – the portfolio is essentially a small but complete portable exhibition. Finally, like the book, the portfolio is not an adjunct to an artist's work but is given as much care and attention as any other part of his activity. There are few artists who when asked about the status of their prints would argue that they are of minor importance. Artists do not distinguish between media. They simply make works of art. Only museums and the art market persist in ghettoising prints and regarding them as poor relations to painting and sculpture.

The formation of Paragon Press: Booth-Clibborn's progress

If the portfolio is essentially a literary genre, it is not surprising that Charles Booth-Clibborn's interest in publishing prints developed out of a passion for collecting books. While a student of history at Edinburgh University he expanded his collection to include illustrated books, that is, limited edition publications containing an original print, often published by small independent presses. During this period his interest in British art began to embrace the contemporary. The publications that interested him most were those put out by Coracle Press, located in Camberwell, London. What struck him in particular was the notion of the collaboration between artist, printer and publisher in the making of an object. Above all Coracle demonstrated the possibility of working with a number of different artists in many different ways.

1985 proved to be a watershed for Booth-Clibborn. Armed with a copy of Sandro Chia's *Bestiary*, he visited New York introducing himself to curators and dealers on the pretext of trying to sell it, while at the same time picking their brains about publishing limited edition books. From New York, where he studied illustrated books and projects in the Museum of Modern Art and the New York Public Library, Booth-Clibborn also went to the West Coast, where he made brief visits to Crown Point Press and Arion Press.

The previous year Booth-Clibborn had seen and purchased the Chia book in Rome and had met Romolo Bulla, a printer and typographer who had published small books and portfolios by the young Italian Transavantgarde. Booth-Clibborn was particularly impressed by the confidence and excitement generated by this Italian school.

The idea of the bestiary had already begun to interest him. At university he had recognised not only a distinctively Scottish sensibility in the 'local' contemporary art but a resurgence of energy and a certain national excitement equivalent to that generated by the Italian Transavantgarde. The combination of an interest in Scottish art and bestiaries led to his first publication.

A context for publishing: Britain and the USA

The Scottish Bestiary was launched in 1986. Booth-Clibborn realised there had been little printmaking activity in the area since the war, in spite of the availability of such excellent print workshops and studios as Peacock Printmakers in Aberdeen. By contrast he was well aware of the revitalisation of English printmaking, which had begun in the late 1950s and which really took off in the 1960s and 1970s. Kelpra Studio, under Chris Prater, had encouraged artists such as Hamilton, Paolozzi, Tilson and Kitaj to develop printmaking skills using modern technology, while Editions Alecto and then Petersburg Press, through an exciting publishing programme in all media, exploited this renaissance to the full. For the first time ever it could be said that there were publishing houses and printers capable of rivalling the great French printer-publishers. Galleries also joined the rush into print including Waddington, which confined its publications to its stable of Pop artists, and Bernard Jacobson, who took a wider view of the field. By the time Booth-Clibborn emerged on the scene in the late 1980s, however, activity had died down. There was a diminished amount of serious publishing activity in Britain.

The history of print publishing in the USA had a similar rhythm. Although there had been a flourishing tradition of printmaking among the Regionalist artists as well as among those who had come into contact with the work of S. W. Hayter, who had moved his workshop from Paris to New York during the Second World War, their productions were usually self-financed and published privately. In the late 1950s, however, print publishing began to take off. The founding of Universal Limited Art Editions (1957), Tamarind Workshop (1960), Crown Point Press (1962) and Gemini GEL (1966) stimulated an increased interest among artists to explore the medium of print. Few artists had been attracted to printmaking among the earlier generation of Abstract Expressionists, partly because in America, as in Europe, printmaking was considered to be a reproductive medium.

It was extremely common in Europe for the painting of an artist to be copied by a printmaker and marketed as an 'original' print. Furthermore, the spontaneous, gestural quality of Abstract Expressionism made the rather slow, cumulative process of making a print seem unattractive and irrelevant to these artists. There was also, however, a strong European tradition of the *peintre-graveur* and it was the possibility of working directly with artists that interested the founders of these new organisations. The formation of these new printing houses was in some senses European in origin; Tatyana Grossman, the founder of ULAE, was Russian by birth and had spent eight years in Paris in the 1930s; June Wayne, who set up Tamarind Workshop, had trained in Paris; Kathan Brown, who established Crown Point Press, had trained at the Slade in London.

Robert Rauschenberg, Jasper Johns, Barnett Newman and Larry Rivers were among the first wave of American artists to take up the challenge of making prints, while Roy Lichtenstein, Ellsworth Kelly, Claes Oldenburg and Andy Warhol followed on. An astonishing surge of activity led to an expansion of the market and an ever increasing number of new publishers. Among the most important of those was Parasol Press, which was responsible in the 1970s for publishing some of the most distinguished portfolios of prints to have come out of the USA. Agnes Martin's *On a Clear Day*, Brice Marden's *Ten Days, Five Plates* and *Five Threes*, Robert Ryman's *Six Aquatints* and *Seven Aquatints*, Robert Mangold's *Seven Aquatints* and almost all of Sol LeWitt's etchings until 1980 were among the many key works it financed. Parasol was an early model for Booth-Clibborn's Paragon Press because unlike ULAE, Tamarind and Gemini, it was not a printing house but commissioned work from Crown Point Press, which specialised in etching. Although Bob Feldman, Parasol's director, used Crown Point Press with regularity he was not tied to it. Thus artists, like Richard Estes, who did not want to make etchings, could work elsewhere. More important, perhaps, was the encouragement he gave to his artists to create suites rather than individual works. While ULAE, notwithstanding Grossman's founding intention to publish illustrated books, tended to concentrate upon the single print – Rivers's and O'Hara's *Stones*, Newman's *Cantos*, Johns's *0–9* and Motherwell's *A la Pintura* were among notable early exceptions – Parasol favoured the portfolio. The artists were given an entirely free hand, although Feldman reserved the right not to publish if he felt there was too great a commercial risk. In the event, in spite of their outstanding quality they did not sell well; his largest market was in Europe, especially among museums. Only since the 1990s have these publications begun to be widely recognised as masterpieces.

Another publisher with a close resemblance to Paragon Press is Peter Blum, again principally a publisher of projects and portfolios and, like Parasol, not tied to any particular press. Booth-Clibborn was particularly struck by Blum's Barbara Kruger portfolio, *We Will No Longer Be Seen and Not Heard*, a set of nine photographic images each bearing a printed word from the assertive statement. Booth-Clibborn was impressed by the coherence and visual impact of word and image and by the integrity and cohesion of the project. He had already published *The Scottish Bestiary*, a collection of images by a wide range of Scottish artists, but within a short time of the appearance of that publication he had formulated the view that the history of significant prints in the twentieth century was essentially the history of illustrated books and portfolios. From that moment onwards, and possibly encouraged by the example of Blum, Booth-Clibborn began to concentrate on portfolios by single artists. He knew that he had to print in small editions because demand would be low and it was necessary to maintain a high value. He also recognised that it would be a disadvantage to be tied to a print workshop. By declining to take this path he could not only restrict his overheads but choose his printers according to the needs of the artist and the project. The artist would have total freedom of choice of technique and technicians. Furthermore he realised that his job was not so much commissioning a specific work but enabling an artist to work in a chosen medium in the manner best suited to them.

Booth-Clibborn's choice of artist was also strategic. Initially he capitalised on the resurgence of Scottish painting and commissioned works from Scottish artists. He knew the Edinburgh and Glasgow scenes well and recognised a literary vein in their work that he felt would translate well into print and which, with his own background of book collecting, had an obvious appeal. It was not until he had published a number of projects that he began to commission work from English artists. In addition to his belief in the strength of contemporary British art, he also was aware of the need to establish an identity for his Press and to be near to the print workshop to deal with the production issues. One of the most important aspects of his publishing programme has been his ability to form a close relationship with his artists, so that a real understanding is achieved between them.

From his study of the history of prints of in the twentieth century he had concluded that most important artists make only one or two significant projects, which tend to occur in mid-career. He regarded Johns's collaboration with Beckett, *Foirades/Fizzles*, and Motherwell's *A la Pintura* as prime examples. Thus Booth-Clibborn generally chooses to work with artists from a generation older than his own. While there is an element of safety in such a choice, the gap in generations permits him to take a more detached and critical view of the artist's work.

A print project for Booth-Clibborn is something of an academic activity involving research, exploration and reappraisal and is not something to be rushed. Whereas Parasol Press would book a finite and limited amount of time on the presses of Crown Point Press – Marden's *Ten Days* takes its title from the period he spent in Oakland on his first visit – Booth-Clibborn imposes no time restrictions but allows his artists to establish the rhythm and pace according to their needs. He generally chooses to work with artists who have little or no post art school experience of printmaking because they arrive with fewer preconceptions. For such an artist the first period of a project is spent acquainting him or herself with the medium and there is no pressure to publish the results.

Paragon portfolios

Painter Christopher Le Brun was given such latitude in 1989. Le Brun's previous exposure to printmaking had been minimal and he had felt restricted by the time limit imposed by financial constraints or the publisher.

Booth-Clibborn suggested lithography to Le Brun as he thought it might suit him. Knowing that the artist was unfamiliar with the medium, he placed him under no time constraint whatsoever. He also made it clear that if any publication were to emerge it would have to be a unified project rather than a single print but that there was no need to embark with a particular project in mind. Thus Le Brun set out merely with the intention of learning about lithography in an unpressured situation. Booth-Clibborn simply hoped that something good would result.

In the event a set of lithographs was published. Le Brun drew the images, destroyed and reworked them in the manner in which he was accustomed when painting. However, whereas in a painting he could rely on a depth of paint to indicate the history of the work and to obscure the preceding image, in lithography it was harder to retain the sense of history. As a planographic process lithography is less suited to layering than is etching and Le Brun came to realise this fairly quickly. Thus, his next project was to be in intaglio. Le Brun rarely makes drawings and tends to paint directly. His paintings of the 1980s were made by applying one image on top of another, drawing the image in and out of the paint, thereby systematically covering and destroying the previous image until he arrived at a final 'state' which satisfied him. In this respect his approach to painting was that of a printmaker. Towards the end of the decade he was becoming increasingly dissatisfied with and nervous of relying on the burial of images to achieve the desired end. Indeed the images he destroyed were in themselves perfectly valid subjects for painting and he wanted to find a way to retain them. Etching was the ideal medium because it is essentially a medium that permits the artist to work in transparent layers.

Le Brun had not predicted that his project would be so extensive when he started out at the Hope Sufferance studios. He tried out various plate sizes but found he was most comfortable with a small one. Working on the plates in groups, he began to draw the images that had not survived in his paintings. The etching series enabled him to show these images, to test them without the need to question whether they had sufficient authority to carry a painting. The concept of a series came naturally for every image was capable of being worked in a different way. The series, therefore, was determined by an inner logic and necessity. Booth-Clibborn's role was to provide encouragement, a little gentle direction and some discreet editing but in essence the artist was allowed to determine the boundaries and extent of the project.

Fifty Etchings, as the series became known, is a sequential narrative of images relating the story of their making and highlighting the process by which an etching is made. The etchings are concerned with the notion of veiling and unveiling, revealing and layering, image-making and mark-making and the tensions between them all. There is a clear structure to the sequence in which they were made and published. The prints are not a random series of experiments. It was not surprising, therefore, that Le Brun should have wanted to reproduce them in a book, for he realised that the only way to understand the full implications of his achievement was to study them close up. Indeed, two bound volumes of the prints themselves were made up so that he could replicate this experience with the actual works. By restricting the number of images he could view at any one time, Le Brun was able to concentrate on the individual differences between each print and regain the intimacy he had experienced while working on the plate. The series thus became an album, an object to study rather than an image to be displayed, a sequence of pages to 'read'.

As a result of exploring a range of images through etching Le Brun felt a greater freedom of expression in his paintings, in particular a freedom to make an image and retain it. He has found that painting and etching are complementary activities, of equal status, which may feed off each other.

The overlap between painting and prints in Le Brun's work is commonly found in the work of many artists. Jasper Johns is perhaps the best known contemporary artist to explore similar images in graphics and painting, but it was Samuel Palmer, whose work Le Brun studied intensively at the outset of the *Fifty Etchings* project, who showed him that an artist's prints could be of a quality and impact equal to, if not greater than, his paintings. His study of Palmer also demonstrated that the greatest prints could be produced by the most economical means.

There is a certain Britishness in this high regard for understatement, but it is precisely this quality which Booth-Clibborn appears to recognise in his policy of promoting exclusively British art (perhaps more accurately English and Scottish).[2] Economy of means but intensity of expression underlie his most successful publications. These are characteristics not only of Le Brun's etchings but of Bill Woodrow's linocuts in his *The Periodic Table*.

Linocut is one of the most direct and simple methods of making prints. Once carved the block may be altered only with difficulty and there is no alchemical process in the plate-making and printing. What you print is what you see on the block. When Bill Woodrow embarked on a project based on Primo Levi's autobiographical novel *The Periodic Table*, he realised that etching would be too time-consuming if he were to make one print for every chapter of the book. He opted for linocut because his memory of making

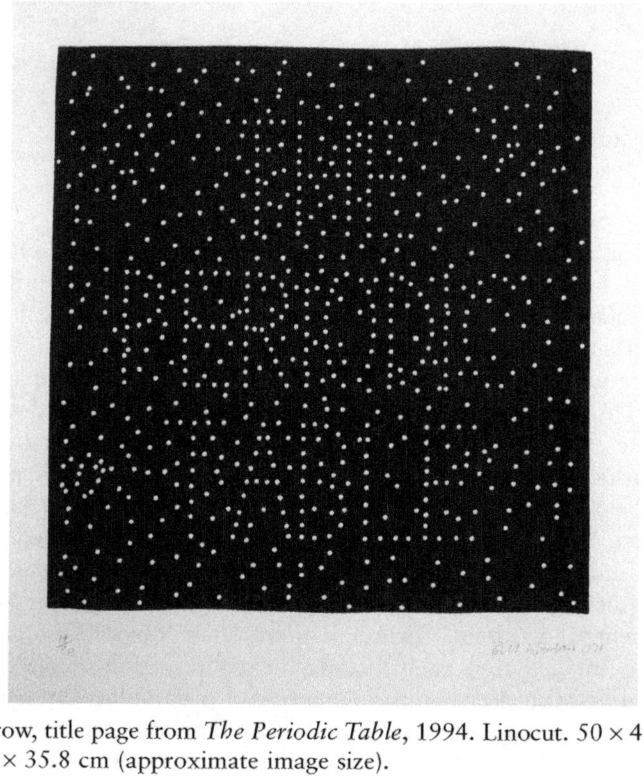

Bill Woodrow, title page from *The Periodic Table*, 1994. Linocut. 50 × 43 cm (page size); 38.3 × 35.8 cm (approximate image size).

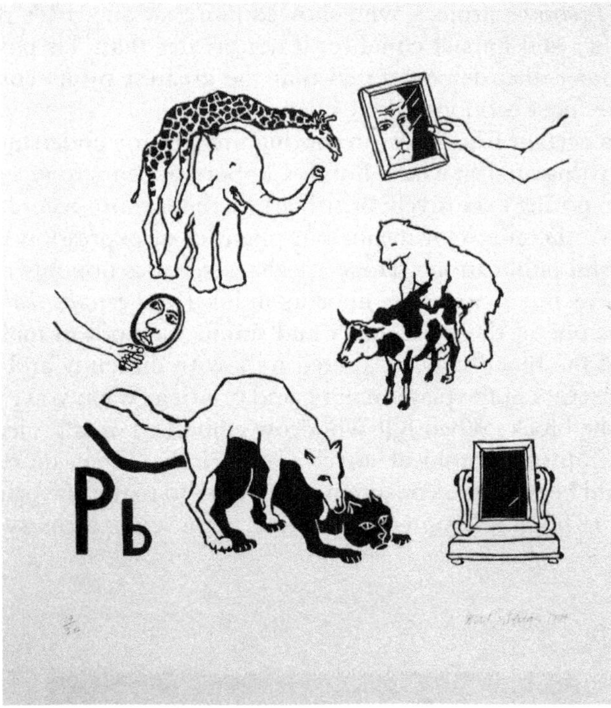

Bill Woodrow, *Pb* from *The Periodic Table*, 1994. 50 × 43 cm (page size); 38.3 × 35.8 cm (approximate image size). Linocut.

one or two at art school led him to believe it would be easy. He also considered that he could achieve greater clarity with this medium and thus mirror the clarity he found in the book. It was only after he had cut the first block that he realised the physical effort required.

The structure of the book determined the structure and sequence of the portfolio. The book is not a straight-forward narrative but does evoke a sense of the passage of time. It is composed more or less as a series of discrete episodes linked by the presence of the author and the common theme of the elements of the periodic table, which form the background for each chapter. Woodrow adopted the episodic form and selected from each chapter an incident or moment that stood out. He did not depict the incident or moment overtly but created a series of symbols and signs to evoke and comment upon them. Although there is no obvious sequential link between the images, they each include the abbreviation of one of the elements. There is also a growing momentum, for cumulatively from first to last they suggest a sense of increasing Fascist oppression, culminating in the print with the symbol for 'Carbon' which depicts a point, a devastating and simple image of finality. The momentum is brought to an abrupt and poignant halt in this final print.

The blocks were carved in the order in which they were published. Each image was mapped out roughly on paper first and then drawn on to the block. There was a certain similarity of concept for Woodrow between making linocuts, in which the image emerges out of the block, and his earlier sculptures, which were cut out of discarded machines. In both cases Woodrow drew on the material before revealing or unravelling an image by cutting. There was a strong notion of sequentiality in both activities and also a sense of unanticipated discovery, of not quite knowing where he was going. Woodrow set out with the intention of making a series of flat sheets but by the time he had executed ten or eleven of them he wondered whether they could also be published in book form. As a book the images would be inseparable, would be seen in the sequence in which they were made and could be looked at privately. The experience would be different from viewing the portfolio which is more declarative. Booth-Clibbom agreed to make a book version. Thus Woodrow's project, which was inspired by a book, ended as a book, indicating once again the essentially literary nature of portfolios.

Woodrow's *The Periodic Table* and Le Brun's *Fifty Etchings* are clearly narrative works. Hamish Fulton's *Fourteen Works* is a series of images thematically linked but which do not recount a story or suggest the passage of time. Fulton has a history of publishing artist's books consisting of photographic images and word pieces or a combination of both. In these books the texts frequently replicate wall paintings while the photographic pages, usually combined with words, reproduce photo-text works. The publications, which are designed by Fulton, serve as mnemonics but they do not replicate the experience of an exhibition. Exhibited works are large scale, books are intimate; a book is read in private, an exhibition is viewed in public; in a book the reader may see only two pages at once; in an exhibition he can see a whole body of work together. Finally, in a book the size of the work is determined by the size of the page; works on the wall can vary in size.

One of the distinctive features of Fulton's publications with Paragon Press is the variety of paper sizes he employs within any one project. This is a clear indication that Fulton has made a project for display. Furthermore, although the portfolios have a unity derived from a common theme – the artist within nature – there is no narrative link between the prints. It is, rather, an exhibition in a box of individual items, portable and durable, unlike his wall works, which are ephemeral and are destroyed at the end of each show. Each print is like a self-contained short story rather than a chapter. There is no obligation to show a portfolio in its entirety. Furthermore, a number of the texts he has printed, particularly in *Fourteen Works*, have previously appeared in books or as wall works. To pursue the literary analogy a little further, this portfolio is more of a lexicon or an index of Fulton's work than a novel.

Print is an ideal medium for Fulton who excludes autographic marks from his work and who dislikes the notion of uniqueness. Reproduction, mechanism and neutrality are at the heart of his work in which he recreates his experiences in nature. His large-scale pieces are derived from notes taken while walking, which are rarely altered when transferred to the wall. He used a similar method in making *Fourteen Works*. There is, therefore, essentially little difference between this portfolio and the large text-pieces other than scale and support and the fact that the texts are printed and framed rather than painted directly onto the wall. In contrast to his books, however, the quality of the printing is such that the works have a greater physicality and presence.

Although Fulton's means of production is relatively neutral the end result is far from impersonal. Indeed his work may be situated within the British Romantic tradition stretching back to the eighteenth century. And although each image may stand alone, there is a unity of intention and approach within each portfolio.

Booth-Clibborn has created a strong identity for his publishing house by concentrating on British artists. Those artists, by and large, have had little previous experience of printmaking. With few exceptions, such as Victor Burgin, John Hilliard and Grenville Davey, Booth-Clibborn's artists have eschewed new technology and to that extent it could be argued that he has facilitated and encouraged the revival of the hand-made print. While his selection of middle generation artists may be unfashionable, his achievement is to have reinvigorated British printmaking in a serious and lasting way by selecting artists for whom, first and foremost, printmaking is about creating works of art with a strong visual impact.

Notes

1 Clark, Thomas A., 'The Gallery and the Book' in *The Coracle*: Coracle Press Gallery 1975–1987, exh. cat., London 1989, p. 70.

2 Since the time of the original publication of this essay Paragon Press has expanded its horizon and now publishes prints by non-British artists.

Gill Saunders

Lasting impressions? A museum perspective on digital fine art printmaking*

In order to understand the V&A* perspective on digital fine art printmaking, and the debates around personalising the surface, I think it is helpful to look back at past print-collecting criteria, particularly as they relate to the contemporary and to new processes. According to the art critic Hilton Kramer, the curator, and by extension, the museum, should exercise a 'disinterested discrimination' in making acquisitions but this is an impossible ideal – and perhaps even more undesirable for a curator charged with collecting the new. Fallibility goes with the territory; the curator must be a speculator, a kind of 'future trader' betting on the 'worth' and longevity of the new, using instinct, intuition and experience to guide their guesses as to what will be valued by posterity. Museum curators talk about acquiring works for the 'permanent' collection; in other words, once formally accessioned, the work cannot be sold or otherwise disposed of without special dispensation in exceptional circumstances. This inalienability is fundamental in shaping and directing the museum's collecting policy, and the choices made by the curators.

The emergence of new technologies has repeatedly challenged curators who are charged with identifying those works of art and design which merit a place in a museum collection dedicated to preserving, documenting and displaying not only the innovative but also the exemplary. The V&A has a great track record in embracing innovation in contemporary practice, and in the field of printmaking the V&A was the first UK national institution to collect the work of contemporary printmakers at or shortly after the time of publication – for example, prints by Manet published in 1862, were

* Gill Saunders. 2009. 'Lasting Impressions? A Museum Perspective on Digital Fine Art Printmaking'. In: Coldwell, Paul and Rauch, Barbara (eds), *The Personalised Surface: New Approaches to Digital Printmaking*. London: Fade Research, pp. 37–44. Reproduced by kind permission of the author and Fade Research. Edited by the author.

* Editor's note: 'The V&A' refers to the Victoria and Albert Museum in London.

acquired in 1864 – and this readiness to embrace the new, without waiting for the benefits of hindsight and the judgements of history has continued. Photographs were acquired early on, and in due course artworks employing other new technologies – notably holography – were added promptly to the collection. In the field of printmaking, processes invented for purely commercial purposes have in turn been taken up by artists. In this new 'fine art' context the status of the process is radically revised and works in the medium have been acquired for the V&A collection. A notable instance was the adoption of Xerography (photocopying) by several artists, including the late Helen Chadwick who used it to create major installation pieces such as *The Oval Court*, acquired by the V&A in the 1980s.

Digital prints – whether output by laser, inkjet or iris printer – have also been acquired, but the collecting in this area is perhaps more tentative. The problems which beset digital printmaking – and the collecting of digital prints (or at least collecting by museums) – have been well-rehearsed and largely overcome but some lingering uncertainties still cohere around the fraught distinction between 'original' and 'reproduction' – a debate which ought now to be irrelevant but continues to influence the perceptions not only of artists and printmakers, but also collectors, curators and the art market. Like a photographic edition, a digital edition is potentially limitless, but editioning is now part of the apparatus of printmaking and print marketing. Of course a digital print edition may be arbitrarily limited, and often is, but a more effective way of counteracting the pejorative associations which attach to digital prints is to 'personalise' the surface in some way. The options for achieving this are many and various: the print may be output on to a variable or unusual substrate, or the artist may introduce additions and variations to the printed surface (collage, drawing, cutting), or he might overprint using a traditional analogue process (screen-print, etching, embossing). In this way the print is made to conform more readily to familiar definitions of 'print', 'edition', and 'original'.

In the debates around the status and character of digital printmaking, it should not be forgotten that for the greater part of its history printmaking has been first and foremost a reproductive process, a means of repeating and disseminating images to further knowledge in fields such as natural history, medical science, and the arts and crafts. Equally it has been a tool of trade and commerce, and a channel for propaganda. Printmaking as a means of reproducing paintings has been secondary, and the practice of producing original works of art in the medium is, again, but a small part of total print production.

But it is the changing status of reproductive and commercial print media which offers a lesson for curators in relation to digital media. Lithography – invented by actor and writer Aloys Senefelder in 1796 as a cheap means of publishing his writings – was quickly co-opted by artists. Screen-printing (basically a sophisticated version of stencilling) was a commercial process used for display advertising until it was adopted by artists in the US in the 1930s. In every case where a commercial technique has been appropriated by fine art, the artists (or those promoting and selling their work) have been at pains to distinguish their application of the process from its commercial origins. For example the print historian Carl Zigrosser coined the neologism 'serigraphy' to differentiate fine-art applications of screen-printing from their commercial equivalents. The term 'Giclée' has likewise been invented to distinguish 'fine art' digital prints.

Through much of its history printmaking has been relegated to a second-class status, considered inferior to painting and sculpture, the arts of 'original invention'. The Royal Academy [in London], founded in 1768, admitted no engravers as such (the well-known and commercially successful engraver Bartolozzi was admitted as a painter). In 1812, an RA committee set up to investigate the inferior position of engravers, concluded that engraving was 'wholly devoid of those intellectual qualities of invention and composition which painting, sculpture and architecture so eminently possess ... its greatest praise consisting in translating with as little loss as possible, the beauty of the original arts of design.' The invention of photography polarised positions, with engraving splitting into two distinct strands – the 'fine art' and the 'commercial'. The introduction of photomechanical processes in fact allowed hand-engravers to argue for an enhanced status, and they were eventually accepted into the Academy on an equal basis with painters and sculptors in 1928. In 1883 Seymour Hayden had argued for etching as 'personal' and thus creative, by comparison with engraving, which was tainted with its earlier applications in reproduction, was 'without personality' and therefore 'merely a craft'.

Societies were founded to promote 'creative' printmaking, and in doing so they stressed how the prints which they promoted differed from those images which employed the new technology. For example, the critic Théophile Gautier introduced the first portfolio issued by the influential Société des Aquafortistes (founded in Paris in 1861) thus: 'In these times, when photography fascinates the vulgar by the mechanical fidelity of its reproductions, it is necessary to assert an artistic tendency in favour of free fancy and picturesque mood'. Subscribers were assured that each impression of the prints sold was an original work of art. In an early instance of 'personalising' the surface, the Society emphasised the variety of effect which could be achieved by inking the plate differently, or by the use of papers of different absorbency, and published an artificial number of states with many proof impressions, thereby denying the basic multiple nature of the print, and making it clear that their publications were rare and precious originals which had no relation to the pedestrian mechanical precision of the photomechanical processes.

The emphasis on the personal 'by hand' intervention of the artist continues to be central to definitions of original printmaking. The International

Congress of Artists in Vienna in 1960 decreed that only prints 'for which the artist made the original plate, cut the wood block or worked on the stone or any other material' could be considered 'originals'. The French National Committee of Engraving in 1965 was even stricter, excluding 'any and all mechanical or photomechanical processes'; this statement was a provocation to the artists of the time, who disputed its validity by making prints which addressed the debate head on. When screen-prints by several British artists including Peter Blake and Richard Smith were sent by the British Council to the Paris Biennale that year, their use of photography sparked a long-lasting debate about their status and acceptability as 'original' prints. This prompted a fierce defence of commercial processes by [British artists] Eduardo Paolozzi and Allen Jones. Paolozzi argued that they 'could provide a complexity and range of possibility not available for normal art/craft printing'. Jones asserted that the crux of 'originality' in printmaking was to conceive a print in the medium of execution and to utilize the specific qualities of that medium. Once we accept this – by now – uncontentious view it is clear that all print technologies which have been tainted by their origins in or sometime application to reproduction or commerce are in fact legitimate means to an end – the end conceived and desired by the artist – and to argue otherwise is to establish a purely artificial division.

Richard Hamilton – who else? – entered the debate with his iconic print, *The Critic Laughs*, 1968, a characteristically witty and sophisticated work which is a dialogue between reproduced and original effects, with hand-made interventions on the surface which were incorporated in the 'reproduction'.* The print was made from a photograph, reproduced as a photo-offset-litho and laminated with plastic film to heighten the photographic quality. The margins were screen-printed with a matt white to give the effect of a photograph mounted on board. Some thick paint was applied to the photographic print prior to reproduction and paint was added by hand to each print after lamination, as was a piece of collage. Consequently every impression has some original work from the artist's hand, and every impression is different.

Hamilton has of course continued to play with the intersections between 'original' and 'reproduction', using digital media; a notable recent instance is *The annunciation*, a digital inkjet print, produced in 2005. The complex process of origination and production of this image has been described in detail by Fanny Singer in *Print Quarterly* (Sept 2008, vol. xxv, no.3). In the catalogue to the exhibition *Painting By Numbers* 2006, which featured this print, Hamilton tells a revealing anecdote which highlights the problems with the perception of digital prints even amongst relatively

* Editor's note: For a reproduction of Hamilton's work, see the chapter by Susan Lambert 'The status of the reproduction' in Part III of this volume.

sophisticated audiences: a collector who had previously bought a copy of each of Hamilton's prints declined to purchase *The annunciation* and when asked why, replied 'It's just a photograph'. Indeed the print has a seamlessly flawless verisimilitude analogous to an 'immaculate conception', a work of art apparently unmediated by human hand. The collector's dismissive verdict is on the one hand testimony to Hamilton's achievement in producing such a convincing approximation of a photograph, but also reveals the pitfalls of such an achievement – and inadvertently shows us why many artists (as Hamilton himself has done elsewhere) might choose to personalise the surface, to add something more explicitly hand-made, to reassure the potential purchaser by reinvesting the printed image with an 'aura' of originality and authenticity. On this occasion Hamilton chose to respond to this misperception that the work was merely a photograph by exhibiting the many stage proofs which led to the final editioned inkjet print – thereby revealing a process that is technically much more complex and challenging than simply taking a photograph.

The debates about 'authenticity' and 'originality' of the various printmaking processes may have exercised the artists, and those charged with protecting and promoting fine-art printmaking within officially sanctioned definitions, but true to its founding principles, the V&A collected prints in all media, with a particular emphasis on new media or innovative applications of traditional media. Indeed whilst the Print Council of Great Britain and its European counterparts were mounting increasingly futile barriers to the recognition of 'reproductive' processes, the V&A was actively acquiring such work. To give just a few examples: Peter Blake's *Beach Boys* (1964) was purchased from the Robert Frazer Gallery in 1965; Richard Hamilton's screen-print *Adonis in Y-fronts* (1963/4) was purchased in 1964; Malcolm Morley's 1969 *Beach Scene* was acquired the year it was published, as were two untitled photo-lithographs by Michael Craig-Martin made in 1970.

Of course it should be said that this enthusiastic collecting of the contemporary and controversial was largely undertaken by the V&A's Circulation Department. This was the department which managed the Museum's extensive programme of touring exhibitions to the regions, where the venues included not only museums, galleries and libraries but also art schools. With a remit to devise and tour inspiring and topical shows, the Circulation Department was able to sidestep some of the constraints which shaped the acquisition policies of the curatorial departments, and with less of an eye on posterity they were empowered to collect new work which blurred the boundaries between 'fine art' and 'commercial' processes. In recognition of its commitment to collecting contemporary prints from its foundation the V&A was designated the 'National Collection of Modern Prints' in the mid-1950s, but in contrast to the adventurous and proactive collecting by Circulation, those responsible for building the permanent collection remained more cautious about the status of the kind of work which was then coming out of print workshops such as Kelpra [in London]. Kelpra had been set up [in 1957] by Chris Prater and Rose Kelly to give artists the opportunity to work with screen-printing, hitherto almost exclusively a commercial process. Photomechanical processes were still regarded with suspicion. Indeed in 1969 Graham Reynolds, then the Keeper of Prints and Drawings, refused a proposed gift of proofs from Prater because, as he later explained in a letter to Tate Curator Pat Gilmour: 'When an artist gives a design in some other medium to another artist for him to make the screens for its reproduction in print form, it is not our practice to regard them as original prints by the first named of these artists.'

Now, of course, the collaborative nature of printmaking is widely accepted – and continues to be a feature of digital printmaking where technical expertise in the use of Epson printers, or computer skills such as programming, are enlisted by artists. On the other hand, the ease and accessibility of many digital print processes have freed many artists from the need for technical support, and enabled them to work alone. For example, one of the attractions for Helen Chadwick of using a photocopier was that it allowed her to work independently of a photographer; Richard Hamilton has a digital-based studio at home, and has developed a mastery in the use of computers and digital printers to originate ambitious digital prints.

But how has the advent of digital print impacted on Museum acquisition policies? What are the criteria in play when a museum selects prints for acquisition? At the V&A there has always been a need to balance the aesthetic value of the work with its character as a print, showcasing either exemplary or innovative technique. What does it mean for an image to be a print rather than a drawing or a photograph? In a museum such as the V&A where there has always been a conscious focus on technique, the rise and rise of digital printmaking brings with it particular challenges – and the need for curators to investigate ever more closely the reasons underlying the choice of digital output media. Is it the logical consequence of originating, manipulating or 'mixing' the imagery digitally? Is it a deliberate choice predicated on the specific qualities of digital print? Or is it simply the easiest/cheapest/fastest means of getting an image published?

What does the choice of a digital output mean, and how is it read by an audience? Most of us grew up in a world of analogue creativity but we are now so immersed in a digital universe that our critical faculties are having a hard time distinguishing the outstanding from the merely competent, the original from the derivative. Like Hamilton's reluctant collector we may find it hard to see beyond the 'surface', mistaking the hard-won illusion of verisimilitude for a straightforward reproduction or reiteration of an original in another medium, be it photography, painting or another print process. Even now, relatively few artists making prints (as opposed to digital artworks) have deployed the new technologies in genuinely creative ways – rather than embracing them as a means of achieving a faster cheaper mimicry of analogue practice, a way of making larger and/or more affordable editions. But like any other print medium, digital print may be chosen by an artist to realise a particular idea, and a successful print is an effective marriage of concept, process and medium. Personalising the surface is one option available to the artist, but sometimes the artist may not wish to remediate the print, because the qualities of the digital surface are those which are best suited to the expression or realisation of the concept.

As I have tried to show, the V&A (despite some unfortunate lapses) has been at the forefront of collecting examples of innovative printmaking which employ new technologies. In part this may be explained by the nature of the V&A's collections, in which the term 'print' encompasses everything from Christmas cards, labels, carrier bags and packaging, advertising graphics, illustration, fashion plates, and wallpapers, to fine art prints, old and new, and in which photographs have enjoyed 'fine art' status from the beginning. And with collections of architectural and design drawings that include CAD files and print-outs, it would be perverse to exclude original fine art which has been created and/or output by digital means. With commercial and reproductive prints enjoying equal status as accessioned museum objects in the permanent collections, the V&A has not erected artificial barriers to exclude specific processes and techniques – and the curators who care for posters and playing cards are also responsible for Old Master and contemporary prints, thus fostering a more open-minded acceptance of work in new media. Indeed the V&A was one of the first – if not the first publicly funded museum in the UK to acquire work by computer artists, notably William Latham in 1988 and James Faure-Walker in 1990.

Most recently, thanks in part to its track record in collecting prints, drawings and photographs in new media, the V&A has received two major gifts of computer art – one a private collection amassed by a percipient American collector, Patric Prince, and the other the archive of the Computer Arts Society. These donations have in turn attracted gifts from a number of the artists who were the pioneers in this field. Amongst the works donated by the CAS are some of the earliest computer graphics – such as a screen-print, *Plastick 1*, by Georg Nees, made after a computer-milled aluminium plate, in the 1960s. Using a programming language designed specifically for scientific computers, Nees created purely aesthetic images. We also have several prints by Mark Wilson; *PCS3 I*, from 2003, was made by using software which he had originally written to generate plotter drawings; he adapted it to create digital files, in this case making 10 different images from 10 runs of the software, which were saved and drawn together to produce a densely detailed final image.

Just as the term 'print' covers a multitude, so 'digital' fine-art printmaking can encompass an unprecedented range of processes and outputs – everything from the computer-guided stereolithography employed by Rachel Whiteread to make her 3D multiple *Secondhand* to the products of the iris and inkjet printers used by artists as diverse as Catherine Yass and Peter Kennard. The V&A collection has embraced digital prints of all kinds, not privileging one kind of 'digital' print over another. In this we have, I think, been in advance of much critical opinion which has tended to favour digital prints which reproduce the effects (often illusory) of the handmade, rather than those which fully exploit the characteristic qualities and capabilities of the digital medium. In an essay for the IPCNY [International Print Center New York] *New Prints* show (Winter 2003) Faye Hirsch lamented that the rise of artists using 'digital modalities' had made it increasingly difficult to discern any difference between art and ads. She singled out for notice those digital prints which looked 'hand-crafted', praising the artists for 'spurn[ing] the slicker effects of the digital medium.' Eschewing this judgemental view of digital print, the V&A has collected with a more inclusive perspective. For us an early laser print by Richard Hamilton, inkjet prints on blue-print paper or adhesive labels by Anne Rook, and glossy iris prints by Willie Cole are as valid as expressions of original fine-art print as are those examples of digital print which have been 'personalised' in some way by the addition of autographic marks, or overlaid by a more traditional print process.

When an artist successfully exploits the potential of digital print media in original and interesting ways, then that work is as interesting to us as the achievements in any other print medium. The V&A does not work with a cut-and-dried definition of print as I hope Rosie Miles and I were able to demonstrate in the book *Prints Now* (V&A, 2006) where we argued for the broadest possible definition of 'print' and showcased work in old and new media, as well as work which pushes against medium-specific boundaries and traditional classifications of object types. To conclude, I will look at some examples where artists have made a deliberate choice of digital print media, analyse their choices and the effects achieved, and explore some of the reasons why the V&A chose to acquire the works in question.

[...]

The use of digital technologies has resulted in the production of some outstanding prints – for example Willie Cole's series of images which exploit the iconographic ambiguity of the domestic iron. Having previously made a series of scorch prints which linked scarification rituals common to African cultures with the branding of slaves, and the floor plans of slave ships with the outlines of African masks, he extended these suggestive analogies in a series of digital iris prints made at the Rutgers Center for Innovative Print and Paper in 2002. He took different models of iron, photographed them from above and then digitally manipulated the images to remove extraneous detail such as the flex, switches and so on, as well as altering and highlighting the colours. When scaled up and output as iris prints on a white ground, the images are ambiguous – still recognisably irons but also imposing mask-like forms. Each of the prints in this series is named for the manufacturer's brand name for the appliance – the V&A

acquired *Loyal and Dependable*. The brand names evoke the claims made in notices advertising slaves for sale in the US before abolition. The appeal of these prints for the V&A is several-fold – first they have a particular resonance in a museum of the decorative (and largely domestic) arts, they are also pertinent to narratives of black history and the work of the African Diaspora which has for some years been a key strand in our collecting policy. They also comment on the ideas of product design, branding (in the commercial sense of the word) and marketing. The use of iris print on glossy paper is suggestive of the superficiality of the advertising message which glosses over the realities of domestic manual labour, and of abuse and exploitation more generally.

Cole's iron prints exploit the cool clinical capacities of digital print but digital print can be as various, as subtle, and as personally inflected as the use to which it is put or the material it is applied to – as we see if we look at the poignant face of Cecilia Mandrile's cloth doll, with its soft blurred features which look worn and well-loved. Mandrile, an Argentinean, left her native country in the mid-1990s for a kind of self-willed exile, and has been on the move ever since. This nomadic life-style is reflected both in her method of working and in its products – she repeatedly refers to questions of identity, and the experience of dislocation and loneliness. As if creating a substitute family to keep her company on her travels she has made a series of dolls – the face of each is made by scanning an old manipulated photo of herself which she then prints onto linen using her Hewlett Packard printer. The V&A doll comes from her *Strategies for Departure* project, made in 1998, and relates to a series of ID cards which feature the dolls photographed on their travels by Mandrile. Here, Mandrile's use of digital print is absolutely essential to her expression of a particular narrative of self and experience. No other medium would have been feasible in the context, or more expressive of the relationship between the life and the work.

As Mandrile's work demonstrates, surface, in digital printmaking, may be an identity or a quality supplied by the substrate on which the print is output or the material of the surface to which it is subsequently applied. Anne Rook's digital prints – replicas of Price Look Up stickers as used by supermarkets to identify loose fruit and vegetables – are applied to apples, tree branches and so on, thereby taking the commodification of nature implicit in our consumer environment back into nature and demonstrating its unnatural relation to the natural world and the food chain. The effect is predicated on the fact that her labels – scanned from the supermarket labels and digitally printed – precisely replicate the originals. Indeed, depending on the substrate she chose, Rook has been able to reproduce a variety of different effects with the same motifs.

[...]

The V&A recently acquired the *Rivington Place* portfolio (2007), a collection of prints by several high-profile Black British and African American

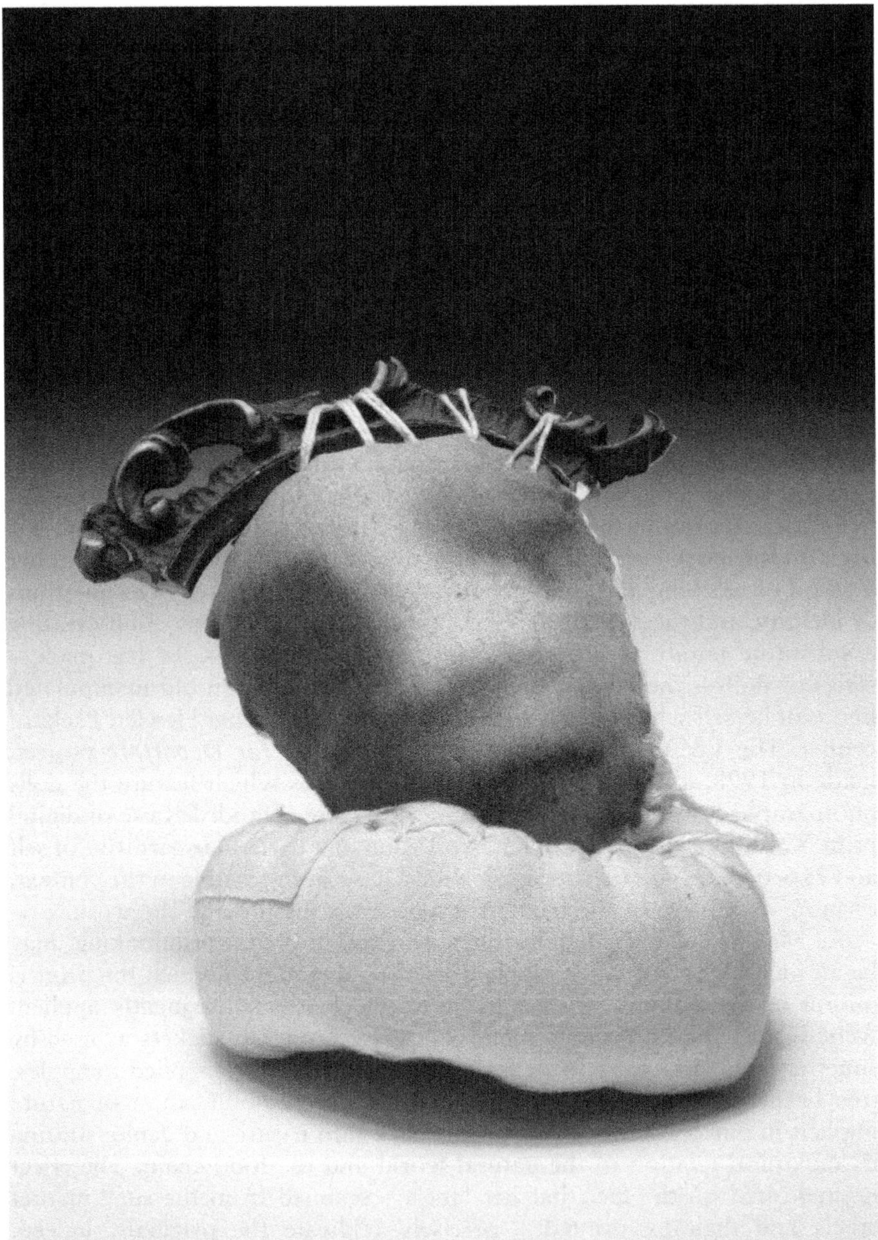

Cecilia Mandrile, *Doll* from *Strategies of Departure*, 1996. Inkjet print on cotton cloth, with thread, acrylic stuffing and plaster moulding. Height: 11.5 cm irregular, overall, including wood, Width: 9 cm irregular, overall.

artists, best known for their works in other media. It includes a mixed media collage print, *The Prize*, by Hew Locke [...]. Locke's piece, constructed like a 3–D jigsaw, is a complex and fragile work involving photography, digital print and screen-printing, as well as digital and manual cutting and pasting. Here digital processes have been deliberately chosen to suggest something cheap and mass-produced, ideas which are inherent in the work's message. The form is based on a chalice he saw in the V&A but here transformed into something flimsy and flash, intended to imply something about the hollowness of trophies and their devalued status in our society. It also alludes, obliquely, to ideas of looting, the forcible taking of 'trophies' of all kinds, which accompanied much of the enterprise of Imperialism and filled Britain's museums with treasures from other cultures.

[...]

My last example is a suite of prints – *Winter Garden*, 2004 by Marc Quinn, 8 pigment prints with varnish applied by hand. (These are not in the V&A, though we would very much like to have them.) The images derive from his photographs of an installation he made in 2000. A commentary on genetic manipulation, the effects of global warming and the disruption of natural cycles and natural processes, they show combinations of hot-house flowers, from different countries and different seasons, frozen in tanks of silicone liquid (giving us 21st-century equivalents of the 17th-century Dutch flower-piece). The photos were scanned and translated into digital files. The photos were not manipulated; instead the implausible saturation of colour was achieved through the use of pigment inks in the printing process, which was done with an Epson 9600 printer. Each print was then sealed by hand with thick coats of gloss polymer varnish, containing Ultraviolet filters. This not only protects the prints, but also enhances the depth and richness of the colours. But the varnish also lends a tactile quality to the surface because individual brushstrokes remain visible. Far from objecting to this intrusion of the hand-made into the apparently flawless surface of his prints, Quinn valued these marks because they gave what he described as 'a reality' to the print, gave it an object-ness which distinguished the print in the flesh from the print as reproduced in a book or a brochure. He wanted to differentiate these two experiences of the prints, and to get away from the idea that seeing the prints illustrated in a book was the same as seeing 'the object itself.' The differences are subtle – but profoundly important – and in this case at least, the differences reside in the surface.

Some artists – and especially those who would identify themselves as printmakers – are pessimistic about the implications of digital processes and their likely impact on how printmaking is defined and practiced. Luis Camnitzer, for example, concluded a recent essay with the assumption that printmaking will soon be relegated to the status of an esoteric craft, with its roles in both image-making and the circulation of ideas superseded by the digital. Certainly there is a likelihood that digital circulation of images will predominate, if it does not already, and that artists will increasingly conceive work only in the digital arena where it will exist as what Camnitzer calls 'pure vision' in 'so many pixels per inch', with no physical aspect at all. But as we know, woodcut survived the invention of engraving, and engraving survived the invention of photography, and so on, with each new process swiftly co-opted to the printmaker's tool-box. The digital media are no different in this respect, and the mix-and-match of processes old and new, hand-made or computer-generated, is just the latest stage in the metamorphosis of printmaking, to which, in turn, curators bring their own apparatus of assessments, evaluations and predictions.

Sheryl Conkelton

Print and the public sphere*

The history of print is closely intertwined with the history of public debate and ideas of shared or common public space. Print has played a key role in shaping public domains as an effective means of distributing information; it served as a primary format for public information and debate well into the twentieth century. That century saw the development of international communication systems that provided a technological base for large mediated public spheres: print, and later other media that extended print's reach, defined common space and a sense of a shared realpolitik, particularly for national contexts. Arguably a key defining element of the modern era, media-based public space became a dislocated and disembodied experience – an abstraction, conceived of as universal and rational, generating authority and mobilizing public opinion. The very publicness of information was valuable: information's generation by and through a public ensured its significance, removing individual prejudice and upholding majority opinion – if not consensus – as a determining process; as democracies emerged around the globe in the late twentieth century, this aspect of 'public' became even more significant.[1]

In the early twenty-first century, transformations of information and its flows significantly altered the conditions and forms of public discourse. Along with technological developments, dramatic changes in socio-political dynamics produced a new consciousness of globally scaled transactions, and the concept of a uniformly constituted public shifted. As globalism's consequences were articulated counter to the singular future that had been intuited and theorized, there arose, instead, a multiplicity of effects determined and mediated by specific, local conditions. What was understood as the public arena has been reformed and decentered; 'the public' is more

* Sheryl Conkelton. 2011. 'Print and the Public Sphere'. In: Moore et al. (eds), *The Graphic Unconscious*. Philadelphia, PA: Philagrafika, pp. 30–41. Reproduced by kind permission of the author and Philagrafika. Edited by the author.

accurately imagined as an arena of different, overlapping social experiences and discourses that are articulated through the continuous activity of multiple evolving publics, rather than as a coherent and monolithic space.[2]

In the developed world, print's functions of reproduction and repetition were largely taken over by electronic media by the late 1990s; the flow of information became instantaneous, simultaneous and, importantly in the last several years, individually customizable. This unraveling of shared experience and mass media has been driven by a new urgency of personal narrative, well supported by technological innovations available in advanced economies. Small consumer devices enabled the replacement of modern public spectatorship with a different kind of participation consisting of active selection and arrangement of information and images on an intimate scale. The shift from public to private was not the only effect. The proliferation of access increased repetition exponentially, without an accompanying extension of stable meaning; images which gained legibility through context (and, as information, often required captioning in order to be specific and useful), are now routinely and constantly displaced, detached from original intentions and redirected by individual users as well as privatized archives via the Web and downloadable content. And while the picture theory of the 1980s accounted for the effects of a mediated 'image world' and the functions of mass publicity, this more recent turn encompassed a dynamics of information flow which produces its own multiple, localized phenomena, utilized as entertainment as well as authority. In this context, print itself became a more complex image, both a type of picture and a system of reproduction and publication that can be referenced to allude to certain aspects of the modern, a type of historical trope that counters or complicates the new publicness.

In the context of these shifts and turns, a consideration of print as contemporary public phenomena must incorporate these dynamics – not merely pointing to the presence and affect of printed material but also examining the ways in which artists engage the ethos of print as a medium whose function has been both to constitute and to reflect public arenas. The artists whose works were included in the *Print and the Public Sphere* section of the exhibition *The Graphic Unconscious*, installed in and around Temple Gallery at Temple University [Philadelphia], share in their practices this basic engagement with print – as a material and, no less importantly, as an imaginary, an animating political or social (read public) force. Some of these projects integrate not only printed images from the public realm but also social and political practices reliant on printed material to communicate the weight of, affinities for, and solidarity with historically and geographically distant counterparts. These artists engage print as a platform for their demonstrations of difference from official and exclusive narratives and structures. In addition to the forms and materials of printmaking, its dynamic and ethics (collaboration, communication, accessibility) are incorporated to support new considerations and conceptualizations of publicness.

Throughout his career Thomas Kilpper has engaged history as a public discourse in projects that wrest control of a common narrative from state authorities. His artistic interventions focus new attention on political and social significance that has been obscured by official narratives. Kilpper's sense of history critiques and expands a revolutionary dynamic, engaging oppositions to manifest a picture of history more diverse and more complicated than those generated by government authority or popular consensus. His history is a monumental collaged space that produces a spectacle of history as a contest – not simply the protestations of unofficial minorities but invigorated, powerful oppositions linked across time and place.

In *State of Control – Out of Control*, 2009, Kilpper challenged the official history of East Germany by siting his project in the very building where the state narrative was erected and enforced by the Stasi (the secret police who relied on a widespread system of informants). Kilpper literally disfigured the building and refigured its political symbolism, replacing a paranoid history with a more expansive one. Working *in situ* constructs a monument to resistance: the hard labor required to carve new images into the floors of the building was available to visitors when the carved and inked 1600-square-meter floor was opened to the public, celebrating labor formerly hidden in the studio as well as the incising process.

In addition to overtly encompassing the labor of making, Kilpper's conceptualization produced large-scale visibility that provokes public dialogue. When the floor was completely covered with carving, he and his assistants used it as a matrix and printed dozens of huge banners, many of which were then installed in an exhibition at the Neuer Berliner Kunstverein. The banner form was another carefully considered element, as it has its own history as mobile propaganda displayed on buildings and carried in parades and political protests. The installation – a forest of images of larger-than-life episodes and looming, monumental portraits – activated this new narrative, making it resonantly public. Print, tangibly present in the paradoxical combination of woodcut-like textures with images known from newspapers and television, proffered a complex perspective on history and the forms with which it is constructed and contested, as well as on its own history as a political medium. In the context of new media, print is anachronistic and obsolete; Kilpper's project recuperates it as a revolutionary form with a specific relationship to histories of resistance.

The projects developed by the Danish collaborative Superflex (Jakob Fenger, Rasmus Nielsen, and Bjørnstjerne Christiansen) also highlight the labor of making to articulate an opposition to dominant discourses and publicity structures. Their installation, *Copy Light*, a workshop project in which paper-shaded hanging lamps were fabricated, challenges the neutral passivity of the gallery's public space by siting a factory within it. Staffed by Tyler School of Art students, the workshop produced paper shades printed with the images of famous copyrighted lamp designs. The lights were hung in the gallery as they were constructed, gradually illuminating the overhead space and serving a secondary, showroom function. The installation thus served to provoke debate about work and its spaces – and how much work is hidden from public view – as well as to complicate ideas about property and ownership.

With *Copy Light*, Superflex also invokes complex issues surrounding art and its operations, among them the democratic intentions of modern 'good design'; the relationships between original and copy, and illustration and object; and key issues surrounding authorship, without providing easy solutions or conclusions. The workers affix the images of well-known and finely crafted modern lighting designs to simply constructed lamps. Most visitors would recognize the designs, but, ironically (in light of their ubiquity and notoriety), they might not know that the designs are copyrighted – privately owned – and so available only to those who can pay for them. Superflex implicated this issue of exclusivity as well as the notion of print as copy; rather than directly challenging the copyright by copying the physical objects, the lamps are only pictured two-dimensionally on substantially simpler objects, referencing rather than reproducing, and pointing towards print's affect as illustration and information. Literally 'on display' in the gallery, the production process alluded to the invisible and often far-flung economies that produce luxury brands (and their unauthorized reproductions). The project challenges entrenched ways of thinking about various kinds of capital – material, intellectual, and historical – not with the usual antagonistic critiques but with projects that expose the attitudes that inform relationships to global consumerism, environmentalism, and Internet copyright.

Carl Pope's practice engages race and other prominent social issues with seemingly modest means: he transcribes marketing slogans, key phrases from Black English and literary quotations, and combines them to represent the competition of ideas and issues that unfold as public cultural discourse, and to insert excluded communities into the mainstream. His billboard project *The Philadelphia Cottage Industry Association Ad Campaign Project*, 2009–10, brought the large scale of public advertising to the small businesses that define the North Philadelphia neighborhood surrounding Temple University. Collaborating with students from the city's Mural Arts Program, Pope worked with business owners in North Philadelphia to develop visual brands and advertising materials to promote them. He then generated large scale designs for billboard ads, placing student-created images of the businesses in locations normally occupied by the franchises of multinational corporations. The insertion of these images of local businesses and non-profit agencies displaced the marketing clichés of advertising

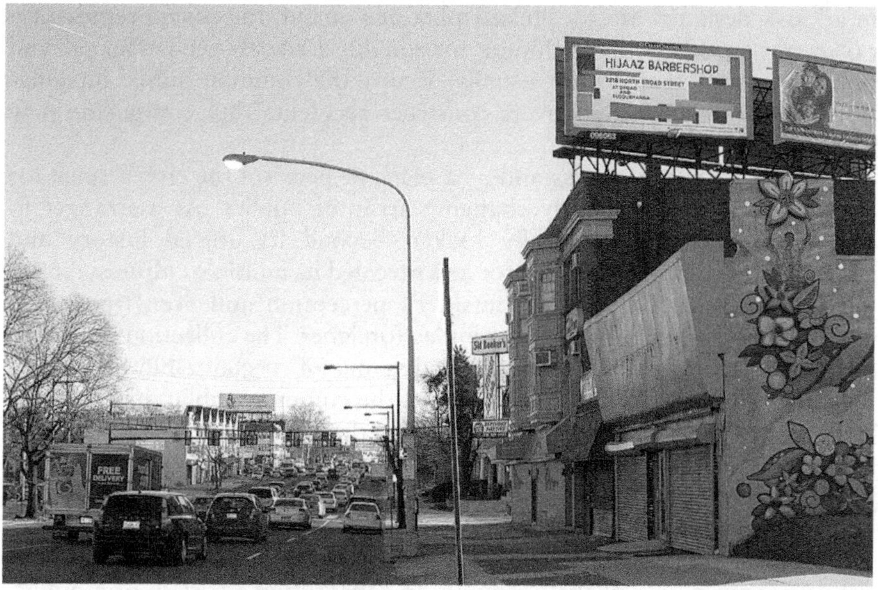

Carl Pope, 'View of the billboard for Hijaz Barbershop', from *The Philadelphia Cottage Industry Association Ad Campaign Project (PICA)*, 2009–10.

products mostly manufactured in distant locations, and substituted emblems of the surrounding local community in a celebration of local dynamics.

Pope's reconceptualization of the public space of advertising projected an unusual agency; it claimed billboard marketing as a means of community activism. By becoming a local space, a corporate, multinational space was made to articulate a different set of values. Pope's project did not simply present the transition from a 'not-being-public' to a 'being-public'; rather, the project offered the possibility of participation: the collaborators, brought together more or less arbitrarily by the artist, were able to organize themselves to produce a new community imaginary, and the community could read themselves in what had previously been an estranging territory.

Francesc Ruiz's *Newsstand (Philadelphia)*, 2010, is an activist construction that generates the possibility of new public dynamics. Following a brief period of residency and research, Ruiz created dozens of covers for imaginary periodicals about Philadelphia. Each cover is a page in a 120-page magazine, taking as inspiration the logos, formats, and typefaces of everything from local businesses and national brands to the layouts and designs of sensationalist tabloids and visually energetic comics and 'zines. The array of covers combines these familiar graphics with idiosyncratic headlines and images, some riffing on recent news events, others satirical. Arranged in a kiosk designed after a Philadelphia newsstand, the covers represent a range of constituencies, including marginalized social, gender/sexual and political groups that do not usually occupy the common public imagination. In combination the covers construct accidental but compelling new narratives.

Ruiz sees the local newsstand as a place to perform the city, a stage for encounters in the constantly changing array of publics. As a stranger to Philadelphia, Ruiz strategically looked beyond its official history and tourism strategies. He searched for and revealed its multiple cultures, retaining the misconceptions of an outsider's perception and even translation errors as markers of his own position as foreigner. The collection presented in the newsstand generates a different dynamic of spectatorship by inscribing smaller publics in the larger space of the common public. Its combinations make visible competing imageries and the flows of ideas and identities in and out of various types of public space. Here, the printed image not only provides platforms for marginalized populations but models dynamic new relationships.

The project by Swoon (Caledonia Curry) perhaps most directly reveals the generative power of the imaginary in constituting a society or a public. For *Print and the Public Sphere*, Swoon installed a series of life-size (and larger) printed paper figures in different locations around North Philadelphia. The figures were based on people she knows – friends, neighbors, acquaintances – posed with friendly gestures and embellished with playful visual characteristics: flamboyant clothing, arbitrary symbols, fictional architectures. Inserting the figures among houses, along sidewalks and on storefronts in the neighborhood very quickly generated an audience and a public.

Swoon underscores the immediacy of these works through an eccentric combination of compelling realism and lively decoration, including intricately cut edges that were left unglued to be animated by the passing breezes. Siting them in transitional street spaces, she activated experiences in unexpected locations, inserting beauty, play, and vitality into ordinary life. Unlike other types of street art, the scale, postures, and accessibility of her printed figures imagined the possibility of social interaction.

Although Swoon's aesthetic can be seen as an outgrowth of street art, her artistic practice specifically engages ethical aspects of ordinary life and manifests a closer kinship with the idealism of off-grid, barter-based cultures and economies based on sharing. Consonant with this idealism, her wheat-pasted figures activate differently contingent social possibilities from seemingly chance encounters; these seemingly simple interventions generate moments of disorientation and anticipation, new and different from usual experience. Their uncanniness complicates the public experience, seemingly manifesting the city's unconscious in their literal figuration of the streetscape. The resulting sense of contingency and delight opens the possibilities of public spaces to all kinds of social transformation, from simple surprise amidst the ordinary to the prospect of alternative societies based in different behaviors and different values.

In both his installations and performances, Barthélémy Toguo works to achieve the scale of public address, but the arena he establishes is distinctly different from the inclusive, consensual platforms of common public space. Through complex and cacophonous works, he engages collective and competitive elaborations of meaning, rather than portraying or alluding to a common good presumed to be at the core of the public sphere. In *Heart Beat (Philadelphia)*, 2008/2010, Toguo, working with teens from community programs in the immediate neighborhood, marked up pages of the city's major newspaper to alter the local public discourse and a narrative 'of record.' Crossed out with thick black markers, the text was literally cancelled, leaving only unlabeled and decontextualized pictures. Installed across the gallery walls like wallpaper, the altered newspapers provided a platform for Toguo's assembly of disparate multiple parts: his own symbolic watercolors, photographed portraits of neighborhood leaders, a video showing Toguo shaving at home in Paris as the local news played on the radio, an oil drum filled with sticks marked with the names of oil-producing nations, and a floor covered with flattened cardboard banana boxes.

Toguo's process of gathering convenes multiple simultaneous narratives and acknowledges the competing lived realities legible in the printed materials that surround us. In *Heart Beat (Philadelphia)* the components provoke the ideas of international economies and the human labor required to maintain them. Events both local and faraway are pictured in the marked-up newspapers, while the layering of other elements complicates the publicness of the gallery space with disconcertingly private experiences.

Consonant with its smash-up of forms, *Heart Beat (Philadelphia)* shifts through an array of representational models – information, sensation, imagined narratives, symbolic figures, everyday objects, and various languages spoken, recorded, and inscribed – and pushes back on oppositions of fiction and truth, local and international, personal and public. Its crowded space presents individual narratives and meanings in conversation with imaginaries generated by community, state and transnational flows of image and information. The mix of readymade, altered, and authored elements is jarring and both complicates and challenges normative ideas of social order.

YOUNG-HAE CHANG HEAVY INDUSTRIES (Young-hae Chang and Marc Voge) have built a substantial body of Web-based works using original music and texts presented with Flash animation. Clicking on a title or a link activates a story that unfurls as type in the browser window, each work experienced at its own nonstop pace, providing an experience that resides somewhere between reading and watching a movie. The works' strong visual and aural rhythms present emphatic and elegant narratives; the artists critique modernist structures, the intelligibility of language and notions of text and subtext, among other issues, relying on satire to write political commentary. In invoking the idea of the novel, the broadside, and other print-based forms of public communication, YHCHI remind us of the print origins of contemporary media even as they engage us in a new consideration of the evolution of print.

At Temple Gallery, *My Pretty Peacenik*, 2010, was installed in a theatre-like setting: a discrete room with dark walls, some seating, and a screen proportionally large for the space set expectations for the expansive experience of cinema. The first-person narrative relayed a bullying incident, introducing issues of conflict and control that loom throughout this work. But while the personal and confessional tone of *My Pretty Peacenik* echoes the model of a novel, its swift pace allows no time for literary reflection; the rhythmic text, punctuated by the sound of synthesized drum and organ, controls the experience of the viewer. Composing in English – a practical choice in terms of accessibility for a large audience – foregrounded the issue of linguistic control and the constitution – and colonization – of the public through language. The rhythm established by the music was relentlessly fast, demanding the viewer read according to the work's terms. The story, through sly comedy, involved and implicated viewers with its personal revelations of private feelings, soliciting identification as well as discomfort and complicity, and reflecting the anxious condition of the individual in society.

Although the seven projects in *Print and the Public Sphere* engaged a wide range of issues and ideas, each of these artists strategically incorporated a consciousness of print and its specific ethos. Their allusions to print and their use of print formats and printed materials provided symbolic leverage (print as a 'modern' medium, with the resonance of history and differently configured values), or marked the territory of a public discourse, rendering visible the fantastic urban unconscious or introducing exchanges among new and multiple publics. Each project also made apparent the evolution of art as a social institution, one that has become a means of rendering intellectual arguments and producing alternatives to mainstream conversations when those conversations become too exclusive.[3] In the rapid succession of forms of communication and their effects on the public sphere, these artists have critically engaged the charged and changing circumstances of public life. They have used print as an image and a trope to point to the evolution of ideas of 'public' and how publics are constituted and reconstituted, not merely how they appear. Rather than publicizing dissident politics, they have directly engaged the flow of information among positions to generate new arenas for the exchange of competing perceptions and ideas. They have created interventions that not only provide entry points into public debate but also open up new collectivities in the spaces of public representation that present the possibility of powerful new social experiences.

Coda

In his *Arcades Project* (1927–40), Walter Benjamin demonstrated how, through advertising, print slipped the bounds of literature in the nineteenth century and infiltrated everyday experience. He wrote, 'Printing, having found in the book a refuge in which to lead an autonomous existence, is pitilessly dragged out onto the street by advertisements [... that] force the printed word entirely into the dictatorial perpendicular.'[4] In the different socio-political circumstances of a globalized world of the twenty-first century, the public sphere in its many manifestations absorbs and commands all forms, from oral exchange to print to digital forms and formats. In these projects print has become mobile and amorphous, diffused as potent imaginary into the flux of multiple publics, yet still urgent.

Notes

1 In the late twentieth century, democracy movements constituted a global phenomenon, and debate about democracy formations occupied academic and artistic circles as well as political discourses. An important resource is Okwui Enwezor (ed.), *Democracy Unrealized* (Ostfildern: Hatje Cantz, 2002), published in conjunction with *Documenta 11*, which Enwezor directed.

2 The loosely presented ideas of 'public' in this essay have been informed by a number of theoretical writings, including Oskar Negt and Alexander Kluge, *Public Sphere and Experience, Toward an Analysis of the Bourgeois and Proletarian Public Sphere* (Minneapolis: University of Minnesota Press, 1993); Michael Warner, 'Publics and Counterpublics,' *Public Culture* 14:1 (Winter 2002): 49–90; and Simon Sheikh (ed.), *In Place of the Public Sphere* (Berlin: b books, 2004).

3 For a discussion of the increasing politicization of art at the beginning of the twenty-first century, see Stefan Jonsson, 'Facts of Aesthetics and Fictions of Journalism: The Logic of the Media in the Age of Globalization,' in *The Green Room: Reconsidering the Documentary and Contemporary Art #1* (ed.), Maria Lind et al. (Berlin/Annandale-on-Hudson, NY: Sternberg Press and Centre for Curatorial Studies, Bard College, 2008), 166–87.

4 Walter Benjamin, quoted in Susan Buck-Morss, *The Dialectics of Seeing* (Cambridge, MA: MIT Press, 1991), 268.

Johanna Drucker

The work event: art in the distributed field and systems of production*

Contemporary artists are taking advantage of digital platforms to create works in what we can call a 'distributed field' of production. In some instances, their approaches follow older models of versioning and iteration. But in other cases, their projects explore contingencies specific to transmedia practices to produce a work that more closely resembles an event (temporal, ephemeral, participatory and/or experiential) than an object. What are the implications of these approaches for book artists or printmakers? What aesthetic possibilities are coming into view as a result of networked technologies? The media environment often produces hybrid works that use every and any available means of analogue, digital and performative experience combined with a wide array of input and output streams. We can certainly point to precedents in early media forms, but the explosive proliferation of these distributed approaches is now pushing against older boundaries in institutional, critical and economic domains, as well as aesthetic ones with unprecedented energy.

For one printerly example of the ways digital production extends traditional versioning, we can examine Sandow Birk's ambitious projects, which reinvent classic texts and graphics in contemporary form. In 2007, Birk created 15 4 × 8 foot woodcuts based on Jacques Callot's seventeenth-century *Miseries of War* (themselves an inspiration for the devastating series by Francisco Goya in the nineteenth century). Titled *Depravities of War*, Birk's edition was limited to a very few copies printed on Japanese paper, and meant for gallery exhibition and/or museum acquisition. The images were reproduced in a coffee-table format catalogue published to accompany its exhibition.

* Johanna Drucker. 2013. 'The Work Event: Art in the Distributed Field and Systems of Production', In: Luke Morgan, (ed.), *Intersections and Counterpoints: IMPACT 7 International Multi-disciplinary Printmaking Conference Proceedings*. Victoria, Australia: Monash University Publishing, pp. 12–16. Reproduced by kind permission of the author and Monash University Publishing.

Birk also engaged in extensive reinterpretation of Dante's *Inferno*, *Purgatorio* and *Paradisio*. His imaginative redrawings were based on imagery by Gustave Doré and other artists. Birk's reworkings follow a long tradition of such reimaginings, but what makes them interesting for my argument is not this updating, but the fact that the artist creates videos, books, prints and exhibits from the same materials as a larger exploration of the themes and imagery. The Dante project includes an animated film starring cut-out puppet figures in an elaborately shot and sequenced collage. The *Depravities* take the form of the large-scale woodblocks just mentioned, a website (where each image could be viewed in thumbnail and enlarged) and a published book. In the first instance, the project has multiple parts, in the second, many instantiations. Multipart works are not new. The distribution of a project across many iterations is almost intrinsic to artistic expression – whether it takes the form of notes, versions, performances – and is certainly central to printing and publishing since their advent.

Why issue a work in these multiple formats? What are the relations between the animation and the source images of Birk's Dante drawings? The gallery installation, the web display of prints and the Chronicle Books editions? Are they versions of a single work, as closely related to each other as the differently coloured prints in an edition of William Blake? Or are they more like Walt Whitman's endlessly re-arranged and re-edited *Leaves of Grass*? Are the cross-platform versions of contemporary artworks verging on a movie product tie-in approach to the consumer items that stretches from Happy Meal™ to action figures and clothing lines?

Theoretical questions arise when a work is produced across many iterations and elements. How is it bounded? Defined? Is each element a stand-alone object, as Birk's projects suggest, or are other formats emerging that make use of transmedia approaches to create more radically distributed works bounded neither in a temporal nor a spatial dimension?

The ongoing community-based engagement of the Los Angeles group, Machine Project, for instance, offers a very different study of distributed platforms. As enablers of other artists' work, hosts of a storefront environment for performance events and gatherings, as individuals who work collectively on installations and public art, they are often as involved with the documentation of their work as with any single instantiation of a piece. Even to say what constitutes a Machine Project 'piece' can be difficult if it is a cheese tasting in which artists draw a collective picture and then post images to Flickr for comment. They consider documentary materials created by themselves as well as by other participants to be integral parts of an ongoing and expanding field that is their work (Lau 2010). For Machine Project, the act of initiating a project with community participation is one milestone in the larger lifecycle of the whole event. The project has no finite form or closure as long as participants continue to contribute. And since their work depends heavily on these multiple levels and types of documentation – their own, promotional materials, critical responses and fan engagement through email, twitter and blog posts – it offers a striking example of ways contemporary artists think self-consciously about archival practices as part of their projects.

Yet another model of distributed work emerges from *The New Ecology of Things*, or *NET*.[1] In 2006 a research team at Art Center College of Design in Pasadena ran a studio class with 'visionary in residence', Bruce Sterling. Led by Phil van Allen and Nik Hafermaas, the goal of the class was to explore suggestions in Sterling's *Shaping Things* – prototypes for networked objects whose activities were enabled by microcomputers that created a modular, fluid environment for the migration and specialisation of information passing through and across them. Designers Anne Burdick and Holly Willis worked with van Allen to create a functioning demonstration of *NET*. This took the form of a poster, a book and web-enabled mobile phones that together constituted a transmedia work. When the poster was opened, the book sat inside a graphic frame that completed the information circuit in the book's design. The mobile phones were activated by codes and signals encoded into the graphic environment. The idea was to imagine a fully ubiquitous and distributed system within which a 'work' was constituted as an event, or an intervention, rather than as a thing.

The science-fiction inspired imagination of the *NET* research project led to the realisation of an actual, integrated, hybrid work. Our cultural imaginary is infused with technophilic musings and aesthetic potentialities. We absorb our ideas of future interface from special effects in films that also offer a vision of space-time transformations, relativistic dreams and mutable conditions of energy and matter. Artists are susceptible to these fantasies and their potential to change the world around us. A wide range of transmedia, cross-platform, altered reality networks and virtual art works are pushing at the edge of traditional boundaries between games and art, literature and theory, analogue and virtual environments – even as their networked entanglements produce curious effects of a work distributed simultaneously across multiple sites.

The autonomous, discrete, thing-ness of objects, as the theoretical subtext of these many projects suggests, is a mere illusion. We imagine we know what a thing is because it has apparent stability. But the idea that a work's identity can reside in a thing comes up for question immediately in these distributed modes. In actuality, any 'thing' is a temporary configuration of complex processes given to our perceptual apparatus in a form that looks fixed and bounded within the temporal frame and spatial scales in which we encounter it. In another frame, all such 'things' are contingent, as dependent on forces and circumstances of their environments and systems of which they partake as the development of embryos or the bonds of subatomic particles. And all works of art, therefore, can be understood as events, snapshots across the interwoven cycles of production and reception that arise in the social, physical, cultural and material worlds at a specific, historically situated, instant.

As the arms of nebulous theory spiral out in one direction and the creation of multiple forms and platforms for artistic publishing spin off in another, the gap between theoretical notions and material practices might seem enormous. Can we connect a theoretical insight at the cutting edge of thingness with the opportunistic approach to multi-platform publishing?

To begin with, working across media platforms is not a new approach. When nineteenth-century publishers advertised their wares by posting announcements in shop windows or newspaper owners recognised the virtues of putting harbinger sheets on hoardings to whet the appetite of readers for their upcoming editions, they were using multiple sites and venues across the media sphere to produce a work whose various dimensions were not consolidated into a single object. Oral reports of a play or performance circulated long before reviews were an established genre. Contemporary urban hacking, or artistic works that are barely visible as such but create a transformative experience in a city environment, can be seen as an extreme version of such activity, or as a stealth action extending the technique of avant-garde sublation of reality and artistic practice. Much depends on the point from which these works are examined, but although specifics vary, the approaches have precedents. Distributed ritual activities have always left traces of their events received by later generations as artefacts in the form of paintings, masks, costumes, or fetish items and so on.

As media historian Sandra Gabriele has recently shown, works in distributed format do not depend on digital technology. What they do depend upon are networks of communication and media ecologies, on the interconnection of various parts and pieces of a project that serve different purposes in the production and reception cycles of its existence. Gabriele has documented the ways late nineteenth- and early twentieth-century newspapers, radio and telegraph could be described as *intermedial* systems in which the benefits of repurposing content were well recognised. For instance, in the 1910s Hearst corporation, the *Chicago Tribune* and other newspaper companies were producing newsreels that were shown with fiction films, using them as promotional tie-ins for their print editions as well as platforms to promote brand identity. Gabriele (2010) shows that the concept of intermediality insists on the value of 'linkages, on activities of appropriation and reversion, on tacit or asserted continuities, on dogged forms of resistance and on eloquent recyclings'. She notes that early pioneers in this cross-platform design 'imagined a new technology bringing together the advances made by the newspaper, wireless, the gramophone, and the telephone separately'. This intermedial device would transform information stored in any one medium into any number of others. Even in the pre-digital era, the fungible character of information across media platforms was easy to envision. Gabriele describes an early twentieth-century notion that a text could be turned into a sound recording, a picture into a description, these in turn could be fed into a machine that would output them as type, or an image on a screen, or as a movie to be viewed in private households and public spaces simultaneously according to the whim and circumstances of consumers (Gabriele 2010).

In a modern era of industrialisation, the promotion of print and theatre productions was accompanied by advertising that brought headline stories, new releases and stage events to the attention of the public through the use of posters propped in conspicuous places in the public eye. The 'work' of a newspaper might consist of its advanced notices and sensational promotions, just as a trailer became part of a film's existence along with production stills of scenes that might never have been part of the actual movie script. The fullest sense of the whole work in these cases would extend to all the many ephemera and documentation that are part of its existence – scripts, notes, rushes, outtakes, annotations and revisions, editing logs and then reviews, promotional material and so on in a continuum of traces that are all part of the work. Independent and industry figures make good use of these ecologies. As the lead up to *The Blair Witch Project* film demonstrated, various teasers and trailers build anticipation and audience when used correctly as advance promotion.

In another media lineage, we can track the history of print editions with its examples of editions and iterations. Compositional genealogies of any particular work comprise the core of the field of bibliographical studies. Interest in retracing the stages of a work's production is motivated differently across the range of intellectual paradigms that mark the shifting goals of bibliography and critical editing. Some figures focused on a task of establishing the authority of biblical texts, creating and constituting the scripture through careful work, as was the case in the early centuries of the Common Era when Church fathers sought to create a biblical text from translations, fragments and variations. In another era scholars attended to the problems of recovering the corpus of classical antiquity through translation back into Greek or Latin from Arabic manuscripts that had preserved the tracts of the ancients in a period when European monasteries had little usage for much that the scholars and scientists of Islamic courts preserved. Throughout, the skills of discerning variations and making judgments about textual validity have been central to humanistic work in preservation of the cultural record. Many decades of scholarly practice have been invested in searches for authentic voices, original texts, or the social production of a work conceived outside of the terms of originality or authenticity. But at the core of such practices is a recognition of the distributed and contingent nature of texts in and across their material witnesses and instantiations.

Closer to our time, the creation of conceptual pieces in which a performance was documented, or an instruction could give rise to multiple versions or instantiations of a work, gave rise to a different conception of artistic practice and objects from the traditional view of a work as a canvas or sculpture. In the 1960s, conceptual artist Robert Smithson created 'non-sites', works designed to expose the distributed field that constituted a work. They consisted of an earthwork, photographic imagery and gallery installations of documents or materials from a site, depending on a project and its specific properties. A pile of dirt from a specific place whose location was shown on a map and in a photograph might be on display in an exhibit, but this was not the representation of an absent place. Rather all elements were elements in pulling apart the illusion of an integral or autonomous object or site for it. Thus these were called non-sites to call attention to their refusal of autonomy and boundedness, and to their participation in and distance from site-specific works. The conceptual move made by Smithson in these projects foregrounded the fractured nature of the aesthetic object – turning it into an intellectual and experiential conundrum as well as a distributed work. To compose the work within a viewer's mind meant holding all parts in relation to each other, possible only as a mental or cognitive exercise, since the pieces of the work could never be co-located physically.

Artists playing with ubiquitous or distributed models sometimes use digital techniques, but analogue and site-specific projects also have a place in this history. For instance, in 2004, Nick Montfort and Scott Rettberg printed sections from a collaborative novel onto crack and peel paper and sent pieces in the mail to a wide assortment of friends and colleagues. The task for each recipient was to put the bit of text somewhere in a public place and photograph it, then return the photograph to them digitally for documentation. Titled *Implementation*, the piece was 'a serial novel' and described by its authors as 'about psychological warfare, American imperialism, sex, terror, identity, and the idea of place, a project that borrows from the traditions of net.art, mail art, sticker art, conceptual art, Situationist theatre, serial fiction, and guerilla viral marketing'.[2] The authors distinguished 'sheet readers' of the work from 'place readers'. The first group had access to the printed sheets and the second to the experience of a single stick in place in an environment. Visitors to the website were 'web readers' and those who listened to a reading in a public venue were 'audience', while the individuals who received, posted and photographed the stickers in sites were 'participants'. Only those who completed the task and returned documentation to the authors were sent the next sheet of sticker texts. I remember nothing of this text piece, just its form. The photograph of Scott and Nick committing an act of public vandalism in Philadelphia and documenting it while being themselves documented exemplifies the self-referential 'implementation' of the work as both subject and method.

Other distributed works also engage with collaboration as a central feature. Gretchen Henderson's *Galerie de Deformité* combines an online collection of texts, or 'Exhibits', as she calls them, that can be downloaded and then transformed. These mini-essays, narrated in the voice of Dante's Beatrice, can be resubmitted electronically to the character of the 'Undertaker' and then considered for inclusion in the online gallery. The gallery will grow as long as contributions continue to be made, but early contributions were considered for publication in the printed volume, so long as they were received by June 2010. The 'gallery' is comprised of the printed work and the online exhibits, the one bounded and the other open-ended.

In another approach to distributed materiality, Amaranth Borsuk's *Between Page and Screen* can be characterised as a virtual pop-up book.[3] It can only be read by closing the circuit of intermedia connections. The pages of her book contain QR markers, black-and-white grids that encode a URL the way a universal price code stores cost information. When held up to the camera eye of a computer, they access a site, and animated poetry begins to display itself.

Multi-platform work also includes the integrative experiments of Alex Galloway and other performers who used video, telepresence and performance in real time to make works that were 'located' in several physical sites simultaneously. Pieces that make use of ubiquitous or distributed media and locations can be analogue as well as digital, with pieces like Montfort and Rettberg's or Borsuk's as examples of distributed pieces that require communication networks as part of their generative infrastructure.

Transmedia storytelling exploits these capabilities to different ends, and has a close affinity with Alternate Reality Games (ARGs). Media theorist Henry Jenkins identifies several key characteristics of this genre, noting the combination of participatory and in-depth capacities of participatory narratives.[4] Immersive platforms promote strong identification with characters, circumstances and also situations of viewing and playing. But the distinguishing feature of ARGs is their blurring of the lines between fictional and actual events. Andrea Phillips's 2001 project, *The Beast*, raised concerns about security and false evidence when it was launched in the immediate post-9/11 era. If mobile devices and media outlets were used to produce simulated news reports and fake documents, how would the public who were not yet clued into the game know they were in an 'augmented' rather than actual situation?

With this range of examples in mind, we can now sketch some tentative categories to describe works that make use of distributed sites and various modes of production: transmedia projects, pieces across distributed platforms, ubiquitous and/or environmental works in a variety of sites, and projects that repurpose their content in different instantiations. Transmedia projects are conceived from the outset as constituted by parts that all relate in a network of production and reception. The *New Ecology of Things* is a dramatic contemporary example, but precedents exist, as we have seen, in print and mass media campaigns where posters, movie trailers and serially released, iterative or cumulative, elements are all integral to a project. More dramatic precedents appear in the mid twentieth century as artists exploded the physical integrity of works into a field of interrelated parts, as in the canonical and paradigmatic non-sites of Smithson. Distributed platforms play a different role – the creation of pieces that integrate mobile, web and sometimes print are typical of fan culture, such as those of Machine Project. Original artefacts spawn a host of responses, remix mash-up and spin-off trails in which role-playing and storytelling take up the characters or scenes of the touchstone piece, in projects that blur boundaries of fictional intervention and reality, as in the example of Andrea Phillips's problematic projects.

When we are in the realm of 'things' that are art objects or aesthetic works, we are even further from the commonplace sense of bounded objects or delimited forms, and closer to the continuum of production/reception cycles. We know this, if we stop to think about any encounter with an aesthetic object. *Jane Eyre* is not the same book for me today as it was when I was 11 years old, any more than the most recent film version is identical to earlier twentieth-century interpretations. The shift is not a mere matter of human subjectivity and individual reading or viewing experience, but is produced at a more fundamental level in which the co-dependent relation between the identity of an object and the circumstances of its existence coincide. A fish out of water soon ceases to breathe, a plate of food in zero gravity disperses its parts, and peas float among the drifting noodles and bits of gravy. So does a work depend upon forces that give it an illusory image of bounded identity within the systems on which it depends for its existence.

The deliberate design of projects engineered to constitute themselves across media platforms is a phenomenon that takes full advantage of the current media ecology. As we have seen, a 'work' can be a transmedia event, a series of interrelated activities sequenced overtime and across multiple spaces and forms of expression. Artists engage with this as an aesthetic investigation, but also as an 'artrepreneurial' aspect of their work.

Works of distributed digital networks involve enhanced reality effects, triggers and keys embedded in the environment that access content stored on servers and which are delivered electronically in real time but in a variety of spaces and places. Works that make use of repurposed content in different output or instantiations are exemplified by Sandow Birk's projects, described above, in which works made for enormous wall display and gallery installation can be readily reproduced in catalogue format and also made available online. Other printmakers, painters and book artists have quickly grasped the value of print-on-demand repurposing of their visual graphics. The possibility of creating multiples in an open-ended edition that requires very little financing up-front, produces no awkward inventory and can be stored for future use across an unforeseen set of projects is of course attractive. Each iteration is a stand-alone element, but the work as a whole makes use of each of these modes to reach a different audience and, of course, market.

While each of these various distributed modes of production creates its own system of products and constituent project elements, they also each offer the chance to think about the ways in which cognitive reception and performance of works is being shaped at the same time. The modes of reading and viewing that are part of spectacle, carnival, even elaborate rituals in religious, political, or other cultural spheres, are multi-part and multi-sensory events. Bringing that model of group authorship, collective subjectivity, participatory production into the world of contemporary art production may shift our sense of what an art object is, but builds on longstanding notions of what an aesthetic experience might and can be. Traditional approaches to the cycles of production and reception that were part of the consumption of discrete seemingly bounded objects (books, magazines, etc.) may turn out to have been a modern anomaly, specific to a historic moment in which market models of 'autonomous' objects worked. The proliferation of multiple outputs and versions of works continues that particular lineage, expanding the range of offerings across broader demographics, reachable because the possibilities of production are so much more flexible than in print media, but the more interesting aspects of the transmedia art production may be in the ways they show us how to understand works of art as events in a distributed field. Not only are works thus part of a social production of objects, but they are embedded in and co-dependent on other systems as well – of distributed material production, lifecycles of consumption, and cognitive experience integrated across numerous points of provocation and perception.

A host of artists are exploring fundamental conceptual issues in more or less direct confrontation with the otherwise long-held belief, rooted in a regular pragmatic positivism, that a work is of course and necessarily a thing, fixed and bounded, no matter how subject to wear, tear, erosion and change it might be under the aggressive vicissitudes of time. Questioning the integrity of 'thing-ness' is not a matter of noting the fraying of edges or the scratched surface of a book or the accumulation of dirt on pages or in the crevasses of a sculpture or niches and crannies of a great cathedral. These new works are instead gesturing towards an ontological reconceptualisation of what a work is – an event – within media systems each of whose affordances and potentialities are realised as a momentary expression. In this conceptual frame, an aesthetic object is an instant, an instantiation, a temporally and spatially ephemeral 'thing' – that we can recognise as the 'work event' in the 'distributed field and systems of production'.

Notes

1 *NET*, newecologyofthings.net.
2 See: http://ruinsorbooks.com/tag/street-art/
3 See: www.thecreatorsproject.com/blog/a-virtual-pop-up-poetry-book.
4 See: http://whatconsumesme.com/2009/posts-ive-written/core-principles-of-transmedia-storytelling.

References

Gabriele, S. 2010. 'Newspapers and the Intermedial Imaginary', Talk delivered on 2 Dec. 2010 in the Art History and Communication Studies Speaker Series, McGill University, Montreal.

Lau, A. J. 2010. '"All Description is a Form of Creation": Constructing the Event through Documentation'. Part of the panel *Finding Community in the Archive: Machine Project as Nexus*. Presented at the *Reimagining the Archive* Symposium at the University of California, Los Angeles, 12–14 November.

Eric Triantafillou

All the instruments agree*

The façade of a now defunct police station in San Francisco's Mission District is plastered with street art. It is a visual cacophony of posters, flyers, stencils, paintings, drawings, and the hand-scrawled responses of passers-by. A remnant of the housing struggles that began in 2000, today this wall is a public commons that transmits information about everything from legal rights workshops to communist party meetings and yoga classes; also occupying its surface are corporate ads cloaked in DIY lino-chic. It is also a screen onto which people project thoughts and feelings about the world they fear and visions of the one they want.

From a distance, all these competing images and ideas side by side create an uneasy harmony, like a Jackson Pollock painting – a kind of abstract social expressionism. Up close, reading the messages, you see a lot of contradiction and tension, evidence of the wall's messy and contentious evolution. The tactile beauty of the wall is immediate, and yet you realize that this wall is not just a space; it also reveals a history – it is a process in time. But what kind of process? Is the wall a representation of a public and participatory experiment, or its actualization? Is the wall a *truly* democratic space in a society that only claims to be democratic? Do these disparate images and contradictory ideas illustrate the diversity of our social, cultural, and political perspectives?

We could view this form of public communication not as constituting a consensus, but as proof that we can have *dissensus* and yet still coexist. After all, no one has to listen to or agree with anyone's opinions; they simply need to tolerate them being expressed. Any idea, any image, can simply be covered over by another, ad infinitum. We could celebrate the wall as a bastion of diversity and dissent, a toehold in a society whose public space

* Eric Triantafillou. 2010. 'All the Instruments Agree'. In: MacPhee, Josh (ed.), *Paper Politics: Socially Engaged Printmaking Today*. Oakland, CA: PM Press, pp. 20–5. Reproduced by kind permission of the author and PM Press.

is increasingly privatized and controlled. But we also have to recognize that the wall can represent a norm for controversy in a society that has not found a way to resolve its conflicts, a society that easily recuperates the meaning of experiments like these and then sells them back to us as aesthetic commodities.

The book you hold in your hands* is also a kind of wall. At one time or another, many of the images in this book have appeared in public spaces across the U.S. and other countries. Like layers of time, these images have been peeled off the palimpsest and placed next to each other on the page. These juxtapositions are both powerful and problematic. Like the wall in the Mission, this book [*Paper Politics*] represents a diverse cross-section of ideas and practices that together form a loose aggregate that we could call 'left political art'. However, viewing all these images next to each other can give the appearance of political unity when there may actually be none.

As printmakers, most of us produce our work with an understanding that we are contributing to and continuing the tradition of politicized printmaking that Deborah Caplow discusses in her essay – a tradition that began with Goya in the early nineteenth century.[1] I often think that we are more preoccupied with continuing this tradition than with asking why the promise it holds out – the promise of universal emancipation – remains so elusive. Our need to be constantly busy, to always be making more, is endemic to the activist compulsion to keep a movement alive, with little sense of what we are moving toward or why. I would go so far as to say that we, the producers of images that are meant to represent social conflict and its antidotes, may actually be complicit in prolonging, as opposed to fulfilling, this broken promise. How could this be?

The graphic art of dissent over the past century and a half is an endlessly twisting, impossibly varied, and fantastically inspired and inspiring maze of imagery. Yet within this multiplicity of signs, symbols, and slogans there are clearly many that are used again and again. The images of past struggles comprise a kind of inventory of left visual tropes that are continuously recycled. New generations of makers adapt the images of previous generations to the social conditions and aesthetic sensibilities of the present. This is in part what it means to operate within a tradition. Images of the past are re-used in order to commemorate them, to create symbolic continuity, to inspire new social movements with the knowledge that they are rooted in the past, to prevent historical amnesia.

Left graphics regularly portray the relationship of social forces as a conflict between two sides: *Us* – children crying, clenched fists, crowds amassing, plants growing, doves alighting – versus *Them* – bombs falling, smoke

* Editor's note: The author is referring to *Paper Politics*, the original source for this essay.

stacks spewing, barbed wire, prison bars, skeletons. In nineteenth-century France, left political cartoons frequently characterized the bourgeoisie as a parasite that sucks the blood of the workers. Many early anarchists and socialists believed that if the workers – whom they believed produced all the wealth – could rid society of the bourgeoisie, they would finally be free. In the history of left political art, this opposition is played out again and again in expressions like 'Capitalists need workers, but workers don't need capitalists.' It is probable that in a society in which workers controlled production there would be a more equitable distribution of material wealth. But I don't think it helps to think of capitalism as something that some people *do* and others *don't*. We are all subjects of the same socioeconomic system. The captains of industry and finance are no less dominated by this system, regardless of the fact that they benefit more, than the billions of people with far less. We are all bound to a system characterized by a blind march toward profit, one that must constantly revolutionize or perish.

In early 2000, during the housing crisis in San Francisco that was caused by the new Internet economy, I produced the image *Cleaner, Brighter, Whiter Tablecloths*. An ironic jab at the hipsters who were moving into the neighborhood, it refers to the ethnic bleaching of the city's predominately lower-income Mission District. The image portrays the immediate reality that was visible in the streets, representing gentrification as an opposition between those perpetrating it and those fighting against it. Representing the 'gentrifiers' makes it unnecessary to represent those fighting against gentrification; the latter are implied. If as a viewer I don't identify with what the symbols in the image signify, I am against *them*; I am one of *us*. And since we tend to affirm symbols of resistance as authentic expressions of suffering, joy, and indignation, we rarely question the thinking or the politics that are bound up with these symbols.

Cleaner, Brighter, Whiter Tablecloths only mirrored the way things appeared, on the surface: young, white, urban professionals move into a 'Latino' neighborhood, driving up real estate values and disrupting the sense of community. This conception reinforces the idea that capitalist society operates and can be understood through binaries like gentrifiers versus indigenous residents. What gets lost is the understanding of gentrification as a consequence of a socio-historical dynamic that shapes the actions of everyone involved: the venture capitalist who invests; the politician who frames the change as the natural course of economic development; the planning commission that rezones the neighborhood to pave the way; the banker who lends; the property owner who borrows to flip a condo or the first-time home-buyer who takes out a mortgage she can barely afford; the developer who controls the building trades or the independent contractor who hires cheap immigrant labor; and the community coalition attempting to get a temporary moratorium on the construction of market-rate housing so a few lower-income families can stay in their homes a little longer. The image of

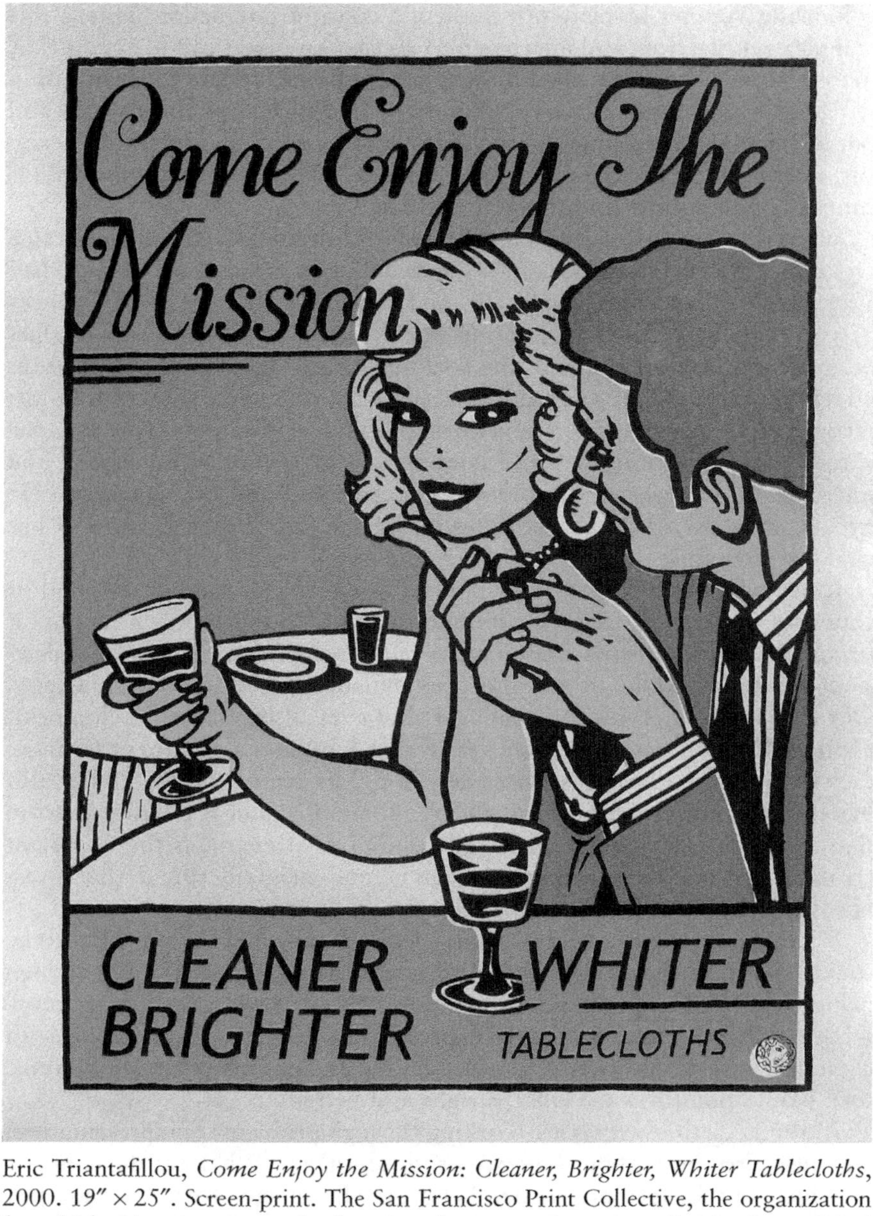

Eric Triantafillou, *Come Enjoy the Mission: Cleaner, Brighter, Whiter Tablecloths*, 2000. 19″ × 25″. Screen-print. The San Francisco Print Collective, the organization for which this print was made, functioned as an anonymous collective for political reasons. The artist claims authorship in this case in order to dissociate the critique he makes in this essay from other members in the collective.

colonizing yuppies in search of authentic cultural interaction flattens this complex set of actors and interests into an easy-to-digest call to action. The more complex challenge of addressing gentrification and anti-gentrification struggles as systemic, as part of a process in which capital moves in and out of the built environment – the spatial component of capitalism's necessity to continuously accumulate and expand – is something these symbols cannot communicate, and, in fact, obfuscate.

What is driving capitalism's imperative to continuously accumulate value and increase that value? Is it old-fashioned human greed or something else? Why does gentrification specifically, and capitalism more generally, appear as a struggle between two opposing sides? Exploitation and social conflict are real and ever-present. But the socio-historical dynamic that structures all relationships, a dynamic that has become increasingly abstract over time, is concealed when it is understood through simple oppositions. This dynamic is rooted in the contingency and symbiosis of all social forces, classes, and interests. To reduce it to a conflict between good and evil does not help explain how this dynamic mediates social life, its origins, or how it has changed over time.

If we continue to express our politics as either choosing to do good or choosing to do bad, we will continue to think of the problem as one of *being*, as something *in* us, and not as a relationship *between* us. Good decisions by good people do not alter this dynamic in any fundamental way. Our focus on the ethical or unethical character of capitalist development, expressed in symbols of altruism versus greed, implies a politics of technocracy (an increase in social services here, a tighter regulation there), but also has the effect of closing off possibilities for more radical politics. Reform that ameliorates immediate material conditions strengthens the dominant thinking that our socioeconomic system is fundamentally sound, that it just needs some tinkering around the edges.

What if our images could do more? What if they had the potential to be radical, to go to the root, to try to represent the relationship that is hidden behind the binary idioms of our tradition? What if we were able to know what determines, and to clearly express, that which is truly wrong with capitalist society? As negative as our thinking and our images might become, they would point toward what is right and better.

At the same time artists are working through problems of representation, we must also think about *how* we produce images. What are the contexts in which our images are made? Who are the images for? Are they just preaching to the converted? If *Cleaner, Brighter, Whiter Tablecloths* was problematic as an image, the context in which it was made – as part of a larger effort to mount a visual response to what was happening in San Francisco's Mission District – had far more potential. In 2000, some fellow printmakers and I began making posters about displacement and evictions. One of the places where we put them was on the old police station wall.

Our group, the San Francisco Print Collective, became the propaganda wing of a neighborhood coalition that had come together to fight gentrification. SFPC members were united by the idea that art is an incredibly powerful tool when rooted in a social movement. We didn't always agree with the political positions or tactics the coalition adopted, but we shared a common goal. The SFPC's images and messages were composed by multiple voices within our collective, but when they hit the streets they spoke with one voice. Our work's constant visual presence in public space helped communicate to others what was happening in the neighborhood. It also inspired and motivated people in the movement, inextricably linking our effectiveness and longevity to the wider community's struggle.

Artists of the past organized large-scale unions and popular fronts in response to the social conditions of their time. Although these forms of organizing shouldn't be ruled out, they haven't materialized in the present. Many artists already work in small collectives, organizing themselves around shared affinities, social values, mutual support, and resources sharing. This doesn't mean that as artists we automatically share a common political vision because of our backgrounds, a certain temperament, the media with which we work, or our relationship to other social actors and institutions. But what if we did? What if, instead of letting this book [*Paper Politics*] or the Mission District wall represent our differences – our pluralism – we began to work towards articulating a shared commonality?

I advocate that we, left printmakers, develop a set of shared goals, and use our powerful ability to intervene in public space, to create new ways of thinking and new meanings that refuse the dominant ones, and to develop tactics that can help us achieve those goals. The voices in this book and on that wall give the appearance of unity, of a unified opposition to capitalist society. But on closer examination, you can see fissures, fractures, and contradictions. If we began to organize ourselves, to create spaces for collective reflection and political education, I think we would find that ideologically we are very atomized, and that many of us would rather remain this way because the concept of unity (and all the past failed attempts at it) means a loss of individual freedom.

The collective articulation of a set of goals (which in and of itself would be an incredible undertaking) would necessitate an in-depth analysis of all the practices we're engaged in. It would mean that we would have to confront the fact that some ways of thinking and some practices are probably better than others as instruments for achieving our goals. This doesn't mean it is wrong to make images that advocate that we 'Support the troops, send the politicians to war' or 'Knit for the revolution.' But it does mean that if these are the kinds of stories we tell ourselves and we attempt to fashion a politics out of them, we may not be getting any closer to our goals. In their broadest sense, these goals would have to involve creating the social conditions in which someone's desire to make whatever she wants, to think and act as she sees fit – without being dominated by time, space or someone else – will have been gained for all.

The wall insists on an encounter. It wants to be used. But it is a space that gestures toward something beyond itself. It is not an end. It is a process of *becoming*. At the same time we create spaces of dialogue and public commons, at the same time we continue our tradition as the archaeologists of dreams and the farmers of inspiration, we can realize the force of unity that lies dormant in our fractured and individualistic practices. Let's investigate our own thinking. Let's look at our practices. Let's collectively reflect on the images we make, and how and for whom we make them. Let's ask if they could do more – if they could reveal the abstract barbarity of our social reality, and still incite and inspire us. As long as our goals are based on an intransigent desire for total social freedom, we have nothing to fear.

Notes

1 Caplow, Deborah, 'Political Art and Printmaking: A Brief and Partial History' in: Josh MacPhee (ed.). 2010. *Paper Politics: Socially Engaged Printmaking Today*. Oakland, CA: PM Press, pp. 12–19.

Mari Carmen Ramírez

Stamping (molding) marks: the San Juan Triennial tracking the new century*

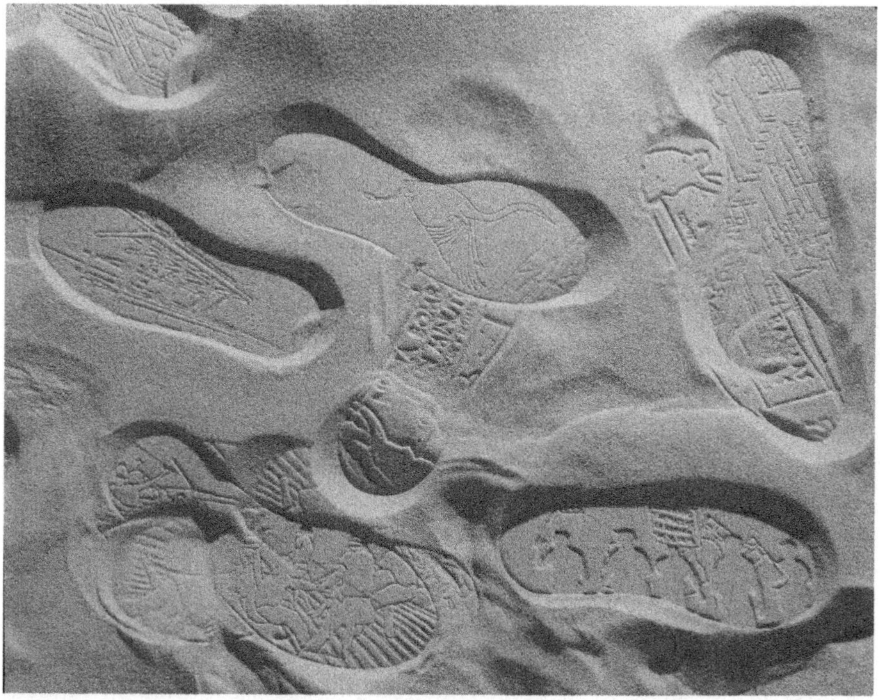

Allora and Calzadilla, *Land Mark (Footprints)*, 2002. Digital C-Print, 20″ × 24″ (50.8 × 60.96) cm.

* Mari Carmen Ramírez. 2004. 'Stamping (Molding) Marks: The San Juan Triennial Tracking the New Century'. In: Ramírez, Mari Carmen et al. (eds), *Trienal Poli / Grafica de San Juan: America Latina y el Caribe and Desplazamientos Precursores en la Grafica LatinoAmericana: Antonio Berni, Beatriz Gonzalez, Inscritos y Proscritos (Poly / Graphic San Juan Triennial: Latin America and the Caribbean)*. San Juan: San Juan Triennial, pp. 14–21. Reproduced by kind permission of the author.

A biennial in crisis

Since their inception at the end of the nineteenth century, art biennials or triennials have functioned as instruments for the promotion and legitimacy of the visual arts within regional, continental or global contexts. These large-scale artistic events, for the most part, share a double purpose. On one hand, by gathering together the latest artistic trends, they stimulate an objective dialogue between artists from a specific country or region and the rest of the world. On the other hand, they agglutinate local economic and political interests around art, whose recasting, in many cases, projects them into a broader arena that encompasses the mainstream. From the pioneer and now venerable Venice Biennale in Europe, to its Latin American counterpart, the São Paulo Biennial, the energizing history of these events confirms their dual role: instruments of cultural diplomacy and symbolic exchange versus tools for the economic validation of emergent regions. In the last decade, the establishment of new biennials in such remote locations as Istanbul (Turkey), Kwang-Ju (Korea) or Dakar (Senegal), as a result of the restructuring of world-systems unleashed by globalization, only serves to reinforce both points.

Despite its undeniable isolation from the international scene – a detachment that, bordering on self-absorption, can be considered a legitimate defense against its endemic colonial condition – the Island of Puerto Rico has enjoyed during the last thirty years a certain prestige in global artistic circuits through the institution of the *Bienal de San Juan del Grabado Latinoamericano y del Caribe* (1970–2001). Established at the peak of the developmentalist project that accompanied the creation of the Puerto Rican Commonwealth, the San Juan Biennial became the most tangible expression of a political and cultural consolidation project, bridging the gap between regional and continental perspectives. From its inception, it served to showcase the latest trends in Latin American graphics, while simultaneously inserting the achievements of Puerto Rican artists – particularly the generation of the 1950s – into the broader continental arena. The fact that this generation had made graphics its signature mode of expression, in turn, influenced the decision to make San Juan a crossroads for the meeting of the best printmakers from Latin America and the Caribbean. In tandem with the socio-political urgency of the 1960s and 1970s, the stimulus that led to the setting up of the San Juan Biennial was also triggered by the desire to provide Puerto Rican and Latin American artists with a forum for technical and conceptual experimentation. During its first edition, the Biennial brought local audiences in touch with the best examples of printing produced throughout Latin America in the 1960s. In doing so, it took the lead in exhibiting the truly cutting-edge character of Latin American graphics during this period.[1] Indeed, together with highly distinguished exponents of traditional media – such as José Clemente Orozco and José Guadalupe Posada – the inaugural Biennial showcased the most iconoclastic graphic artists of the period: Jesus Rafael Soto, Luis Camnitzer, Liliana Porter and Omar Rayo among others.

The radical implications of such a project for a truncated *island-nation* like Puerto Rico should not be underestimated. By making Latin America its sphere of action, the Biennial was staking out a place for Puerto Rican artists in this geo-political enclave to which it was connected by history, language, culture, and religion. At the same time, it was resisting absorption into the American way of artistic life. Hence, despite the radical ups and downs which the event suffered over its three and a half decades of existence, the San Juan Biennial did succeed, however modestly, in its goal of projecting the vitality of Puerto Rican graphics to the continent and vice versa. To this day, the Biennial stands out as one of the few bold initiatives of its kind in the highly strategic yet underestimated Caribbean region that, with the exception of Cuba, has thus far remained somewhat indifferent to large-scale international events.

By the end of its 13th edition in 2001, however, it was clear that, despite having made it into a new century, the San Juan Biennial had reached a critical quagmire. Since the late 1980s a handful of factors oscillating from the ongoing fluctuations of local political life to the institutional sclerosis of its host institution (the Institute of Puerto Rican Culture) – not to mention financial bankruptcy – significantly curtailed the quality of its presentations as well as its scope of influence both regionally and internationally. Yet, it would be unfair to exclusively attribute the conceptual and practical obsolescence of the Biennial to insular political or institutional woes.

In order to fully assess the magnitude of its crisis, we must ponder at least two other factors. First, there was the Biennial's inability to transform itself in light of the profound decline in status and relevance suffered by graphics at that time. In such a period, the renewed popularity of painting, together with the innovative emergence of image technologies exemplified by digital photography, the internet, and installation art, led many artists to either abandon graphics altogether or to approach them as ancillary elements of broader conceptual or process-oriented strategies. In this regard, the Biennial's blind adherence to a conservative definition of printmaking as the basis for the selection of artists and works made it increasingly unattractive to both established and emerging graphic artists focused on expanding the technical or conceptual limits of these media. Hence, rather than staying true to its original experimental impulse, the San Juan Biennial barely survived by eliminating radical innovation and promoting instead a guild-oriented, fundamentalist approach to printmaking.

A second factor that explains the impasse confronted by the Biennial concerns the way in which its structure – based on the nineteenth-century model of national artistic representations, combined with a selection jury and prize system – increasingly hindered its competitive edge vis-a-vis other events of its kind worldwide. We must bear in mind that since the late 1980s, globalization – understood here in terms of the crisis of nation states, and the continuous displacement of individuals across national borders, among other considerations – not only stimulated the implementation of new biennials everywhere but also forced a profound alteration of their structure and organization to meet the demands of a more porous world order. The most evident sign of this transformation was the abandonment of the wasted (and, in many cases, highly corrupt) model of national representations in favor of a thematic or issues-orientated scheme more in tune with the extreme malleability that characterizes contemporary art, including graphics. This model, widely adopted throughout the 1990s by both established and emergent biennials, as well as other global exhibitions, relied on the active role of the curator in shaping the overall substance and reach of these events.

In this context, curatorial authority not only came to substitute the hierarchical apparatus that had characterized past biennials but also proved to be a catalyst for a prize-less art-world. That is to say, one that responds, more and more, to horizontal mechanisms of organization, non-hierarchical channels of distribution, and modes of production that are both multicultural and polyvalent in scope.

All of these determinants combined to raise serious doubts about the San Juan Biennial's continued relevance for the rapidly evolving field of Latin American graphics as well as for contemporary art by and large. In 2001, the broad consensus was that, unless the institution reinvented again, it would either disappear altogether or, even worse, face downgrading to the level of a purely local exhibition. With regards to the new scenario, the key questions confronting the Biennial organizers were: What special role, if any, could a graphic arts biennial oriented towards Latin America and the Caribbean fulfill today? How could the Biennial's mission and structure be updated so that it could effectively meet the present needs of both Puerto Rican artists as well as of their counterparts in the region? During the last two years, the attempt to answer these questions in a way that was creative, as well as future-oriented, led to the complete transformation of the San Juan Biennial into its current format: The SAN JUAN POLY/GRAPHIC TRIENNIAL: Latin America and The Caribbean. This new configuration resulted from an intensive reflection about two fundamental aspects of this challenging undertaking. First, a strategic consideration of the role Puerto Rico can play as a dynamic hinge between artists and peoples of Latin America, the Caribbean, and the United States. Secondly, the extraordinary change undergone by graphics worldwide over the last fifteen years and their implications for the expanding field of Puerto Rican and Latin American graphics.

A new territory of action for the triennial

If the arena of graphics has changed since the first edition of the San Juan Biennial, so have the political conditions that justify and make such an event viable for the Island and the continent. Hence, before considering the transformations undergone by graphics two decades ago, a new action territory for the Triennial must be mapped. The ideas of Trans/Migration – which, in the view of the curators, defines the developments affecting contemporary graphics – find a direct correlation in the situation of Puerto Rican (as well as Caribbean and Latin American) culture today. Trans/Migration refers to the constant displacement of disenfranchised peoples across borders, particularly the borders that separate the First World from the Third. Over the last fifteen or twenty years this flux of peoples and cultural goods has left a deep dent in the way we define the identity of the entire region. At the present time, it is impossible to consider either Puerto Rican society or its Latin American counterparts as 'homogeneous entities' contained within their national frontiers, or subject to strict regional or communal limits. On the contrary, these societies embody a discontinuous and, above all, fragmentary ensemble of races in formation, mainly social groups in process adopting brand new conducts in their milieus thus carrying out important migratory displacements.

In this context, the United States has emerged in recent times as the new stage of action for a vital mise-en-scene of Latin American culture. According to the numbers put forth in the last census, the 'latino' population of this country already surpasses 37% of the population; this means that one out of three Americans belongs to our cultural background. For better or for worse, Puerto Ricans – divided between the continental United States and the Island – comprise a considerable share of this reality. Separated by the same language as well as by unbearable affinities, the unavoidable reconciliation among our communities – whether Puerto Rican, Nuyorican, Chicano or Latino – becomes a priority for our own cultural survival again. Therefore, beyond the wasted debate about its political status – and far from defending a servile position with regards to a declining superpower – Puerto Rico can neither escape such an impending reality nor can it cede a relevant position within the new panorama that international geo-politics imposes upon it.

While taking stock of the current state of graphics in Latin America, the Triennial thus will be in a condition to capitalize on Puerto Rico's hinge position between North and South America to highlight, for the first time in an event of this nature, the production of artists from Mexico, the Caribbean, and Central and South America, side by side with the work of Latino artists from the United States, Canada, and Europe. In doing so, it is setting out to map a new territory of cultural and artistic relations that stands above the imposed limits of geography or nationhood. Indeed, at the core of this policy shift there is a symbolic capital operation that implies the only possibility of survival for colonial peoples. I refer to the *empowerment* of the margins. As the periphery of the periphery, Puerto Rico's only hope for the future lies in the strategic alliances with Caribbean and Latin American countries. Alliances based on cultural as well as economic exchange.

All of the above presupposes a fact that, perhaps, was not evident in the realm of previous editions of the San Juan Biennial which, today, has become the sine qua non issue not only of international biennials but of artistic process itself. I refer to the need to adopt a flexible model whose less absolute idea of identity is constantly redefined by movable margins and other porous forms of real and symbolic exchange. This model presupposes that 'identity' as such cannot be predetermined by national frontiers or community borders. Instead, the fluidity of this identity model allows us to access the dialogue between Puerto Rico and the U.S. Latino communities in a more consistent way. In this sense, such a shifting position offers the best alternative for a successful and effective integration of Puerto Rican artists to the rest of the Americas.

Graphics in an expanded field

During the period under discussion, graphics went from being hypothetical tools for forming the identity of countries and specific communities in the region to critical elements of broader technologically-based discursive strategies. This transformation was influenced on one hand by what I have referred to elsewhere as the 'conceptual shift' that took place in the 1960s in Western art; on the other hand, it was the result of artists' assimilation of technological advances in printing and image processing techniques.[2] In order to fully grasp the depth of this change in the status and function of graphics I must first outline – however sketchily – the factors that initially justified and made visible a poly/graphic biennial focused on Latin America and the Caribbean.

The formulation of the San Juan Biennial directly reflected the international *boom* of graphics in the period of expansion and development that followed the end of World War II. This phenomenon first appeared at the grassroots levels in Europe and the United States in the 1950s, only to consolidate itself as an international current in the 1960s. Without doubt, the undeniable ascendancy of the national middle class during this period – together with the emergence of a market designed to suit both its budding taste for art as well as its limited pockets – led to the flourishing of printmaking worldwide. This graphics renaissance took on a critical urgency in countries like Puerto Rico or the Latino communities of the United States where artists either lacked or did not have equal access to fully consolidated art markets, museums, and other institutionalized venues of distribution.

Hence, as in the case of drawing, which also flourished as an autonomous medium during this period,[3] artists throughout the region turned to prints on account of their low cost, their accessibility to broad audiences, and their potential to function – as in the case of the Puerto Rican silkscreen – as a sort of surrogate painting endowed with its own alternate channels of marketing and distribution. In this context, for instance, the well-known art critic Marta Traba vehemently appealed to the artists of the continent to consciously engage graphics and drawings as media appropriate to comprehend the true precariousness of their surroundings.[4] Traba's position conflated graphics with a form of artistic essentialism, grounded in the matrix that became the hallmark of the medium in Latin America. Further stimulating this essentialist orientation of graphics was the ideological role they came to play in the political struggles of the period. Through their combination of potent images and their serial multiplication, graphics reached out and gave visibility to the conditions of oppression that affected the peoples of their communities.

In the 1970s, however, conceptualism stimulated a profound questioning of the nature and function of art in favor of more strategic approaches whose tactics were guided by the need to produce and circulate meanings of another type. This led to the transformation of graphics from their passive role of prints to one more resource in the debates surrounding the notion of 'representation.' In the face of conceptual expediency, technological or aesthetic preciousness ceased to be the most fundamental concern of the printmaking operation. In this context, the irreducible core of graphics, its matrix, underwent a progressive devaluation. Since then, together with photography, prints became integrated into a more ample redefinition of the very ideas of language or of space. These changes were manifested in the substitution of the supports – which encompass wallpaper to ready-mades and billboards – as well as in experiments with the actual tools of impression, mainly Xerox copiers and printers hooked to laptops.

The irruption of the digital image, midway through this critical decade, introduced an unedited resource whose potential is still undergoing exploration, thereby further destabilizing the landscape of conventional printmaking. The use of computers – together with developments in photography, video, and digital image – opened up unsuspected horizons of expression for these media that may well end up redefining them altogether. In this regard, as José Ramón Alcalá has argued, the main issue at stake is oriented not only towards the ongoing substitution of updated technologies, but rather to the vanishing of the matrix as a physical, tangible object. The fact that now both the image and the representation are the product of a virtual or electronic support, has led to an unprecedented displacement: the objective of art is neither the work nor the artist but its *discursive efficiency*.[5] An efficiency that manifests itself in its unlimited capacity to generate, process, and distribute images in an interactive, multi-medial way through a broad array of supports which include, but are no longer limited to, paper. Hence the appeal of this new digital graphic art influenced new generations of artists not only in Latin America but worldwide.

It is important to underscore, however, that despite the impact of the new image technologies on traditional graphics, the latter have not disappeared as valid means of expression for a sector of contemporary art. On the contrary, as demonstrated by the recent editions of the Krakow Triennial, the Sapporo International Print Exhibition, the Havana Biennial, and other similar international events, large numbers of artists worldwide continue to practice lithography, etching, silkscreen, and woodcut in both pure or hybrid forms. These artists, however, confront a particular dilemma: they operate at a crossroads where both traditional practices and new opportunities opened by advanced technologies intersect. Their work, then, not only leads to technological hybridization but also raises a question that has been central to this Triennial: to what extent do traditional graphics harbor possibilities for renovation?

The profound transformations in the nature of contemporary prints suggest that, rather than graphics, it may be more pertinent to develop the notion of *poly-graphic strategies for the multiple image*. Strategies as such involve a deep questioning of the basic notions that have traditionally defined prints such as: register, support, permanence, the series, and reproducibility. In a similar way, rather than insist on the centrality of the matrix as the mandatory condition of printmaking, it makes more sense to elevate the notion of the *imprint* – all this understood as a deep mark left on the ground or surface by a living organism – as a valid point of reference for graphics in this expanded field.

The poli/graphic triennial: a new parameter for Latino-America

From all of the above, it is clear that an international graphics event organized in the twenty-first century cannot but promote and stimulate the advances that can result from the combination of these media with the broad gamut of technological achievements that have emerged in this field over the last two decades. To close itself to these possibilities or to sideline their potential can only result in an attitude that is both retrograde and limiting to the core objectives of any exhibition of this nature. Not only the development of visual arts practices today but Puerto Rico's historical moment cannot be read with eyes upon the past. To deny the reality of transformation is not an option when confronted with the artistic and political stimuli of contemporary reality.

In an attempt to effectively engage the conditions of contemporary graphics in Latin America, the curatorial team chose to focus *on the expanded role of graphics in contemporary artistic practice*. That is to say it set out to explore the *technological displacements* and *conceptual trajectories* experienced by classical printmaking over the last three decades in the region. Understood in this way, the purpose of this Triennial is not to necessarily do away with the qualities and attributes of traditional printmaking, but to reframe them within the postmodern scenario.

Both individually and as a whole, the works gathered in this first edition of the San Juan Triennial attest to the vital role which an expanded notion of graphics is playing in the field of contemporary Latin American and Latino art. From different, often contrasting, perspectives these innovative insights are critically opposing the values of the hegemonic centers. Whether by means of politically updating the rebuttal tradition of graphics – instigating images in public circuits, mapping new coordinates for artistic or social activism, or offsetting the clean registers of traditional representation – their work shows an axiology whose flexibility is meant to engage the challenges posed by both globalization and the proliferation of new image technologies in the present century. It is ultimately their flexibility to adjust to the new panorama of printmaking that is allowing them to actively intervene in the social process confronting their societies and communities. In this regard, the San Juan Triennial is not only about art and culture-in-the-making but, undeniably, about fostering radical change in the region.

Notes

1 Alegría, Ricardo E. Introduction to the catalogue of the First San Juan Biennial (San Juan, PR: Instituto de Cultura Puertorriqueña, 1970).
2 See Ramírez, Mari Carmen, 'Tactics for Thriving in Adversity: Conceptualism in Latin America, 1960–80' in *Inverted Utopias* (Houston/London: The Museum of Fine Arts, Houston and Yale University Press, 2004), pp. 425–6.
3 For this phenomenon, see Ramírez, *Re-Aligning Vision: Alternative Currents in South American Drawing* (Austin: Archer M. Huntington Art Gallery / The University of Texas Press, 1997).
4 Traba, Marta, *Dos décadas vulnerables en las artes plásticas latinoamericanas* (Mexico City: Singlo XXI Editore, 1973), pp. 87–153.
5 Alcalá, José Ramón, 'La gráphica digital y el nuevo mercado de arte' in *Las tecnologias digitales de la imagen en la praxis artistica moderna* (Pontevedra, 1998).

Shang Hui

Chinese printmaking in the twenty-first century: new horizons and energies*

Since the beginning of the twenty-first century, printmaking in China has shown a distinct contemporaneity. The keen awareness on the part of many printmakers of participating in contemporary art draws on two sources. One is an aesthetic need of Chinese society, which has turned to prints as a meaningful visual expression of recent cultural developments. The other is a growing interaction with global art. From its inception in the 1930s, the woodcut as a modern art form in China has moved through several pivotal stages: critical engagement with reality, representations of life experiences, and an emphatic return to the properties of the medium itself. In the new century, printmakers have begun exhibiting a contemporary outlook in their works by further asserting a creative subjectivity and by their commitment to conceptual innovations, as well as to experimentation with new media.

The newly energized and expanding field of printmaking in China in the twenty-first century is all the more remarkable when viewed against the backdrop of the previous decades. The 1980s was an exciting period of general revival, a decade in which printmakers were particularly active and adventurous in pursuing their individual artistic visions. It was also a decade when many regional schools emerged and a great number of exhibitions took place across the country. The ninth National Print Exhibition, held in 1986, was widely regarded as the most successful of its kind in the new era of reform and opening up that followed the Cultural Revolution (1966–76). At the second National Congress of Printmakers, which coincided with this historic exhibition, delegates declared that 'diverse and multiple aesthetic pursuits are our goal,' marking a resolute departure from the stylistic and ideological uniformity of the previous era.

* Shang Hui. 2011. 'Chinese Printmaking in the Twenty-First Century'. In: Tang, Xiaobing, Hui, Shang and Farrer, Anne (eds), *Multiple Impressions: Contemporary Chinese Woodblock Prints*. Ann Arbor, MI: University of Michigan, Museum of Art, pp. 18–21. Reproduced by kind permission of the author and the University of Michigan. Translated by Xiaobing Tang.

While on the one hand printmakers sought to 'purify' their visual language by calling attention to the unique qualities of the medium, on the other hand there was an attempt to go beyond the dominant medium of woodblock prints. The rise of etching, lithography, and silkscreen prints during this period was part of a drive towards modernization in the field. Four national exhibitions devoted to these three relatively new printmaking methods between 1981 and 1991 considerably boosted their growing popularity. Even more significant was the fact that numerous programs aimed at promoting prints were developed, enjoying broad public support. In January 1985, for instance, the Chinese Print Society for Young Children was formed, going on to sponsor shows of prints by children in the following years. Indeed, a true measure of the great appeal of printmaking as a public art form during this time was the introduction of related educational programming for young children.

This vibrant printmaking revival stagnated in the 1990s, even though the period witnessed the emergence of many exciting new developments in the art scene at large. In contrast to media such as oil and ink-and-brush painting, where a culturally grounded conception of contemporary art began to be articulated, the field of printmaking appeared subdued and diminished. The decline is attributable to inertia on the part of printmakers and to lack of interest on the part of critics and researchers, which resulted in printmaking's being largely insulated from contemporary artistic developments. Many printmakers in the 1990s continued to work with ideas and models from the 1980s, turning images of regional and ethnic customs into lifeless imitations. Formal innovations became flat and staid decorative exercises. Moreover, misguided and facile explorations were widespread and exhibited nothing more than feeble pretensions to 'modernity.' Some printmakers immersed themselves in craftsmanship, their chief concern being the special effects of printing or the achievement of making a large number of prints, and offered scant reflection on or grasp of contemporary culture and society. In the meantime, preoccupied with setting out research agendas and articulating values and standards based on native traditions, art critics in general paid much more attention to oil and ink-and-brush painting and were little invested in studying contemporary prints or scholarly research related to printmaking.

In the 1990s, as the new market economy in China consolidated, the art market emerged along with the changes in the socio-economic structure and cultural life in general. With this transformation, works of art were no longer circulated through official exhibitions or publications, but more and more often directly entered the market as commodities. Because of the stagnation in the field, prints did not gain recognition as valuable cultural products on the art market. The stagnation in printmaking was also observable in the fact that, compared to the previous decade, far fewer print-focused exhibitions or activities were held in the 1990s. As the number of publications shrank and viewership dwindled, many artists turned away from making prints altogether. A structural shift occurred: while in the 1980s most printmakers were supported by various cultural organizations, by the 1990s the majority were based in the academy. A significantly reduced number of printmakers resulted in the field's being viewed sometimes as elitist, one consequence of which was that both prints and their audiences became ever more specialized. And, indeed, a noticeable feature of prints from the 1990s is their strong group identity. Yet, the apparent isolation of printmaking from both the art market and developments in other artistic fields may be regarded in a different light. With the unmistakable passing of political passions that marked the 1960s and 1970s, and with the disappearance of the ideological pressures that historically shaped printmaking, what quietly revealed itself away from the sound and fury of the new art market may well be a true and natural state in the art of printmaking.

Chinese prints in the new century, in comparison with those from the 1990s, express a greater contemporary consciousness in their humanistic concern with current social realities. Large-scale urbanization and an ever more robust market economy have contributed to the steady accumulation of wealth and brought about a gradual transformation of China from a production-oriented society to a consumer society. 'The age of consumption' is now a broadly accepted description of this period. And while a consumer culture makes it possible for people to enjoy many material goods, it also gives rise to numerous anxieties and dissatisfactions in spiritual and emotional life. Addressing these new conditions became a pivotal point around which printmakers could productively move beyond preoccupations with technical concerns and reaffirm as well as explore art as an expression of human compassion.

The prevailing desire to create contemporary art has necessarily given rise to theoretical reflections. Over the past decade critical commentary and scholarly research on printmaking has been both active and far-reaching. In particular, many fruitful discussions have been conducted over topics such as the defining nature and morphology of prints, the implementation of a productive critical mechanism, changes in the vocabulary of printmaking in the context of contemporary art, and the creation of a contemporary discourse on Chinese prints that is intrinsic to native culture. The concepts of 'multiplicity' and 'mediatedness' were advanced in the late 1980s in an effort to describe and theorize the unique properties of printmaking, namely the possibility of multiple reproductions and the inevitable mediation involved in image making. In 2007, Zhao Kun proposed the notion of 'creative imprints' as essential to the process of making a print:

> Creative imprints are the material form of an artist's spirituality and creativity. They embody and crystallize the artist's understanding of the world, whereas texture, the feel of the wood grain, the mark of the carving knife, and the

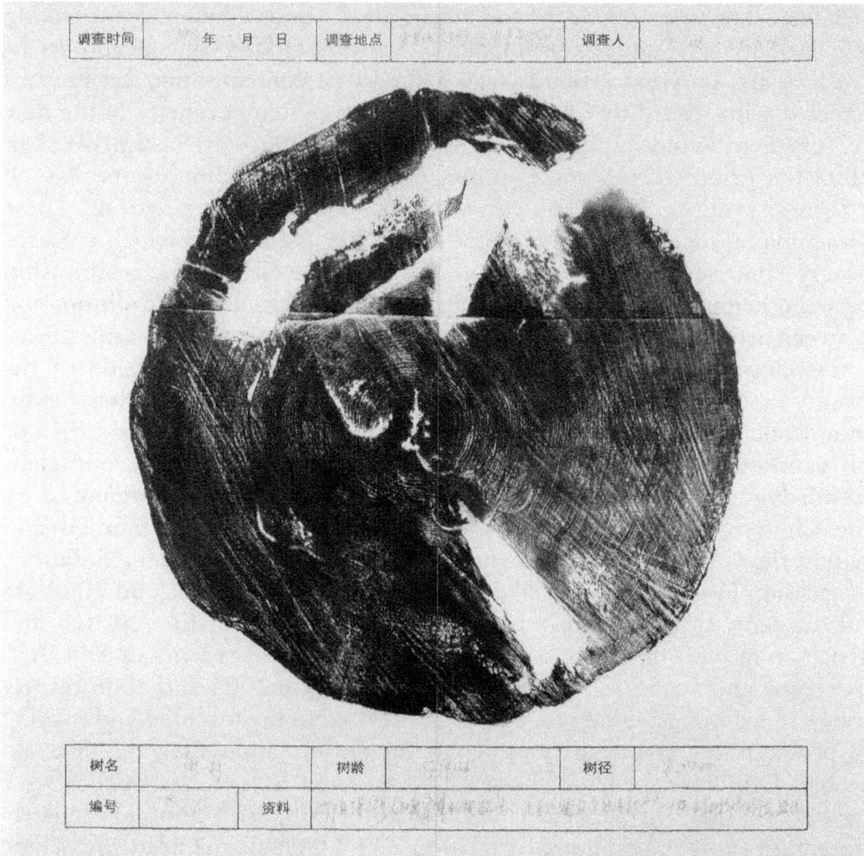

Cai Feng and Shen Ligong, *In Memory of an Ancient Tree*, 1999. Impression made with oil-based ink, of a thousand-year-old fir tree that was illegally cut down in the Tianmu Mountain National Nature Reserve in Zhejiang. 180 × 180 cm.

> innate pattern of the conveying material (i.e., paper) are all an accidental material form. When an artist follows his conception and makes selective use of those components, be it to integrate them or transform them, he harmonizes them with his vision and achieves imprints that are imaginative, creative, and aesthetically meaningful. The various components become a spiritual object full of life. By conjoining material forms and the artist's soul, creative imprints enable him to express his spirit.[1]

Such inquiries into the nature of printmaking affirm the creative role of the artist. They also help overcome a single-minded preoccupation with printing effects, a tendency encouraged by the twin notions of 'multiplicity' and 'mediatedness.'

Given that there was a period when ideas about Chinese printmaking fell into disarray under the impact of various modernist conceptions of Western art, on what grounds may a theory of contemporary art be constructed with regard to Chinese prints if their contemporaneity in the new century is to avoid duplicating ideas of contemporary art in the West? In 2003 the printmaker Wang Lianmin proposed three components of such a theory: synthesization, contemporaneity, and self-determination.[2] These three pivotal ideas underscore some of the key issues with which contemporary Chinese printmakers have to contend: the challenging relationship between belonging both to the modern world and to a long tradition, and between artists' cultural embeddedness and their cosmopolitan aspirations.

Developments in Chinese printmaking during the first decade of the twenty-first century were steady and significant. The number of print exhibitions increased, even if it never reached that of Chinese ink-and-brush or oil painting. Major events included the sixteenth, seventeenth, and eighteenth National Print Exhibitions in 2001, 2005, and 2007 organized by the Chinese Artists' Association (CAA) and the Print Art Commission within the CAA. These two institutions also mounted national exhibitions of etching, lithography, and silkscreen prints in 2001, 2003, and 2009. As the academy now provides crucial institutional support for research and artists, two meetings were convened at the Central Academy of Fine Arts in Beijing and at the Tianjin Fine Arts Academy, in 2004 and 2006 respectively, to examine a wide range of topics related to the teaching and making of prints in fine arts academies across the nation. Soon after, the first and second Exhibition of Contemporary Prints from Chinese Academies were successfully held in Shenzhen in 2006 and 2008, with another similarly organized show opening in Shanghai in 2007. Outside the academy, which remained the central base for creative work, a small number of printmaking institutes and workshops continued to function in some provinces (such as those in Heilongjiang and Jiangsu) and large cities (such as the Peninsula Printmaking Workshop in Shanghai). These organizations play an important role in promoting printmaking and supporting amateur printmakers.

Another phenomenon in the new century: some major art dealers began to recognize the medium's commercial potential and thus helped to propel the rise of a market for prints. This led in 2006 to the creation of the China Guanlan Original Printmaking Base in Shenzhen, also known as the Guanlan Prints Village, a joint venture between the CAA and local governments. The venture, which combines a residential program for international printmakers, printmaking workshops, exhibition facilities, museums, and international marketing of prints, aims to develop a profitable cultural enterprise. Since its formation the Guanlan Prints Village has successfully organized two international print biennials and has expanded both the scope and reach of the exhibitions; the second Guanlan International Print Biennial in 2009, for instance, received 2,894 works by 1,604 artists from seventy countries. Indeed, since the year 2000, there has been a steady increase in international print exhibitions organized by various research institutions across China, for example the 2003 Beijing International Print Biennial and the 2008 Yunnan International Print Biennial. Such exhibitions have gained broad recognition and attracted more and more artists from abroad, creating a situation markedly different than that of the last decades of the twentieth century, when Chinese prints were mostly shown abroad.

International exhibitions have greatly increased Chinese viewers' appreciation of prints. They have also helped establish a set of internationally accepted curatorial standards and procedures and a jury system. But the purpose of holding international art exhibitions in China in the new century is not simply to give Chinese artists some clout. Far more important is recognizing and respecting the values and cultures of different places, nations, and artists from around the world while remaining situated within one's own cultural tradition. Only then may we hope to create a forum for world art in which truly equal dialogues may take place. The energy generated by events such as the Guanlan International Print Biennial reveals that the contemporaneity of Chinese printmaking in the new century rests squarely in such self-consciousness in a global context, conceptual innovations, and experiments with new media.

Notes

1 Zhao Kun, 'Shixi banhua de benzhi tezheng-chuangyi yinhen' (An essay on the essential feature of prints-creative imprints), *Zhongguo banhua* (Chinese prints), no. 29 (2007), 7.

2 See Wang Lianmin, 'Lun Zhongguo banhua yishu linian de goujian' (On the construction of a concept of the art of Chinese printmaking), *Zhongguo banhua* (Chinese prints), no. 21 (2003), 9–10.

Matthew Perkins

What is 'studio' in the post-disciplinary age?*

In the contemporary educational context the term photography has in many cases metamorphosed into such phrases as photomedia to reflect not only the adoption of a number of lens-based media, but also the move to digital media technologies. The idea of the *studio*, from the perspective of the educational curriculum is at an interesting juncture. The utilisation of similar technologies across a number of studios raises a number of issues for discussion in relation to recent notions of the *post-disciplinary* and what this means to the definition of the studio within an art school context.

The educational environment raises a number of questions concerning the role of the studio and its relationship to materials and processes. In this essay, I question how does a photomedia-based studio respond to this evolution in art-practice? Within fine art degrees what is the role of the studio in the twenty-first century? Is the studio as a *field* of research on the verge of becoming an anachronism?

I present a discussion that addresses issues regarding the studio model of art education and the curriculum in a post-disciplinary era. Whilst the studio approach to the curriculum has largely been an organisational structure, rather than an imperative to art practice, do we need to rethink this approach or to rethink how we define the term *studio*? Suggesting an examination of the nature of the studio within the fine-art educational context immediately brings to mind two central ideas for discussion: of the *discipline* and of the *medium*. These terms need to be interrogated further in order to understand what is involved in their 'post' condition.

* Matthew Perkins. 2011. 'What is "Studio" in the Post-Disciplinary Age?' In: Hoskins, Stephen et al. (eds), *IMPACT 6 Multi-disciplinary Printmaking Conference Proceedings*. Bristol: Impact Press, pp. 86–90. Revised by the author. Reproduced by kind permission of the author and Impact Press.

Defining discipline within the educational context

There are a number of well-established disciplines within the context of art and design such as design, digital media, architecture and fine art. Within fine art, there are a number of specialist areas or subsidiary disciplines such as photography, printmaking, painting and sculpture. These are commonly referred to as the 'studios'. The idea of the discipline and the studio are interchangeable. Traditionally, the studio placed primary significance on the acquisition of knowledge relating to materials and processes. Lessons focused on the technical aspects of practice; critique then addressed the conceptual elements of the work and its relationship to the aesthetic qualities used by the student. The emphasis here was that the materials were a given in relation to the particular studios and this was relatively unquestioned. For example, in the photographic studio students used photographic material and in the printmaking studio students used printmaking materials. In the painting studio students would utilise paint while in the sculpture studio there was an expectation of working with three-dimensional objects. The conditions of production within the studios had a number of predetermined boundaries.

In order to develop this discussion further I will now examine the definition of discipline, and thus the 'studio'. Geoffrey Squire suggests that on one-hand, a discipline corresponds to an abstract idea of an essential corpus within a structure of a given framework; while on the other, a discipline is an artificial construct, determined by relations of power and authority.[1] Elizabeth Bird comments that disciplines are a question of tribes and territories; they are groups of people occupying both physical and intellectual spaces, who fiercely defend these spaces, and regard those, who either intrude or disrupt with suspicion.[2] Patrice Ossona de Mendez says that, over time, the disciplines have developed a specific methodology as well as a specific vocabulary.[3] For Basil Bernstein, knowledge is controlled by codes of framing that maintain strong disciplinary boundaries, and individuals are socialised into the discipline; the subject [or discipline] becomes the linchpin of the identity'.[4] We can use the photography studio to illustrate these ideas in the fine art context. Reflecting on my own time as an undergraduate student in the late 1980s if you wanted to utilise photography as your creative medium you applied to be placed within the photography studio. It was only the students from the photography studio who learnt photographic processes and this knowledge was not readily shared outside of this privileged group. Critiques were also managed within the studio. So themes such as the environment were only debated within the photographic context rather than involving, for example, the painting studio where depictions of the environment through landscapes have had a long history and this perspective could have made an important contribution to the discussion. At that time the idea of an interdisciplinary practice or moving between studios was not overtly discouraged but strong organisational boundaries made it an unlikely occurrence. In fact, once artists were practicing outside of the art institution there was often a need to identify what type of artist they were. It was clear that disciplinary commitment was entrenched and the boundaries were difficult to break. More recently, as a lecturer within an art school I still witnessed the same territorial boundaries and the same codes of framing with this artificiality being continually emphasised by the students' ever more divergent activities.

It becomes evident that the studio is not purely physical and technical but also an intellectual entity, which is bound in its own specific knowledge. As such the photography studio may entail the physical aspects of having lighting-studios, darkrooms, computers, printers, video-cameras and projectors, in addition to technical processes such as colour correcting, enlarging, editing, printing, authoring and burning. These aspects bind the creative tools and processes to specific intellectual knowledge (themes and contexts), specific methodologies (hypothesis and analysis) and specific pedagogical strategies (relation of power to knowledge). Reflecting on the ideas of Squire, Bird, de Mendez and Bernstein this would suggest that the studio has become an enclosure for medium-specificity and has inadvertently imposed boundaries that prevent cross-border ideas to flow freely. If culture is moving in a different direction then the traditional idea of the discipline should be questioned.

Defining the *medium* within a fine art context

Contributory to destabilising the idea of the disciplines is the changing and evolving concept of *medium*. Sven Lütticken states that the term medium only came to be associated with our current cultural and aesthetic understanding in the later nineteenth and early twentieth century.[5] According to Lev Manovich in the last third of the twentieth century, various cultural and technological developments such as happenings, installation, time-based art and the dematerialisation of the art object have rendered the concept of the term 'medium' as meaningless.[6] The assumption that artistic practice can be neatly organised into a small set of distinct mediums has continued to structure the organisation of art schools and other cultural institutions even though this assumption no longer reflects the actual functioning of culture.[7] Further, Diarmuid Costello remarks that what constitutes a given medium today need no longer do so tomorrow, indeed what counts as a work in one medium today need no longer count as a work in the same medium tomorrow.[8] As the influence of this perceptual shift begins to work its way through art schools, teachers must question the strong association of the medium to the 'studio'.

Rosalind Krauss describes the destabilising of the medium in contemporary art as the 'post-medium condition' of artistic production.[9] Krauss focuses on the integration of the conceptual into art as well as the assimilation of photography into art in order to clarify her argument. She reminds us that art had adopted photography, not so much as a medium with specific aesthetic qualities, but as a 'theoretical object' historically aligned to the issue of the copy and a reliance, in its mass media manifestations, on the written caption.[10] Krauss is referring to the artistic practices of artists such as Jeff Wall, Sophie Calle and Dan Graham; sharing a conceptual attitude based on a reflective distance to the medium that underpins their work.[11] In this way, they are appropriating the medium as a conceptual vehicle, rather than primarily expressing a concern through a given medium with specific qualities. This development moves away from the Greenbergian modernist aim of finding the unique formal essence of the medium or medium-specificity. Mary Ann Doane suggests that medium-specificity identifies the crucial recursiveness of that structure that is a medium; meaning there is both a resistance to resistance and a continual presentation of those material constraints as its field of operation.[12] *Medium-specificity* thus falls into the same restrictive regime as *discipline*. This presents us with a paradoxical situation where the studio's being, defined as a discipline that deals with a specific medium, has less validity if the educational aim of art schools is to produce contemporary artists who produce new cultural forms, rather than becoming the champions of existing ones. This logic reconfirms a need to rethink the approach to the studio.

Proposing a post-disciplinary approach

Post-disciplinary performance theorist Jon McKenzie has suggested that, in the present era, a broad social emphasis and concern with disciplinarity is waning.[13] There is an increased interest and emphasis on inter-disciplinary practice; the term 'post-disciplinary' is beginning to evolve. But while *inter-disciplinary* connotes a sense of a unified field of practices and social structures, 'post-disciplinary' suggests that the structures of the disciplines themselves are at question. Sue-Ellen Case states that the *post-disciplinary* retains nothing of the notion of a shared consciousness, or of a shared objective that brings together a broad range of discrete studies. Instead, a post-disciplinary condition suggests that the organising structures of the disciplines themselves will not hold.[14] Diana Taylor defines post-discipline as a field of intellectual endeavour that is no longer determined by an ideal object of inquiry, or an ideal method of analysis, as has historically been the definition of an academic discipline. A post-discipline is thus characterised by an irreducible element of debate and difference as to what to study, how to study it, and why. Post-disciplines proliferate in an era of radical uncertainty as to the foundations and orderings of knowledge.[15]

Discipline boundaries are currently undergoing considerable redefinition. New and hybrid forms of interdisciplinary research not only test existing disciplinary limits, they also produce new objects for study which, in turn, require new methodologies. Eleanor Gates-Stuart and Jenny Wolmark suggest that tentatively emerging post-disciplinary practices are porous, fuzzy-edged and indeterminate.[16] The basic qualities of this new production of knowledge are: complexity, hybridity, non-linearity, reflexivity, heterogeneity, and transdisciplinarity. This hybridisation reflects the need to accomplish tasks at the boundaries and in the spaces between different communities.[17] Post-disciplinary practices are well placed to refuse to accept hierarchies of knowledge that are offered as repositories of universal values. As cultural hybrids, post-disciplinary practices retain knowledge of the specificities of disciplines and of their histories, but they are also inherently transgressive and capable of operating outside the limitations imposed by those disciplines.[18] In this way, the idea of the post-disciplinary does not negate the idea of the studio but considers new approaches to practice initiated by a questioning of the disciplines within which we find ourselves.

So let us return to the main question proposed: what is *studio* in the post-disciplinary age? In addition to the structures of the studio being under pressure, as I have suggested, the importance of material mastery has somewhat diminished. With a greater emphasis on conceptual development rather than technical skills training we must question the viability of the traditional studio model of art education. What the traditional studio model does offer is a specific approach to conceptualising creativity that contextualises art making in both historical and contemporary perspectives grounded in a medium. New studio labels such as ‘photomedia’ highlight the expanding field of processes and materials that are taking hold within these traditions, but they also propose questions about their future directions. It is not a simple task and history is a stoic force. Marvin Carison suggests that many scholars have entered the new century with one face looking backward to an academic world of established disciplines and sealed boundaries; and another looking forward to an intellectual world that allows, indeed encourages, the free flow of study and insights across the old barriers.[19] Carison’s suggestion is a good starting point for a post-disciplinary approach to the pedagogical process. This approach allows enough scope to continue the work of the traditional studio model, most common in art schools, while also introducing the idea of a counter-disciplinary praxis.

Case study

A case in point might be the evolution of the studio of photography into photomedia. It would be naïve to consider that this evolution simply concerns the physical state of these materials. With the introduction of materials previously unheralded within the studio we must also consider the alternative contexts and histories of these materials. Traditionally photography entailed the development of photographic prints and that was the limit of the studio in relation to materials. Photomedia on the other hand opens the studio to a great number of material options from lens-based media, such as photography and video, to various digital imaging technologies. Digital imaging allows for the printing onto different materials such as fabric or printmaking-paper. Vector graphics allows for both figurative and abstract rendering of designs onto two-dimensional surfaces. It also allows students to interface with laser cutters using a wider range of materials such as wood, glass, metals and plastics. The historical contexts that might apply to these materials range from photography, video art and cinema to textiles, printmaking, sculpture and painting. While an expanded field of material options would be part of a post-disciplinary approach to the curriculum, the dialogue between the various historical contexts that underpin them is of greater importance. It is this dialogue that exposes the entrenchment of specific signs, vocabularies and methodologies in addition to the particular structures that hold them together within the educational context. This is an important educational strategy in a post-disciplinary approach to the studio because it empowers students to experiment between the disciplines while giving them a broader understanding of the historical and cultural context of their ideas. Within the context of a degree programme a post-disciplinary approach may manifest itself in greater cross-studio interaction through the sharing of staff expertise and resources. Further, the development of an *access to an all-areas* philosophy could drive curriculum development where students are exposed to all technical workshops within the art school rather than single studios. This would reflect developments taking place in contemporary practice and allow students greater flexibility in mapping their own development.

Conclusion

A post-disciplinary approach to the studio may signal new spaces for scholarly work and new ways of thinking about how fine art studios function. It will encourage artworks that are positioned at the boundaries between studios and thus encourage the exploration of new forms and concepts with the mediums at hand. The studio as a field of research is not on the verge of becoming an anachronism but there is a need to maximise students' exposure to the myriad of new and stimulating artistic and critical discourses surrounding evolving contemporary art practices. The role of the studio has been and will continue to be an integral part of achieving the broader objectives of the curriculum. If the primary objective is to empower students as future contemporary art practitioners, both conceptually and technically savvy, and able to work in alternative ways, then how the studios interact with one another needs to be reconceptualised.

Notes

1 Squires, Geoffrey, *First Degree: The Undergraduate Curriculum* (Buckingham: SRHE and Open University Press), 1990, p. 101.
2 Bird, Elizabeth, 'Disciplining the Interdisciplinary: Radicalism and the Academic Curriculum', in *British Journal of Sociology of Education*, Volume 22, Number 4, The Sociology of the Curriculum (Dec., 2001), p. 467.
3 Ossona de Mendez, Patrice, 'The Risks and Challenges of Interdisciplinarity', in Dan Sperber, *Why Rethink Interdisciplinarity?* (on-line discussion), www.interdisciplines.org/interdisciplinarity/papers/1/2#_2, accessed 10 December 2008.
4 Bernstein, Basil, 'On the Classification and Framing of Educational Knowledge', in M. F. D. Young (editor) *Knowledge and Control: New Directions for the Sociology of Education* (London: Collier Macmillan), 1971, p. 56.
5 Lütticken, Sven, 'Undead media', in *Afterimage* Volume 31, Number 4 (Jan–Feb 2004), p. 12.
6 Manovich, Lev, 'Post-media Aesthetics: Medium in Crisis', www.manovich.net/DOCS/Post_media_aesthetics1.doc, accessed 9 April 2009.
7 Ibid.
8 Costello, Diarmuid, 'Pictures, Again', in *Post Medium, Australia & New Zealand Journal of Art*, Volume 8, Number 1 (20070), p. 24.
9 Krauss, Rosalind, 'Reinventing the Medium', in *Critical Inquiry*, Volume 25, Number 2 (Winter 1999).
10 Ross, Toni, 'Art in the "Post-Medium" Era: aesthetics and conceptualism in the Art of Jeff Wall', in *The South Atlantic Quarterly*, Volume 101, Number 3, Summer 2002. http://muse.jhu.edu/journals/south_atlantic_quarterly/v101/101.3ross.html, accessed 6 April 2009.
11 Hinderer, Max, 'Unwanted Positivism: On the Term "post-Medium Condition" in the Work of Rosalind Krauss', translation Helen Ferguson, in *Springerin*, Issue 1, 2009, www.springerin.at/dyn/heft_text.php?textid=2160&lang=en, accessed 3 April 2009.
12 Doane, Mary Ann, 'Indexicality and the Concept of Medium Specificity', in Robin Kelsey and Blake Stimson (editors) *The Meaning of Photography* (Massachusetts: Sterling and Clark Art Institute), 2008, p. 4.
13 McKenzie, Jon, *Perform or Else: From Discipline to Performance* (London: Routledge), 2001. http://en.allexperts.com/e/p/po/post-discipline.htm, accessed 10 June 2009.
14 Case, Sue-Ellen, 'Feminism and Performance: A Post-Disciplinary Couple', in *Theatre Research International*, Volume 26, Number 2, pp. 145–52 (United Kingdom: International Federation for Theatre Research), 2001. http://journals.cambridge.org, accessed 23 August 2009.
15 Taylor, Diana, *The Archive and the Repertoire: Performing Cultural Memory in the Americas* (Durham, NC: Duke University Press) 2003. http://en.allexperts.com/e/p/po/post-discipline.htm, accessed 10 June 2009.

16 Gates-Stuart, Eleanor and Wolmark, Jenny, 'Cultural Hybrids, Post-Disciplinary Digital Practices and New Research Frameworks: Testing The Limits', Conference paper & proceeding publication, PixelRaider2. Sheffield Hallam University, UK, 2004. dspace.anu.edu.au/bitstream/1885/41954/1/GCWPixel_Raiders.pdf, accessed 10 July 2009.

17 Ibid.

18 Ibid.

19 Carlson, Marvin. 'Theatre and Performance at a Time of Shifting Disciplines', *Theatre Research International*, Volume 26, Number 2, p. 140 (United Kingdom: International Federation for Theatre Research), 2001. http://journals.cambridge.org, accessed 23 August 2009.

Amanda Thomson

Making a place: art and a multi-modal, multi-disciplinary approach*

Introduction

In this paper I will explore the nature of how place has been conceptualised by subjects including geography and anthropology, and discuss the ways in which a contemporary arts practice intersects with such concerns, before moving to address the ways in which art can contribute and add to such disciplines. I will draw on my work on the forests of Morayshire and the native pinewoods of Abernethy in Scotland, which relates to an interdisciplinary arts practice-based PhD completed in 2013. My research involved repeated visits to these places and incorporated ethnographic fieldwork, walking with foresters and ecologists, and working as a volunteer on a nature reserve. By incorporating these methods of gathering information, elements of these places hitherto unknown to me were revealed. Repeated visits meant that different aspects of place were revealed at different times, and using ethnographic methods allowed other people's expert knowledge of these places to influence and impact on my work.

Theoretical approaches to place and landscape

In considering the range of disciplines that have engaged with the 'everyday', Stephen Johnstone draws parallels between theoretical writing and

* Amanda Thomson. 2014. 'Making a Place: Art and a Multi-Modal, Multi-disciplinary Approach'. In: Harrison, Paul Liam, Shemilt, Elaine and Watson, Arthur (eds), *Borders & Crossings: The Artist as Explorer: IMPACT 8 International Printmaking Conference*. Dundee: Duncan of Jordanstone College of Art & Design, University of Dundee, pp. 210–15. Reproduced by kind permission of the author and DJCAD.

the preoccupations of artists: 'all of those interested in the everyday search to find a language or form that can adequately convey its complexity, ambiguity and elusiveness' (2008, p. 16). The same might be said about how we try to understand place. An engagement with writing from subjects such as geography and anthropology adds layers to how our entanglements with places can be understood. Such writing deals with the dynamics of places and how we come to know them (Shotter 2005, Ingold 2000, 2011), and the fact that places are 'made', 'unfinished' and ongoing, and always 'becoming' (Ingold 2000, Dewsbury et al. 2002). Such accounts also engage with the significance of atmosphere and 'affective responses' (Thrift 2004, Anderson 2009). I am interested in the ways in which an arts practice, and particularly printmaking, can usefully engage with, and add another dimension to, these conceptions of place and landscape.

I will begin by considering the ways in which geographers and anthropologists have explored our relationship to landscape and place. Many of these writers, in the latter part of the 20th century and into the 21st, have questioned what has been described as the Cartesian dualism between the viewer and viewed, and have attempted to collapse what has been a separation of the distinctions between person and landscape (Wylie, 2007). I will then explore the ways in which an arts practice can address and enhance some of these same concerns by giving the context of my own work, which is rooted in printmaking and bookworks.

The geographer John Wylie contends that 'landscape is tension' (2007) and in doing so he complicates and makes sense of relationships that are always in flux. As he sets out tensions such as body/mind, culture/nature, distance/proximity (impartial) observation/ (sensuous) inhabitation, he draws out complexities which are not set in stone, but which ebb and flow. It is within these tensions that the entanglements of life arise – in terms of human interactions and entwinings, as well as ideas of vitalism, and human to non-human relationships (Greenhough, 2010). Elsewhere, Wylie (2005) uses a solitary long distance walk to consider his experience of the walk itself in relation to theories of place and landscape. His exploration of 'self and landscape' reveals the ways in which our relationship can shift from an intense awareness of what is around us, to day-dreaming and thoughts wandering off in any number of directions, shifting from an interiority to an exteriority that can happen from moment to moment. Anthropologist Tim Ingold has long explored the notion of the 'lifeworld' (Ingold, 2000, 2011). In developing a 'dwelling perspective' to explore how we become 'at home' in the world, he explores how our lives consist of constant interactions with other people, and the 'things' of the world. For Ingold, the significance of activity is central. He states 'through living in it, the landscape becomes a part of us, just as we are a part of it' (2000, p. 191).

Thus, as Barbara Bender points out, landscapes have become 'part of the world of movement, relationships, memories and histories' (2001, p. 76). Many writers explore the multisensorial, subjective and emotional nature of our interactions and responses to these places, and ideas of 'atmosphere' and 'affect' (Anderson 2009, Thrift 2004). John Wylie, for example, describes affect as being 'the shifting mood, tenor, colour or intensity of places and situations ... domains of experience that are more than subjective' (2005, p. 236).

Nigel Thrift's 'non-representational theory', which he describes as being 'the geography of what happens' (Thrift, 2007, p. 2), calls for explorations of the processes and practices that make up our lived lives. Hayden Lorimer's overview of some of the research that adopts this broad approach sees it as being concerned with the processes of how places come to be made, rather than 'the place portrayed by the end product' (2005, p. 85). For example, Owain Jones and Paul Cloke's work on 'tree cultures' (2001, 2002) is described by Lorimer as being 'attentive to the intimacies and intersubjectivities shared between plants, trees and people' (2005, p. 85). Their research considers trees in a variety of settings, seeing them not as static, unchanging, separate entities, but as having to be contextualised in terms of silviculture, their cultural significance, history, economics and human interactions, and the interactions and complexities of nature and culture. Cloke and Jones see places, and the trees that can 'make' them, as, 'dynamic entities, constituted by human and nonhuman actants alike' (2001, p. 650). From an engagement with writers such as Shotter (2005), Bender (2001), Ingold (2000, 2011), Thrift (2004, 2007), and Wylie (2005) come perspectives that see places as being fluid, constantly shifting and dependent on activity in them, characterised by different atmospheres and subjectively and multisensorially experienced. Such perspectives have led some writers to assert that 'the world is more excessive than we can theorise', and that 'the world does not add-up' (Dewsbury et al. 2002, p. 437). Such conceptualisations of place also ask questions as to the best ways to describe, articulate and convey these differing material, immaterial and affective aspects. Writing of this nature can feel quite abstruse and academic, and at odds, sometimes, from the very qualities of place that they seek to describe. Indeed, there have been explicit calls for approaches that would better take account of the complexities and intensities of place (Wylie 2005), and what Hayden Lorimer refers to as 'the rich lore of place' (2008, p. 182).

I contend that art can make an important contribution to these debates and discussions through the multiple forms that it can take, its non-linearity, and its ability to create often (though not always) wordless explorations of place that allow for the insertion of imagination and through providing alternative ways of encountering, experiencing and responding to these complexities.

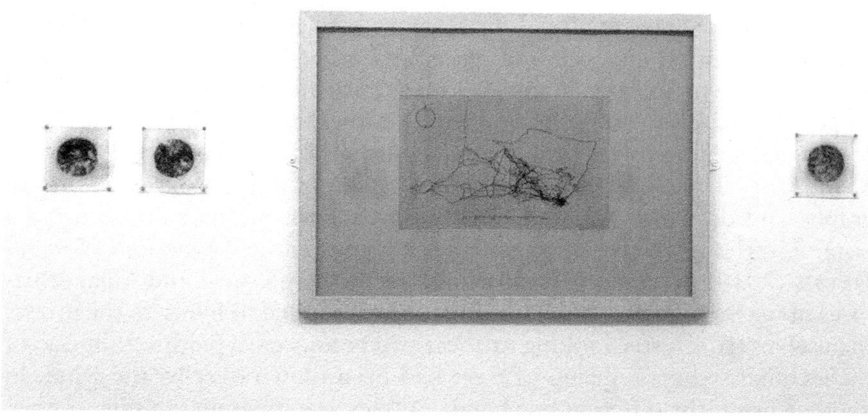

Amanda Thomson, *Dead Amongst the Living: Field Etchings, WalkDrawing, Fieldguide*, 2010/2013.

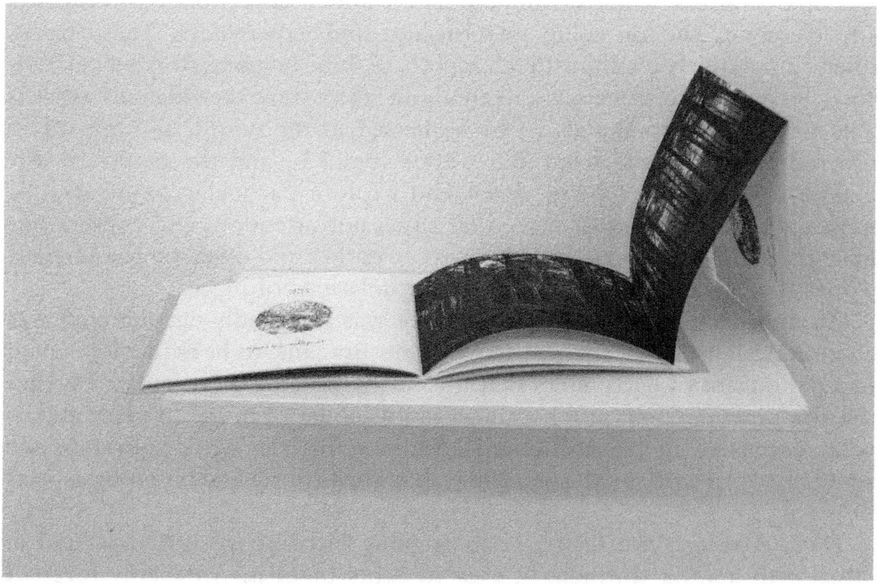

Amanda Thomson, *Dead Amongst the Living: Fieldguide* (2nd edition), 2013.

A temporal and multi-modal approach to art-making and place

As some writers have explored the tensions between presence and absence, distance and proximity, self and place, and other human (and nonhuman) activity inherent to how places are made, artistic engagement with landscape and place also straddles and explores these relationships. Sometimes, our engagement involves standing back and observing. For example, some of the work I make is two-dimensional: etchings and lithographs, photographs and drawings that one might approach as one might look upon a vista. A series of twelve photopolymer etchings entitled *Overlook: Several Forests* (2010) precipitates a close looking at the physical and tonal structures of masses of trees, where the images are cropped to focus on the forests themselves. A forester looking at these prints noticed windthrow in one of the etchings, where a group of trees had been blown over by the wind. In another print, the different age bands of trees are apparent, and in another, one can see a clump of broadleaved trees, their leaves turning in the autumn day that the photograph was taken on, paler among the conifers.

Some pieces are potentially more immersive and interactive: for example soundworks, videos and the haptic interactions intrinsic to bookworks. In these works, the back-and-forth between the two- and three-dimensional, the looking at and being within, are haptic and visceral iterations of different, changing and on-going relationships and experiences. These pieces often cumulatively combine to tell aspects of these ongoing stories of experience. Stephen Johnstone has talked about 'the extent to which an artist is able to get close to things, to be immersed in the world, as opposed to observing and judging from afar' (2008, pp. 13), and the nature of art-making means that we can dwell and explore particular moments, the intricacies and nuances of place that catch our attention, and capture our imagination. Should we choose to, we can gather and dwell on the smallest stories that make up these broader encapsulations of place.

An approach in which the same place was repeatedly encountered was an important aspect of the way in which my art came to be made. It resulted in a palimpsest of encounters that thereafter came to be articulated within the arts practice itself, and became a multi-modal response to place and to what happened in my encounters. Additionally, the work speaks to the simultaneity of stories (Massey, 2005) that are intrinsic and on-going aspects of place.

Dead Amongst the Living is an ongoing piece of work that started in 2005 with a walk through an area of Scots pines in Abernethy forest. I became interested in the dead trees that punctuated these woodlands, and when I researched their ecology, I became aware of their vital importance in the health of the ecosystem of these woods. In fact the number of saproxilic species – that is species dependent on dead wood – includes mosses and lichens, fungi, and insects such as rare beetles and hoverflies, as well as significant Scottish species such as the crested tits that rely on the holes of dead trees for their nests. This body of work now consists of etchings and photopolymers, bookworks, soundworks, prints, digital photographs, videos, as well as essays. I was interested in the allegorical quality of these trees – how the dead, the overlooked, the often invisible continue to be important and give succor and support to that which lives on.

The work consists of repeated walks and time spent in a particular piece of woodland, looking for its standing deadwood – often referred to as 'snags' – and different ways of recording the snags that I found. Elsewhere, I have described these walks as hidden performances (Thomson, 2012), and also discussed the significance of walking as markmaking in my work in an article in the *Geographical Review* (Thomson, 2013).

In these walks, I used a GPS to mark the co-ordinates of any of the dead trees I found, took photographs of them, sketched them, and tried to find ways of describing what I would take to be their key qualities as aide-mémoires. For example, in my sketchbook I noted how one tree reminded me of a stag's antlers, and how another tree's bark had shed so it looked as though all that remained were its bare bones. At one point I took steel etching plates, the edges of them blocked by an acid-resistant (and so also water-resistant) ground, and placed them on the North side of each of the dead trees I found. After three months, I retrieved these plates, now rusted, and where the raw steel had been exposed, the weather had etched patterns of rust. Once I removed the hard ground from them, I printed them as I would an acid-dipped etching plate. The resulting series of prints, together with some of the descriptive texts above became the basis for a bookwork: *Dead Amongst The Living: Fieldguide*.

The original version of this book was made by printing these etchings, dry, onto Fabriano paper, which had already been run through a digital printer with my handwritten descriptions, notes and mappings from sketchbooks scanned and digitised, and so able to be incorporated into the book. In a second incarnation the etchings have been scanned, and the whole book made digitally, using Somerset Book and Somerset Text Laid papers. Making this book in this way allowed for a double-sided book, stitched using a three-hole pamphlet stitch as opposed to a concertina book.

In bookworks, the artist can play with the relationship of content to format and layout, and the very nature of a book creates yet another iteration of how place becomes conceptualised. Johanna Drucker has described a zone that sees artists' books 'at the intersection of a number of different disciplines, fields and ideas, rather than at their limit' (2004, p. 1), and the books I make consist of prints and photographs, drawings and text, influenced variously by geographical, ecological, historical and anthropological writings. Text and information can sit with images in unexpected, and sometimes curious, ways. The bookworks made as part of *Dead Amongst the Living* can be read in conjunction with other elements of the project that include soundscapes (a list of the birds that can be heard on the soundscape *Still Life, Abernethy, Dawn* (2011) is given in the *Fieldguide*), videos (a list of moth names in the *Fieldguide* alludes to a video, titled *imago/imagines* (2012), which is a film about a moth trap and the moths of a pinewood, and an essay, 'Moths to light', which explores the ecological significance of moths to birdlife). A digital print *Treescape* (2012), which ordinarily is printed at 110 centimeters in length, is re-versioned in the bookwork.

In a gallery space, the work can be read together. The digital prints, etchings, videos and soundworks all come together to create different aspects of place that have been 'found' at different times. These aspects of place are sometimes familiar, sometimes uncanny and sometimes they ask the audience to consider what is often overlooked, or what appears familiar, in new ways. The subject of two photopolymer etchings of nightscapes might at first appear to be the moon, but it is the silhouettes of the trees, and how they can be identified by the silhouettes of the leaf-shapes, which are of equal significance.

Dead Amongst the Living is a mixture of still and moving image, sounds, material objects (the wood of the place) and words. The work sometimes asks the viewer to stand back and look – sometimes, by placing headphones on and listening to the sounds of place, almost to be within. Videos take the viewer to the smallest of moments – the movements of coal tits, or a night-time world rarely encountered. The haptic quality of the bookwork invites the viewer to physically enter its space. Combined, the pieces aim to create encounters that are informational, evocative, affective, and sometimes disconcerting.

While books can be standalone productions, they can also, as is the case of the *Fieldguide* (2nd edition), pull together different strands of a project and here the book feeds back into the 'essence' of what the project is about. This *Fieldguide* exists as a portable iteration of the project as a whole, and also articulates, albeit in a more poetic form, the subject matter of the project. Further, it has an ongoing relationship to the site of the fieldwork as, essentially, the *Fieldguide*, containing my descriptions of these dead trees and their coordinates, could be taken back into the field to (re)find them. However, with the inaccuracies inherent in how the GPS records coordinates, which can run to being several metres out, the subjectivity of my descriptions and with the inherent change that time, the trees' decay, and new growth will bring, it will become more inaccurate and less of a 'guide' as time goes on. This itself speaks to the changing nature of place and its constant 'becoming'.

Drucker has observed that 'every book is a metaphor, an object of associations and history, cultural meanings and production values, spiritual possibilities and poetic spaces, and all of these are part of the field from which the artist's book derives its identity, its shared connections and distinguishing features as a book whose realized forms and thematic intentions are only the most evident aspects of its totality as an idea' (2004, p. 42). Here, the artist's book forms part of an ongoing story and investigation about a particular place, but it can also hold its own self-contained narrative and rationale.

An arts-based approach that is multi-modal in its outputs, together with a methodology that takes into account and responds to what happens, provides an intensely productive way of exploring the layers of encounters and interactions, connections and disassociations that make up our lives, and how places come to be made and experienced. This work demonstrates a way of taking into account the complexities of place described by writers such as Ingold, Thrift and Wylie, and a way to take into account these aspects of place that are subjective, nuanced, affective, immaterial and subjective. The artmaking, and the artworks that have been made, are liminal spaces of thought, reflection and making between the artist and the places themselves. The nature of art making allows the artist to follow, variously, people, ideas, and very specific aspects, nuances and 'moments' of place. It shows what has come to be known in a variety of ways, including bookworks, prints, photographs and other media. Thus these entanglements can be articulated in multiple ways, creating complex and multiple articulations and iterations of ongoing stories of place, which can speak and contribute to these other languages of place, as well as being significant in their own right.

Acknowledgements

Amanda Thomson's PhD was supported by Forestry Commission Scotland, The University of the Highlands and Islands, and Highlands and Islands Enterprise.

References

Anderson, B. 2009. 'Affective Atmospheres', *Emotion, Space and Society*, 2 (2), 77–81.

Bender, B. 2001. 'Landscapes on-the-Move', *Journal of Social Archaeology*, 1 (1), 75–89.

Cloke, P. and Jones, O., 2001. 'Dwelling, Place and Landscape: An Orchard in Somerset', in: *Environment and Planning* A, Vol 33, 649–66.

Dewsbury, J. D., Harrison, P., Rose, M. and Wylie, J. 2002. 'Introduction: Enacting Geographies', *Geoforum*, 33 (4), 437–40.

Drucker, J. 2004. *The Century of Artist's Books*. New York, Granary Books.

Greenhough, B. 2010. 'Vitalist Geographies: Life and the More-Than-Human'. In: B. Anderson and P. Harrison, eds, *Taking-Place: Non-Representational Theories and Geography*. Farnham: Ashgate, 37–54.

Ingold, T. 2000. *The Perception of the Environment: Essays on Livelihood, Dwelling and Skill.* London, Routledge.

Ingold, T. 2011. *Being Alive.* London: Routledge.

Johnstone, S. (ed.), 2008. 'Introduction/ Recent art and the Everyday', in: *The Everyday.* London, Whitechapel Gallery.

Jones, O. and Cloke, P. 2002. *Tree Cultures.* Oxford: Berg.

Lorimer, H. 2005. 'Cultural Geography: The Busyness of Being "More-Than-Representational"', *Progress in Human Geography*, 29 (1), 83–94.

Lorimer, H., 2008. 'Poetry and Place: The Shape of Words', *Geography*, 93 (3), 181–2.

Massey, D. 2005. *For Space.* London: Sage.

Shotter, J., 2005. 'Goethe and the Refiguring of Intellectual Enquiry: From "Aboutness"-Thinking to "Withness"-Thinking in Everyday Life'. *Janus Head*, 8 (1), 132–58.

Thomson, A. 2012. 'Walking Among the Dead Amongst the Living', *Performance Research: On Ecology*, 17 (4), 27–32.

Thomson, A. 2013. 'Making a Place: Art, Writing and a More-Than-Textual Approach', *The Geographical Review* 103 (2), 244–55.

Thrift, N. 2004. 'Intensities of Feeling: Towards a Spatial Politics of Affect', *Geografiska Annaler Series B: Human Geography*, 86 (1), 57–78.

Thrift, N. 2007. *Non-Representational Theory.* London: Routledge.

Wylie, J. 2005. 'A Single Day's Walking; Narrating the Self and the Landscape on the South West Coast Path', *Transactions of the British Institute of Geographers*, NS 30, 234–47.

Wylie, J. 2007. *Landscape.* London: Routledge.

R. L. Tillman

Failures, irritations and grief in printing: in search of Manly Banister, an excerpt from an unpublishable memoir*

I admit that when I picked up the book I was only interested in the author's name, which seemed straight from the pages of pulp fiction. After all, I didn't need another printmaking manual. But a printmaking manual written by Manly Banister? Yes, please.

With a bit of digging, I learned something about the life and work of Manly Banister. I suppose it's unlikely that I will ever know much more, and I'm not sure that I would care to. In my imagination, the man has assumed a mythic stature proportionate to his name.

Banister had a wide-ranging career as a writer, driven by an amateur's interest in art, science fiction, and mechanical tinkering. He had been a fireman, a Marine on Okinawa, and a self-taught translator of French, German, and Dutch. In the 1950s, he self-published an early science fiction fanzine, *The Nekromantikon*. His own sci-fi stories were printed in *Weird Tales* and other magazines, and a novel called *Conquest of Earth* was published by Avalon Books in 1957.

Banister also wrote a tremendous amount of instructional material for *Popular Mechanics* magazine in the 1960s and 70s. He published a series of purposeful articles for the do-it-yourselfer, complete with step-by-step instructions and exploded diagrams. In one case, there was an illustration of a handsome homeowner in a crisp button-down shirt, proudly pushing a leaf-blower, presumably made with his own two hands.

In the course of my research, I became a bit intimidated by the breadth of Manly's mechanical experiments. My family recently moved into an old house, where I often find myself faced with difficulties that I am wholly incompetent to solve. 'Make Yourself a Leaf Blower,' Manly says. I can't

* R. L. Tillman. 2014. 'Failures, Irritations and Grief in Printing. In Search of Manly Banister, an Excerpt from an Unpublishable Memoir'. In: Emmons, Amze, Tillman, R. L. and Urban, Jason (eds), *Manual: An Anthology of the Manual.* 2014. Austin, Texas: Printeresting, pp. 17–20. Reproduced by kind permission of the author and Printeresting.

even commit to *buying* a leafblower. 'Here's an alternate way to fire the boiler,' Manly says. I find the workings of our boiler impenetrable, and even calling the service company gives me a headache. Let's just say that by the time I got to Manly's article 'Build your own Steam Engine,' I was a bit discouraged.

And thus we return to his name, which is like an unsubtle jab at my own heteronormative insecurities. OK, so I'm not a handy man. I don't build things, and I have a preternatural tendency to strip screws. I'm not proud of it. But do I really need some hairy-armed ghost named 'Manly Banister' to remind me?

In this regard, one *Popular Mechanics* article was of special concern: 'Build A Table Top Printing Press.' As a printer, I'm capable enough with the tools of my trade, and I know my way around a press. But I've never been a technician. Even if I did manage to assemble my own printing press, I'm certain that I could make better prints on a George Foreman Grill. And yet many printers I know are also highly competent builders, who might tackle these instructions as a weekend project, just for fun. So this essay felt like a special affront to my competence and my authority, issued by Manly Banister himself from beyond the grave. It was time to take a stand.

So I acquired the essential works of Manly Banister, which have been published under various names over the years: a book on lithography, a book on etching, another on relief printing, and still another on bookbinding. I even got my hands on a copy of *Conquest of Earth*. Bluntly, I hoped to discover errors in these books that would ease my own creeping sense of inadequacy. On a book arts forum, I had read some uncomplimentary reviews of Banister's texts, which were especially disdainful of his use of Elmer's Glue as an adhesive. Perhaps this character was a jack of all trades but master of none. I have learned that sometimes the guy who can do everything, actually can't do anything right.

*I may not be qualified to assess the quality of your steam engine instructions, but I can and will judge your printmaking acumen. You may be t*he king of your castle, but you're on my turf now, Banister!

So I read Manly's manuals. And damn it, I loved them.

Naturally, like all manuals, these do contain some questionable information. The books are full of impractical DIY tips, and the illustrations are odd. In particular, the reproductions of Banister's own ham-fisted woodcuts and lithographs do not do these volumes any favors. (There is one picture of a donkey so perverse in its form that I fear I will never forget it.) But the books are written with an idiosyncratic clarity that reveals something strangely intimate about the author. Who could dislike a book with a chapter titled 'Failures, Irritations, and Grief in Printing'?

The fact is, Manly Banister was a proud amateur. An amateur, in Manly's own words, is 'one who does something for the pure love of it.' Banister's own love for printing is evidenced by the many photographs of his deeply unphotogenic hands, blunt instruments deeply engaged in delicate activities.

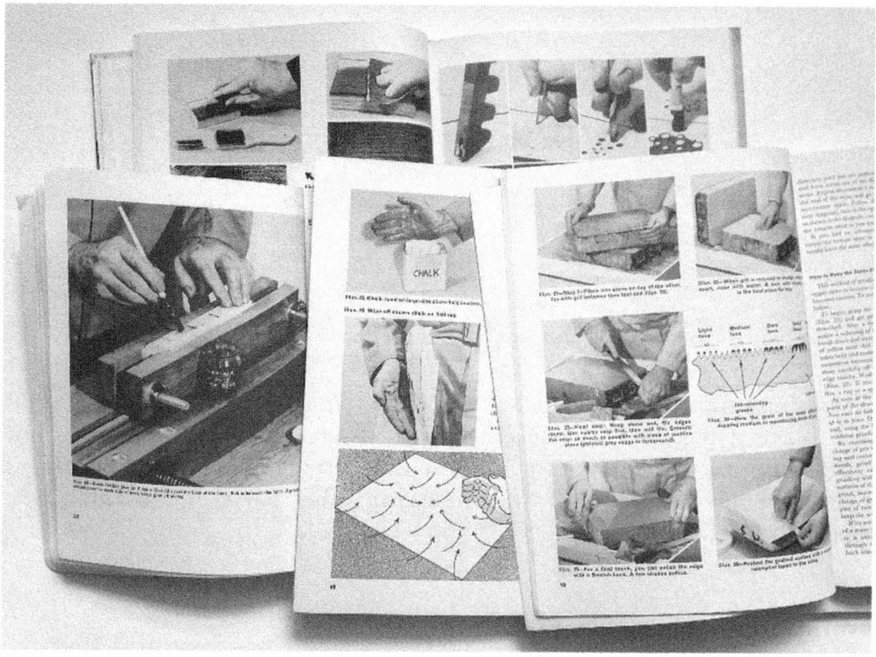

Assorted publications by Manly Banister.

In his important book *The Craftsman*, Richard Sennett wrote: 'it might be argued that high levels of technical skill can be reached only by people with objective standards of truth.' This may be the source of my own detachment from technique; my standards of truth are wholly unobjective. But if it's necessary for the craftsman to apply objective standards, this is not the case for the artist, or for the amateur. And this is where I found common ground with Manly Banister. By objective standards, Banister made crude prints and wrote a largely unreadable novel. Who knows, maybe by objective standards the guy wasn't even a good craftsman. But here's the unobjective truth: as an amateur, he was an artist.

And that's all that I need to know about Mr. Manly Banister.

References

Banister, Manly. 1973. *Lithographic Prints from Stone and Plate*. N.p.: Cork Publishing.

Banister, Miles Manly. 1986. *Practical Guide to Etching and Other Intaglio Printmaking Techniques*. Mineola, N.Y.: Dover Publications.

Sennett, Richard. 2008. *The Craftsman*. New Haven: Yale University Press.

Part IV Further reading

Please note that the headings are not definitive and many texts relate not just to one category. When several keywords are mentioned, this does not mean that every text links to ALL the categories. Individual publications also often refer to keywords mentioned in other parts of the anthology, especially Part III.

Workshops/publishing/portfolio

Brown, Kathan. 1996. *Ink, Paper, Metal, Wood: Painters and Sculptors at Crown Point Press*. San Francisco: Chronicle Books.

Cooney, Lynne. 2012. 'Ink, Paper, Plates: The Legacy of Printmaking in South Africa and the Caversham Press'. *African Arts* 45 (2): 36–45.

Cullen, Deborah. 2012. 'Contact Zones: Places, Spaces, and Other Test Cases'. *American Art* 26(2): 14–20.

Drucker, Johanna. 2014. 'Concepts of Production'. *Afterimage* 42 (1): 2–5.

Gilmour, Pat. 1992. 'Artists' Workshops: An Historical Perspective'. In: Turner, Sylvie (ed.), *British Printmaking Studios*. London: Estamp.

Goodsir, Jane and Phillips, John. 1999. 'London Print Workshop'. *Grapheion*. 26–28 Jan. (Interview).

Hopkinson, Martin J. 1991. 'The Scottish Printmaking Workshops'. *Print Collector's Newsletter* 22 (5) (Nov.–Dec.): 166–8.

Law, Jenn and Cooper, Tara (eds), 2016. *Printopolis*. Toronto: Open Studio. Chapter 4: 'Reflections on Open Studio's 45 years', 216–87.

McDonald, Katherine. 2002. Contemporary Print Collecting: Melbourne's Print Workshops and Publishers. *Art & Australia* 40 (2): 298–301.

Phillips, John. 2005. *Transforming Print: Key Issues Affecting the Development of Londonprintstudio*. PhD Dissertation, University of Brighton.

Rexer, Lyle, Camnitzer, Luis and Porter, Liliana. 2008. 'Roundtable: New York Graphic Workshop'. *Art On Paper* 13 (1): 50–9.

Scott, Sue and Towle, Tony. 1998. *Proof Positive: Forty Years of Contemporary American Printmaking at ULAE, 1957–1997*. London: Harry N. Abrams.

Sidey, Tessa and Mellor, David Alan. 2003. *Editions Alecto*. Aldershot: Lund Humphries.

Turner, Silvie (ed.), 1992. *British Printmaking Studios: A Survey of Artists Open Print Workshops in the UK*. London: Estamp.
Turner, Sylvie. 1990. 'Printmaking Studios in Britain: The Continuing Tradition'. *Print Quarterly* 7 (4) (December 1): 397–413.

Collaboration

Bartlett, Jennifer, Berdan, Michael, Field, Richard S., Johnson, Robert Flynn, Katz, Alex *et al.* 1986. 'Collaboration East & West: A Discussion'. *Print Collector's Newsletter* 16 (6) (Jan.–Feb.): 196–205.
Book, Andrew and Trent, Walter. 2013. 'Copying Collaboration: A Dialogue between Brook Andrew and Trent Walter'. In: Morgan, Luke. *Intersections and Counterpoints: IMPACT 7 International Multi-disciplinary Printmaking Conference Proceedings*. Clayton, Victoria: Monash University Publishing, 1–6.
Cuccio, Claire. 2010. 'When a Copy is an Original – the Satō Woodblock Print Workshop and Rebecca Salter'. Blog *The Journal of Modern Craft Website*: http://journalofmoderncraft.com/author/clairecuccio [Accessed 11 December 2016].
Davila-Villa, Ursula. 2012. 'El Panal/The Hive: The Anataomy of Collaboration'. In: Cullen, Deborah et al. *El Panal/The Hive: The Third Poligraphic Trienal of San Juan*. San Juan, Costa Rica: Programa de Artes Plásticas Instituto de Cultura Puertorriqueña, 217–37. http://jasonmena.com/files/PDF/Trienal_Poligrafica_de_San_Juan.pdf [Accessed 27 January 2016].
Davis, Julie Nelson. 2015. *Partners in Print: Artistic Collaboration and the Ukiyo-e Market*. Honolulu: University of Hawai'i Press.
Drucker, Johanna. 1999. 'Collaborative TY/opography'. *Afterimage* 27 (3): 9.
Gilmour, Pat. 2000. '"The Curious Pavane": Tamarind and the Art of Collaboration'. In: Devon, Marjorie (ed.), *Tamarind 40 Years*. Albuquerque: University of New Mexico Press, 37–59.
Grishin, Sasha. 2006. 'The Gentle Art of Collaboration'. *Art and Australia* 44 (1): 104–9.
Hansen, Trudy V. et al. 1995. *Printmaking in America: Collaborative Prints and Presses 1960–1990*. New York: Harry Abrams.
Laidler, Paul. 2011. *Collaborative and Digital Wide Format Printing: Methods and Considerations for the Artist and Master Printer*. PhD Dissertation, University of the West of England, Bristol.
Merrill, Hugh. 2008. 'Printmaking Artists and Master Printmakers'. *Contemporary Impressions* 16 (1): 19–23.
Zammiello, C. and Hodermarsky, E. 2012. *Conversations from the Print Studio: A Master Printer in Collaboration with Ten Artists*. New Haven: Yale University Art Gallery.

Collecting

Cherix, Christophe. 2005. 'Breaking down Categories: Print Rooms, Drawing Departments, and the Museums'. In: Altshuler, Bruce (ed.), *Collecting the*

New: Museums and Contemporary Art. Princeton: Princeton University Press, 55–64.

Gilmour, Pat. 2005. 'Setting up Departments I, Prints at the Tate Gallery'. *Print Quarterly* 22 (2) (June): 159–62.

Gilmour, Pat. 2005. 'Setting up Departments II: Prints at the National Gallery of Australia'. *Print Quarterly* 22 (3) (Sept.): 307–11.

Grishin, Sasha. 2000. 'The Making and Collecting of Graphic Arts in Contemporary Australia'. *Grapheion* 15 (3–4): 64–79.

Law, Jenn and Cooper, Tara (eds), 2016. *Printopolis*. Toronto: Open Studio. Chapter 1: 'Print Collections: The Collector's Impulse', 16–75.

Rainbird, Sean and Tyler, Kenneth E. 2004. *Print Matters: The Kenneth E. Tyler Gift*. London: Tate Publishing.

Book art

Bechard-Léauté, Anne and Oncins, Valentine (eds), 2014. *Le livre d'artiste depuis 1980 en France et au Royaume-Uni/Developments in the Field of the Artist's Book Since 1980 in France and the United Kingdom*. Saint-Étienne: Publications de l'Université de Saint-Étienne.

Brody, Jacqueline. 1994. 'A Century of Artists' Books: Between the Pages'. *Print Collector's Newsletter* 25 (5) (Nov.–Dec.): 172–6.

Burkhart, Anne L. 2006. 'Mongrel Nature: A Consideration of Artists' Books and Their Implications for Art Education'. *Studies in Art Education* 47 (3): 248–68.

Bury, Stephen and Rossi, Daniella. 2015. *Artists' Books: The Book as a Work of Art, 1963–2000*. London: Quaritch.

Drucker, Johanna. 2014. 'Material And/or Virtual: Hybrid Forms of Artists' Books'. In: Kroman, Thomas Hvid et al. *Danish Artists' Books*. Cologne, Germany: Møller and Verlag der Buchhandlung Walther König, 133–46.

Drucker, Johanna. 1998. *Figuring the Word: Essays on Books, Writing, and Visual Poetics*. New York: Granary Books.

Drucker, Johanna. 1995. *The Century of Artists' Books*. New York: Granary Books.

Jones, Phil. 2011. 'Looking Through, Looking into and Looking at the Book: The Materiality of Message and Medium'. *Book 2.0* 1 (2): 255–71.

Kwinter, Sanford. 2014. 'Plumbing the Urban Azimuth (at the End of the Age of the Book)'. *Harvard Design Magazine* (38): 41–53.

Moeglin-Delcroix, Anne. 1997. Esthétique du livre d'artiste: 1960–1980. Paris, Jean-Michel Place/Bibliothèque nationale de France.

Phillpot, Clive and Cherix, Christophe. 2012. *Booktrek: Selected Essays on Artists' Books Since 1972*. Zurich: JRP Ringier.

Spector, Buzz. 1995. *The Bookmaker's Desire*. Pasadena, CA: Umbrella Editions.

Wasserman, Krystyna, Niffenegger, Audrey and Drucker, Johanna. 2007. *The Book as Art: Artists' Books from the National Museum of Women in the Arts*. New York: Princeton Architectural Press.

White, Tony. 2012. 'From Democratic Multiple to Artist Publishing: The (R)evolutionary Artist's Book'. *Art Documentation: Journal of the Art Libraries Society of North America* 31 (1): 45–56.

Wye, Deborah and Weitman, Wendy. 2006. *Eye on Europe: Prints, Books and Multiples, 1960 to Now*. New York: The Museum of Modern Art.

Biennales

There are (almost) as many biennale catalogues as there are print biennales. This is just a small selection.

Cullen, Deborah et al. 2012. *El Panal/The Hive: The Third Poligraphic Trienal of San Juan*. http://jasonmena.com/files/PDF/Trienal_Poligrafica_de_San_Juan.pdf, San Juan, Costa Rica: Programa de Artes Plásticas Instituto de Cultura Puertorriqueña.

Philagrafika (Organization), Moore College of Art and Design., Pennsylvania Academy of the Fine Arts., Philadelphia Museum of Art, Temple Gallery (Philadelphia, PA) and Print Center for Prints and Photographs (Philadelphia, PA). 2011. *The Graphic Unconscious*. Philadelphia, PA: Philagrafika.

Rees, Simon and Näripea, Eva (eds), 2011. *The 15th Tallinn Print Triennial: For Love Not Money*. Tallinn: Tallinn Print Triennial.

Global

Amir-Ebrahimi, Samila. 2009. 'Printmaking in Iran'. *Printmaking Today* 18 (3): 22–3.

Arnold, Marion (2013) 'The Imprint of South Africa: Naratives by Some Black Women Printmakers at the Caversham Press'. In: Morgan, Luke. *Intersections and Counterpoints: IMPACT 7 International Multi-disciplinary Printmaking Conference Proceedings*. Clayton, Victoria: Monash University Publishing, 30–6.

Candiani, Alicia. 1999. 'From the Margins: Latin American Printmaking in the Era of Digital Technology'. In: Parraman, Carinna and Brewer, Emmeline (eds), *IMPACT International Multi-disciplinary Printmaking Conference Proceedings*. Bristol: Impact Press, 53–62. www.uwe.ac.uk/sca/research/cfpr/dissemination/conferences/IMPACT%20PROCEEDINGS%20copy.pdf [Accessed 25 January 2018].

Chan, Leong K. 2013. 'The Printed Image and Nation Building in the Republic of Singapore'. In: Morgan, Luke. *Intersections and Counterpoints: IMPACT 7 International Multi-disciplinary Printmaking Conference Proceedings*. Clayton, Victoria: Monash University Publishing, 100–5.

Farrer, Anne and Barker, David. 2003. *Chinese Printmaking Today*. London: British Library.

Freitas, Artur. 2010. 'Gravura Expandida: As Mostras Da Gravura Dos Anos 1990'. *Visualidades* 8 (2): 31–47. www.revistas.ufg.br/VISUAL/article/viewFile/18274/10913 [Accessed 10 November 2016].

Hobbs, Philippa and Rankin, Elizabeth. 1997. *Printmaking in a Transforming South Africa*. Claremont: David Philips Publishers.

Jiang, Xu. 2015. 'The Phantom of Print'. In: *Academic Papers, Illustrated Talks, Themed Panels: IMPACT 9 International Printmaking Conference Proceedings*. China: China Academy of Art Press, 7–17.

Kirker, Marjorie Ann. 2009. *Printmaking as an Expanding Field in Contemporary Art Practice: A Case Study of Japan, Australia and Thailand*. PhD Dissertation, Queensland University of Technology.
Kornhoff, Oliver, Schenk-Weininger, Isabell, Schlegel, Birgit, Völkle, Monika, Hill, Katie, Farrer, Anne and Huang, Liaoyuan. 2008. *China macht Druck: zeitgenössische chinesische Druckgrafik*. ['China Presses On: Contemporary Chinese Printmaking'.] Heidelberg: Kehrer Verlag.
MacWhirter, Peter. 2008. 'Contemporary Chinese Printmaking'. *Contemporary Impressions* 16 (1): 6–10.
MacWhirter, Peter. 2001. 'Contemporary Printmaking in Korea'. *Contemporary Impressions* 9 (1): 12–15.
Tang, Xiaobing. 2015. 'Where to Look for Art in Contemporary China'. In: *Visual Culture in Contemporary China: Paradigms and Shifts*. Cambridge: Cambridge University Press, 210–49.
Tang, Xiaobing, Hui, Shang and Farrer, Anne. 2011. *Multiple Impressions: Contemporary Chinese Woodblock Prints*. Ann Arbor, MI: University of Michigan, Museum of Art.
Tang, Xiaobing, Hui, Shang and Farrer, Anne. 2007. *Origins of the Chinese Avant-Garde: The Modern Woodcut Movement*. Berkeley: University of California Press.

Education

Ganter, Jo. 2005. 'Craft Versus Concept'. *Grapheion* 1 (18): 4–7.
Kent, Corita and Cage, John. 1967/68. '10 Rules for Students and Teachers (and Life)'. https://corita.myshopify.com/products/ten-rules-poster [Accessed 10 December 2016].
Lovett, Steve. 2013. 'Where is the Next Generation of Printmakers and Who Will Follow After Them?' Unpublished paper.
Lovett, Steve. 2009. 'Making Friends with Digital Natives'. *Scope (Art & Design)*, 4, Nov, 215–20. www.thescopes.org/assets/Uploads/04-215-Lovett-11-09.pdf [Accessed 4 April 2016].
Merrill, Hugh, Ganson, Adelia and Rehagen, Amanda. 2014. *Shared Visions. Thoughts and Experiences in Social Arts Practice*. Kansas City: Chameleon Press.

Research

Harrison, Paul Liam. 2015. 'Teleportation and the Printed Human'. In: *Academic Papers, Illustrated Talks, Themed Panels: IMPACT 9 International Printmaking Conference Proceedings*: China: China Academy of Art Press, 382–9.
Hodes, Charlotte and Treadaway, Dr Cathy. 2011. 'At the Cutting Edge: An Investigation into the Role of Digital Print within Creative Practice'. In: Stephen Hoskins et al. (eds), *IMPACT 6 Multi-disciplinary Printmaking Conference Proceedings*. Bristol: Impact Press, 110–14.

Langerman, Fritha (2011) 'Defining Order: Print, Representational Taxonomies and Encyclopaedic Knowledge Systems'. In: Stephen Hoskins et al. (eds), *IMPACT 6 Multi-disciplinary Printmaking Conference Proceedings*. Bristol: Impact Press, 16–20.

Mosely, Tim. 2014. 'A Definitive Haptic Practice, and a Methodological Model for an Artist's Book Practice'. In: Harrison, Paul, Shemilt, Elaine and Watson, Arthur (eds), *Borders & Crossings: The Artist as Explorer: IMPACT 8 International Printmaking Conference*. Dundee: Duncan of Jordanstone College of Art & Design, University of Dundee, 162–7.

Princenthal, Nancy. 1994. 'Artist's Book Beat: Johanna Drucker Interview'. *Print Collector's Newsletter* 25 (1) (Mar.–Apr.): 31–4.

Shemilt, Elaine. 2010. 'Limited Edition – Unlimited Image: Can a Science/Art Fusion Move the Boundaries of Visual and Audio Interpretation?' In: Gardiner, Hazel and Gere, Charlie. *Art Practice in Digital Culture*. Farnham: Ashgate, 139–51.

Activism/political print/self-publishing

Aarons, Philip and Bronson, A. A. (eds), 2008. *Queer Zines*. New York: Printed Matter Inc.

Eichhorn, Kate. 2016. *Adjusted Margin: Xerography, Art, and Activism in the Late Twentieth Century*. Cambridge, MA: MIT Press.

Gilbert, Annette. 2016. *Publishing as Artistic Practice*. Berlin; New York: Sternberg Press.

Latitudes #Open Curating. 2012. 'Books – Expanded – Field: An Interview with BADLANDS UNLIMITED'. 2012. Web. www.lttds.org/assets/OpenCurating_Badlands.pdf [Accessed 11 May 2016].

Ludovico, Alessandro. 2012. *Post-Digital Print: The Mutation of Publishing Since 1894*. Eindhoven: Onomatopee.

MacPhee, Josh. 2009. 'Street Art and Social Movements'. Justseeds Artists' Cooperative. 17 February. http://justseeds.org/street-art-and-social-movements/ [Accessed 28 February 2017].

MacPhee, Josh (ed.), 2010. *Paper Politics: Socially Engaged Printmaking Today*. Oakland, CA: PM Press.

Maurer, Philipp. 2010. 'Druck in Köpfe. Politische Und Kritische Druckgraphik Im Alltäglichen Kampf Um Köpfe' ['Imprints in Heads: Political and Critical Graphic Art in Everyday Fighting For Heads'.] In *im:print 2010. zustandsprotokolle aktueller druckgrafik / journal of the current state of printmaking*. Edited by Schneider, Michael, Maurer, Philipp and Lebzelter, Georg. Wien: Springer Verlag, 29–45.

Merrill, Hugh. 2001. 'Prints and Politics: Boundaries or Connections?' *Contemporary Impressions* 9 (1): 19–21.

Miller, Kimberly. 2003. 'The Philani Printing Project: Women's Art and Activism in Crossroads, South Africa'. *Feminist Studies* 29 (3): 618–37.

Montgomery, Harper. 2011. 'Enter for Free: Exhibiting Woodcuts on a Street Corner in Mexico City'. *Art Journal* 70 (4): 27–39.

The Piracy Project. 'The impermanent book'. Blog 19 April 2012: http://rhizome.org/editorial/2012/apr/19/impermanent-book/ [Accessed 11 November 2016].

Princenthal, Nancy. 1996. 'Books to Billboards: Crossing the Boundaries'. *Moma*, no. 22. The Museum of Modern Art: 14–19.

Princenthal, Nancy. 1988. 'Political Prints: An Opinion Poll'. *Print Collector's Newsletter* 19 (2) (May–June): 45–7.

Saunders, Gill. 2011. 'Street Art – Prints and Precedents'. *Art in Print* 1 (3). http://artinprint.org/article/street-art-prints-and-precedents/ [Accessed 3 March 2017].

The Serving Library. www.servinglibrary.org/words.html?id=96 [Accessed 6 February 2013].

Tallman, Susan. 2000. 'Socks, Politics, and Prints'. In: Devon, Marjorie (ed.), *Tamarind 40 years*. Albuquerque: University of New Mexico Press, 97–115.

Thomas, Susan E. 2009. 'Value and Validity of Art Zines as an Art Form'. *Art Documentation: Journal of the Art Libraries Society of North America* 28 (2). [The University of Chicago Press, Art Libraries Society of North America]: 27–38.

Triantafillou, Eric. 2010. 'Printmaking as Resistance?' In: *The Brooklyn Rail, Critical Perspectives on Art, Politics and Culture*, 4 May 2010. http://brooklynrail.org/2010/05/express/printmaking-as-resistance [Accessed 15 June 2017].

Tyler, Linda P. and Walker, Barry (eds), 1993. 'Hot Off the Press: Prints and Politics'. *The Tamarind Papers* 15 (1993–4). Albuquerque: University of New Mexico Press.

Van Leijsen, Rob. 2017. 'Copy, Tweak, Paste: Methods of Appropriation in Re-Enacted Artists' Books'. *Journal for Artistic Research* (JAR), 22 June. www.researchcatalogue.net/view/231490/328418 [Accessed 5 July 2017].

Weinmayr, Eva. 2014. 'One Publishes to Find Comrades'. In: Klimpel, Oliver (ed.), *The Visual Event: An Education in Appearances*. Leipzig: Spector Books, 50–9. http://evaweinmayr.com/wp-content/uploads/Eva-Weinmayr%E2%80%93One-publishes-to-find-comrades.pdf [Accessed 7 April 2016].

Williams, Matt. 2015. 'Self-Publishing is Political: An Interview with Dan Mitchell and Sara MacKillop'. www.ica.org.uk/bulletin/self-publishing-political-interview-dan-mitchell-and-sara-mackillop [Accessed 28 February 2017].

Wye, Deborah. 1988. *Committed to Print: Social and Political Themes in Recent American Printed Art*. New York: The Museum of Modern Art.

Index